READING, WRITING, AND BOOKISH CIRCLES IN THE ANCIENT MEDITERRANEAN

EDUCATION, LITERARY CULTURE, AND RELIGIOUS PRACTICE IN THE ANCIENT WORLD

Series Editors: Sean A. Adams (University of Glasgow, UK) and Catherine Hezser (SOAS, University of London, UK)

Editorial Board: Jim Aitken (University of Cambridge, UK), Jeanne-Nicole Saint-Laurent (Marquette University, USA), David Carr (Union Theological Seminary, New York, USA), Raffaella Cribiore (NYU, USA), Matthew Goff (Florida State University, USA), Marc Hirshman (Hebrew University of Jerusalem, Israel), Sylvie Honigman (Tel Aviv University, Israel), Jan Stenger (Julius Maximilian University of Würzburg, Germany).

This interdisciplinary series provides a space for the exploration and advancement of the study of education and literary culture in antiquity and its intersection(s) with religious practice. Specifically, it covers the geography of the Mediterranean basin from the beginning of literary culture until late antiquity. Books in the series are at the cutting edge of research, challenging traditional scholarly boundaries by engaging with the lived elements of literary culture, religion, and education.

By advancing theoretical and methodological approaches from inter/transdisciplinary perspectives, books in this series make important contributions to discussions of textuality, history, material culture, and cultural studies. Interactions with material and literary culture are core elements to this series and scholars will wrestle with how practices change over time and locality. Attention to interreligious and intercultural interaction will deepen our understanding of religious experiences, communities, institutions, and individuals in antiquity.

Lived Wisdom in Jewish Antiquity, Elisa Uusimäki

READING, WRITING, AND BOOKISH CIRCLES IN THE ANCIENT MEDITERRANEAN

Edited by

Jonathan D. H. Norton, Garrick V. Allen,
and Lindsey A. Askin

BLOOMSBURY ACADEMIC
LONDON • NEW YORK • OXFORD • NEW DELHI • SYDNEY

BLOOMSBURY ACADEMIC
Bloomsbury Publishing Plc
50 Bedford Square, London, WC1B 3DP, UK
1385 Broadway, New York, NY 10018, USA
29 Earlsfort Terrace, Dublin 2, Ireland

BLOOMSBURY, BLOOMSBURY ACADEMIC and the Diana logo
are trademarks of Bloomsbury Publishing Plc

First published in Great Britain 2022
Paperback edition published 2024

Copyright © Jonathan D. H. Norton, Garrick V. Allen, Lindsey A. Askin, and contributors, 2022

Jonathan D. H. Norton, Garrick V. Allen, and Lindsey A. Askin have asserted their rights under the Copyright, Designs and Patents Act, 1988, to be identified as Editor of this work.

For legal purposes the Acknowledgments on p. xi constitute an extension of this copyright page.

Series design: Charlotte James

Cover image: CBL W 139 f.1v © The Trustees of the Chester Beatty Library, Dublin.
Photographed by CSNTM

All rights reserved. No part of this publication may be reproduced or transmitted in any form or by any means, electronic or mechanical, including photocopying, recording, or any information storage or retrieval system, without prior permission in writing from the publishers.

Bloomsbury Publishing Plc does not have any control over, or responsibility for, any third-party websites referred to or in this book. All internet addresses given in this book were correct at the time of going to press. The author and publisher regret any inconvenience caused if addresses have changed or sites have ceased to exist, but can accept no responsibility for any such changes.

A catalogue record for this book is available from the British Library.
Library of Congress Control Number: 2021951977

ISBN:	HB:	978-1-3502-6502-8
	PB:	978-1-3502-6506-6
	ePDF:	978-1-3502-6503-5
	eBook:	978-1-3502-6504-2

Series: Education, Literary Culture, and Religious Practice in the Ancient World

Typeset by Trans.form.ed SAS

To find out more about our authors and books visit www.bloomsbury.com
and sign up for our newsletters.

To the memory of Heythrop College

CONTENTS

List of Contributors		ix
Acknowledgments		xi
List of Abbreviations		xiii
1.	READING, WRITING, AND BOOKISH CIRCLES IN THE ANCIENT MEDITERRANEAN: AN INTRODUCTION Jonathan D. H. Norton	1
2.	THE SOCIAL STRATIFICATION OF SCRIBES AND READERS IN GRECO-ROMAN JUDAISM Lindsey A. Askin	12
3.	ASPECTS OF SCRIPTURALITY IN THE *COMMUNITY RULE*: A KEY TO THE HISTORY OF QUMRAN LITERATURE Annette Steudel	22
4.	THE MAKING OF THE THEME OF IMMORTALITY IN THE WISDOM OF SOLOMON Ekaterina Matusova	28
5.	BOOKISH CIRCLES? THE MOVE TOWARD THE USE OF WRITTEN TEXTS IN RABBINIC ORAL CULTURE Catherine Hezser	53
6.	SYMPOTIC LEARNING: SYMPOSIA LITERATURE AND CULTURAL EDUCATION Sean A. Adams	71
7.	TEACHING AND LEARNING IN PHILOSOPHICAL SCHOOLS OF THE SECOND CENTURY AD: ARRIAN'S EPICTETUS AND AULUS GELLIUS'S CALVENUS TAURUS Michael Trapp	88

8. THE LONE GENIUS AND THE DOCILE LITERATI:
   HOW BOOKISH WERE PAUL'S CHURCHES?
   Jonathan D. H. Norton   105

9. READING THE NEW TESTAMENT IN THE CONTEXT OF OTHER TEXTS:
   A RELEVANCE THEORY PERSPECTIVE
   Steve Smith   134

10. DIVINE DISSIMULATION AND THE APOSTOLIC VISIONS OF ACTS
    John Moxon   150

11. SCRIPTURAL LITERACY WITHIN THE CORINTHIAN CHURCH:
    FROM THE CORINTHIAN CORRESPONDENCE TO 1 CLEMENT
    H. H. Drake Williams, III   168

12. LIBRARIES, SPECIAL LIBRARIES, AND JOHN OF PATMOS
    Garrick V. Allen   183

Bibliography   204
Index of References   232
Index of Authors   246

List of Contributors

Sean A. Adams is Senior Lecturer in New Testament and Ancient Culture at the University of Glasgow, UK.

Garrick V. Allen is Senior Lecturer in New Testament Studies at the University of Glasgow, UK, and a research associate in the School of Ancient and Modern Languages and Cultures, University of Pretoria, South Africa.

Lindsey A. Askin is Lecturer in Jewish Studies at the University of Bristol, UK.

Catherine Hezser is Professor of Jewish Studies at SOAS, University of London, UK.

Ekaterina Matusova is a Heisenberg Fellow at Eberhard Karls University, Tübingen, Germany.

John Moxon is Head of Philosophy, Theology, and Religious Studies, University of Roehampton, UK.

Jonathan D. H. Norton is Lecturer in Second Temple Judaism and Christian Origins at King's College London and Honorary Research Fellow of the University of Roehampton, UK.

Steve Smith is Tutor and Lecturer in New Testament Studies, St Mellitus College, UK.

Annette Steudel is Professor in Early Judaism at Georg-August University, Göttingen, Germany.

Michael Trapp is Professor of Greek Literature and Thought at King's College London, UK.

H. H. Drake Williams, III is Associate Professor of New Testament at ETF Leuven, Belgium.

Acknowledgments

Our thanks go to all those who contributed papers at the Bookish Circles and Echoes of Audience colloquia at Heythrop College between 2016 and 2018, including Sascha Stern, Francesca Middleton, Matthew C. Nicholls, Bart J. Koet, Greg Woolf, Joan E. Taylor, Tim J. G. Whitmarsh, Ingo Kottsieper, Max Leventhal, Srecko Koralija, James K. Aitken, and Sean M. Ryan. Their papers, which belong to material published elsewhere, can be viewed on the Heythrop Centre for Textual Studies webpage.

We also want to take this opportunity to thank all those who helped in the creation and running of the Heythrop Centre for Textual Studies, from its inception in 2013 until the close of Heythrop College in August 2018. Thanks go to Heythrop colleagues and staff: Martin Poulsom, Karalina Matskevich, Marthe Kerkwijk, Charlotte Naylor Davis, Jonathan Gorsky, Michael Barnes, Tony Carol, Nick King, and Nadeem Ahmad. Special thanks go to Heythrop Colleagues: Bridget Gilfillan Upton, who proposed the centre in the first place, Sean M. Ryan and Ann Jeffers, whose support and involvement in the colloquia was invaluable throughout. Thanks go colleagues from other institutions who participated in colloquia over the years: John Barton, Jon Riding, Joe Norton, Matthew Kimberley, Mark Scarlata, Stacey Gutkowski, and Rebekah Welton. Thanks also to Mark Krycki, VictorFilms Limited, for the filming and production of all footage now available online. Special thanks go to Joe Norton and Kay Pickering for the excellent emergency catering services they provided at the Echoes of Audience colloquium in 2018, and for distributing leftovers among the rough-sleepers of Kensington.

Many thanks also to the editors of *Temas Medievales*, who allowed Catherine Hezser to substantially revise her article originally published in that journal as 'Bookish Circles? The Use of Written Texts in Rabbinic Oral Culture', *Temas Medievales* 25 (2017): 63–81.

Finally, we would like to express our gratitude to Heythrop College as an institution, and to the members of the Academic Research Committee between 2013 and 2018, for supporting and funding the Centre and its work. The closure of Heythrop College in August 2018, just after its 400th birthday, has been a matter of great sadness to those of us who studied, taught, and collaborated within its strangely peaceful walls next to the Sisters of the Maria Assumpta in the midst of bustling Kensington. It is with great fondness that we remember Heythrop's students, staff, colleagues, friends, and oddly sloping floors.

Abbreviations

AB	Anchor Bible
ABD	*Anchor Bible Dictionary*. Edited by David Noel Freedman. 6 vols. New York: Doubleday, 1992
AC	*L'Antinquité Classique*
AGAJU	Arbeiten zur Geschichte des antiken Judentums und des Urchristentums
AJEC	Ancient Judaism and Early Christianity
AJP	*American Journal of Philology*
ANTF	Arbeiten zur neutestamentlichen Textforschung
ANWR	*Aufstieg und Niedergang der römischen Welt*
ASNU	Acta Seminarii Neotestamentici Upsaliensis
ATD	Das Alte Testament Deutsch
AYB	Anchor Yale Bible
BBR	*Bulletin for Biblical Research*
BECNT	Baker Exegetical Commentary on the New Testament
BETL	Bibliotheca Ephemeridum Theologicarum Lovaniensium
BICS	*Bulletin of the Institute of Classical Studies*
BJS	Brown Judaic Studies
BT	*The Bible Translator*
BTB	*Biblical Theology Bulletin*
BZAW	Beihefte zur Zeitschrift für die alttestamentliche Wissenschaft
BZNW	Beihefte zur Zeitschrift für die neutestamentliche Wissenschaft
CB	Coniectanea Biblica
CBET	Contributions to Biblical Exegesis and Theology
CBQ	*Catholic Biblical Quarterly*
CBR	*Currents in Biblical Research*
CFQ	*California Folklore Quarterly*
CW	*Classical World*
DJG	*Dictionary of Jesus and the Gospels*. Edited by J. B. Green, J. K. Brown, and N. Perrin. Downers Grove: IVP, 1992
DSD	*Dead Sea Discoveries*
FAT	Forschungen zum Alten Testament
FRLANT	Forschungen zur Religion und Literatur des Alten und Neuen Testaments
GRBS	*Greek, Roman, and Byzantine Studies*
HTR	*Harvard Theological Review*
IBS	*Irish Biblical Studies*

ICC	International Critical Commentary
ISBL	Indians Studies in Biblical Literature
JAJ	*Journal of Ancient Judaism*
JANEH	*Journal of Ancient Near Eastern History*
JBL	*Journal of Biblical Literature*
JGRChJ	*Journal of Greco-Roman Christianity and Judaism*
JHelStud	*Journal of Hellenic Studies*
JHI	*Journal of the History of Ideas*
JHPh	*Journal of the History of Philosophy*
JJS	*Journal of Jewish Studies*
JLS	*Journal of Literary Semantics*
JQR	*Jewish Quarterly Review*
JRS	*Journal of Roman Studies*
JSJ	*Journal for the Study of Judausm*
JSJSup	Supplements to the Journal for the Study of Judaism
JSNT	*Journal for the Study of the New Testament*
JSNTSup	Journal for the Study of the New Testament Supplement Series
JSP	*Journal for the Study of the Pseudepigrapha*
JTS	*Journal of Theological Studies*
LHBOTS	Library of Hebrew Bible/Old Testament Studies
LNTS	Library of New Testament Studies
LSTS	The Library of Second Temple Studies
NIGCT	New International Greek Testament Commentary
NovT	*Novum Testamentum*
NovTSup	Supplements to Novum Testamentum
NRth	*La nouvelle revue théologique*
NTS	*New Testament Studies*
OLA	Orientalia Lovaniensia Analecta
OSAPh	*Oxford Studies in Ancient Philosophy*
PRSt	*Perspectives in Religious Studies*
RAC	*Reallexikon für Antike und Christentum*
REP	*Routledge Encylopedia to Philosophy*
RevQ	*Revue de Qumran*
RhetR	*Rhetoric Review*
SBB	Stuttgarter biblische Beiträge
SBLSP	Society of Biblical Literature Seminar Papers
SEP	*Stanford Encyclopedia of Philosophy*. Edited by E. N. Zalta. https://plato.stanford.edu/info.html
SJT	*Scottish Journal of Theology*
SNTSMS	Society for New Testament Studies Monograph Series
SP	Sacra Pagina
SPB	Studia Post Biblica
STDJ	Studies on the Texts of the Desert of Judah
SPhilo	*Studia Philonica*
StPatr	*Sudia Patristica*
TENT	Texts and Editions for New Testament Study
TJ	*Trinity Journal*

TNTC	Tyndale New Testament Commentaries
TSAJ	Texte und Studien zum antiken Judentum
TynBul	*Tyndale Bulletin*
VC	*Vigiliae Christianae*
VT	*Vetus Testamentum*
WBC	Word Biblical Commentary
WUNT	Wissenschaftliche Untersuchungen zum Neuen Testament
ZNW	*Zeitschrift für die neutestamentliche Wissenschaft und die Kunde der älteren Kirche*

1

Reading, Writing, and Bookish Circles in the Ancient Mediterranean: An Introduction

Jonathan D. H. Norton

Anyone in the Greco-Roman era bound to complete all three cycles of Greek literary education (*enkuklios paideia*) was on a gilded path. As writers like Quintilian, Tyconius, Pseudo-Plutarch, Philo and Seneca tell us, such levels of attainment were reserved for élite men of senatorial, equestrian or decurion *ordine*, whose public careers in law or politics required the highest levels of literacy.[1] The papyri have shown how 'the majority of women who attained a degree of literary education belonged to the upper strata of society and came from propertied environments'.[2] Yet the vast majority of students who embarked on a Greek literary education would not attain its highest levels.[3] People from the sub-decurion strata (about 95% of the population) exhibited huge variety of educational achievements at the primary and secondary levels, ranging from complete illiteracy to varying levels of functional semi-literacy.[4] Many of those who had received some level of literary education were 'able to read and write short texts, slowly'.[5]

---

[1] Teresa Morgan, *Literate Education in the Hellenistic and Roman Worlds* (Cambridge: Cambridge University Press, 1998), 226–34. With reference to Quintilian, Sean Ryan says, 'completion of the cycle of ἐγκύκλιος παιδεία prepared an élite minority of students for an oratorical career in law or politics' (*Hearing at the Boundaries of Vision: Education Informing Cosmology in Revelation 9* [London: T&T Clark, 2012], 13).
[2] Raffaella Cribiore, *Gymnastics of the Mind: Greek Education in Hellenistic and Roman Egypt* (Princeton: Princeton University Press, 2001), 75.
[3] This has long gone without saying for men. It is worth noting that pockets of evidence exist for female scribes and teachers from sub-decurian ranks (Ryan, *Hearing*, 23).
[4] Cribiore, *Gymnastics*, 18.
[5] Ryan, *Hearing*, 9.

Greco-Roman authors' own depiction of Greek literary education, then, has two significant features. First, education is viewed predominantly from the perspective of the élites. Second, the three-tiered cycle they present is readily conceived as a scale upon which any given ancient person might be placed. Modern enquiry into ancient literacy has reflected these two features of ancient élite preoccupation. Mid-twentieth-century study tended to focus on how the emergence of an organized writing system affected Greek culture (a discussion inevitably skewed toward the perspective of the ruling classes).[6] As long as writing was viewed principally as an agent of social change, 'literacy' remained a monolithic category in analysis. Secondly, such an undifferentiated conception of literacy readily translates into a single *scale of literacy* that reflects Roman social stratification. It is hardly surprising, then, that William Harris' magisterial study, *Ancient Literacy* (1989), whose influence on scholarship is universally acknowledged, focused precisely on *levels* of literacy. But as Ramsay MacMullen had already declared: 'there are plenty of studies on literacy, none on its use, that I know of'.[7]

In the past twenty or so years the study of literacy in the ancient Mediterranean has undergone a transformation. The quantitative conception of literacy levels (what percentage of ancient people could read and write, and to what extent) has given way to increasingly qualitative discussion. Historians now seek not only to distinguish *kinds* of literacy associated with textual activity but also, through appeal to material culture and social-historical data, to understand how these kinds functioned within particular *contexts*. Thus, discussion of the ways in which people from various social circles engaged with texts, alongside the practicalities and economics of text-production, have become prominent in the wider discussion of literacy. This development undoubtedly picks up the interest in the subaltern, which has grown among historians, archaeologists and social scientists over the past seventy or so years.[8] Recent publications in Classics demonstrate the success of this approach[9] and enquiry is now burgeoning in the fields of Hebrew Bible, Second Temple Judaism, early Rabbinics, and early Christian studies. Refined by social scientific insights, and fuelled by continued publication and study of Judaean manuscripts, Egyptian papyri, and collections from Vesuvian Pompey, the study of Jewish reading and writing cultures in ancient Near Eastern and Greco-Roman contexts is likewise blooming.[10] As we peer

---

[6] William A. Johnson, 'Introduction', in *Ancient Literacies: The Culture of Reading in Greece and Rome*, ed. W. A. Johnson and H. N. Parker (Oxford: Oxford University Press, 2009), 3.

[7] Ramsay MacMullen, 'The Epigraphic Habit in the Roman Empire', *AJP* 103 (1982): 233–246, here 233; cited by Shirley Werner, 'Literacy Studies in Classics', in Johnson and Parker, eds., *Ancient Literacies*, 333.

[8] See Stephen Morton, 'The Subaltern: Genealogy of a Concept', in *Gayatri Spivak: Ethics, Subalternity and the Critique of Postcolonial Reason*, ed. Stephen Morton (Malden: Polity, 2007), 96–7.

[9] Werner, 'Literacy', gives an excellent overview of work done within the Classics from around 1990. Two volumes which have particularly influenced the present publication are: Johnson and Parker, eds., *Ancient Literacies*; Jason König, Katerina Oikonomopoulou, and Greg Woolf, eds., *Ancient Libraries* (Cambridge: Cambridge University Press, 2013).

[10] Building on earlier work by, for example, Birger Gerhardsson and Werner Kelber, enquiry into the culture of early Jewish and Christian reading and writing in an oral world has been progressed in particular by Catherine Hezser and Martin S. Jaffee (cited in this volume). See also A. K. Bowman and G. Woolf, eds., *Literacy and Power in the Ancient World* (Cambridge: Cambridge University Press, 1994), as well as studies cited in this volume by Sean Ryan, David Stern, Alan Millard, and

more closely at surviving *realia* of ancient literary culture, so grows our interest in the mechanics and socio-economic implications of textual production, on the one hand, and ancient audiences' literary experiences, on the other.

Yet it can be difficult to locate a mainstream in discussion, since an old tendency to silo studies off into departmental subject areas persists. As a result, a significant amount of data from the Greco-Roman period remains understudied. Much of this evidence falls within the scope of biblical and post-biblical studies. In our view there is still great potential for efforts in these areas to be shared and integrated into a larger discussion of ancient Mediterranean life. For example, in his study of the reading culture of Roman statesmen, William A. Johnson has emphasized that, far from being some closed end in itself, reading served a complex of social functions that were 'tied *essentially* to particular contexts'.[11] Johnson's study focuses on élite reading circles, for whom there is plenty of evidence. But he notes how his approach could be fruitfully applied to non-élite circles, too. As several essays in the present collection show, early Christian and rabbinic writings provide excellent material for studying reading practices in such provincial, sub-decurion circles.

Our aim in this volume, then, is to put our shoulder to the wheel of ongoing efforts to bring these sub-disciplines into closer dialogue. We hope that these studies help not only to enrich the seams available for Classicists to mine but also enliven discussions of material that is often specially fenced off as religious or theological. As these chapters show, the historical context of textual activity in the ancient Mediterranean casts significant new light on older questions of the emergence and transmission of sacred scripture in early Judaism and Christianity. Likewise study of the ancient Jewish and Christian materials have great potential to shape research in Classics in ways that have yet to be fully exploited.

The participants in this project gathered from 2016 to 2018 at a series of colloquia and seminars at the *Heythrop Centre for Textual Studies*, Heythrop College, University of London. Many of the papers were filmed and can be viewed on the *Heythrop Centre for Textual Studies* web page. Although publication has been delayed due to the closure of Heythrop College in 2018, this volume is the published result. Some of those who contributed to the colloquia had already published their work elsewhere.[12] Their contributions to the proceedings, which can be viewed online, have helped to shape the work and thought in this volume.

In fact, this volume contains contributions to two related projects. The *Bookish Circles* colloquia took place at Heythrop College during 2016–2017 under the full title: *Bookish Circles – Varieties of Adult Learning and Literacy in the Greco-Roman Mediterranean*. Focusing on varieties of adult literary education in ancient

---

Chris Keith. Understanding of Jewish scribal culture has been progressed by, among others, Michael Fishbane, Emanuel Tov, Karel van der Toorn, Eibert Tigchelaar, D. Andrew Teeter, Sidnie White Crawford, Philip Davies, and Philip Alexander.

[11] William A. Johnson, *Readers and Reading Culture in the High Roman Empire: A Study of Elite Communities* (Oxford: Oxford University Press, 2010), 20 (italics original).

[12] Francesca Middleton, Srecko Koralija, Max Leventhal, Sascha Stern, Greg Woolf, Joan E. Taylor, Tim J. G. Whitmarsh, Matthew C. Nicholls, Bart J. Koet, Ingo Kottsieper, James K. Aitken, and Sean M. Ryan presented material that has been published elsewhere. Their contributions have played an important role in informing the discussion published within these pages.

Mediterranean contexts, the participants pursued the ongoing quest to distinguish kinds of literacy and their social functions. Several of the essays in this study pursue the lines of enquiry chosen for these colloquia, that is: how 'bookish' various reading communities really were in late antiquity; what forms of adult education are discernible in texts of the period; in what sort of social contexts people read and learned, and why they did so.

When we look at varieties of textual encounter, audiences emerge more clearly from the shadow normally cast by authors and their writings, especially when those writings have long been enshrined in classical canons. In further pursuit of this question the 2018 Heythrop colloquium, *Echoes of Audience in Ancient Writings* focused on what texts can reveal about their audiences. Attending to what a text implies about its own context is a stock-in-trade of historians. The process of inferring past context from literature (known colloquially in New Testament studies as 'mirror-reading') includes the drawing of inferences about a text's first author(s) and audiences(s), the relationships among them, and what role reading played in defining those relationships. The literary-critical and historical techniques involved in correlating *implied* and *past* audiences hold considerable potential for the wider task of studying how kinds of literacy functioned in the lives of ancient people. As some of the following chapters seek to show, attention to what a text implies about its audience can help to bring ancient audiences into clearer view while preventing literary élites from eclipsing those audiences and their literary encounters.

The questions posed in both projects inevitably raise further sets of issues. If an ancient reading community was not 'bookish' in the modern sense of the term, then how did its members encounter texts? What kinds of texts did they encounter? Were they literary, administrative, documentary, contractual, personal? What did the scrolls or books on which the texts were inscribed look like? How were they made, by whom and for whom? How were they housed and where? What role did these books play in a community's shared ideology, sense of place-in-the-world and ability to meet changes in that world? All of the essays in this volume address these questions.

In her essay, 'The Social Stratification of Scribes and Readers in Greco-Roman Judaism', Lindsey Askin questions a hierarchical assumption that characterizes much enquiry into ancient Jewish literacy. That is, while Second Temple Jewish scribes are usually imagined as rather solitary literary élites, or as quasi-monastic sages engaged solely in copying and editing literary texts, their *readers* are pictured as simultaneously privileged and indiscriminately passive audiences. According to Askin, this assumption perpetuates an impression that *literature* is the only type of text encountered by a scribe or reader, and, indeed, that reading and writing are socially stratified activities which take place within a hierarchy. However, the 'context of letters' for Jewish scribes and readers includes *non*-literary texts, such as correspondence, wages, catalogues, labels, and other types of writing. Askin argues that, contrary to the common assumption, the boundaries between scribe and reader are often more permeable than widely supposed. She seeks to investigate how documentary and inscriptional evidence might allow us to place scribes' and readers' experiences into a more coherent historical picture, in which the two groups are not socially estranged in such a polar manner. When this is done, says Askin, the close interaction between the makers and users of text makes more realistic sense in historical terms. This point is supported by other essays in this collection.

In her 'Aspects of Scripturality in the *Community Rule*: A Key to the History of Qumran Literature', Annette Steudel looks at the scribal voluntary association which lies behind key sectarian texts found among the Dead Sea Scrolls. Looking at manuscript evidenced, Steudel observes the way in which members of this Jewish movement composed, transmitted, and edited their own religious texts as their circumstances changed over time. She finds that the members of this association did not merely pursue literacy for literacy's sake. Rather, their literary pursuits were undertaken in the service of adapting their worldview as the world around them changed. Drawing inferences from some rare autograph material found in the caves at Qumran, Steudel is able to trace the process by which a small group of collaborating scribes developed their messianic reading of prophetic writings in response to developments in the political and religious landscape of Hasmonaean Judaea. An intimate glimpse into the literary life of one particular scribe's contribution to his group's outlook shows once again how literary pursuits were embedded in social contexts. Although this sectarian group seems to comprise an unusually literate membership, Steudel's study tends to support Askin's broader contention that the boundary between those who produce texts and those who use them is much more permeable than often assumed.

In 'The Making of the Theme of Immortality in the Wisdom of Solomon', Ekaterina Matusova continues to explore the way in which Jewish writers in the Hellenistic period pursue ideological debates with contemporaries through literary composition. Regarding the subject of immortality in the Wisdom of Solomon, she proposes a certain correction of focus. Rather than asking whether the author holds a Greek or Jewish view of immortality, she looks into how his statements on immortality have been formed. Engaging in debates reflected in other contemporary Jewish texts, in Greek and in Hebrew, she finds that the author is drawing on a framework of Platonic theology to formulate his polemics against the theology of 'creation with hatred' and 'predestination for destruction' expressed in the Greek text of Ben Sira and the first three columns of the Damascus Document. Elements of Plato's *Republic* and *Timaeus* help to explain why he turns to Platonic philosophy to formulate his polemic. Matusova's study shows that the author of Wisdom, untroubled by differences between the Jewish and Platonic attitudes to immortality, was attracted by the support which Greek philosophical ideas could lend to his Jewish position.

In 'Bookish Circles? The Move toward the Use of Written Texts in Rabbinic Oral Culture', Catherine Hezser asks to what extent the Sages were 'bookish circles'. The answer depends on what period is in view. Hezser distinguishes three stages in the use of written material, which she treats backwards. Only in the latest stage, from the tenth century onwards can we 'hesitatingly' talk about 'bookish' circles in Jewish culture. This is the post-Talmudic period leading to the Middle Ages, the period when the large written documents existed and when rabbinic academies for the study of the Talmud emerged. Moving backwards to the period from the fifth to tenth centuries – that is, the time when the Talmud and Midrash were edited – she finds a mixed use of oral and written sources. The evidence does not indicate that written sources were valued more highly than orally transmitted material in this period. Moving back again to her earliest period – that is, the amoraic period – there is only scanty evidence of a rabbinic use of written texts, whether rabbinic or biblical. In this period, Torah memorisation established in school and supplemented in weekly synagogue readings made recourse to written texts largely unnecessary. Since rabbinic study was meant to make Torah relevant for contemporary circumstances, this endeavour went far beyond Torah on which it was based, creating a new and continuing (Oral) Torah to which each generation of scholars contributed.

In 'Symptotic Learning: Symposia Literature and Cultural Education', Sean A. Adams investigates the ways that learning is represented in ancient symposia. Like the best of Greek literature, a good symposium was written to be both entertaining and instructive. Tracing how authors redeployed and developed the symposium genre, Adams examines the authors' view on who should learn, what they should learn and when they should learn it. Symposia promote the value of learning by depicting the characters within the text as eager students, although they tend to be extremely well educated, privileged people. Symposia texts are partly self-referential in that readers of symposia participate in the process through the act of reading itself. The authors tend to reinforce the centrality of Greek culture and the inherent importance of learning, even for those of lower social rank. Although the ideal learner is a free, Greek male who starts young, the authors also favourably depict women and late starters who embark on modest learning. Adams also shows how symposia refer to their own literary heritage, meaning that those readers who know the literary archetypes – the symposia of Plato and Xenophon – will gain most from reading them. Authors of Jewish symposia make use of this awareness to present Jewish culture favourably in terms of this Greek heritage.

In 'Teaching and Learning in Philosophical Schools of the Second Century AD: Arrian's Epictetus and Aulus Gellius's Calvenus Taurus', Michael Trapp seeks to look into the classrooms of the second century CE. While two of Lucian's dialogues, *Hermotimus* and *Nigrinus*, initially promise a glimpse into what adult learning looked like in a philosophical school, neither text makes the task easy, in the first case, because *Hermotimus*' teacher has a hangover, in the second, because Nigrinus's teacher suffers a fit of verbosity. Arrian's account of the discourses of the Stoic Epictetus and Aulus Gellius' *Attic Nights* seem to offer a little more hope. But Trapp must warn us of obstructions to visibility: the philosophers presented in these texts are mediated through the literary artifice of their authors.[13] We never encounter Taurus presenting himself but rather the character that Gellius constructs. Likewise, we never read Epictetus' self-presentation but Arrian's depiction of him. In the end, argues Trapp, neither Gellius nor Arrian give us more than very partial glimpses of Taurus' or Epictetus' classroom procedures, and even these are offered *en passant* in the pursuit of other ends. But Trapp's salutary study still provides helpful conclusions. Since these accounts of Taurus and Epictetus are driven by Arrian and Gellius's own

---

[13] The same problems also beset those who quest among the Gospels to find the Historical Jesus.

agendas, which allow a degree of representative background detail, the accounts must be broadly faithful to the kinds of context and procedure with which their subjects worked. So in the end, they do furnish us with some kind of overview of classroom modes and procedure. If we read these accounts for what they tell us about Gellius's and Arrian's expectations of a philosophical teacher's ethos and impact, then we may learn some of what we wanted to know.

In 'The Lone Genius and the Docile Literati: How Bookish Were Paul's Churches?', Jonathan Norton questions the way many modern interpreters characterize Paul's communication with his audiences. Scholars often treat Paul as an active thinker presenting his "Thought" to mutely passive auditors. This portrait implies that Paul's audiences possessed extensive familiarity with large swathes of text but remained devoid of any doctrinal conviction about its meaning. This is an historically very unlikely combination. To catch the communicative coherence of Paul's letter, we should rather view Paul engaging in a conversation in which the audience themselves are also keenly engaged. We should not see Paul aloofly disseminating religious wisdom to audiences capable only of mute admiration. In particular, we should see Paul and his first audiences as a group of Christians engaged in a lively and well-informed dialogue that is more evenly balanced than we often suppose. Most early Christians may not have been bookish. But they do seem to have entered a voluntarily religious movement with an explicitly literary and exegetical ethos. Paul seems to have taken their exegetical aspirations seriously.

In his chapter, 'Reading the New Testament in the Context of Other Texts: A Relevance Theory Perspective', Steve Smith applies relevance theory to the question of early Christian reading. In describing an almost instantaneous interaction in the reader's mind between the words on the page and the interpretive context of the reader, the theory shows how the reader actively constructs meaning in a process that revolves around relevance. Smith argues that, when they engaged with texts, ancient readers added new knowledge to what they already knew. While this process is common to all readers, Smith shows how the theory: makes a particular contribution to understanding how ancient readers approached texts; and explains how readers can read at more superficial or at deeper levels. While different readers bring different configurations of encyclopaedic information to the texts they read, the author of the ancient text takes care to ensure that the reader is likely to understand the text in a manner that will ensure the communication unfolds as the author wants, that is, provided the reader reads in a manner that looks for optimal relevance. Smith's case study of Acts helps to show how, although a reader's encyclopaedic information is rich and elastic, the way that Luke has written his text suggests that he expected a good level of biblical competence in his readers.

In his 'Divine Dissimulation and the Apostolic Visions of Acts', John Moxon examines Luke's use of a Socratic–Cynic device in Acts 9–10 and asks what this might imply about Luke's early Christian audience. The device of didactic dissimulation was characteristic of Socratic tradition and Cynic pedagogy. It was also a characteristic of divine speech in the Greco-Roman world. But while Greco-Roman people were familiar with enigmatic utterance in divine speech, Jewish writers of the Hellenistic and early Roman eras were not comfortable with the idea that God might encrypt important warnings in coded messages. Nevertheless, this ploy is attributed to the divine voice in the visions of Paul and Peter in Acts 9:1–9 and 10:9–16. These dialogues in Acts see an anonymous interlocutor using enigmatic challenges, feigned ignorance, and misdirection to trap the subjects into confessing ignorance, prejudice, or wrong-doing. Although apparently visible in the Jesus tradition, other New Testament texts seem to discourage this approach to teaching. The fact that Luke uses the device here may suggest that his readers were developing cultural assimilation to popular Roman expectations of divine speech. Or Luke may be using the device to locate the characters' 'conversions' within a broader cultural narrative, where Christianity's role might otherwise be questioned. Finally, by 'parallelising' Peter and Paul – two central characters in the narrative – Luke may be working to reconcile two factions within Luke's audience, which may still be struggling with the remnants of the Jew-Gentile problem which appears in other New Testament texts.

In his essay, 'Scriptural Literacy within the Corinthian Church: From the Corinthian Correspondence to *1 Clement*', Drake Williams examines three documents written to a predominantly Gentile-Christian community in Corinth – 1 Corinthians, 2 Corinthians, and 1 Clement. Williams argues that this community developed its level of 'scriptural literacy' over time. That is, the 'bookish ethos' within the community grew between the writing of 1 Corinthians and the writing of 1 Clement, and it grew in part as a result of receiving the first two letters. Shifting away from characterizing literacy as a scale between illiterate and literate, Williams introduces 'appreciation of text' as a separate designation of literary competence. When viewed through this lens, Williams is able to conclude that the Corinthian congregation was growing increasingly literate with regard to its *appreciation* of scripture, even if its members were not more able to read as such. Their appreciation of the books of Deuteronomy and Isaiah at the time of 1 Corinthians came to encompass a few more texts by the time of 2 Corinthians. By the time of 1 Clement their textual appreciation had increased considerably. Here Williams emphasizes the dynamic effect that texts have on the literary competence of those who read them.

Garrick Allen's examination of the Revelation of John of Patmos, 'Libraries, Special Libraries, and John of Patmos', reveals the author's expert engagement with Greco-Roman and Jewish literature. Although John purports to be recounting a heavenly vision, his modes of composition suggest that he was a well-educated individual who combined extensive use of written copies with his own capacious memorisation of traditional literature. Allen concludes that direct appeal to written texts as well as memorisation of their contents played an important combined role in the literary life of the upper classes in Judaea and the diaspora, in both Hellenistic and Jewish circles. Allen's survey of known Jewish and Greco-Roman book collections shows that books, book collections, and special libraries played an important role in John's composition process, both in terms of the education on which John drew as he composed his revelation and in terms of his ongoing encounters with literature in the process of writing. Allen observes how John is able to offer a commentary on contemporary imperial politics to Christians in Asia Minor framed as a visionary experience and interpreted through traditional Jewish scripture.

By attending to what texts reveal about their own contexts, we have sought to recover the experiences of and relationships among the ancient people who made and used texts. In various ways, the contributors have responded to Askin's call to degrade the hierarchical distinction often proposed between ancient text-makers and text-users. Contributors have likewise responded to Hezser's observation that our own idea of 'bookishness' may not suitably describe how ancient people – even those who seem to us archetypally 'bookish' – really engaged with texts. The essays have explored how ancient writers and text-users pursued ideological debates with their contemporaries and adapted their worldviews through particular cultures of reading in response to changes in the world around them. Such reading cultures are discernible across the breadth of ancient Mediterranean life. This breadth should warn us against bounding the 'Classical' literature off from the Jewish and early Christian literatures as separate *corpora* to be studied by distinct guilds of theological specialists. This point bears underscoring once again. Although many of the papers presented at the *colloquia* from 2016 to 2018 dealt with Classical literature 'proper',[14] the majority of essays in this volume concern Jewish or early Christian writings. Yet we have not felt impelled to change the title – *Reading, Writing, and Bookish Circles in the Ancient Mediterranean* – so as to signal some special interest in things theological. Our contention is precisely that Jewish or early Christian writings often play a central role in illuminating ancient Mediterranean life. Far from being religious and provincial *marginalia*, or the remit of strictly theological enquiry, Jewish and Christian writings bear lucid witness to central movements in Mediterranean life during the first and second centuries.

The point has been made by Tim Whitmarsh in his contribution to the Bookish Circles *colloquia*.[15] He notes the importance of Jewish and early Christian writings as witnesses to the 'literary bug' pervading the Roman Empire by the second century CE. The idea that owning a Greek literary canon sealed imperial legitimacy was a notion the Roman élites had inherited from the political jostlings of the Ptolemaic and Seleucid Empires, whose rulers had made ownership of Greek literary canons a principal tool of cultural warfare. From at least the age of Augustus, the Roman élite had increasingly sought to develop its own canon in imitation of classical Greek literary culture. But by the second century the impulse was not a solely imperial, political one confined to the Roman political classes. Works like Pseudo-Aristeas or *Ezekiel the Tragedian* show that Jews, too, were re-writing their traditions in Greek literary styles. Likewise, by the second century a Syriac literature was being developed from scratch around Edessa while a Coptic literature was being developed, again, from scratch, in Egypt. Later, in the age of Augustine, Latin Christianity would strive to develop its own Latin literature. As Whitmarsh notes, by the second century the Mediterranean was an environment in which people sought 'to create large networks of cultural unity through the circulation of texts'. He points to early Christianity, with

---

[14] The contributions of Francesca Middleton, Sean M. Ryan, Tim Whitmarsh, Greg Woolf, and Matthew Nichols (most of which can be viewed online) all broached 'classical' material.

[15] Tim Whitmarsh, 'The Paper With No Name', presented at Heythrop College, University of London, 11 January 2017. This can be viewed online.

its preference for letters (which can be collected and re-circulated), as 'one of the first manifestations of this internationally text-networked world'.

In recent years a growing number of enquiries into ancient Mediterranean life have depended principally on early Christian or Jewish sources. For example, in her 2016 monograph, *At the Temple Gates*,[16] Heidi Wendt examines 'the religion of "freelance experts" in the Roman Empire'. This wide-ranging study, which treats a huge sample of Greek and Roman material, sits squarely within the field of 'classical studies'. Yet it is a corpus of early Christian writings that constitutes Wendt's central evidence for phenomena which, she contends, pervaded daily life from one end of the Mediterranean to the other. Paul's letters illuminate and unite the many scattered clues peppering the classical corpus which testify to the economy of 'freelance religious experts' that Wendt explores.[17] This kind of approach to Paul's letters underlies the contributions of Drake Williams and Jonathan Norton in this volume.

Comparable is the growing body of literature on Greco-Roman guilds and associations. Scholars in various disciplinary fields increasingly invoke the Jewish and Christian materials as witnesses to various religions, associations, and mystery cults to be found throughout the Greco-Roman Mediterranean.[18] Meanwhile, several scholars specializing in Jewish and early Christian studies are increasingly examining Jewish and Christian groups as well-documented examples of Hellenistic associations.[19] Essays in this volume develop this line of enquiry. Annette Steudel's study of a sectarian scribe provides an intimate glimpse into literary activity within a Jewish religious voluntary association. Ekaterina Matusova casts light onto debates between Jews of distinct intellectual movements of the Hellenistic era, which includes Jewish appeal to Platonic traditions. John Moxon shows how the author of Acts draws on classical Greek literary heritage to edify his early Christian audiences.

A final example, the study of ancient libraries, shows how the classical, Jewish, and Christian materials illuminate common areas of ancient Mediterranean life. The 2013 collection, *Ancient Libraries*,[20] which provided a major impetus for this volume, deals with Greek and Roman materials. Yet, as recent publications show,[21] the study of

---

[16] Heidi Wendt, *At the Temple Gates: The Religion of Freelance Experts in the Roman Empire* (Oxford: Oxford University Press, 2016).

[17] Wendt's approach stands in a lineage of New Testament scholarship exemplified by the work, for example, of Wayne Meeks, Bernadette J. Brooten, Abraham J. Malherbe, Stanley Stowers, Clarence Glad, Troels Engberg-Pederson, and Paula Friedrickson.

[18] For example, Marvin W. Meyer, *The Ancient Mysteries. A Sourcebook of Sacred Texts* (Philadelphia: Temple University Press, 1999); Mary Beard, John North, and Simon Price, *Religions of Rome: Volume 1. A History* (Cambridge: Cambridge University Press, 1998); Mary Beard, John North, and Simon Price, *Religions of Rome: Volume 2. A Sourcebook* (Cambridge: Cambridge University Press, 1998); John S. Kloppenborg and Richard S. Ascough, *Greco-Roman Associations: Texts, Translations, and Commentary* (Berlin: de Gruyter, 2011).

[19] For example, Yonder M. Gillihan, *Civic Ideology, Organisation and Law in the Rule Scrolls* (Leiden: Brill, 2012); Pieter B. Hartog and Jutta Jokiranta, 'The Dead Sea Scrolls in Their Hellenistic Context', *DSD* 24 (2017): 339–55; Benedikt Eckhardt, *Private Associations and Jewish Communities in the Hellenistic and Roman Cities*, JSJSup 191 (Leiden: Brill, 2019); Richard S. Ascough, *Paul's Macedonian Associations: The Social Context of Philippians and 1 Thessalonians* (Eugene: Wipf & Stock, 2020).

[20] König, Oikonomopoulou, and Woolf, eds., *Ancient Libraries*.

[21] For example, Cecilia Wassen and Sidnie White Crawford, eds., *The Dead Sea Scrolls at Qumran and the Concept of a Library* (Leiden: Brill, 2015); Jonathan Norton, 'The Qumran Library and

libraries, book collections, and the social circles that curated and used them spans the breadth of available literary and artefactual materials from the ancient Mediterranean, including Greek, Roman, Jewish, Christian, and other ancient Near Eastern traditions. Garrick Allen's essay develops this insight with reference to John of Patmos and the first readers of his apocalypse.

We are bound to view the ancient Mediterranean largely through texts. Endlessly agreeable as it is to study this literature, we are well reminded to keep reading *through* the texts if we want to find the lives behind. Those lives did not retreat neatly into academic subject areas. The circles overlapped. We hope that the readers of this volume enjoy entering our own bookish circle. And we hope that these chapters show the value of drawing the early Jewish and Christian materials into the mainstream of ancient literacy studies.

---

the Shadow it Casts on the Wall of the Cave', in *Ancient Readers and Their Scriptures: Engaging the Hebrew Bible in Early Judaism and Christianity*, ed. G. V. Allen and J. A. Dunne (Leiden: Brill, 2019), 40–74.

2

The Social Stratification of Scribes and Readers in Greco-Roman Judaism

Lindsey A. Askin

Jewish scribes in the Greco-Roman period and their respective readers have been a topic of interest in recent research. Modern discussions outline ancient scribes and readers as somewhat theatrically juxtaposed: active/passive, creative/receptive, elite/popular, literary/non-literary. Jewish scribes are presumed to be literary elites or proto-monastic sages engaged solely in copying or editing sacred literature, while lesser scribes do administrative tasks, running the economy elsewhere. Readers are imagined collectively as simultaneously privileged and indiscriminate audiences: highly educated and expecting a high sophistication of thought and style. Such readers are often conflated with a nebulous catch-all category, the so-called scribal circle. Reading is not a passive activity, however, but rather the force that steers textual transmission.

We know that scribes in the Hellenistic and Roman periods were often of low status and largely administrative, as Carol Bakhos has argued, yet much research on Jewish scribal culture preserves a vision of scribes as largely literary copyists.[1] This picture creates an impression that literature is the only evidence we have of scribal culture in Second Temple Judaism, or if not the only, then perhaps the more accessible evidence – or that the main type of text encountered by a Jewish scribe or Jewish reader in antiquity is literature. Reading and writing is then socially stratified between a minority of elite literati and a mass population of semi-illiterates who may or may not read letters and documents, let alone a short book or two. It is arguable, however, that research on scribal culture methodologically is only reliable and useful if it integrates both documentary and literary sources. By doing so, scribes can be

---

[1] Carol Bakhos, 'Orality and Memory', in *The Oxford Handbook of Jewish Daily Life in Roman Palestine*, ed. C. Hezser (Oxford: Oxford University Press, 2010), 488.

placed back into their natural environments in the landscape of early Judaism: not just Qumran and the Temple of Jerusalem, but also homes, farms, villas, cities, banks, and courts. Examining how scribes interact with common readers, in turn, sheds light on textual processes.

In studies, Jewish scribes seem to be socially separated from readers and most of society, as well as physically and temporally removed from the landscape and daily life of Second Temple Judaism. William V. Harris' study imagined two types of literacy in pre-modern societies: a scribal literacy (about 5–10 % of the population) and a professional or craftsman's literacy.[2] While more recent studies differ on the proportion of literacy and types of literacy, such research tends to maintain or even increase the boundaries between scribal literacy and that of everybody else. Research of this kind often can shape and influence where, what, and how we look for evidence of scribal culture,[3] thus often limiting discussion to ancient literature rather than incorporating documentary sources.

Mroczek disputes the categories of the 'biblical', and related searches for the 'biblical' in Second Temple literature, especially in pseudepigrapha and rewritten scripture, are unhelpful and dichotomizing. Using the 'biblical' as a lens and framework limits the scribal imagination of Jewish authors, and removes from view the variety of authors' strategies and interests besides the 'biblical' and questions of canon.[4] Yet as we search for ways in which the practices of scribes tell us about the formation of the Bible, or ancient Jewish literature overall as Mroczek does, we have relegated other categories of evidence as less helpful than literature is for understanding how scribes worked.[5]

A different picture is presented in studies of scribes in, for example, Hellenistic Egypt, where scribes were the backbone of administrative, financial, and economic work, with a similar structure in place throughout the Greek and Roman world.[6] In Classical studies, scribes are mainly administrators, servants and sometime copyists, below the level of the intellectual elite.[7] Since many documentary sources of education survive from Greco-Roman Egypt, we now know that some level of scribal education was available for any who could afford it. Most school pupils with access to this

---

[2] William V. Harris, *Ancient Literacy* (Cambridge, MA: Harvard University Press, 1989); cited in Bakhos, 'Orality and Memory', 485.

[3] Some recent studies include: David M. Carr, *Writing on the Tablet of the Heart: Origins in Scripture and Literature* (Oxford: Oxford University Press, 2005); Carr, *The Formation of the Hebrew Bible: A New Reconstruction* (Oxford: Oxford University Press, 2011); William M. Schniedewind, *How the Bible Became a Book* (Cambridge: Cambridge University Press, 2004); Eva Mroczek, *The Literary Imagination in Jewish Antiquity* (Oxford: Oxford University Press, 2016); Karel van der Toorn, *Scribal Culture and the Making of the Hebrew Bible* (Cambridge, MA: Harvard University Press, 2007).

[4] Mroczek, *The Literary Imagination in Jewish Antiquity*, 8–9, 11.

[5] Ibid., 6–7.

[6] Michael Ivanovitch Rostovtzeff, *The Social & Economic History of the Hellenistic World*, 3 vols. (Oxford: Clarendon, 1941), 1.266.

[7] Raffaella Cribiore, *Writing, Teachers, and Students in Graeco-Roman Egypt* (Atlanta: Scholars Press, 1996); Cribiore, *Gymnastics of the Mind: Greek Education in Hellenistic and Roman Egypt* (Princeton: Princeton University Press, 2001); William A. Johnson and Holt N. Parker, eds., *Ancient Literacies: The Culture of Reading in Greece and Rome* (Oxford: Oxford University Press, 2009); Jocelyn Penny Small, *Wax Tablets of the Mind: Cognitive Studies of Memory and Literacy in Classical Antiquity* (London: Routledge, 1997); Rosalind Thomas, *Literacy and Orality in Ancient Greece* (Cambridge: Cambridge University Press, 1992).

education did not become scribes.[8] Reading, then, is not merely an activity of the scribe, but an activity available to most people in the ancient Mediterranean world by at least the Hellenistic era.

The 'context of letters' for Jewish scribes and readers might be extended then beyond literary sources, to include epigraphy, documents, receipts, wages, petitions, and identifying markers such as labels and seals. With this study, I propose a few ways in which documentary and other 'non-literary' evidence might illuminate further scribes' and readers' practices and concerns in their social and historical contexts. These contexts ought to help us place Jewish scribes in secular, not just sacred, settings.

The first problem, then, is that 'literary' scribes tend to eclipse other types of late Second Temple Jewish scribes. This view is problematic given bureaucratic innovations witnessed in the Hellenistic and Roman periods. The methodological hurdles in successfully integrating such documentary evidence is pointed out by Catherine Hezser – archaeological and documentary sources risk serving as handmaidens to other disciplines of history, biblical and rabbinic studies.[9]

The second, related problem is how to imagine the typical Jewish reader. While it is sometimes acknowledged that reading was far more common than writing in the ancient world, stereotyped Jewish readers remain mirror reflections of the scribe: a scribe's 'audience'. The reader is also passive and receptive, interested only in elite reading, appearing in quiet, solitary settings of sacred reading or oral performance. In this framework, little room remains for the reader to decide to read anything else besides sacred texts. Yet 'readers' and audiences underpin any discussion of the formation of ancient texts. Why then, do we continue to imagine Jewish scribes in such one-dimensional ways, or place literature on a higher tier than documents and wall scratchings? It could be that most readers read more inventories and contracts every day than literature, and encountered literature only once a week or even less, a few times a year. Likewise it may be that scribes tallied accounts and copied repetitive formulae most of the year or for much of their career, and copied texts only infrequently. Does such a mixture of exposure have an effect on how those scribes and readers understood each other, how they understood texts, or how they approached lists and contracts in Hebrew scripture and Second Temple literature?

Wages, Archives, Inventories

In historical writings, numeracy is taken with a pinch of salt. Numbers and even lists, such as inventories or genealogies, become interpretive political or religious statements. If mostly symbolic, when do exact numbers matter? In Classical Hebrew literature, numbers do not need to be exact for armies, tribes, the tally of Solomon's wives, and the size of royal treasuries. Symbolic round numbers tend to look nicer and provide the sense both that numbers mean whatever the scribe wants them to

---

[8] Cribiore, *Gymnastics*.
[9] Catherine Hezser, 'Private and Public Education', in *The Oxford Handbook of Jewish Daily Life in Roman Palestine*, ed. C. Hezser (Oxford: Oxford University Press, 2010), 465–81; Hezser, *Jewish Literacy in Roman Palestine* (Tübingen: Mohr Siebeck, 2001).

mean, and that readers have a similar liberal or symbolic sense of numeracy. For example, during the imprisonment of the bad king Jehoachin, Neco's tax on Jerusalem in 2 Kgs 24:33 seems to be quite accurate: one hundred talents of silver and one talent of gold. In 2 Kgs 6:25, the siege of Samaria by Ben-Hadad king of Aram lasts so long that 'there was a great famine in the city; the siege lasted so long that a donkey's head sold for eighty shekels of silver, and a quarter of a cab of seed pods for five shekels'. The price of a chariot imported from Egypt for Solomon's stables in 2 Chron. 1:16 is exactly 600 shekels of silver, and a horse costs 150, although one might suppose that perhaps some bargaining took place. Solomon employs exactly 70,000 basket carriers, 80,000 quarriers, and 3,600 supervisors for his mines (2 Chron. 2:1). After the census of David, a divine pestilence is sent as a punishment, killing an even 70,000 of people from Dan to Beer-sheba (2 Sam. 24:1-9). Perhaps it was because David rounded off the numbers.

Wages, taxes, and prices in the Hebrew Bible do have a nicely realistic sound to them. Yet in other numbers, especially of people and in genealogies of chronological ages as in Genesis, numbers shift to estimates and often get inflated. This tells us something about human ability to imagine very large numbers of populations and crowds, but we might also see these types of numbers in light of documentary texts. Thus we can compare the attitudes towards numeracy in literature to those of daily life, which is important since scribes are the administrative and economic backbone of a society, writing receipts and balancing the books, and yet are also the copyists of literature in which we have a mix of realistic and symbolic numbers.

For example, we have a case of a petition of a Jewish man against the village scribe:

CPJ I 43. Tcherikover and Fuks.

P.Ryl. 578, from Philadelphia (Fayum), 17.5 x 12cm. Mid-second century BCE

Petition of a Jewish peasant.

A petition of a Jew, Judas son of Dositheos, to epimeletes Zopyrion re the action of his village scribe, Marres who has raised the rent on him.

[*broken*] 29. To Zopyrus epimeletes from Judas son of Dositheos, Jew. I am a farmer of around 3 arourai of dry ground near Philadelphia at the pre-existing annual rental of 4 artabai of wheat per aroura. This dry ground I have cultivated with great distress and expense, and have completed the annual payments for rent satisfactorily up to the 23rd year. But now Marres the village scribe (Μαρρῆς ὁ κωμογραμματεὺς) has entered me, contrary to what is right, for the amount of 5 2/3 artabai of wheat per aroura over and above the amount of rent, though I have never paid this sum. Therefore I appeal to your clemency and request you, if you will, to write to the proper authority for accurate details to be submitted to you, so that if the facts are as I state them, you may take care that I do not have to pay any improper exaction, and I myself may obtain my just rights. Farewell. [*broken*]

In this case, a Jewish farmer has submitted a petition. Hellenistic petitions are quite formulaic and we might imagine he had some conversations with the scribe who helped him make his case. The scribe of this petition then makes two copies, one for the office, and one for Zopyrus, the higher official, the addressee. In the Ptolemaic government, the village scribe (*komogrammateus*) and the village chief together had the important role of annually reviewing the land holdings – numbers which then go to higher levels up to toparchs, nomarchs, and then to Alexandria, and this is where things have gone wrong for Judas son of Dositheos, of Philadelphia. Marres has, for whatever reason, increased the rental of his land tenancy by a considerable amount, by 30 percent. The reason he has done this is unclear: Marres probably gets no considerable profit from increasing the numbers at this stage, and Judas appears to be looking back to previous years' rent for reference. As Rostovtzeff notes, government officials at the village level had very little profit in compensation for the dangerous nature of their jobs.[10] Tax collector was not a popular job, either today or in the past. Marres might have made a mistake, and it went to the higher levels and Judas finds himself in a very dangerous and risky position where Marres' bookkeeping might leave him penniless.

Comparing this kind of scribal error is interesting because often we look for scribal errors in literary manuscripts, but seldom elsewhere. In this case, accounting might have gone wrong – or perhaps there is no mistake and Marres just has a grudge against Judas. Unfortunately, we do not know the outcome of this case, as the copy of this petition is broken off and shows no record of the decision.

Another example from Hellenistic-period Egypt are receipts issued by Jewish tax-farmers:

CPJ I 107. Probably Thebes. 154/3 BCE.[11]

(2nd hand) I have received…

(1st hand) Simon son of Jazaros, tax-farmer controlling the 25 percent of fisher's tax for the 28th year, to Mesoeris, greetings. I have received from you, in respect of tax for you and your sons, in the month of Tybi, four thousand drachmai in copper, total 4000.

Written by Dellous at the request of Simon, because he is illiterate.

CPJ I 108. Thebes. 155/4 BCE.

Adaios to Simon, greetings. You have paid in respect of the pasture-tax for the land at Thebes for the 27th year three thousand seven hundred and forty drachmai in copper, total 3740.

---

[10] Rostovtzeff, *Social & Economic History*, 319.
[11] CPJ I 111 was probably dictated for someone who was illiterate like 107. For CPJ I 107, see A. H. Sayce, 'Jewish Tax-Gatherers at Thebes in the Age of the Ptolemies', *JQR* 2 (1890): 401–5. Sayce found this ostracon among several others on a trip to Karnak.

In the above cases and several others, the tax-farmers writing the receipts are likely Jewish, and in some cases the recipient is also probably Jewish (CPJ I 107–111).[12] These are examples where tax was paid, and the taxpayer received their written evidence of the transaction. Copies were also made for the record office. Perhaps these were cases where the taxpayer had absolutely no care for what is written exactly, as in the case of the illiterate man (CPJ I 107), and Simon son of Jazaros (Eleazar) simply holds onto his valuable slip of papyrus to show the authorities if they come calling. It is not clear whether Simon is illiterate in the sense of being unable to read, or simply unable to write his name. Perhaps he might have poor handwriting. But in the other cases, the tax receipt is addressed directly to the taxpayer, the reader. Here the numbers matter exactly, the writing is driven towards the service-user, and the written formula strictly adheres to the rules of accounting. The scribe may be either the tax-farmer or an assistant scribe.

Another reason that taxes are interesting is because of the care taken in the Ptolemaic period to record what people have paid. The Ptolemaic banking system was rather sophisticated. During this time, we can see good reason for having records in written form: when injustice strikes, written documents help. These items are not merely mundane articles of daily life, but lifesaving tax receipts for their recipients, and perhaps for the tax-farmer as he depends on their accuracy not to be lynched. Accounting documents such as these might be kept safe in one's house, with copies housed in official archives, alongside household property deeds, tenancy agreements, contracts, and other 'written' sources. In this light it is unfair to suggest these documents were all either just completely illegible to their owners, or if readable, they were ordinary pieces of papyrus that held far less meaning for most people than literary texts. If an important tax document can be produced at a time of injustice or trouble, would the owner of the document be able to point out which words refer to their correct rent? We could imagine perhaps, Judas digging out a previous rental agreement and pointing to the correct numbers to prove his case. It might be asking too much to suggest that farmers in such precarious financial situations rely completely on the honesty of scribal administrators to kindly tell them what their own tax documents say. It might also be helpful to recall that reading was far more common than writing skills in the ancient world.

Among these documentary sources, readers of all levels are expected to interact with the scribes, tax-farmers, about the contents and numbers of taxes, of inventories, and of censuses, on a number of levels. The scribe has to interact with the people around him and cannot be removed into a different solitary environment when considering questions of accuracy and scribal error. Errors can come from anybody in the vicinity speaking with the scribe. In the case of genealogies and symbolic numbers, we might ask whether scribes held onto a different set of literary or oral-literary expectations in storytelling, representing and communicating with an audience in symbolic numbers.

---

[12] CPJ I.104–111: CPJ I 104, 105, 106?, 109, and 110 are similar addressed directly '<name> to <name>'.

Funerary Inscriptions

A different type of writing and reading in Greco-Roman Judaism consists of inscriptions. Schwartz argues that ancient Israel and Second Temple Judaism are part of Mediterranean culture, meaning that the Mediterranean pre-modern societies functioned in an environment of limited resources, distributed between individuals and levels primarily by means of reciprocity, the classical definition of the bonds of friendship.[13] While it has often been said that ancient Israel and early Judaism rebelled against such ideas on the grounds of charity, Schwartz shows that most Mediterranean societies used charity to offset ingrained reciprocity-based systems. Charity kept the system of reciprocity in balance.

In funerary inscriptions, we have another resource of evidence for Jewish patronage in at least the Roman period. For example this inscription:

CIJ I.256 (=Noy II 218). Third/fourth century CE. Vigna Randanini catacomb, Via Appia[14]

NIKETE·PROSELYTO | DIGNO ET BENEMERENTI | DIONYSIAS · PATRONA FECIT

'For Niketas, the proselyte, a worthy and well-deserving man, Dionysias, his patroness, has set up (this tomb)'

There are around fourteen surviving Jewish inscriptions which mention proselytes, mostly from Italy and Judea. Reflecting a slightly different scenario of patronage, other inscriptions mention Jewish patrons gifting land to clients for tombs, such as the example of Livius Dionysius and Antonius. This type of patronage for burial space is comparable to Roman practices.[15]

CIJ I.533 (=Noy I 18). Second century CE. Castel Porziano (10km SW of Ostia)

[synagoga] IUDEORVM·
[in col(onia) ost(iensi) commor]ANTIVM QUI COMPARA
[verunt.ex.conlat]IONE·LOCVM·C·IVLIO·IVSTO
[gerusiarchae.ad.m]VNIMENTVM · STRVENDVM
[donavit.rogantib]VS·LIVIO·DIONISIO·PATRE·ET
[……………..]NO·GERVSIARCHE·ET·ANTONIO

---

[13] Seth Schwartz, *Were the Jews a Mediterranean Society? Reciprocity and Solidarity in Ancient Judaism* (Princeton: Princeton University Press, 2010).

[14] Jean-Baptiste Frey, ed., *Corpus Inscriptionum Judaicarum*, 2 vols. (Rome: Pontifical Biblical Institute, 1936); David Noy, *Jewish Inscriptions of Western Europe*, 2 vols. (Cambridge: Cambridge University Press, 1993). For another example of a Jewish patronized client named Theomnestos, see Libanius, *Epistulae* 1097.

[15] CIJ (Frey) I 533 (= Noy I 18) – second century CE, Castel Porziano (10km SW of Ostia). A similar inscription of patronage from Jerusalem is written in Greek for the *archisynagogos* Rufina, dating at earliest to the third century CE. CIJ II 741 (= IK Smyrna 295).

[..........diab]IV·ANNO·IPSORVM·CONSENT·GE[r]
[us.C.Iulius.Iu]STVS·GERVSIARCHES·FECIT·SIBI
[et.coniugi] SVAE·LIB LIB·POSTERISQUE·EORVM·
[in fro]NTE·P·XVIII·IN AGRO ·P· XVII

[The community] of Jews living in the colony of Ostia who from [the proceeds of a collection?] have acquired a plot of land (gave it) to C(aius) Iulius Iustus, [gerusiarch], to construct a tomb on, [have presented it] to him. [It was on the motion] of Livius Dionysius, the patron, and [...]nus, gerusiarch and Antonius ...[archon for] life, in their year (of office), with the agreement of the gerusia. [C(aius) Iulius Iu]stus, gerusiarch, made (this tomb) for himself [and his wife], his freedmen and freedwomen and their descendants. 18 feet across, 17 feet away from the road.

There are many hints of Jewish participation in the system of reciprocity earlier in the mid-third century BCE, such as the reciprocity between Zenon, the right-hand man of Apollonios, Ptolemy's finance minister, and Tobias. Tobias sends gifts to Zenon and to Ptolemy several times, a practice demonstrating the strengthening of a reciprocal friendship. Later examples from Judea would be the building projects of Herod the Great. While these projects partly functioned as means of increasing employment and as economic injection, they also represent an established means in Hellenistic society of a ruler developing a stronger relationship of reciprocity with the people.[16] This is done for example in the support and tax relief given by the Seleucid ruler to Jerusalem in the Seleucid charter of Jerusalem recorded by Josephus.[17]

Patronage or reciprocity become quite formalized in Roman times, but their basic principles were well established in the Mediterranean from an early stage. Reciprocity is an important relationship to publicly announce in writing, and therefore it is remarkable to have some written expressions of Jewish patronage in epigraphic form.

The readers and writers behind funerary inscriptions are interesting for another reason besides patronage: who reads tomb inscriptions? And who writes them? Are the readers of inscriptions only other wealthy literate people, or as in the case of patronage inscriptions, do readers include clients? This turns us towards the idea of functional or professional literacy, a question approached recently by Johnson and Parker, as well as Woolf, who argue for numerous kinds of literacy.[18] In the two inscriptions above, one is in the Jewish catacombs of Rome, where only 18 percent of inscriptions are

---

[16] Peter Richardson, *Herod: King of the Jews and Friend of the Romans* (Columbia: University of South Carolina Press, 1996); Samuel Rocca, *Herod's Judaea: A Mediterranean State in the Classical World*, TSAJ 122 (Tübingen: Mohr Siebeck, 2008); Norman Gelb, *Herod the Great: Statesman, Visionary, Tyrant* (Lanham: Rowman & Littlefield, 2013).

[17] Elias J. Bickerman, 'The Seleucid Charter of Jerusalem', in *Studies in Jewish and Christian History: A New Edition in English Including* The God of the Maccabees, ed. A. D. Tropper (Leiden: Brill, 2007), 315–56; Ronald Wallenfels, 'Seleucid Babylonian "Official" and "Private" Seals Reconsidered: A Seleucid Archival Tablet in the Collection of the Mackenzie Art Gallery, Regina', *JANEH* 2 (2015): 55–89.

[18] Johnson and Parker, *Ancient Literacies: The Culture of Reading in Greece and Rome*; Greg Woolf, 'Ancient Illiteracy?', *BICS* 58 (2015): 31–42.

in Latin, the rest mostly in Greek and Aramaic or Hebrew. The second is within the Jewish catacomb in Castel Porziano, near Ostia. There are other patronage-related funerary inscriptions in Judea which are in Greek. Who are their intended audiences? The sense is that they are meant to be read by other Latin-speaking Jews, prioritising the communication of status rather than imparting new information.

Several recent studies on Seleucid propaganda and monuments suggest that ordinary people were expected to be able to read the state language.[19] This theory explains why such great expense goes to creating them, and it explains why inscriptions are so formulaic. Formulas are easy to learn and recognize if you can expect them on every stele or inscription. Many funerary inscriptions follow similar patterns. One of the reasons why such monumental writing is formulaic is because it might be easier to read for those with some functional literacy. To press further, however, inscriptions are driven by the service user, implying meaningful interactions between scribe and 'author'. One may consider the implications of such interaction for other factors such as audiences, notions of posterity, communication of status and the purpose of public forms of writing.

Finally, below is an example of the last few words of an inscription from Jerusalem concerning Rufina, an *archsynagogos*, who offers an account of her deeds of patronage for her buried freedmen and slaves (CIJ II 741 [= IK Smyrna 295], no earlier than third century CE, Jerusalem). The inscription then offers a curse for those that disturb the tomb, and finally concludes confidently:

Α ΤΑΥΤΗΣ ΤΗΣ ΕΠΙΓΡΑΦΗΕ
ΤΟ ΑΝΤΙΓΡΑΦΟΝ ΑΠΟΚΕΙΤΑΙ
ΕΙΣ ΤΟ ΑΡΧΕΙΟΝ

'A copy of this inscription has been deposited in the record office'.

Conclusion

To conclude, a related example from Egypt may be helpful. For a long time it was assumed, owing to Herodotus, that the physicians of Egypt never spoke to the embalmers, the people who perform mummification, because embalmers were a 'hereditary and socially ostracized caste'.[20] Recent studies on Egyptian medicine show this not to be the case. There is no evidence that embalmers were ostracized or held only hereditary positions. They communicated fairly often with physicians, with whom they shared professional knowledge of anatomy.

The integration of documentary and literary products of Jewish scribes, however, needs some addressing, so that artefacts and documents do not become the handmaidens of studies that place an emphasis on sacred literature as the sole index

---

[19] Wallenfels, 'Seleucid Babylonian'.
[20] Kent R. Weeks, 'Medicine, Surgery, and Public Health in Ancient Egypt', in *Civilizations of the Ancient Near East*, ed. J. M. Sasson, G. M. Beckman, and K. S. Rubinson (Peabody: Hendrickson, 2000), 1787–98.

of scribal practices. Such a circular model tends to perpetuate the unhelpful habit of juxtaposing literature and documentary sources. One of the side effects of leaving documentary sources out of literary analyses, usually justified for reasons of existing specialisations or simplifying discussion, is that solely literary analyses produce narrow, literary results, which in turn produce 'literary-only' scribes. Fortunately, the surviving corpus of evidence for Greco-Roman Jewish writing and reading is impressive. By integrating artefacts and documents with literary texts, the researcher may discover more about how scribes and readers interacted. In turn, this information would shed more light on textual transmission and other processes.

The idea in the title of this study remains a problem for scribal culture and the literary atmosphere of Second Temple Judaism. Future studies would benefit from more methodological balance in the selection of data. One type of evidence cannot simply serve to inform another: documentary texts do not merely serve to inform us about Jewish literature, they inform us about the activity (and interactivity) of scribes and readers. Scribes must be placed back into their natural, highly social environment to see them more clearly among the landscape of early Judaism: courts, temple, households, villas, urban centres, banks and offices, unsafe roads through farming villages in Egypt. Along the way, documentary sources bring into focus the various characters – good, shady, passive, lively, honest, dishonest – with whom they interacted. A redefinition of scribal culture would be unnecessary. The definition of scribal culture is adequate: the textual and material products of scribes and systems of scribal education. Rather, one might suggest, even insist, that the term 'scribal culture' simply not be misconstrued and coopted by research which is selectively literary. Discussions of the nature of scribal circles, for example, might resist reification of such groups as rather ossified audiences, and leave room for scribal interactions with readers. A balanced methodology might consider the idea that scribe–reader interaction might mutually shape and inform reader (and writer) expectations of texts of all kinds, bringing documentary expectations to literature or vice versa. Before the subject of scribal culture becomes a servant to studies of the formation of sacred literature, researchers may consider reintegrating scribes and readers into the same physical environment, and into our analyses of the various roles these groups are required to perform in our modern debates.

3

Aspects of Scripturality in the *Community Rule*: A Key to the History of Qumran Literature

Annette Steudel

The nearly one thousand manuscripts recovered from the caves near the ruined settlement Khirbet Qumran are ideal examples for studying scripturality in antiquity,[1] even if it remains uncertain whether the evidence allows for general conclusions about scripturality among Jewish groups from the Second Temple period. Much remains historically unknown about the ancient group or groups responsible for the Qumran material, material that is almost exclusively literary and not documentary. Identifications of the movement and its leading members, whose names are never clearly mentioned, depend on the interpretation of the scrolls and their contextualization. Regardless of the results, it is clear that a significant number of members of the Qumran group was able to read and write. We see in these texts the capability to communicate in writing,[2] to compose literary texts,[3] to copy,[4]

---

[1] Cf. on the topic most recently Charlotte Hempel, 'Bildung und Wissenswirtschaft im Judentum zur Zeit des Zweiten Tempels', in *Was ist Bildung in der Vormoderne?*, ed. P. Gemeinhardt (Tübingen: Mohr Siebeck, 2020), 229–44.

[2] See the letter 4QMMT published in E. Qimron et al., eds., *Qumran Cave 4.V: Miqṣat Maʿaśeh Ha-Torah*, DJD 10 (Oxford: Clarendon, 1994). It exists in several copies and seems to address a leader of Israel.

[3] Certain criteria, like vocabulary and exegetical formulas, are traditionally used to define, which texts among the Qumran findings were composed by the movement, see e.g. Charlotte Hempel, 'Kriterien zur Bestimmung "essenischer Verfasserschaft" von Qumrantexten', in *Qumran kontrovers: Beiträge zu den Textfunden vom Toten Meer*, ed. J. Frey and H. Stegemann (Paderborn: Bonifatius, 2003), 71–85. At least at its fringes it is difficult to decide which texts actually belong to it.

[4] The exact number of scribes who copied the scrolls from the caves is unknown, but astonishingly the vast majority of scrolls were copied by different scribes, a fact that poses the question of where the manuscripts where copied. It is certain that many of them came from places other than the Qumran settlement, which had not been in use when the oldest manuscripts were written. Under the leadership of Mladen Popović the Groningen Qumran Institute is running a project on the development and application of digital research methods for a palaeographical analysis of the Dead Sea Scrolls.

to rewrite,[5] to hand down their authoritative scriptures,[6] to develop new worlds of thought,[7] and to find new genres in which to express them.[8]

In the following I will demonstrate different fields of scripturality at Qumran by looking at one of its major and best-preserved compositions, the *Community Rule* (S). I will also briefly sketch how these manuscripts fit into the yet-to-be written history of Qumran literature. The *Community Rule* exists in multiple copies which reflect different literary stages of the work. Its fullest copy, 1QS, is dated around 100 BCE or slightly later, that is, the work itself was composed and had already developed its most elaborate form by this date.[9]

The first example comes from the oldest literary layers of the composition.[10] It gives us a glimpse in the beginnings of the movement and concerns the requirement of communal study:

> In a place where the Ten (i.e. the quorum of ten Jewish men) are, there must not be lacking someone (איש) studying/interpreting (דרש) the Tora, day and night, 7 continually alternating[11] from one to another. And the many (הרבים) shall be awake together (יחד) for one third of every night of the year, reading aloud (קרא) in the Book, studying/interpreting (דרש) the law (משפט), and 8 praising (ברך) together (יחד). (1QS VI 6)

Thus, according to the *Community Rule*, every full member[12] of the group was able and obliged to read and to study/interpret Scripture. The process was done communally on a regular and frequent basis. A similar passage from the same scroll that

---

[5] Numerous rewritings of Scripture were found in the caves, and rewriting was also practiced with rule texts from Qumran, see Anette Steudel, 'The Damascus Document (D) as a Rewriting of the Community Rule (S)', *RevQ* 100 (2012): 605–20.

[6] Among the findings are about 200 copies of books that later on became part of the Bible.

[7] The dualistic so-called Treatise of the Two Spirits (1QS III 13–IV 26) and also the Songs of the Sabbath Sacrifice (ShirShabb) belong to the most unique pieces of Qumran literature, see e.g. M. Christian, 'The Literary Development of the "Treatise of the Two Spirits" as Dependent on Instruction and the Hodayot', in *Law, Literature and Society in Legal Texts from Qumran*, ed. J. Jokiranta and M. Zahn, STDJ 128 (Leiden: Brill, 2019), 153–84, and Noam Mizrahi, 'The Songs of the Sabbath Sacrifice and Biblical Priestly Literature: A Linguistic Reconsideration', *HTR* 104 (2011): 33–58.

[8] Unattested genres in Jewish literature before the Qumran era had been the thematic midrashim and the pesharim, which appeared around the end of second century BCE and prevailed until around 50 BCE. See e.g. James H. Charlesworth et al., eds., *The Dead Sea Scrolls: Hebrew, Aramaic, and Greek Texts with English Translations*, vol. 6B Pesharim, Other Commentaries, and Related Documents (Tübingen: Mohr Siebeck, 2002).

[9] See the most recent edition of Sarianna Metso, *The Community Rule: A Critical Edition with Translation* (Atlanta: SBL, 2019).

[10] The traditional view was that 1QS VIII–IX were the oldest parts of the work, but Sarianna Metso, *The Development of the Qumran Community Rule*, STDJ 27 (Leiden: Brill, 1997) and Reinhard Kratz, 'Der "Penal Code" und das Verhältnis von Serekh ha-Yachad (S) und Damaskusschrift (D)', *RevQ* 25 (2011): 199–227 and others have proved that 1QS V–VII is the most ancient core of the text.

[11] 'Alternating', חליפות, is the common conjecture for the reading of על יפות, literally meaning 'concerning the being-beautiful', which is nevertheless maintained by Geza Vermes, *The Dead Sea Scrolls in English* (London: Penguin, 2004), 77, J. Maier, *Die Qumran-Essener: Die Texte vom Toten Meer* (Munich: Reinhardt, 1995), 182, and others who understand the phrase 'concerning the right conduct of a man with his companion'.

[12] Column VI depicts the many as full members.

speaks of the group as a kind of (probably inner) exilic community reveals another aspect of scripturality:[13]

> ...When such men as these come to be in Israel, 13 conforming to these doctrines, they shall separate from the session of perverse men to go to the wilderness, there to prepare the way of truth, 14 as it is written, 'In the wilderness prepare the way of the LORD, make straight in the desert a highway for our God' (Isa. 40:3). 15 This means the expounding of the Law, decreed by God through Moses for obedience, that being defined by what has been revealed for each age, 16 and by what the prophets have revealed by His holy spirit. (1QS VIII 12)

In this passage again the group is demanded to interpret scripture, namely the Torah of Moses and the books of the Prophets. Especially new is the usage of a quotation from an authoritative text, the book of Isaiah, to make clear that by the study of the Law and Prophets the group fulfills what is written in scripture, that is, it fulfills God's will. Furthermore, the technical side of this passage – that is, having an explicit quotation introduced by a quotation formula and the interpretation separated from the quotation by an interpretation formula – was an innovation among Qumran compositions. In a shorter, earlier versions of the Community Rule represented the manuscript 4Q258 frg. 6 6–8, the quotation is missing in this passage. Thus, the different manuscripts open a very rare window and let us observe the redactional reworking of an ancient Jewish text. And while we do not exactly know when this quotation was introduced into the Community Rule, the following example offers even deeper insight into the development of this composition.

1QS IX 10–11 is perhaps the only case of which we get to know the backstory of a scribe's unique idea. It says, 'They shall govern themselves using the original precepts by which the men of the Yahad[14] began to be instructed, doing so until there come the Prophet and the messiahs of Aaron and Israel'.[15]

While the Damascus Document attests to the expectation of a messiah of Aaron (priest) and of Israel (king),[16] a prophet is never explicitly mentioned in messianic contexts.

Nevertheless, there is a single sheet of leather – written by the same scribe as 1QS! – that contains three quotations from scripture, one about a king (Num. 24:15-17), one about a priest (Deut. 33:8-11), and a first one about a prophet like Moses (Exod. 20:21, according to the Samaritan Pentateuch). At the bottom of the page, a fourth figure is introduced, a negative one, contrasting the three positive ones. This sheet of leather, 4QTestimonia (4Q175), is one of two identified autographs that exist in the Qumran corpus.[17] A combination of different aspects identifies 4QTestimonia as an

---

[13] Translation with M. O. Wise, M. Abegg, and E. Cook, Accordance, Oak Tree, 2009.
[14] *The Yahad* (היחד) is one of the earliest self-designations of the Qumran community.
[15] Translation with Wise, Abegg, and Cook, Accordance, Oak Tree, 2009.
[16] See e.g. CD XIX 10–11.
[17] The other autograph is 4Q340 (List of Netinim).

autograph and not a copy: the text is written on a sheet of leather instead of a scroll, its handwriting is far less careful than in other manuscripts, and there are a number of mistakes, much more than in the other scrolls which the scribe has copied, namely 1QS and (part of) 1QIsa^a and 4QSam^c.[18] This private note might have been made for discussion with other members of the group, or simply in order not to forget about an idea.[19] Whatever its exact purpose was, the person who noted down these lines in 4QTestimonia introduced the idea of a prophet, a priest, and a king in one of the most important community rules, in 1QS IX 10–11. This observation touches the question of what a trained Qumran scribe was allowed to do. Obviously more than only copying and making minor corrections or insertions. It seems that at least in this case, he was also a 'scholar', searching in the authoritative writings for evidence of what he wanted his community to expect for the future – in this case, the coming of three distinct eschatological figures. Probably, this example tells us even more: the fourth person, mentioned at the bottom of his private note, the only negative one, has been identified with the Hasmonean ruler John Hyrcanus I, who, according to Josephus was seen as prophet, ruler, and high priest. If this identification was correct, and good reasons seem to speak for it,[20] we have an outer political claim that necessitated religious learning inside the group. As the scribe sought to made clear, our group is waiting for three figures, not one. Only they will be the ideal king, the ideal high priest, and the ideal lawgiver like Moses of the future. The lack of further resonance of this idea in the context of 1QS IX in other Qumran texts is remarkable, unless we perhaps assume that important roles in the subsequent literary history of the community, namely 'the Interpreter of the Law' and/or 'the Teacher of Righteousness' were prophetic in character.[21]

Looking at the broader context of our examples, we can make a number of observations. First, a religious forerunner group, obviously a bookish circle of well-educated members, is literarily visible in the early stages of the Community Rule. At some point in the second century BCE it seems to have come under the strong influence of the priestly Sons of Zadok and their followers who joined the group.[22] The influence of a Zadokite contingent profoundly changed what we used to call the Qumran movement. A broad spectrum of literature arose, the community rules were elaborated, if not written down for the first time, re-written later on when necessary.[23] An enormous

---

[18] See e.g. Eibert Tigchelaar, 'The Scribes of the Scrolls', in *T&T Clark Companion to the Dead Sea Scrolls*, ed. G. J. Brooke and C. Hempel (London: T&T Clark, 2018), 524–33, cf. most recently M. Popović, M. Dhali, and L. Schomaker, 'Artificial Intelligence Based Writer Identification Generates New Evidence for the Unknown Scribes of the Dead Sea Scrolls Exemplified by the Great Isaiah Scroll (1QIsa a)', *ArXiv* (2020).

[19] On this view see Annette Steudel, 'Testimonia', in *The Dead Sea Scrolls Encyclopedia*, ed. L. Schiffman and J. C. VanderKam (Oxford: Oxford University Press, 2000), 936–8.

[20] Cf. H. Eshel, 'The Historical Background of the Pesher Interpreting Joshua's Curse on the Rebuilder of Jericho', *RevQ* 15 (1992): 409–20.

[21] See this H. I. Kirchheiner, 'Revitalization in Judea: An Anthropological Study of the Damascus Document' (PhD diss., University of Birmingham, 2018), 88–113.

[22] See e.g. 1QS V 9.

[23] The Damascus Document presents itself as the final of such rule texts, see the end of the composition, preserved in 4Q270 frg. 7 ii 15 par 4Q266 frg. 11 20.

process of religious learning and of intellectual debate was initiated in this period and it is visible with the development of the Community Rule.[24]

Second, it seems that changes within the group's orientation were not inaugurated via executive orders by the new leaders, but rather in an ongoing and enduring sophisticated process of exchanged arguments, of clarifications, and modifications. This process at its beginning is reflected in the literary development of the community rules S and D, which grew side by side, mutually influencing one another; but it is reflected also in other literature like the War Rule where we can observe a priestly rewriting of its earliest core.[25] It is not only that the priests wrote themselves into many of these texts, but they and/or their followers seem to have started a process of learning and thinking that formed the community over many decades. Three major features were introduced:[26] (1) scripture was introduced as an authoritative source to explain the community's history, which can best be seen in the long admonition in the Damascus Document; (2) exegetical techniques, like midrashic interpretation, quotation, and interpretation formulas, were found on the literary level of the manuscript 1QS (it is missing on the 4QS level) for the first time, and also in the Damascus Document, followed later on in the new genres of thematic midrashim and pesharim; (3) eschatology became a significant focus, which interestingly goes hand in hand with the first two points. After roughly 100 BCE all compositions of the Qumran movement where exegetical, eschatological texts.

Third, sometimes intellectual trends arose that became influential and widespread among the community texts for a while, but then disappeared, and were never taken up again. A nice example is a dualistic 'Sons of Light'-era, which seems to have started with the famous Doctrine of the Two Spirits in the Community Rule. From there it influenced other rule texts, like the fragmentarily preserved beginning of the Damascus Document and also the beginning of the War Rule, and perhaps also other compositions like the large wisdom composition Instruction, the so-called *Musar leMevin*, of which the very beginning, where we usually find traces of this redactional intervention, is lost. While it is prominent in the Midrash on Eschatology (4Q174 + 4Q177), no traces of the 'Sons of Light' dualism are found in the pesharim, the latest texts known to be composed by the movement.

Thus, constant rethinking and reworking of the group's own compositions was a major endeavour, reflecting the fruits of their religious learning. More questions than answers remain. Why did the literary activity seem to have stopped with the pesharim around the middle of the first century BCE and only copies of other texts were still

---

[24] Literary growth – each layer reflecting a different stream of thoughts – is visible in many of the major texts from Qumran, a phenomenon that prevailed until the end of the literary production of the movement, where it is found e.g. in 1QpHab II.

[25] See Steudel, 'Damascus Document (D) as a Rewriting', 605–20, and Steudel, 'Biblical Warfare Legisslation in the War Scroll (1QM VII:1-7 and X:1-8)', in *The Reception of Biblical War Legislation in Narrative Contexts: Studies in Law and Narrative*, ed. C. Berner and H. Samuel, BZAW 460 (Berlin: de Gruyter, 2015), 183–91.

[26] See on the following Annette Steudel, 'The Development of Essenic Eschatology', in *Apocalyptic Time*, ed. A. I. Baumgarten (Leiden: Brill, 2000), 79–86, and Steudel, 'Dating Exegetical Texts from Qumran', in *The Dynamics of Language and Exegesis at Qumran*, ed. D. Dimant and R. Kratz (Tübingen: Mohr Siebeck, 2009), 39–53.

made? Do the inkwells, which were found in the settlement Khirbet Qumran, connect to the findings in the scrolls caves near by, and do they mean that manuscripts were written at Qumran?[27] And do the few documents from the caves in which scribes had tried their 'pens' before writing,[28] speak in the same direction? What does the huge number of manuscripts in the caves, around 1000, tells us about the scripturality of the Qumran movement? Did the scrolls belong to the inhabitants of the settlement, and were they hidden during the times of the war against the Romans around 70 CE? It might well be. But we could also think of other possibilities:[29] What if the people of the Qumran movement, bookish as they were, rescued books from places destroyed or endangered by the Roman army, not the Temple library as some thought, but the treasures of other communities who dedicated, like them, their lives to the Torah. The huge number of different scribes found in this corpus might speak for such a scenario. Phenomenological parallels for such acts of book rescuing exist throughout history. Perhaps the most recent might be found in modern-day Syria where people, trying to survive the terrible war, collected books from destroyed buildings and hid them in a safe 'library', actually in a basement of a house where people can come to and study or simply rest for a safe moment from the terror outside.[30] They collect everything, holy books and cooking books, poems and children's literature, classics and modern fiction novels. In that way they try to maintain life, rescuing books for a future life and, by building up this library, giving their own life meaning in a senseless war.

Methodological questions have to be raised as well. Do the rule texts reflect the real situation of the Qumran movement, or do they rather describe an ideal situation? Especially texts that talk about the movement in the biblical terms of Israel seem to raise doubt about the historic reliability of what we read there.[31] While in our first example from 1QS VI, which is an old text in the history of Qumran literature, all members of the group are described as being able to read and study, later on in the admonitions of the Damascus Document the repeated refrain 'listen to me' could speak to a contrary situation, if the sapiential formula had to be taken literally and the admonitions had not been meant to be orally performed on the feast of the renewal of the covenant.[32]

---

[27] On the archeology of settlement see e.g. Joan Taylor, 'The Archaeology of Qumran and the Dead Sea Scrolls', in *The Archaeology of the Holy Land: From the Destruction of Solomon's Temple to the Muslim Conquest*, ed. J. Magness (Cambridge: Cambridge University Press, 2012), 108–32.

[28] Cf. most recently Émile Puech, 'Exercices de deux scribes à Khirbet Qumrân: KhQ 161 et KhQ 2207', *RevQ* 32 (2020): 43–56.

[29] Alternative interpretations of the Qumran Side are numerous, see e.g. Daniel Stökl Ben Ezra, *Qumran: Die Texte vom Toten Meer und das antike Judentum* (Tübingen: Mohr Siebeck, 2016).

[30] See https://www.bbc.com/news/magazine-36893303 (accessed 21 January 2021).

[31] See e.g. the War Scroll with its priestly lead eschatological battle and its rewritings.

[32] See Ben Zion Wacholder, *The New Damascus Document. The Midrash on the Eschatological Torah of the Dead Sea Scrolls: Reconstruction, Translation and Commentary*, STDJ 56 (Leiden: Brill, 2007).

4

The Making of the Theme of Immortality in the Wisdom of Solomon

Ekaterina Matusova

The Wisdom of Solomon is the first book in the Bible to contain certain novel theological statements on immortality when compared with the previous biblical tradition, statements that are of extraordinary importance for the development of Christian theology. It explicitly formulates the idea that human beings were created immortal and were intended to be so forever (Wis. 2:23-24). It frees God from any suspicion of introducing death into the world (1:12-16). And it refers unequivocally to the possibility of eternal life after physical death (3:2-4; 5:15-16).

Of course, the Wisdom of Solomon did not develop this view of immortality independently of previous biblical tradition. On the contrary, its dependence on Proverbs, for instance, is quite obvious in some of the aforementioned passages. Wisdom shares with Proverbs a general opposition between life, associated with righteousness and the righteous (Prov. 3:18, 22; 4:22-23; 8:35; 10:2-3, 10-17, 25; 11:19, 30; 14:27), and death, connected to wickedness and the wicked (Prov. 1:17-19; 2:12-19; 5:5; 7:26-27; 8:36; 12:28; 18:6; 24:8). This influence is very clear in Wis. 1:12-16: Wis. 1:12 (μὴ ζηλοῦτε θάνατον ἐν πλάνῃ ζωῆς ὑμῶν//μηδὲ ἐπισπᾶσθε ὄλεθρον ἐν ἔργοις χειρῶν ὑμῶν) clearly echoes Prov 1:10-19, 4:14-16 and 24:1-2, while Wis. 1:16 (Ἀσεβεῖς δὲ ταῖς χερσὶν καὶ τοῖς λόγοις προσεκαλέσαντο αὐτόν) is a reformulation of Prov. 18:6 (τὸ δὲ στόμα αὐτοῦ τὸ θρασὺ θάνατον ἐπικαλεῖται). Similarly, Wis. 1:15 (δικαιοσύνη γὰρ ἀθάνατός ἐστιν) paraphrases Prov. 10:2 (δικαιοσύνη δὲ ῥύσεται ἐκ θανάτου).

However, despite Wisdom's clear dependence on Proverbs, the differences between the two books are immediately perceptible. Proverbs speaks about death and life, but never about 'eternal life' or 'immortality'. It presents the notions of life and death in a vague, broad sense that recalls typical biblical usage (e.g. Deut. 30:15) and allows for metaphorical interpretations in every verse. By contrast, the Wisdom of Solomon is very clear on these points: humanity was meant to be immortal and, therefore, the righteous will be immortal. Wisdom's new level of theological reflection manifests itself in the choice of vocabulary used to express these ideas. The author of Wisdom uses the words ἀφθαρσία/ἄφθαρτος and ἀθανασία/ἀθάνατος (Wis. 1:15; 2:23; 3:4; 6:18, 19; 8:13; 12:1; 15:3), which do not occur in the LXX and do not correspond to any biblical Hebrew expression. Outside of Wisdom, these terms are found only in 4 Maccabees, which is a late book, full of Greek philosophical vocabulary, and in one special passage in Ben Sira which we discuss below. These terms are borrowed from the Greek intellectual context and carry strong philosophical connotations.

The following example illustrates how Wisdom's concept of immortality, expressed using the term ἀθανασία, specifies some of the statements from Proverbs. Proverbs 11:7 (LXX) says: τελευτήσαντος ἀνδρὸς δικαίου οὐκ ὄλλυται ἐλπίς, 'When a righteous man dies, hope does not perish' (NETS). The nature of this hope, which does not die with the death of a righteous person, is unclear. Wisdom 3:2–4 specifies: καὶ ἐλογίσθη κάκωσις ἡ ἔξοδος αὐτῶν ... οἱ δέ εἰσιν ἐν εἰρήνῃ ... ἡ ἐλπὶς αὐτῶν ἀθανασίας πλήρης, 'And their departure was considered to be suffering ... but they are at peace ... their hope full of *immortality*' (NETS). Thus, Wisdom clarifies the notion of hope by specifying that the righteous who died may hope to be *immortal*.

When attempting to assess the notion of immortality in Wisdom, scholars commonly consider whether the author's ideas draw primarily on a Jewish religious or Greek philosophical background. They question whether the author speaks about the immortality of souls, in the Platonic sense, or the resurrection of body, as in some Jewish traditions which influenced early Christian teachings.

Thus, Émile Puech, following in the footsteps of others, has drawn attention to Jewish parallels in 2 Macc. 7:21-23 and some texts from Qumran. He radically insists that the Jewish context overwhelmingly shapes Wisdom's theology of immortality. According to Puech, all Greek terms used by the author of Wisdom convey exclusively Jewish notions and are only chosen to accommodate the tastes of the Hellenized audience; the author intends immortality in terms of the resurrection of bodies, similar to what Paul describes in 1 Corinthians 15.[1] On the other hand, other scholars have emphasized Greek Hellenistic influences.[2] Passages like Wis. 8:20 support the

---

[1] Émile Puech, 'Il Libro della Sapienza e i manoscritti del Mar Morto', in *Il libro della sapienza (tradizione, redazione, teologia)*, ed. G. Bellia and A. Passaro, Studia Biblica I (Rome: Città Nuova, 2004), 131–55. In particular, he draws attention to 4Q521 5 ii + 7, 4Q521 2 ii 12–14, 4Q418 69 ii. See also Pierre Grelot, 'L'eschatologie de la Sagesse et les apocalypses juives', in *À la rencontre de Dieu. Memorial Albert Gelin*, ed. M. Jourgion et al. (Mappus: Le Puy, 1961), 165–78; Paul Beauchamp, 'Le salut corporel des justes et la conclusion du livre de la Sagesse', *Biblica* 45 (1964): 491–526, here 495; M. Delcor 'L'immortalité de l'âme dans le livre de la Sagesse et dans les documents de Qumran', *NRTh* 77 (1955): 614.

[2] The view that the author of Wisdom speaks about immortality of souls is represented by John Collins, 'The Reinterpretation of the Apocalyptic Traditions in the Wisdom of Solomon', in *The Book of Wisdom in Modern Research*, ed. A. Passaro and G. Bella (Berlin: de Gruyter, 2005), 143–58; idem, 'The Root of Immortality: Death in the Context of Jewish Wisdom', *HTR* 71 (1979): 177–92, here 186. David Winston also thinks in this vein in *The Wisdom of Solomon: A New Translation with Introduction and Commentary*, AB 43 (Garden City: Doubleday, 1982), 25–32. See also Chrysostomos Larcher, *Études sur le livre de la sagesse* (Paris: Gabalda, 1969), 326, and George W. E. Nickelsburg, *Resurrection, Immortality and Eternal Life in Intertestamental Judaism and Early Christianity* (Cambridge, MA: Harvard University Press, 2006), 87–90. For further bibliography, see Puech 'Il libro della Sapienza', 147–8 n. 51.

view that the Greek philosophical context has left distinctive traces in the author's presentation of the theme.[3]

The approaches insisting on the theological uniformity of the immortality theme in Wisdom are based on a modern view of the history of religion and philosophy that strictly differentiates between the Jewish-Christian and the Greek philosophical perspectives on immortality. These approaches demand an equally neat theological vision from a Hellenistic Jewish text written in Egypt, probably in Alexandria, around the time of Philo's activity. However, the history of scholarship has shown that any one-sided interpretation of Philo or even his predecessors Aristobulus and Aristeas is inadequate or unsatisfactory. A careful study of these Alexandrian authors reveals a dual background to their thought, especially in theological matters. To properly understand it, one must focus on how its heterogenous elements interact. A similar strategy, appropriate to the text's location and time period, might also be more promising in the case of Wisdom. But in order to apply this perspective, one has to find a proper point of departure. I think that an attempt to inquire why and how statements of such extraordinary theological novelty appeared in this text can serve as such a starting point. In other words, I would like to focus on the formation of these statements, allowing us to clearly trace the traditions that influenced the author and to analyze their interaction and eventually to draw conclusions about his strategies and concerns in using them. This approach may help to specify the level and focus of his theological reflection better than an attempt to answer questions traditionally asked from a modern perspective and shed light on the intellectual and educational background of Wisdom's author. I will begin this investigation by considering the importance of the author's Jewish background.

Level 1: Jewish/Hebrew Tradition of Immortality Behind the Author's Innovative Thoughts

Immortality at Creation

The idea that human immortality was intended by God at the creation is introduced in Wis. 2:23-24, using the term ἀφθαρσία:

ὅτι ὁ θεὸς ἔκτισεν τὸν ἄνθρωπον ἐπ' ἀφθαρσίᾳ
καὶ εἰκόνα τῆς ἰδίας ἀϊδιότητος ἐποίησεν αὐτόν·
φθόνῳ δὲ διαβόλου θάνατος εἰσῆλθεν εἰς τὸν κόσμον,
πειράζουσιν δὲ αὐτὸν οἱ τῆς ἐκείνου μερίδος ὄντες.

---

[3] As Sterling has recently stressed while revising an old discussion (Gregory E. Sterling, 'The Love of Wisdom: Middle Platonism and Stoicism in the Wisdom of Solomon', in *From Stoicism to Platonism: The Development of Philosophy, 100 BCE–100 CE*, ed. T. Engberg-Pedersen [Cambridge: Cambridge University Press, 2017], 202–3). Cf. also Winston, *The Wisdom of Solomon*, 26. This despite the reluctance of many scholars to accept that the passage bears a distinctively Platonic connotation, e.g. Chrysostom Larcher, *Le livre de la sagesse, ou, La sagesse de Salomon*, 3 vols. (Paris: Gabalda, 1984), 2:552–6.

Because God created human beings for incorruption and made them the image of his own nature,⁴ but through the envy of the devil death entered the world, and those who belong to his party experience it. (NETS)

As already noted by scholars, the context of this passage is connected to the realm of biblical interpretation.⁵ If the expression καὶ εἰκόνα in the phrase καὶ εἰκόνα τῆς ἰδίας ἀϊδιότητος immediately refers to Gen. 1:26 (καὶ εἶπεν ὁ θεός [אלהים] ποιήσωμεν ἄνθρωπον κατ'εἰκόνα ἡμετέραν καὶ καθ' ὁμοίωσιν [בצלמנו כדמותנו]), the thought that death was not intended by God in the creation of humanity can be deduced from Gen. 2:17 and 3:19.

In Gen. 2:17, God warns Adam that death will be the outcome of his transgression of the command not to eat from the tree: 'but of the tree for knowing good and evil, of it you shall not eat; on the day that you eat of it, you shall *die by death* (θανάτῳ ἀποθανεῖσθε)' (NETS). In Gen. 3:19, God says that returning to earth is the main result of Adam's disobedience: 'By the sweat of your face you will eat your bread until you return to the earth from which you were taken, for you are earth and to earth you will depart' (NETS). These verses suggest that God's original plan in the creation of humanity was for human immortality and that death only came into the world through the serpent's plotting (apparently alluded to in the mention of the envy of the *diabolos* in Wis. 2:24) and the disobedience of Adam. However, Wis. 2:23 clearly shows that this idea, deduced from Gen. 2:17 and 3:19 and their immediate context, was read back into Gen. 1:26, where the expression καὶ εἰκόνα comes from. This is a sign of intentional work on the biblical text in terms of its interpretation. Adam's original immortality is taken as the explanation of his likeness to God, and this explanation derives from the suggestions contained in the text of Genesis itself. A very different understanding of likeness, in terms of rationality, i.e. the likeness of the human mind to the mind of God (*logos, nous*), features, for instance, in Philo (e.g. *Opif*. 69). The Philonic interpretation has a thoroughly Greek philosophical background, based on Plato's Timaeus,⁶ whereas the biblical interpretation behind Wis. 2:23–24 points to a Jewish tradition available to the author of Wisdom in some form.

Faint traces of this tradition in Hebrew can be seen in Ps. 82:6-7 (LXX 81:6-7) and probably in 4QInstruction. Psalm 82:6-7 contrasts the Godlike status of human beings with their death, thus suggesting that humanity's Godlikeness implies immortality: 'I said, "You are gods (אלהים), and all of you are sons of the Most High. But you die (תמותון) as men and fall as one of the princes"'. Here, we see a contrast between אלהים, used in Gen. 1:26 and 27 where humanity's creation in the likeness of God is mentioned, and תמותון, echoing God's sentence for human transgression (מות תמות) in Gen. 2:17.

---

⁴ NETS follows Ziegler's ἰδιότης here, whereas Rahlfs prefers ἀϊδιότης. See G. Scarpat, *Libro della Sapienza*, vol. 1 (Brescia: Morcellana, 1989), 198. In any case, the reading ἀϊδιότης only highlights the meaning already present in the text: likeness is immortality.
⁵ E.g. Puech, 'Il Libro della Sapienza', 142–5.
⁶ Ekaterina Matusova, 'Genesis 1–2 in *De opificio mundi* and its Exegetical Context', *SPhilo* 31 (2019): 57–94.

It is possible that a similar contrast based on the same biblical verses occurs again in 4QInstruction (4Q418) 69 ii 6, which uses the verb יצר in opposition to the idea of death:

אֹתָֹ֯ם[ ]ל נוצרתם ולשחת עולם תשובתכם[7]

The verb יצר is one of the verbs used to describe the creation of humanity in Genesis 1-2: עשה (Gen. 1:26), ברא (Gen. 1:27), and יצר (Gen. 2:7). It is said in Gen. 1:26-27 that Adam was created 'in our image, according to our likeness' (בצלמנו כדמותנו), and the verb יצר occurs several times in collocations expressing the 'creation in likeness' in the Qumran texts. Thus, we see it in combination with דמות in 4Q504 (4QDibHam^a) col. 1, frag. 8, line 4: 'You fashioned [Adam], our [fa]ther, in the image of [Your] glory (אדם אבינו יצרתה בדמות כבודכה)'. We see this word used in a similar collocation in 4Q417 1 i 17 in reference to the creation of man, or Enoch, 'according to the likeness of the holy ones (כתבנית קדושים יצרו)'. It could be possible therefore that a similar theme was present in 4Q418 69 ii 6 as well. I would not stress the likelihood of this conjecture were it not for the broader context of this line and other fragments from this Qumran composition, which are remarkably similar to the next two passages about immortality in Wis. 3:1-9 and 5:15-23.

Immortality After Physical Death

These next two passages contain the second aspect of the theme of life that distinguishes Wisdom from Proverbs, namely, life as a possible condition *after* physical death. This possibility is expressed in two phrases: ἡ ἐλπὶς αὐτῶν ἀθανασίας πλήρης (Wis. 3:4) and Δίκαιοι δὲ εἰς τὸν αἰῶνα ζῶσιν (Wis. 5:15). Here is the full context of both quotations:

Wis. 3:1-9
But the souls of the righteous are in the hand of God, and no torment will ever touch them. In the eyes of the foolish they seemed to have died, and their departure was considered to be suffering, and their going from us to be destruction, but they are at peace. For even if in the sight of human beings they were punished, their hope is full of *immortality* (ἀθανασίας). And having been disciplined a little,

Wis. 5:15-23
But the righteous *live forever* (εἰς τὸν αἰῶνα ζῶσιν), and in the Lord is their reward, and the care of them with the Most High. Therefore they will receive *a glorious crown* (τὸ βασίλειον) and a beautiful diadem from the hand of the Lord, because with his right hand he will protect them and with his arm he will shield them. He will take his zeal as his whole armour and make creation his weapons for vengeance on his

---

[7] The reconstruction of the missing letters is different in different editions and the reconstruction of the missing words varies as well. Thus, Strungell and Hurrington suggest: 'you were fashioned [by *the power of* G]od, but to the everlasting pit shall you return' (DJD XXXIV, 1999, 283). The reconstruction by Puech is 'vous été façonnés pour [le Shé]ôl', for which reading no particular reasons from the context of the document or elsewhere are adduced. See É. Puech, 'Les fragments eschatologiques de 4QInsruction (4Q416 I et 4Q418 69 ii, 81–81a, 127', *RevQ* 22 (2005): 89–119, here 99.

they will be greatly benefited, because God tested them and found them worthy of himself; as gold in the furnace he tested them, and as a sacrificial burnt offering he accepted them. And in the time *of their visitation* (ἐν καιρῷ ἐπισκοπῆς αὐτῶν) they will shine out, and as sparks through the stable, they will run about. They *will judge nations* (κρινοῦσιν ἔθνη) and rule over peoples, and the Lord will be king over them for ever. Those who trust in him *will understand truth* (συνήσουσιν ἀλήθειαν), and the faithful will remain with him in love, because grace and mercy is upon his holy ones, and he watches over h*is chosen ones* (τοῖς ἐκλεκτοῖς αὐτοῦ) (NETS)

enemies; he will put on righteousness as his breastplate and wear *impartial justice* (κρίσιν ἀνυπόκριτον) as a helmet; he will take holiness as an invincible shield and will sharpen stern anger for a sword, *and creation will fight with him against those without sense* (συνεκπολεμήσει δὲ αὐτῷ ὁ κόσμος ἐπὶ τοὺς παράφρονας). Well aimed shafts of lightening will fly out and from the clouds, as from a well-drawn bow, will leap to the target, and hailstones full of wrath will be hurled as from a catapult; the water of the sea will rage against them and rivers will overwhelm them relentlessly; a mighty wind will rise against them, and like a hurricane will winnow them away. And lawlessness will make the whole earth desert (or: *will desert the whole earth*), and evil-doing will overturn the thrones of rulers (καὶ ἐρημώσει πᾶσαν τὴν γῆν ἀνομία, καὶ ἡ κακοπραγία περιτρέψει θρόνους δυναστῶν) (NETS)

In 4Q418 69 ii, the idea of the restoration of life after death immediately follows lines 6–7, discussed above. This text too presents a contrast between the righteous and the sinners, with justice to be restored at the last judgement. Specifically, it is said that the righteous 'shall rouse' (יעורו).

Here is the full context of the quotation 4Q418 69 ii 7-15:

> ...and all who exist forever (וכול נהיה עולם), those who seek truth, will rouse themselves to yo[ur] judgment [...] .⁸ And then all the foolish of heart will be destroyed, and the sons of iniquity will be found no more, and all who seize wickedness will wither [away. And then] ⁹ at your judgment the foundations of the firmament will shout, and all…will thunder [...]. ¹⁰ But you, O chosen of truth, who earnestly follow [...] seek[ers of insight ... and] the watchful ¹¹ for all knowledge. How can you say, We are weary of insight, and we have been careful to pursue true knowledge [...] ¹² and untiring in all the years of eternity. Indeed he will take delight in truth forever and knowledge [eternally] will serve him; and [the sons of] ¹³ heaven, whose inheritance is eternal life, will they truly say, We are weary of deeds of truth, we worked hard [...] ¹⁴ of every era. Indeed, in eternal light they will wa[lk...] glory and great honor you [...] ¹⁵ in the sky [...] council of the divinities all [...] But you, O [enlightened] son [...] ⁿⁿⁿⁿ

Let us compare the stressed elements in the two Wisdom passages with this Qumran fragment and its context. The notion of ἀθανασία in Wisdom 3 is connected to the notion of ἐπισκοπή (Wis. 3:7; cf. 3:13, 4:15), which is the traditional rendering of פקדה as 'visitation' or 'retribution'.[8] This word, although not present in the fragment quoted above, is of supreme importance in other extant fragments of this Qumran composition. It occurs in these fragments 15 times, most importantly in 4Q417 1i 7.

It is stressed in Wis. 3:7 that at their 'visitation' the righteous will 'shine out', ἀναλάμψουσιν (cf. Wis. 5:6), which may correspond to the theme of light in 4Q418 69 ii 14 ('in eternal light they will wa[lk]').

It is said in Wis. 3:8 that the righteous will 'judge' nations, κρινοῦσιν ἔθνη. This corresponds to the active positions of the righteous as judges in 4Q418 69 ii 7, who 'will rouse themselves to yo[ur] [sinners'] judgment'.[9]

It is stressed in Wis. 3:9 that when justice triumphs, the righteous will understand the truth, συνήσουσιν ἀλήθειαν; they are also called 'his chosen', τοῖς ἐκλεκτοῖς αὐτοῦ, in the same verse. This corresponds to the description of the righteous in 4Q418 69 ii as 'those who seek truth' in line 7 and to their epithet as the 'chosen of truth' (line 10). Furthermore, συνίημι is a traditional rendering of the root בין,[10] one of the most important roots in 4QInstruction, which in its verbal forms and in the participial form מבין occur 44 times, also in combination with the notion of truth: מבין באמת (4Q418 frag. 102 a+b 3).

It is said in Wis. 5:15 that the righteous 'will live eternally', εἰς τὸν αἰῶνα ζῶσιν. This expression recalls the notion of ζωὴ αἰώνιος known to us from the book of Daniel and New Testament texts.[11] It has a recognizable Hebrew formula behind it: judging from the translational equivalents in the Septuagint, it can correspond to the notions of חיי עולם (Dan. 12:2) or חיי נצח[12] which are used at Qumran to express eternal life (e.g. CD 3:20; 1QS 4:7). However, 4Q418 69ii 7 has the verbal expression with the verb היה: כול נהיה עולם ('all who exist forever') which better corresponds to the verbal expression in Wisdom. The potential confusion between ח and ה in Hebrew manuscripts (חיה instead of היה) makes the possibility of a direct coincidence even stronger.

The reference to God's 'impartial judgement' (κρίσιν ἀνυπόκριτον) in Wis. 5:18 corresponds to the reference to God's judgement ('at your judgment') in 4Q418 69 ii 9. Wisdom's subsequent extensive elaboration on the involvement of the cosmos similarly matches the next thought in 4Q418 69 ii 9: 'the foundations of the firmament will shout, and all…will thunder'.

---

[8] Cf. Job 10:12; Ps. 108:8; Isa. 10:3, 15; 11:23.
[9] This motif is also present in Dan. 7:22; 1QpHab V 4; Mt. 19:28; 1 Cor. 6:2; and Rev. 20:4, as noted by Winston, *Wisdom of Solomon*, 128.
[10] See E. Hatch and A. Redpath, *A Concordance to the Septuagint, And the Other Greek Versions of the Old Testament*, 2nd ed. (Grand Rapids: Baker, 1998), 1315–17.
[11] See Dan. 12:2; Mk 10:30; Lk. 10:25; 18:30; Mt. 19:16, 29; 25:46; Jn 3:15; 4:14, 36; 5:39; 6:27, 40, 47; 10:28; 17:2; Rom. 2:7; 5:21; 6:22; Gal. 6:8; 1 Thess. 1:16.
[12] נצח is a difficult word that has many divergent translations in the LXX. However, αἰών or εἰς τὸν αἰῶνα χρόνον is one of them and it is found in the translations of Jeremiah and Isaiah, e.g. Jer. 50:39 (LXX 27:39) and Isa. 33:20.

Wisdom 5:20 and 23 describes 'those without sense' as the target of God's cosmic fighting (συνεκπολεμήσει δὲ αὐτῷ ὁ κόσμος ἐπὶ τοὺς παράφρονας) and predicts their final annihilation (καὶ ἐρημώσει πᾶσαν τὴν γῆν ἀνομία,[13] καὶ ἡ κακοπραγία περιτρέψει θρόνους δυναστῶν). The same idea is found in 4Q418 69 ii 8: 'And then *all the foolish of heart* will be destroyed, and the sons of iniquity will be found no more, and all who seize wickedness will wither [away]'.

Beyond the passages currently under discussion, but in direct connection to the theme of immortality and the content of 4QInstruction, the author of Wisdom also connects the comprehension of post-mortem immortality with knowledge of the divine 'mystery' (Wis. 2:22; see, e.g., 4Q417 2 i 10-11).[14] The word μυστήριον (μυστήρια) used in Wis. 2:22 can render the Aramaic word רז, used in 4Q417 2 i 10-11, a word centrally important for this Qumran composition.[15]

The Combination of Originally Intended and Restored Immortality

As I have suggested thus far, the combination of the themes of immortality implied at the creation of human beings and the subsequent restoration of immortality after death may be present already in 4Q418 69 ii. The reference to the creation of humanity in line 6 is immediately followed by the reference to resurrection in line 7. While the gaps in the text in line 6 prevent overconfidence about its content, a similar combination of themes occurs in 2 Macc. 7:23. This book reveals a significant number of parallels with Wisdom, one of the most important of which is the topic of the death of the righteous at the hands of sinners. This feature unites both compositions, in contradistinction to Proverbs, which never speaks about sinners actually triumphing over the righteous.

2 Maccabees 7:23 reads: 'But doubtless the Creator of the world, *who formed the generation of man, and found out the beginning of all things* (ὁ πλάσας ἀνθρώπου γένεσιν καὶ πάντων ἐξευρὼν γένεσιν), *will also of his own mercy give you breath and life again* (καὶ τὸ πνεῦμα καὶ τὴν ζωὴν ὑμῖν πάλιν ἀποδίδωσιν), as ye now regard not your own selves for his laws' sake' (KJV).[16] This text suggests that the restoration of life after martyrdom follows naturally from the thought of the creation of humanity. This view corresponds to the combination and order of thoughts in Wis. 2:23 and 3:4 where immortality is discussed in the context of the creation of humanity, followed by the promise of hope for immortality after death.

Conclusion

The two concepts of immortality – connected to the creation of humanity and restored to human beings after death (especially death at the hands of sinners), which distinguish Wisdom from one of its important sources, Proverbs – have a specific Jewish

---

[13] I think that the meaning of this phrase in its context is 'lawlessness will desert the whole earth'. See LSJ s.v. ἐρημόω III.
[14] See Goff, *The Worldly and Heavenly Wisdom of 4QInstruction* (Leiden: Brill, 2003), 60. On the connection with Wisdom, see Puech, 'Il Libro della Sapienza', 144 n. 47.
[15] See Dan 2:18, 19, 28.
[16] Cf. 2 Macc 14:46.

background behind them. This background is reflected most obviously in 2 Maccabees and 4QInstruction (and later in the New Testament). Correspondence to the Hebrew context can be stressed using other sources too,[17] although the number of parallels with 4QInstruction is overwhelming. While not touching upon the question of how systematic this Qumran composition was in presenting the theme of immortality, nor intending to say that 4QInstruction alone is sufficient to explain the development of this theme in Wisdom, I would like to stress that the parallels discussed above support Puech's observation that 4QInstruction or the tradition reflected in it must have influenced the author of Wisdom.[18]

Level 2: Polemics

In this section of this study I wish to draw attention to the fact that some thoughts are formulated negatively in Wisdom as it related to immortality, especially in Wis. 1:13-14 ('because God did not create death nor does he delight in the destruction of the living…and there is no destructive poison in them, nor is the kingdom of Hades on earth') and 11:24 ('For you…detest none of the things that you have made, for you would not have formed anything out of hatred').

Thoughts formulated as negations imply a kind of argument against something. For instance, Xenophanes' insistence that God is 'neither in bodily frame similar to mortals nor in thought' (οὔτι δέμας θνητοῖσιν ὁμοίιος οὐδὲ νόημα, B 23 DK) and that 'He always stays in the same place, not moving at all, and it is not fitting that he travel now to one place, now to another' (αἰεὶ δ᾽ ἐν ταὐτῶι μίμνει κινούμενος οὐδέν // οὐδὲ μετέρχεσθαί μιν ἐπιπρέπει ἄλλοτε ἄλληι, B 26 DK), functions as a polemic against the epic tradition's understanding of gods as similar to humans. Similarly, when Plato in the Republic formulates the famous foundations of his theology as 'God does not cheat' (380d), 'God does not change' (381b) and 'God does not lie' (382a), he does so as an intentional antithesis to Homer, Hesiod, and popular religious opinions. In the case of Wisdom, against what or whom is the author arguing? Who says that God has created death, or that Hades rules on earth, or that God had hatred toward creation?

Wisdom 1:13-16 and 2:23 and Ben Sira

Four negations are accumulated in Wis. 1:13-16: the author negates God's creation of death, his pleasure at humans death; the presence of some chemical ingredient in the world that secures its dying; and, finally, the rule of Hell on earth:

---

[17] Thus, for instance, the Rule of the Community, 1QS IV 7–8 has *hai nezah*, 'perpetual life', in combination with '*the crown of glory* (וכליל כבוד) with a garment of majesty in light'. Similarly, the matching Greek expression εἰς τὸν αἰῶνα ζώσιν in Wis. 5:15 is accompanied by the description of 'a glorious crown and a beautiful diadem' (τὸ βασίλειον τῆς εὐπρεπείας καὶ τὸ διάδημα τοῦ κάλλους).

[18] Puech, 'Il Libro della Sapienza', 144 n. 47: 'Si potrebbe pensare che l'autore di Sapienza abbia conosciuto tale tipo di composizione sapienziale', 150–2, with reference to 4QInstruction.

because God did not make death nor does he delight in the destruction of the living. For he created all things that they might exist, and the generative forces of the world are wholesome, *and there is no destructive poison in them, nor is the kingdom of Hades on earth.* For righteousness is immortal. But the impious by their deeds and words summoned it. (NETS)	ὅτι ὁ θεὸς θάνατον οὐκ ἐποίησεν οὐδὲ τέρπεται ἐπ' ἀπωλείᾳ ζώντων. ἔκτισεν γὰρ εἰς τὸ εἶναι τὰ πάντα, καὶ σωτήριοι αἱ γενέσεις τοῦ κόσμου, καὶ οὐκ ἔστιν ἐν αὐταῖς φάρμακον ὀλέθρου οὔτε ᾅδου βασίλειον ἐπὶ γῆς. δικαιοσύνη γὰρ ἀθάνατός ἐστιν. Ἀσεβεῖς δὲ ταῖς χερσὶν καὶ τοῖς λόγοις προσεκαλέσαντο αὐτόν

It has been noted that certain texts in the Jewish wisdom tradition, although roughly contemporary with 4QInstruction, have no expectations of the afterlife in any form.[19] In particular, a rather sinister view of death is presented in Ben Sira. Death is an eternal predestination for all humans, there is no way to avoid it. God ordained it: 'the covenant of old is: "By death you shall die"' (Sir. 14:17, ἡ γὰρ διαθήκη ἀπ' αἰῶνος Θανάτῳ ἀποθανῇ). Human beings are 'dust and ashes' (Sir. 17:32, γῆ καὶ σποδός). It is interesting that Ben Sira uses expressions and words from the same passages in Genesis on which the author of Wisdom based his interpretation of original immortality, especially Genesis 1–2: 'By death you shall die' (Θανάτῳ ἀποθανῇ) comes from Gen. 2:17 and 'earth and ashes' (γῆ καὶ σποδός) is inspired by Gen. 2:7; 3:19 (with an allusion to Gen. 18:27). In Ben Sira's interpretation, the focus is on the opposite aspect: predestination for death instead of envisioned immortality. He even uses a remarkably generalizing phrase: 'because the son of man is not immortal' (Sir. 17:30, ὅτι οὐκ ἀθάνατος υἱὸς ἀνθρώπου). The Hebrew *Vorlage* of this passage has not come down to us, so we cannot judge which Hebrew notion was behind it, but to express it, the grandson uses the Greek word (οὐκ) ἀθάνατος – which is *the first and only occurrence of the root in the LXX* before its appearance in Wisdom and later 4 Maccabees. He uses this Greek term, which has strong philosophical connotations, to deny human immortality. Wisdom's pointed affirmation of human immortality using the same Greek terms (ἀθανασία and its close synonym ἀφθαρσία) is clearly antithetical to Ben Sira:

Sir. 17:30, 32	Wis. 2:23
ὅτι οὐκ ἀθάνατος υἱὸς ἀνθρώπου. καὶ ἄνθρωποι πάντες γῆ καὶ σποδός.	ὅτι ὁ θεὸς ἔκτισεν τὸν ἄνθρωπον ἐπ' ἀφθαρσίᾳ καὶ εἰκόνα τῆς ἰδίας ἀϊδιότητος ἐποίησεν αὐτόν
because a son of man is not immortal and all human beings are earth and ashes. (NETS)	Because God created human beings for incorruption, and made them image of his own nature (or: eternity). (NETS)

---

[19] Matthew Goff, *Discerning Wisdom: The Sapiential Literature of the Dead Sea Scrolls*, VTSup 116 (Leiden: Brill, 2007), 125–30.

Ben Sira says that humanity is not immortal; Wisdom says that humanity was created immortal. Ben Sira stresses that humanity is *earth* and *ashes*; the author of Wisdom stresses that humanity was created in God's *likeness*, and is *God-like* in its originally intended immortality.

The question is whether this clear antithesis is also intentionally polemical. To answer this question, we must determine whether the aforementioned negations in Wisdom can be read as deliberate negations of Ben Sira's work. I will start by discussing the negation of the creation of death by God: 'because God did not make death' (Wis. 1:13, ὅτι ὁ θεὸς θάνατον οὐκ ἐποίησεν).

In Ben Sira's translation we have the following combination of passages on death. God ordained death for humans 'from the beginning' (ἀπ' αἰῶνος), and everything which was created decays and dies: 'All flesh becomes old like a garment, for the covenant of old is, "By death you shall die (Θανάτῳ ἀποθανῇ)"' (14:17), and 'Every work decays and ceases to exist' (14:19). This thought is resumed and expanded in Sir. 17:30-32, where, in addition to the noteworthy formula that the 'son of man is not immortal' (17:30), a thought about the possible decline of the created world is included: 'What is brighter than the sun? Yet even it ceases to exist (suffers an eclipse) (ἐκλείπει)' (17:31). Although the verb ἐκλείπει can have an astronomical meaning (to 'suffer eclipse'), it can also mean 'to die', and it was previously used in this sense in the previous passage on death: 'Every work decays and *ceases to exist* (ἐκλείπει)' (Sir. 14:19). In this passage the verb is used of the rotting and ceasing to be of every created object, which allows for a similar understanding of the verb in 17:31 where it refers to the sun. On this reading, the idea of predestined death refers not only to human beings, but to the created world in general. This cosmic nuance is suggested by the word ἔργον in the previous passage (Sir. 14:19), which refers to anything that came to be by someone's hands. But in Ben Sira 17 the idea is developed more explicitly into the concept of the entire created world as symbolized by its highest representation – the sun.

Ben Sira continues: 'He who lives forever created all together' (Sir. 18:1, Ὁ ζῶν εἰς τὸν αἰῶνα ἔκτισεν τὰ πάντα κοινῇ). In our modern editions, this line is considered the beginning of ch. 18 and thus it is printed separately from the end of ch. 17, which prevents us from reading it as a continuous text. But our ancient manuscripts, like Codex Sinaiticus and Codex Vaticanus, have the continuous text of Ben Sira without division into chapters. In Codex Vaticanus, chapter divisions were added in the margins by a second hand, apparently at a considerably later date. The break between chapters 17 and 18 does not correspond to any structural division that has been suggested for the Hebrew text either.[20] There is almost no doubt that the author of Wisdom understood Sir. 18:1 as a continuation of the previous passage, whose subject is death, predestined for all humans and the created world. If this is the case, what would be the meaning of 'created all together' (ἔκτισεν τὰ πάντα κοινῇ)? As death, i.e., predestined mortality, is the subject of the previous passage, the phrase must

---

[20] Jeremy Corley, 'Searching for Structure and Redaction in Ben Sira. An Investigation of Beginnings and Endings', in *The Wisdom of Ben Sira: Studies on Tradition, Redaction, and Theology*, ed. A. Passarro and G. Bellia (Berlin: de Gruyter, 2008), 21–47.

include death within the range of created things, because how else could the emphatic function of κοινῇ be explained? Death was created *in addition to* all the other things God created. On this reading, τὰ πάντα would refer to the created world in general, with human beings as its integral part, *and* to death, which, being created *with them*, is their natural end as predestined by God.

The combination of passages which, if read together, convey this meaning that I have outlined:

Sir. 14:17-19

πᾶσα σὰρξ ὡς ἱμάτιον παλαιοῦται.//ἡ γὰρ διαθήκη ἀπ' αἰῶνος Θανάτῳ ἀποθανῇ; ...
πᾶν ἔργον σηπόμενον ἐκλείπει.

Sir. 17:30-32

οὐ γὰρ δύναται πάντα εἶναι ἐν ἀνθρώποις,
ὅτι οὐκ ἀθάνατος υἱὸς ἀνθρώπου.
τί φωτεινότερον ἡλίου; καὶ τοῦτο ἐκλείπει·
καὶ πονηρὸν ἐνθυμηθήσεται σὰρξ καὶ αἷμα.
δύναμιν ὕψους οὐρανοῦ αὐτὸς ἐπισκέπτεται,
καὶ ἄνθρωποι πάντες γῆ καὶ σποδός. Ὁ ζῶν εἰς τὸν αἰῶνα ἔκτισεν τὰ πάντα κοινῇ (Sir. 18:1)

This reading of Ben Sira shows how Wis. 1:13-15 can be read as a direct polemic against it. Wisdom 1 denies that God created death and predestined the world and humans to die. Specifically, the phrase 'because God did not make death' (Wis. 1:13) denies that God 'created all things [including death] together' (Sir. 18:1). Wisdom 1:14 follows the use of ἐποίησεν in 1:13 with the word ἔκτισεν, thus directly repeating the word used by Ben Sira in Sir. 18:1. The use of τὰ πάντα also directly echoes Ben Sira's wording, but in a way that gives the sentence an antithetical meaning. Instead of being destined for death, Wisdom replies to Ben Sira that τὰ πάντα was created 'that they might exist' (εἰς τὸ εἶναι). τὰ πάντα is thus used in reference to the whole world, with human beings as its integral part, and as a synonym for ὁ κόσμος, which is introduced in the next line (Wis. 1:14): 'and the generative forces of the *world* (τοῦ κόσμου) are wholesome, *and there is no* (οὐκ ἔστιν) *destructive poison in them* (φάρμακον ὀλέθρου)'. Wisdom's cosmic viewpoint echoes Ben Sira's references to every created thing (πᾶν ἔργον), culminating in the failing sun (ἥλιος), while the denial of any 'chemical' ingredient (φάρμακον) in the world that causes it to die constitutes an antithesis of the idea of 'the sepsis of death' present in still living things in Sir. 14:17-19.

However, there are two more negations in this passage in Wisdom 1: the denial of God's pleasure at human death (Wis. 1:13) and the denial that Hell's kingdom is on earth (Wis. 1:14). To elucidate these negations, we will now turn to Sir. 41:1-4 where the theme of death is resumed. Here, an apostrophe addressed to death, illustrating its inevitability for all (41:1-2), is followed by a moral (3-4):

τοῦτο τὸ κρίμα παρὰ κυρίου πάσῃ σαρκί,
καὶ τί ἀπαναίνῃ <u>ἐν εὐδοκίᾳ</u> ὑψίστου;
εἴτε δέκα εἴτε ἑκατὸν εἴτε χίλια ἔτη,
<u>οὐκ ἔστιν ἐν ᾅδου ἐλεγμὸς ζωῆς</u>

This is the judgement from the Lord for all flesh.
And why should you reject the *pleasure* of the Most High?
Whether ten or hundred or thousand years,
in Hades there is no *reproving* of life.

In this text we see the perspective of God's εὐδοκία ('satisfaction/approval; good will, contentment') at human's death.[21] This line sets up an opposition between what humanity *rejects* or *is averse* to and what God ethically or 'emotionally' *approves* or *accepts*. This is, however, precisely what Wisdom denies in 1:13: 'nor does he delight in the destruction (ἀπωλείᾳ) of the living', with ἀπώλεια meaning not only 'destruction' in the active sense but also 'ruin' or 'death' in the passive sense. Thus, Wisdom's denial of God's delight at human death (οὐδὲ τέρπεται) can be taken as directly refuting the idea of εὐδοκία in Ben Sira.

But the last line in this Ben Sira passage presents an interpretative problem and deserves some more attention. The text reads, 'Whether ten or hundred or thousand years, in Hades there is no ἐλεγμός of life' (Sir. 41:4). The word ἐλεγμός occurs in Greek sources from the LXX onwards. In the LXX it has the following meanings: (1) 'chastising' (most often of people by God, or of people by other people) (Lev. 19:17; Judg. 2:10; 4 Kgdms 19:3; 1 Macc. 2:49; Pss. 38:12; 149:7; Sir. 20:29; 21:6; 32:17; *Pss. Sol.* 10:1; Isa. 37:3, 15) *or* (2) 'unmasking, disclosure' (presumably of guilt, but also of innocence) (Num. 5:18, 19, 23, 24, 27).

The word is formed from the verb ἐλέγχω, whose meanings oscillate between investigating and bringing the truth to light and bringing to light a negative truth, hence 'chastise, rebuke by unmasking the sin'. Both of these contrasting meanings – neutral detection vs. negative rebuke – are typical of its derivate ἔλεγχος as well. The word ἐλεγμός in the LXX mostly occurs in contexts of chastisement. Nevertheless, its use in Num. 5:18, 19, 23, 24, and 27 shows that the alternative meaning of testing and disclosure was associated with this word too. For example, τὸ ὕδωρ τοῦ ἐλεγμοῦ was meant to reveal whether the woman was guilty or not, rather than to 'chastise' her sin.

However, the translators of the KJV took the word in its better testified meaning. They thought that this chastisement applied to sins committed in a person's life. Such accusation in the grave can only have God as its agent and thus implies the situation of a post-mortem trial. They translated Sir. 41:4 as 'there is no inquisition in the grave, whether thou have lived ten, or a hundred, or a thousand years', i.e. no one will inquire into a person's bad deeds and punish for them. This understanding, correct as to the

---

[21] This line has no equivalent in the Masada manuscripts. It corresponds to the Hebrew from the Cairo Genizah: ומה תמאס בתורת עלי[ון], (Sir[B] 41:4). Torah, 'the law', cannot be translated as εὐδοκία. Either Ben Sira's grandson had a different *Vorlage* or he intended the different meaning of pleasure.

meaning of the Greek word, is difficult to reconcile with the context that speaks about any life being doomed to death, rather than about the moral irrelevance of anyone's actions in life. This is also difficult to reconcile with the general moral message of the book and explicit statements that God will repay 'mortals according to their deeds' (Sir. 35:24 [35:22 LXX]).

Therefore, subsequent modern translations have not retained the KJV interpretation. They deviate from it in different ways. Rudolf Smend, for instance, keeps the KJV interpretation of the word's meaning as 'chastisement for something really committed', but he changes the scene in which this chastisement takes place. He suggests that one person in the netherworld rebukes another person for the shortness of the other person's life. In this interpretation, the meaning would be that no one in the netherworld can boast of the length of his own life by humiliating another's, because death makes all people equal.[22] This interpretation is good in that it avoids the inappropriate implications of moral relativism while still remaining sensitive to the meaning of the Greek word. But it is a forced interpretation in that it requires many allowances to arrive at it, and it does not easily fit into its immediate context. For example, why should one 'chastise' or 'rebuke' the shortness of another person's life when in Hell? And how does this correspond with the possibility of living for one thousand years?

Later translators did not follow Smend's interpretation, instead adopting the sense suggested by the Hebrew version of this passage: איש <אין> תוכחות בש[אול] חיים (Sir[B] 41:4). This medieval Hebrew manuscript with its slightly odd syntax implies that there is no man who would 'berate' life itself when in Hell, as any life, long or short, is always better than being in Hell. The Hebrew should be translated as 'no man berates life in Hell', that is, 'complains about life, when he is in Hell'. Whether this meaning of berating, without chastisement for a real misdoing, is appropriate for תוכחות or not, this is certainly a different idea of 'accusation' from the one implied in the Greek word ἐλεγμός.

Therefore, Skehan translates Sir. 41:4 thusly: 'Whether one has lived ten years, a hundred, or a thousand, in the netherworld there are no arguments about life'. Or, as Di Lella clarifies, 'Simply because nothing takes place there except dark, dismal, shadowy existence devoid of any real life or joy'.[23] Sauer translates: 'Ja, zehn Jahre oder hundert oder tausend,//es gibt keine Beschwerde in der Unterwelt über das Leben'. His interpretation is: 'Ob wir nun auf 1000 Jahre oder zehn oder 100 zurückblicken, es gibt keine Instanz, bei der eine Beschwerde für dieses Geschick eingebracht werden könnte. Der, der in der Unterwelt versammelt ist, hat sein Leben beendet und ist nach alttestamentlicher Anschauung getrennt von Gott, vgl. Ps. 88.'[24]

---

[22] Rudolf Smend, *Die Weisheit des Jesus Sirach* (Berlin: Reimer, 1906), 382: 'in der Hölle, wo sie alle tot sind, kann keiner dem anderen die Kürze seines Lebens vorhalten und damit gegen ihn grosstun'.
[23] Patrick W. Skehan and Alexander A. Di Lella, *The Wisdom of Ben Sira: A New Translation with Notes*, AB 39 (New York: Doubleday, 1987), 474.
[24] Georg Sauer, *Jesus Sirach/Ben Sira*, ATD Apokryphen B.1 (Göttingen: Vandenhoeck & Ruprecht, 2000), 282–3.

As noted above, neither 'arguments' nor 'Beschwerde' or 'Rüge' correspond to the idea of ἐλεγμός – 'chastisement' or 'rebuke' for something bad that has already taken place. But the grandson apparently did not have איש in his *Vorlage*. His translation (οὐκ ἔστιν ἐν ᾅδου ἐλεγμὸς ζωῆς) would correspond to אין תוכחות חיים בשאול. The word תוכחות, however, is mostly used in the Bible in moral contexts, of God blaming humans or of humans rebuking each other for their moral misbehaviour toward each other. Consequently, ἐλεγμός is a standard Greek equivalent of תוכחות in these biblical passages.[25] When translating from his *Vorlage*, the grandson used this standard equivalent which resulted in the meaning reflected in the KJV translation.

The verse with this meaning, not only confused the majority of modern translators of Greek Ben Sira, but its Hebrew variant might have been a problem for later Jewish scribes who produced Hebrew manuscripts and added the gloss איש in the beginning of the phrase.[26]

Against this background we may suspect that the author of Wisdom too may have seen the difficulty in reading this phrase as referring to the absence of any trial and retribution after death. To solve this difficulty, he may have opted for a different interpretation of ἐλεγμός. As I stressed earlier, the meaning of ἐλέγχω is essentially twofold, implying either exposing a negative truth and rebuking someone for it, or neutrally detecting and unveiling a situation as it is. The verb and its derivatives are used in this neutral sense not only in classical literature, but also in Ben Sira (19:13-15) and Wisdom themselves. Thus, in Wis. 1:5 it is said that 'the holy spirit of education… will disclose itself (ἐλεγχθήσεται) when unrighteousness comes'.[27] And in Wis. 2:11 it is said that 'what is weak is proved to be useless (ἀσθενὲς ἄχρηστον ἐλέγχεται)'. This meaning of ἐλέγχω presents the possibility of interpreting the phrase οὐκ ἔστιν ἐλεγμὸς ζωῆς as 'life cannot be disclosed (i.e. detected) in Hell'.

Given the possibility of understanding Hades not only as a place where people go after death, but also as a metaphor for death itself,[28] this reading of Sir. 41:4 makes perfect sense as the culmination of the preceding three verses' emphasis on the universality of death: 'Whether life lasts for ten years or a hundred or a thousand, it cannot be detected in Death (Hades)', i.e., death is existentially overwhelming in any case. This is admittedly a somewhat sinister interpretation, but not only is it highly appropriate to its immediate context, it is also consistent with other passages in Ben Sira where dying is presented as innate in the life of any created being (e.g. Sir. 14:17-19). On this reading, Wisdom's denial of death's dominion on earth, expressed using the image of Hades (1:14), echoes Ben Sira's imagery, being antithetical to his thought.

---

[25] See Takamitsu Muraoka, 'Hebrew/Aramaic Index to the Septuagint', in *A Concordance to the Septuagint and the other Greek versions of the Old Testament* (Grand Rapids: Baker, 1998), 365.

[26] The later Jewish scribes, wishing to exclude the possibility that God does not chastise humans for their sins after death, might have resolved the ambiguity of the phrase by adding איש (thus excluding the possibility that God was the agent of תוכחות), which would explain the odd syntax of the phrase. This change would also have created a new context for תוכחות in which it means general 'cursing' rather than disclosure of misdeeds.

[27] The phrase is normally misunderstood in modern translations. KJV understood it correctly but rendered it rather freely: 'The holy spirit of discipline…will not abide when unrighteousness cometh in'. For this reason, this version has not influenced subsequent translations.

[28] See Hos. 13:15; Ps. 17:7. This usage is explicitly present in Sir. 14:12; 28:21.

Thus, all the negative statements in Wis. 1:12-16 can be understood as polemics against Ben Sira. Wisdom's negative assertions that God did not create death (Wis. 1:13) and that there is no destructive germ of rotting inherent in all things (1:14) deny the statements in Sir. 14:17-19 and 17:30-18:1. Wisdom's denials of God's pleasure at human death (1:13) and of Hell's kingdom on earth (1:14) likewise respond to Sir. 41:1-4. Consequently, the contrast between the presentations of human immortality and God-likeness in Wis. 2:23 to human mortality and earthiness/dustiness in Sir. 17:30-32 can also be considered deliberately polemical.

The fact that all these negations in Wisdom are elements of a single coherent passage (1:13-16), combined with the fact that Sir. 17:30-18:1 was most likely read by the author of Wisdom through the lens of statements in 14:17-19, strongly suggest that the author of Wisdom read Ben Sira by excerpting from his translation and combining passages referring to the same theme. This is a strategy well known to us from a variety of Jewish sources, including the Reworked Pentateuch/Rewritten Bible traditions, Targumim, Philo's commentaries, and Midrashim.[29] In this case it may be a sign that this method of reading was familiar to the author of Wisdom from his educational background. Alternatively, we could suggest that Ben Sira's translation had become part of Jewish school education by the time that Wisdom was composed and that Ben Sira was available to the author of Wisdom in thematic excerpts.

Wisdom 11:17–12:22 and the Damascus Document

The theme of the immortality of human beings and the created cosmos appears again in Wisdom 11. The context in which it appears develops the thought that God does not kill even bad human beings, even the enemies of the Jews. For example, although God was able to annihilate the Egyptians, nevertheless he only punished them in order to bring them to an understanding of his existence (e.g. 11:15-23). This thought is developed in the following chapter with the example of the original inhabitants of the promised land (12:3-22). Contrary to the biblical narrative, in which the annihilation of the local peoples is prescribed by God,[30] the author of Wisdom asserts that God spared them (12:8), 'giving them time and opportunity in which to free themselves from their wickedness' (12:20), showing that 'the righteous one should be loving towards human beings' (12:19).

In this context, a passage addressing the theme of immortality appears (11:23–12:1). The author repeats that all beings have the immortal spirit of God in them (12:1) and that everything stands (one surmises, forever, without dying) (11:25):

---

[29] On the Reworked Pentateuch/Rewritten Scripture see Michael Segal, 'Biblical Exegesis in 4Q158: Techniques and Genre', *Textus* 19 (1998): 45–62; Sidnie White Crawford, *Rewriting Scripture in the Second Temple Times* (Grand Rapids: Eerdmans, 2008), 39–59; Molly M. Zahn, *Rethinking Rewritten Scripture: Composition and Exegesis in the 4QReworked Pentateuch Manuscripts*, STDJ 95 (Leiden: Brill, 2011), 25–134. On Targumim, see Martin McNamara, *Targum Neophiti 1: Deuteronomy* (Collegeville: Liturgical Press, 1997), 1–15. On the Midrashim, see Herbert W. Bateman IV, *Early Jewish Hermeneutics and Hebrews 1:5-13* (New York: Peter Lang, 1997), 153–206.

[30] See Deut. 7:22-24; 9:3; 12:29; 19:1; 31:3; Josh. 23:4, 9.

ἐλεεῖς δὲ πάντας, ὅτι πάντα δύνασαι, | You have mercy on all, because you can do all things,
καὶ παρορᾷς ἁμαρτήματα ἀνθρώπων εἰς μετάνοιαν. | And you overlook the sins of human beings that they may repent.
ἀγαπᾷς γὰρ τὰ ὄντα πάντα | For you love all things that exist
καὶ οὐδὲν βδελύσσῃ ὧν ἐποίησας· | and loath none of the things that you have made,
οὐδὲ γὰρ ἂν μισῶν τι κατεσκεύασας. | For you have not formed anything out of hatred (with hatred).
πῶς δὲ διέμεινεν ἄν τι, εἰ μὴ σὺ ἠθέλησας, | How would anything have endured if you have not willed it?
ἢ τὸ μὴ κληθὲν ὑπὸ σοῦ διετηρήθη; | Or how would anything not called by you have been preserved?
φείδῃ δὲ πάντων, ὅτι σά ἐστιν, δέσποτα φιλόψυχε· | You spare all things, because they are yours, O Sovereign Lord, you who love human beings.
τὸ γὰρ ἄφθαρτόν σου πνεῦμά ἐστιν ἐν πᾶσιν. | For your incorruptible spirit is in all things.
(Wis. 11:23–12:1)

I wish to draw particular attention to how easily the author of Wisdom again switches between the immortality of human beings and the created world. God's mercy towards humans (Wis. 1:23, ἐλεεῖς δὲ πάντας; cf. 11:26, φιλόψυχε) is explained by his love toward the entire creation (ἀγαπᾷς γὰρ τὰ ὄντα πάντα) and developed by using neuter pronouns and participles (οὐδέν, τι, κληθέν), which apparently refer to created things in general, rather than to humans. The idea that the immortal divine spirit is present in human beings is taken by the author from Gen. 1:26 and 2:7, which he draws upon for his conclusion about human immortality in Wis. 2:23, an interpretation of Gen. 2:7 that is also explicitly mentioned in Wis. 15:11. At the same time, the divine spirit's presence throughout the whole created world (Wis. 1:7) may also be an allusion along these lines. This makes the border between the two subjects of immortality – people and the world – even blurrier and illustrates how easily the author fluctuates between them.

The idea that God does not wish to kill people also echoes a key element of the theme of immortality as introduced in Wisdom 1, namely the author's denial of God's pleasure at humans' death. But here, by denying that God kills even notoriously bad people and by introducing considerations on how power should be exercised by an unlimited ruler, the author of Wisdom also gives an ethical-political dimension to this denial.

This is the general context in which two further negative statements appear: 'and you loath none of the things you have made, for you would not have made any thing with hatred' (Wis. 11:24). To better understand these negative statements, I wish to draw attention to the next sentence, specifically, to the line 'Or how would anything not called by you have been preserved?' (ἢ τὸ μὴ κληθὲν ὑπὸ σοῦ διετηρήθη, Wis. 11:25). Where, in any context, does the idea of 'bestowing a name' or 'calling' connect to the idea of eternal existence? Nowhere in Greek thought, to the best of my knowledge. In

Genesis, the idea of bestowing a name (καλέω) is used in the creation account, when God gives names to the newly created world (Gen. 1:5, 8, 10), but it is not connected with the idea of the world's preservation. On the other hand, the idea of the (ever) lasting existence of the world occurs in Ps. 118(119):90, but it is not connected to the idea of calling.[31] In Isaiah, the idea of calling, or calling by name (καλέω/καλέω τὸ ὄνομα, קרא\קרא בשם) and the idea of everlasting existence appear within one book, but they are still contextually separate (e.g. Isa. 40:26; 41:4; 43:1; 45:3–4; 49:1; 66:22). These ideas grow together in some late Second Temple texts, particularly in CD II 11 and IV 3–4:[32]

CD II 11–12: 'But during all those (years), (God) raised up for himself *those called by name* so as to leave the remnant for the land' (ובכולם הקים לו קריאי שם למען התיר פליטה לארץ)

CD IV 3–4: 'and "the Sons of Zadok" are the chosen ones of Israel, *those called by name, who stand* in the end of the days'[33] (ובני צדוק הם בחירי ישראל קריאי השם העמדים באחרית הימים)

In both quotations, there are people 'called by name' (קריאי שם), the expression deriving from Isaiah and translated in LXX Isaiah using the verb καλέω. In the last quoted line, the idea of survival is expressed using a participial from of the verb עמד, used for the idea of everlasting existence in Ps. 118:90 and Isa. 66:22. This meaning of the verb can be translated into Greek using διατερέω (cf. Exod. 9:19) and, more often, (δια)μένω (e.g. Ps. 118:90; Isa. 66:22).[34] We see these two verbs accompanying the thought of calling by name in Wis. 11:25: πῶς δὲ διέμεινεν ἄν τι, εἰ μὴ σὺ ἠθέλησας, ἢ τὸ μὴ κληθὲν ὑπὸ σοῦ διετηρήθη.

In the Damascus Document, these elements occur in a context that speaks about God's wrath directed towards sinners. The theme starts in column I (CD I 2–4, 17–18) and stretches down to the end of column III. In particular, it is said that God 'annihilated the lot' of the sinners (CD I 1) leaving them 'without remnant or survivor' (CD I 6–7); 'Everything mortal on dry land expired and became as if they had never existed' (CD II 20). He 'exterminated' the sons of Noah (CD III 1) as well as the sons of Jacob with their descendants (CD III 6, 9–12). By way of summary, the text says: 'Those who reject this water ("the law") He will not allow to live' (CD III 17).

These quotations speak for themselves. They convey an idea systematically refuted in Wis. 11:27–12:22, which asserts that God, even if he can exterminate, nevertheless spares even the worst of sinners. Most importantly, the Damascus Document explains God's extermination of sinners by saying that God did not choose them primordially (from the beginning of the world):

---

[31] 'Thou hast established the earth, and it abideth' (KJV); εἰς γενεὰν καὶ γενεὰν ἡ ἀλήθειά σου ἐθεμελίωσας τὴν γῆν καὶ διαμένει (לדר ודר אמונתך כוננת ארץ ותעמד).
[32] Cf. also 4Q521 frag. 2 ii + 4 5: 'For the Lord attends to the pious and calls the righteous by name' (וצדיקים בשם יקרא).
[33] Here and below, I am using J. M. Baumgarten's translation of the CD (DJD XVIII).
[34] See also: Pss. 118:91; 18:10; 101:27; Sir. 41:13.

Col. II

6. in the han[d] of all the angels of destruction for those who wilfully depart from Way and despise the statue, *leaving them neither remnant*
7 *nor survivors. For God did not choose them primordially* (מקדם עולם); before they were established he knew
8. their works. *And he despised the generations (in which) they [st]ood* and hid his face from the land
9. from (...) until their completion. And he knew years they would stand and the numbers and details of their times, during all
10. the existence of eternity and being before they came to be in their respective times during all the years of eternity.
11. But during all those (years), (God) raised up for himself *those called by name so as to leave the remnant* for the land and fill
12. the face of the world with their seed. And he informed them through those anointed in his Holy Spirit and who view
13. his truth of *the details of their names. But those whom he hated he caused to stray.* (CD II 6–13)

מקדם עולם in CD II 7 introduces the theme of the creation of the world,[35] as well as an idea popular in the Qumran documents that some are 'chosen' by God from the moment of the creation, while others are not. CD II 13 says explicitly that God's hatred was the reason of their misbehaviour and II 8 ascribes to God a loathing of these people: 'And he despised the generations (in which) they [st]ood'. Thus, the text presents God as having chosen between good and bad people before the world came to be. God's hatred is the reason why they are bad. Based on this presentation, the conclusion that God had hatred at the creation is inevitable. God loathes those who came into being by his hatred.[36]

Loathing is expressed using the verb תעב, the standard correspondence of which in Greek is βδελύττω (e.g. Lev. 18:30; 20:23, 25; 21:14; 26:11; Deut. 7:26; 23:7; 3 Kgs 20[21]:6), while hatred is expressed using the verb שנא, typically rendered by μισέω. Both verbs occur in Wis. 11:24, which denies the perspective of CD, asserting that God did not have hatred at creation and does not loathe anyone: 'For you love all things that exist and *loath* (βδελύσσῃ) none of the things that you have made, For you have not formed anything *out of hatred* (μισῶν)'. Wisdom's general argument in 11:17–12:22 stands opposed to the argument of the Damascus Document in columns

---

[35] On the creational meaning of the expression, see Ekaterina Matusova, 'A New Translation of Ps. 78:2 (LXX 77:2) in Matt. 13:35', in *History and Theology in the Gospels*, ed. T. Nicklas, K.-W. Niebuhr, and M. Seleznev, WUNT 447 (Tübingen: Mohr Siebeck, 2020), 271–88, here 274–9.

[36] This idea has a broader context in the Qumran documents. The notion of God's hatred at creation with reference to the two spirits, rather than to the righteous and sinners, is also present in the Rule of the Community (1QS III 25–IV 1): 'It is actually He who created the spirits of light and darkness, making them the cornerstone of every deed, their [ ] the premise of [eve]ry [ ]. God's love for one spirit lasts forever. He will be pleased with its actions for always. The counsel of the other, however, He abhors, hating its every impulse for all time.' Cf. 4Q509 VII 3.

I–III and the antithetical correspondence of the arguments is supported by the correspondence on the lexical level.

The standard technical use of Greek lexemes suggests that either this text (or a very similar one) was known to the author of Wisdom in Greek translation or that he was a trained translator himself and rendered phrases that were important *ad hoc*. Whichever way it happened, it is interesting that while the Damascus Document speaks exclusively about the relationship of God with people, the author of Wisdom uses the notions of calling, hating, and loathing in application to neuter subjects. In so doing, he shifts the picture by enlarging it to include the entire created world. In the case of calling and preservation, expressed using the verbs καλέω and διαμένω, he may have had other biblical texts in mind that facilitated this shift (e.g. Gen. 1; Isa. 40; 48; 66; Ps. 118). But in the case of hating and loathing, he must have been guided solely by his own strategy of blurring the line between human beings and the cosmos as aspects of one and the same creation.

Another interesting aspect of this adaptation is that, while negating some points in the discourse, the author of Wisdom seems to accept others, all of which are present together in column II of the Damascus Document. These include not only the connection between calling and preservation, but also, inconsistently enough, such peculiar notions as the inborn wickedness of the wicked. For example, the author asserts that God knew 'that their origin was evil and their wickedness inborn and their way of thinking would never change; for they were an accused race from the beginning' (Wis. 12:10-11) and refers to God's 'hatred' toward these people (Wis. 12:4). The presence of these elements in an argument aimed at proving the opposite thought makes an odd impression, and I do not see any other way to explain it except with reference to the view's incontestable popularity.[37]

It requires more discussion, and is beyond the scope of the present study, to determine whether the author of Wisdom had the Damascus Document to hand, or another source in which the major outline and specific details coincided with CD I–III. It is enough to say that although many of these elements certainly have a broader context and parallels in other texts from Qumran (particularly in 1QS), they are nowhere else presented in such a clear and concise form that enables us to explain the polemical message and the inner logic of Wisdom 11–12.

Level 3: Platonic Philosophy and its Part in the Author's Polemics

The motif of the immortality of human beings and the cosmos appears in Wisdom 1–2 and 11 in connection with the polemics against Ben Sira (in Wis. 1–2) and the ideology of the first part of the Damascus Document (in Wis. 11). How are these two Jewish 'philosophies' connected to each other as targets of Wisdom's polemics? Formally speaking, they convey different ideas. Ben Sira speaks about the predestination to death ordained by God in the universe for people and for created things. The

---

[37] Even Philo alludes to God's wrath as the cause of the origin of sinners at one point (*Deus* 70), which is otherwise totally atypical of him.

Damascus Document is not necessarily of this opinion. It says that some people were created bad because of God's (primordial) hatred towards them and that only these people are predestined to be exterminated in the course of history.

On the one hand, a thread connecting these two approaches is the motif of God's acceptance of human death. Wisdom 1:13 argues against God's εὐδοκία at human death mentioned in Sir. 41:4. This helps to explain the author's polemics against the Damascus Document's tendency to ascribe to God a desire to cut short some people's life (cf. CD III 17).

On the other hand, why is the author of Wisdom so opposed to the idea that God might have feelings of hatred and loathing towards anyone, even the adversaries of the Jews? And why does he generalize the discussion of God's attitude by extending it from humans to the created world in general? While Ben Sira's text may contain an impulse to such a conflation of animated and non-animated nature, no comparable impulse is found in the Damascus Document. But the author of Wisdom is very consistent in pursuing this strategy. What is he guided by?

I suggest that the answers to these questions can be found by taking into account the Platonic attitude to the problem. According to the basics of Plato's theology, God does not have any bad feelings or intentions: he is not the cause of any evil (*Resp.* 379b1; 379c2-7); the evil existing in the world is the result of human choice (*Resp.* 617e4-5). God is entirely good, ἀγαθός (*Resp.* 379c2; *Tim.* 29d), and his goodness is the only *cause* of *the creation of the world* as well as the warrant of its *immortality*. These postulates are clearly laid out in the Timaeus, an extraordinarily popular dialogue in late antiquity. Specifically, Plato says:

> Let us now state the Cause wherefore he that constructed it, constructed Becoming and the All. He was good, and in him that is good *no envy ariseth ever concerning anything* (ἀγαθὸς ἦν, ἀγαθῷ δὲ οὐδεὶς περὶ οὐδενὸς οὐδέποτε ἐγγίγνεται φθόνος); and being devoid of envy he desired that all should be, so far as possible, like unto himself. This principle, then, we shall be wholly right in accepting from men of wisdom as being above all the supreme originating principle of Becoming and the Cosmos. For God desired that, so far as possible, all things should be good and nothing evil (ἀγαθὰ μὲν πάντα, φλαῦρον δὲ οὐδέν). (*Tim.* 29d–30a)

Plato continues with the postulate that to destroy something which is good would be an act of a wicked one. But God is perfect. Consequently, he cannot want to destroy the world. Although the world was created, and although creation implies dissolution, this principle does not apply to the world. It will last forever by God's will:

> Gods of gods, those works whereof I am framer and father (Θεοὶ θεῶν, ὧν ἐγὼ δημιουργὸς πατήρ τε ἔργων), you came into being by me, but you *are indissoluble as I am unwilling* (ἐμοῦ γε μὴ ἐθέλοντος). For though all that is bound may be dissolved, yet to will to dissolve that which is fairly joined together and in good case were the deed of a wicked one. Wherefore ye also,

seeing that ye were generated, are not wholly immortal or indissoluble, yet in no wise shall ye be dissolved *nor incur the doom of death* (οὐδὲ τεύξεσθε θανάτου μοίρας), because in my will ye possess a bond greater and more sovereign than the bonds wherewith, at your birth, ye were bound together. (*Tim.* 41a7-b6)[38]

'Gods' in Plato's text refer to planets, the main constituents of the cosmos; all created elements are referred to as ἔργα. Together they form part of the notion of the cosmos. To them it is promised by God that they will not experience death (θάνατος). All these elements – θάνατος, ἔργον, ἥλιος (which is one of the planets in Greek astronomy) – also occur in Ben Sira's passages (Sir. 14:17-19; 17:30-32), against which Wisdom takes a polemical stance. When Wisdom says 'because God did not make death nor does he delight in the destruction of the living. For he created all things that they might exist, and the generative forces of the world (τοῦ κόσμου) are wholesome' (Wis. 1:13-14), this sounds Platonic. In these passages, Wisdom introduces the concept, unprecedented in the LXX, of the cosmos (ὁ κόσμος) in the sense of the created world (as a synonym of τὰ πάντα),[39] a centrally important concept in the Timaeus. Its use in Wis. 11:17 in connection with the idea of its creation from 'formless matter' (ἐξ ἀμόρφου ὕλης) clearly shows the direct influence of the Timaeus, as this expression corresponds to the standard first-century BCE Platonic interpretation of *Tim.* 30a.[40] At the same time, the references to the world as an animated being in Wis. 12:1 and 1:7, and to the providence of God in Wis. 6:7, 14:3, and 17:2, correspond to *Tim.* 30b.[41] In all likelihood, Plato's text, standing in contrast to Ben Sira, becomes a strong theoretical basis and support for the author of Wisdom in emphasizing the immortality of the cosmos in general, rather than only human immortality.

Taking into account the crucial Platonic postulate that God's 'goodness' is the only cause of creation and that no bad intention can be predicated of him, Wisdom's emphatic denial of God's hatred as the cause of creation and of God's loathing of people becomes much more understandable. It is consistent with this suggestion of Platonic influence that in the context of this argument (Wis. 12:22), as well as elsewhere in the text (Wis. 7:26), we encounter the notion of 'goodness' (ἀγαθότης)

---

[38] Plato, *Plato in Twelve Volumes*, vol. 9, trans. W. R. M. Lamb (Cambridge, MA: Harvard University Press, 1925), with minor emendations.

[39] Outside of Wisdom, in the LXX it appears in the sense of 'world' only in 2 Maccabees, written around the first century BCE and highly relevant to Wisdom, owing to its many significant parallels of various kinds. The other books of the LXX, even including Ben Sira, have the word κόσμος only in the meaning of 'ornament' or 'order'.

[40] See *Tim.* 30a: 'He took over all that was visible, seeing that it was not in a state of rest but in a state of discordant and disorderly motion, he brought it into order out of disorder (οὕτω δὴ πᾶν ὅσον ἦν ὁρατὸν παραλαβὼν οὐχ ἡσυχίαν ἄγον ἀλλὰ κινούμενον πλημμελῶς καὶ ἀτάκτως, εἰς τάξιν αὐτὸ ἤγαγεν ἐκ τῆς ἀταξίας), deeming that the former state is in all ways better than the latter'. See, for instance, Philo, Aet. 13.

[41] Despite the Stoic appearance of the phrase, the thought is genuinely Platonic, deriving from *Tim.* 30b: 'Thus, then, in accordance with the likely account, we must declare that this Cosmos has verily come into existence as a Living Creature endowed with soul and reason owing to the providence of God' (τόνδε τὸν κόσμον ζῷον ἔμψυχον ἔννουν τε τῇ ἀληθείᾳ διὰ τὴν τοῦ θεοῦ γενέσθαι πρόνοιαν).

applied to God. The idea that God causes death to the cosmos, emphatically denied by Plato because it represents a potential 'bad intention', is also emphatically denied by the author of Wisdom, but he extends it to include both the world in general and humanity in particular. Plato's theodicy, according to which any evil in a human's life is rooted in that human's choices rather than in God's will, is congruent with Wisdom's statement that the cause of death is people's choice of behaviour, rather than God. For example, Plato states that 'the guilt is his who chooses: God is innocent' (*Resp.* 617e4-5), while Wisdom notes that 'God did not create death…but the impious by their deeds and words summoned it' (Wis. 1:13, 16).

The influence of the Timaeus explains not only Wisdom's general philosophical stance towards the ideology of Ben Sira and the Damascus Document, but also some more specific elements in the Wisdom passages analyzed above. This includes, for instance, the notion of the devil's 'envy' (φθόνος) by which death entered the world despite humanity's original creation in God's likeness (Wis. 2:23-24).

In the Genesis creation narrative nothing is said about the 'envy' of the serpent. However, Plato explicitly denies this quality to God in the passage from the Timaeus discussed above: 'He was good, and in him that is good no *envy* (φθόνος) ariseth ever concerning anything'. Moreover, Plato does this in a sentence that stresses that God wanted to create the world 'similar' to himself: 'and being devoid of envy he desired that all should be, so far as possible, like (παραπλήσια) unto himself' (*Tim.* 29e). This same combination of notions occurs in Wis. 2:23-24: God created the first human similar to himself (κατ' εἰκόνα [καὶ καθ'ὁμοίωσιν]; cf. Gen. 1:26), but it was someone's else 'envy' that deprived him of this similarity.

Another distinctive textual allusion can be seen in Wis. 11:25, where the author, speaking about the immortality of the world, addresses God: 'How would anything have endured if you have not willed it (εἰ μὴ σὺ ἠθέλησας)?' This wording corresponds precisely to the famous phrase in the Timaeus, attributed to God, whose goodness and sovereign will are the reason for the world's immortality: 'but you *are indissoluble as I am unwilling* (ἐμοῦ γε μὴ ἐθέλοντος)' (*Tim.* 41a).

Conclusion

In this study, addressing the subject of immortality in the Wisdom of Solomon, we suggested a certain correction of focus on this text. Rather than posing a common question as to what specific view on immortality – Greek or Jewish – the author holds, we inquired how his statements on immortality are actually formed. The study confirmed that the idea of immortality defended by the author of Wisdom points us towards the Jewish context of 4QInstruction, 2 Maccabees, and biblical interpretation. However, we found that his statements, particularly those which are expressed negatively, have a strong polemical impulse. The majority of them are conceived as polemics against corresponding statements in the Greek text of Ben Sira. This conclusion becomes clear if the Greek text of Ben Sira is viewed through more appropriate lenses, paying deeper attention to the subtle area of Greek semantics, and emulating methods of reading texts that were practiced in Second Temple Jewish tradition. The other evident target of his polemics turns out to be the theology of 'creation with hatred' and 'predestination for destruction' as presented in the first three columns of the Damascus Document.

The general framework of Platonic theology explains the missing points of departure in Wisdom's polemics. We knew that, with the strong support of some elements in the Jewish culture, the author of Wisdom wanted to emphasize humanity's originally intended immortality and potential eternal life. But we did not know why he necessarily connected this with the immortality of the cosmos, or how Ben Sira and the Damascus Document are connected as targets of his polemics. Now we see that both texts contain thoughts that make them equally antithetical to the Platonic theology of the Republic and of the Timaeus: neither the destruction of the world, nor God's bad intentions are acceptable from the Platonic point of view. Particularly, the Timaeus helps us to understand why, when speaking about God's hatred at creation, the author of Wisdom repeatedly shifts his focus to the created world in general, rather than humans only.

In Wisdom 11–12, when asserting that God does not wish to annihilate anyone, the author draws not only on Platonic theology, but also on Hellenistic treatises on royalty which emphasize the philanthropy of the ideal ruler.[42] Thus, the influence of the Greek context here is multifaceted and even wider than Plato alone. The question, however, is whether this Greek influence, evident as it is, was *alone* responsible for the author's rejection of the Damascus Document ideology, or whether, as in the case of Ben Sira's attitude to immortality, there was a diversity of perspectives within Judaism itself on this issue. Passages like Ezek. 33:10-20, denying that God wills for sinners to die and arguing against any predestination for them to die, could serve as a basis for an ideology strongly dissenting from that in CD I–III, whereas passages like Mt. 5:43-48 and Jn 3:16-17, which emphasize God's love towards all human beings, good and bad, without hatred towards anybody, might be a sign of the existence of such a trend within Judaism which was manifested in the New Testament texts. Thus, the question is, could not the Wisdom of Solomon also be reflecting a Jewish tradition dissenting from that of the Damascus Document, just as it reflects the immortality trend dissenting from Ben Sira's? However, in the absence of a Jewish source predating the Wisdom of Solomon with which this text can be compared, this suggestion remains hypothetical.

What is not hypothetical, however, is that in looking for a philosophical ally against Jewish ideologies which the author wants to reject, he turns to Plato. Wisdom's understanding of the originally intended immortality of humans is based on an interpretation of the creation account in Genesis 1–3, and Ben Sira's assertion of human mortality is based on his (or his tradition's) interpretation of these very same biblical chapters. Consequently, Plato's dialogue on the creation of the world, the Timaeus, is adapted to serve as a philosophical foundation and support for Wisdom's interpretation of the Genesis creation account. Significantly, this strategy constitutes a neat

---

[42] As noted already by J. M. Reese, *Hellenistic Influence on the Book of Wisdom and its Consequences* (Rome: Pontificio Istituto Biblico, 1970), 76–7.

methodological parallel to what we find in Philo's approach to the biblical creation narrative. In his treatise *De opificio mundi*, as well as in his other treatises where he touches upon the subject of creation, the biblical narrative is interpreted through the narrative of the Timaeus.[43] However, besides some very basic elements like the goodness of the creator and the immortality of the world, Philo's interpretation differs from that of the author of Wisdom. For example, humanity's likeness to God is explained in terms of the rationality of the human soul, rather than immortality, while the creation in Genesis 1–2 is explained as an essentially twofold process whereby the world is created first in the form of ideas and then afterwards in physical form. By contrast, some elements emphasized by Wisdom (e.g. the metaphysical role of envy) are irrelevant for Philo, as is the issue of God's attitude towards death in general. The reason for this is clear. The author of Wisdom had specific polemical concerns and turned to Plato as an ally in his argumentation, which gave particular prominence to the notions of the devil's envy and God's unwillingness to cause death. Philo was writing *De opificio* without a polemical motivation, but rather with the purpose of giving a systematic and programmatic philosophical interpretation of the Genesis account. However, it remains significant that Wisdom's author shows no trace of any familiarity with the Philonic interpretation of Genesis. Given Philo's prominence as a Jewish philosopher in Alexandria and the sensitivity of Wisdom's author to the philosophical ideas present in his environment, this must imply that the author of Wisdom was writing before Philo, or, at least, prior to Philo's *acme*.[44] Nonetheless, this indicates the existence of a cultural context within Hellenistic Egyptian Judaism that favoured a theological strategy of adapting Platonism to Judaism, developed later by Philo.[45]

In the light of this strategy, the commonly asked question as to whether the author has a specifically Jewish or Greek view of immortality makes little sense because it presupposes a modern understanding of the history of philosophy and religion which separates entities and evaluates them as discrete alternatives. In contrast, one may suggest that, for the author of Wisdom, the possibility of using Greek philosophical ideas to corroborate and underpin his Jewish material was a more important theological agenda than investigating differences between the Jewish and Platonic attitudes to immortality. In marked contrast to modern scholarly tendencies, the author of Wisdom intentionally brings doctrines together with pioneering boldness and has little concern for the essential differences between them.

---

[43] See David T. Runia, *Philo of Alexandria and the 'Timaeus' of Plato* (Leiden: Brill, 1986), and Matusova, '*De opificio mundi*', 57–94.

[44] James Aitken and Ekaterina Matusova, 'The Wisdom of Solomon', in *The Oxford Handbook of Wisdom and the Bible*, ed. W. Kynes (Oxford: Oxford University Press, 2021), 599–615, here 611–13.

[45] On the author's use of the Platonic teaching about souls, see Ekaterina Matusova, 'The Platonic Influence in the Passages on Soul in the Wisdom of Solomon', in *XVII Congress of the International Organization for Septuagint and Cognate Studies, Aberdeen 2019*, ed. G. Kotze, M. N. van der Meer, and M. Rösel (Atlanta: SBL, 2022) (in print).

5

BOOKISH CIRCLES?
THE MOVE TOWARD THE USE OF WRITTEN TEXTS
IN RABBINIC ORAL CULTURE

Catherine Hezser

When setting out to examine the role of written texts in late antique Palestinian Judaism one should avoid certain pitfalls that may arise from arguing retrospectively, based on the later literary evidence and the study of rabbinic texts in institutional contexts. These developments, that is, the creation of the large rabbinic encyclopaedic collections (the Palestinian and Babylonian Talmuds also called Yerushalmi and Bavli) and the study in permanent rabbinic academies or *yeshivot*, point to post-Talmudic, Gaonic times as a period of social, administrative, and educational changes,[1] culminating in the circulation of the first Jewish 'books' in the form of codices in the Near and Middle East of the tenth and eleventh centuries.[2] The Mishnah, Tosefta, and Talmuds have been studied in *batei midrash* (study houses) and *yeshivot* (lit.: sittings or sessions) since the Middle Ages.[3] The various forms of rabbinic study that

---

[1] Jeffrey L. Rubenstein has argued that references to Babylonian rabbinic academies belong to the stammaitic, post-amoraic layer of the Bavli. See Rubenstein, 'The Rise of the Babylonian Rabbinic Academy: A Reexamination of the Talmudic Evidence', *Jewish Studies, an Internet Journal* 1 (2002): 55–68. For a critique and rejection of the traditional view that permanent academies existed in amoraic Palestine, see David M. Goodblatt, *The Monarchic Principle: Studies in Jewish Self-Government in Antiquity* (Tübingen: Mohr Siebeck, 1994), and Catherine Hezser, *The Social Structure of the Rabbinic Movement in Roman Palestine* (Tübingen: Mohr Siebeck, 1997), 195–214.
[2] See the important article by David Stern, 'The First Jewish Books and the Early History of Jewish Reading', *JQR* 98 (2008): 163–202, here 163. Stern suggests that the origins of the codex in Jewish culture lie in the eighth century (p. 164). Its use in the Middle Ages 'mark[s] a watershed moment in the history of Jewish reading and its technology' (p. 165).
[3] On the development of Ashkenasic *yeshivot* in the Middle Ages, see especially Ephraim Kanarfogel, *Jewish Education and Society in the High Middle Ages* (Detroit: Wayne State University Press, 1992), 56–7 and elsewhere. Gaonic *yeshivot* in Babylonia were organized differently. On these see Moshe Gil, *A History of Palestine, 634–1099* (Cambridge: Cambridge University Press, 1992), 569–75.

developed once the written documents were compiled, once codices had replaced scrolls, and once Talmud academies had been established in Babylonia and elsewhere cannot be considered representative of rabbinic study practices in Roman Palestine in the first four centuries CE. To use our contemporary knowledge of rabbinic texts and ways in which they are used in 'traditional' (usually identified with ultra-Orthodox) contexts and assume that these forms of study can be traced back to late antiquity is therefore methodologically inappropriate.[4] Later outcomes and developments cannot be used to make sense of earlier – different, diverse, and uncertain – circumstances.

How can we assess and make sense of the earlier situation, then? Palestinian rabbis of the first five centuries CE had limited access to texts in scroll format. How prevalent biblical scrolls were and whether and to what extent written rabbinic texts existed, who had access to them, how they were used and in which contexts remains uncertain. What is clear, though, is that throughout tannaitic and amoraic times rabbinic study and discourse took place in an oral cultural context whose parameters are difficult to reconstruct.[5]

1. Is the Term 'Bookish' Applicable to Ancient Rabbis?

Whether and to what extent rabbis belonged to 'bookish circles' and were 'literate' obviously depends on the definition of these terms. Does 'bookish' merely refer to the valuation of written texts – or one text in particular – or also imply the reading of 'books', in scroll format, on a regular basis? Can 'bookish' describe the oral discussion of memorized rules and narratives or does it require access to written texts? How can we distinguish between the mere self-presentation as a 'bookish' public persona, fashionable among wider circles of the middle and upper strata of society in late antiquity, and intellectuals?[6] Should we call those individuals scholars who had memorized and were able to recite a circumscribed number of traditional religious texts, even if they lacked access to Torah scrolls and were unable to write (more than) their own names?

The term 'bookish', in the way in which it is used in popular parlance nowadays, cannot be applied to ancient societies and especially not to rabbis. Rabbis were not 'bookish' in the sense of being surrounded by books, consulting them on a regular basis. For them, only one 'book' was worthy of discussion. They did not perceive the Torah as a 'book' like other books that circulated at their time. As divine tradition turned into discourse and emulated practically in daily life, the Torah was much more than a book. As divine revelation and holy object, the Torah could not be treated like

---

[4] This was the approach of almost all earlier scholarship until the 1990s. Scholars such as Alon assumed that the rabbinic academy was a fixed institution in the first centuries CE already and 'had the last word on all halakhic questions'. See Gedaliah Alon, *The Jews in Their Land in the Talmudic Age (70–640 C.E.)*, 3rd ed. (Cambridge, MA: Harvard University Press, 1989), 10.

[5] See Catherine Hezser, *Jewish Literacy in Roman Palestine* (Tübingen: Mohr Siebeck, 2001), especially 190–209, 451–73, 496–504.

[6] Paul Zanker, *The Mask of Socrates: The Image of the Intellectual in Antiquity* (Berkeley: University of California Press, 1995), brings many examples of funerary images of the deceased (both men and women) depicted with scrolls in their hands. The desire for an 'intellectual look' seems to have been widespread in late antiquity (see ibid., 224).

other text scrolls.⁷ Whether and to what extent rabbis had access to written Torah scrolls and whether at least some rabbinic traditions circulated and were consulted in written form remains uncertain.⁸

Rabbis were also not 'bookish' in the way in which ivory tower academics are perceived by the public nowadays. Study was not conducted in isolation but in lively discussion and debate with colleagues and in the presence of students. Actual practice in daily life counted as much as theoretical instruction and debate. Rabbis had ordinary professions and reacted to actual issues they encountered in the marketplace and on the road. They lived their lives amongst the public rather than receding to enclosed spaces to engage in speculations of the mind. Their topics of discussion were concrete and material rather than the remote theoretical speculations of philosophers and theologians.

2. Structure and Main Argument

In the following, I shall investigate the question of rabbis' use of written texts from a chronologically reversed perspective, moving backwards from the time of the editing of the Talmud and Midrash (fourth and fifth centuries CE) to the amoraic period (third to fourth centuries CE). The first part examines rabbis' access to written versions of rabbinic traditions, whereas the second part focuses on the availability and use of written biblical texts.

I shall argue that competition with the knowledge culture of Christianity in the early Byzantine period made rabbis question the usefulness of maintaining the 'Oral Torah' format and decide to preserve rabbinic knowledge in written form. The expanding literature of the church fathers, with their competing theology and biblical interpretation, seems to have made it necessary to create an equivalent body of written rabbinic knowledge that could be studied and expanded by future generations. Roman-Byzantine imperialism was also an imperialism of one knowledge culture over another. To persevere in such a context, rabbinic scholars probably considered it necessary to adopt the written transmission format of the competing religion.

3. The Creation of the Larger Rabbinic Compilations in Early Byzantine Times: From Oral Transmission to Written Texts

Although we lack information about the editors who created amoraic Midrashim and the Talmud Yerushalmi, they lived in a cultural environment in which the written preservation and compilation of earlier traditions was held in high esteem. These scholars would have been guided by the desire to preserve the teachings,

---

⁷ See also William Scott Green, 'Writing with Scripture: The Rabbinic Uses of the Hebrew Bible', in *Writing with Scripture: The Authority and Uses of the Hebrew Bible in the Torah of Formative Judaism*, ed. J. Neusner and W. S. Green (Minneapolis: Fortress, 1989), 14.
⁸ See the discussion in Hezser, *Jewish Literacy*, 202–7; Martin S. Jaffee, *Torah in the Mouth: Writing and Oral Tradition in Palestinian Judaism, 200 BCE–400 CE* (Oxford: Oxford University Press, 2001), 101, 124–5, 140.

precedents, and stories of their rabbinic predecessors, whom they considered superior to themselves in wisdom.⁹ They were eager to transmit that body of knowledge to later generations of sages.¹⁰ The desire to collect rabbinic traditions of previous centuries and to transmit them to later generations in written form stood in marked contrast to the earlier amoraic aversion against writing down rabbinic traditions, an aversion which also found expression in the concept of the Oral Torah. According to *y. Meg.* 4:1, 74d, 'things that were stated orally [must be presented] orally'. In its literary context the statement supports *ad hoc* translations from Hebrew into Aramaic and rejects the use of written targumim. Another text is even more forceful against the circulation of written aggadic texts: 'as to an aggadic passage, one who writes it down has no share in the world to come...' (*y. Shab.* 16:1, 15c). A story tradition immediately follows as an example: 'R. Hiyya b. Ba saw a book containing aggadic writings. He said: If what is written in that book is correct, let the hand of the one who wrote it be cut off.' These traditions suggest that great value was placed on the oral circulation of rabbinic traditions. Some written collections – e.g., student notes, Aramaic translations of Hebrew biblical texts, story collections, rabbinic exegetical commentaries – may have nevertheless existed in amoraic times. Such written collections were probably made unofficially, below the radars of prominent rabbis, perhaps by scribes in the margins of the rabbinic movement who tried to make some money from selling them.

Why did late antique rabbis insist on oral transmission at a time when writing had already been used for centuries in their own Jewish culture and in the Graeco-Roman context they lived in?¹¹ In amoraic times, the insistence on oral transmission had specific functions that benefited rabbis' social status, identity, and halakhic creativity: (a) it served to link disciples and followers to their rabbinic masters as incorporations of Torah knowledge; (b) it kept rabbinic halakhah flexible and adaptable to specific circumstances; (c) it helped representing the rabbinic movement in analogy

---

⁹ The model suggested by Peter Schäfer and Hans-Jürgen Becker, according to which the large rabbinic documents grew organically, without the conscious input of a group of editors, from individual traditions to medieval manuscripts, and were basically open ended as far as changes and were basically open ended as far as later changes are concerned, does not seem logical on practical grounds. For this model, see Peter Schäfer, 'Research into Rabbinic Literature: An Attempt to Define the Status Quaestionis', *JJS* 37 (1986): 139–52; Hans-Jürgen Becker, *Die grossen rabbinischen Sammelwerke Palästinas. Zur literarischen Genese von Talmud Yerushalmi und Midrash Bereshit Rabba* (Tübingen: Mohr Siebeck, 1999). How could such large bodies of material, even if in written form, be transmitted from one generation to the next, over hundreds of years? In addition, the logical and formal structure of the *sugyot* and tractates suggests a more conscious editorial intervention than this model assumes.

¹⁰ As David Kraemer has already stressed in connection with the Babylonian Talmud, rabbinic literature is school literature, created for study by future generations of rabbinic scholars; see his 'The Intended Reader as a Key to Interpreting the Bavli', *Prooftexts* 13 (1993): 125–40.

¹¹ Not only the Torah but also other books of the Hebrew Bible such as prophetic texts existed in written form by then. On the move from orality to writing in the transmission of prophesy in Second Temple times see the contributions in Michael Floyd and Robert D. Haak, eds., *Prophets, Prophecy, and Prophetic Texts in Second Temple Judaism* (New York and London: T&T Clark, 2006); Brian B. Schmidt, ed., *Contextualizing Israel's Sacred Writings: Ancient Literacy, Orality, and Literary Production* (Atlanta: SBL, 2015); Susan Nidich, *Oral World and Written Word: Ancient Israelite Literature* (Louisville: Westminster John Knox, 1996). Furthermore, works created in pre-rabbinic times such as the Qumran literature and Philo's and Josephus's writings were available as manuscripts.

to philosophical schools with their emphasis on the 'living voice' of the wise teacher.[12] Memorizing the words and practices of a chosen teacher was very different from reading Talmudic *sugyot* that present disputes between masters with whom the reader would not have been familiar through first-hand knowledge. The opinions and stories that appear in the written Talmud lack their original contexts. They are reformulated and adapted to serve as parts of *sugyot* that the editors constructed. In the original oral context students had to live with and accompany their masters to listen, observe, and memorize their wisdom. Rabbinic halakhic rules were case-specific, they were geared at the specific circumstances encountered in real life situations and flexible with regard to variations of details. By contrast, the written Talmud, once it existed, allowed everyone to access a vast range of variant and partly contradictory rabbinic teachings. Whereas the student would be devoted to his master and value his views over those of other rabbis, on the page of the Talmud all rabbinic opinions are presented side by side as equally true and relevant. The written format fixed these views in time. Altogether, then, memorizing and transmitting an individual master's views and practices was very different from studying rabbinic disputes by reading written Talmud pages.

The third possible reason for the insistence on oral transmission in late antiquity may have been Palestinian rabbis' desire to present themselves as intellectuals similar to Graeco-Roman philosophers, who were held in high esteem. As Stowers has emphasized, 'what was important was not abstract information but living models of character who embodied philosophical doctrines'.[13] Despite the fact that Seneca also wrote letters, he stated: 'Of course, the living voice and the intimacy of a common life will help you more than the written word. You must go to the scene of action, first, because men put more faith in their eyes than in their ears, and second, because the way is long if one follows precepts, but short and helpful, if one follows examples' (*Ep.* 6.3-5). Like philosophers, rabbis provided specific examples of what the life of a (Torah) sage would entail. Their students were like apprentices who learned this lifestyle through serving their masters (*shimush hakhamim*). This learning-by-listening-and-observing-model was also adopted by the early church. As Papias (first to second century CE) has stated: 'For I did not suppose that information from books would help me so much as the word of a living and surviving voice' (Eusebius, *Hist. eccl.* 3.39.4). These statements stress the preference for having direct access to a wise man rather than consulting less trusted written material.[14]

This reliance on the living voice seems to have changed in rabbinic circles of the early Byzantine period. According to a statement attributed to R. Abin, who belonged to one of the last two generations of Palestinian amoraim, one of the major differences between Jews and non-Jews was the phenomenon of the Oral Torah: 'If I [God]

---

[12] See Loveday Alexander, 'The Living Voice: Scepticism Towards the Written Word in Early Christian and Graeco-Roman Texts', *Journal for the Study of the Old Testament* 87 (1990) 221-47.

[13] Stanley K. Stowers, *Letter Writing in Graeco-Roman Antiquity* (Philadelphia: Westminster, 1986), 38.

[14] On the ancient distrust in written texts, see also Yoon-Man Park, *Mark's Memory Resources and the Controversy Stories (Mark 2:1–3:6): An Application of the Frame Theory of Cognitive Science to the Markan Oral-Aural Narrative* (Leiden: Brill, 2010), 67.

had written down for you the larger part of my Torah, you would not be considered a stranger anymore [cf. Hos. 8:12]'. Jews differed from Greeks and Romans because they owned a large body of Oral Torah, whereas others produced books (the term *sefer* is used here) and other pieces of writing (*diphthera*) (*y. Pe'ah* 2:6, 17a, par. *y. Hag.* 1:8, 76d).[15] It seems that the later amoraim were quite aware of the production and circulation of books in Roman and Byzantine Christian society. The reliance on orality, which had seemed an advantage in the first centuries CE, became a liability in later times. Rabbinic scholars of early Byzantine times probably realized that the continued oral transmission of rabbinic traditions put them in danger of being forgotten and eventually disappearing over time. Therefore, the reliance on oral transmission could put rabbis at a disadvantage in comparison to non-Jews, whether Christian, Greek, or Roman, whose knowledge was safely stored in books.

The experience of Roman and Byzantine Christian imperialism might also have played a role in the rabbinic move toward written compilations. König and Woolf have suggested that Roman imperialism may have been one of the reasons for Roman encyclopedism to develop in imperial times. There may have been a 'connection between acquisition of territory and acquisition of knowledge'.[16] Especially when the empire had become Christian and Christians circulated books that provided alternatives to the rabbinic interpretation of the Torah, some rabbinic scholars may have decided to divert from their traditional oral ideal and to create 'real' material evidence of rabbinic wisdom of the past.

Early Christians derived power from literacy: 'they met to read, hear and discuss their holy texts', which, from the second century onwards circulated in the much more practical and portable codex form.[17] Christians who stemmed from pagan backgrounds would have been familiar not only with written records in pagan cults but also with the vast Greek and Latin literary tradition that ranged from tragedy to philosophical treatise and historiography. Although Greeks and Romans considered themselves superior to other cultures on the basis of their rhetorical excellence, this oral discourse was based on the reading, study, and interpretation of written texts of the past.[18] By the fourth century CE rabbis would look back at the Written Torah as their main cultural heritage but lacked a comparable 'library' of their own more recent intellectual activity except, perhaps, for the Mishnah. The early Byzantine proliferation of patristic literature and legal codices may have made them aware of the power that lies in writing and its dissemination. Through writing and its oral

---

[15] Marcus Jastrow, *A Dictionary of the Targumim, the Talmud Babli and Yerushalmi, and the Midrashic Literature* (Jerusalem: Horev, 1985), 304, derives *diphthera* from the Greek διφθέρα, 'hide prepared for writing' with 'salt and flour'. Since the material was precious and costly, one may assume that only the most important documents and records were written on this material (rather than on papyrus or ostraca). Therefore, Jastrow suggests to translate *diphthera* with '(national) records' here.

[16] Jason König and Gregg Woolf, 'Encyclopedism in the Roman Empire', in *Encyclopedism from Antiquity to the Renaissance*, ed. J. König and G. Woolf (Cambridge: Cambridge University Press, 2013), 29.

[17] Robin Lane Fox, 'Literacy and Power in Early Christianity', in *Literacy and Power in the Ancient World*, ed. Alan K. Bowman and Greg Woolf (Cambridge: Cambridge University Press, 1994), 126.

[18] For the emphasis on speech, see Greg Woolf, 'Power and the Spread of Writing in the West', in Bowman and Woolf, eds., *Literacy and Power in the Ancient World*, 84.

distribution – whether in the form of letters, written sermons and commentaries, or legal edicts – Christian clergy and Byzantine rulers established and expanded their power throughout the Mediterranean world.

We do not know what proportion of the material collected by the editors of the Talmud and Midrashim came down to them in written form. A mixture of both written and oral transmission is most likely, especially if one reckons with several stages of editing. For example, the editors of the Yerushalmi may have used lists of case stories arranged thematically or under the names of individual rabbis.[19] Shared formal features and parallel formulation could have served memorization. These stylistic features seem to indicate that an editor, either the one who integrated traditions into *sugya*-format or the editor of a story collection, homogenized the texts to some extent. More common than biographical collections are thematic collections of halakhically relevant stories and statements that seem like variants on the same theme. If they fit smoothly into the context of a particular *sugya*, it is more likely that the editors of the *sugya* (identical with the editors of tractates or the Yerushalmi as a whole?) were responsible for formulating the sequences. As far as the Babylonian Talmud is concerned, one must reckon with the possibility that the editors composed larger narrative story cycles, as Rubenstein has pointed out.[20]

Whether and to what extent the editors of the Talmud had written tractates of the Mishnah and Tosefta available and whether they quoted on the basis of (memorized) written texts or oral traditions remains uncertain. Again, combinations of these modes of transmission are possible. Whereas Lieberman has supported the theory that the only authoritative version of the Mishnah was the one that was composed orally and circulated orally,[21] in the context of ancient book composition and publication this theory seems rather unlikely.[22] There is no analogy in Graeco-Roman society for the centuries-long oral transmission of a textual corpus as large as the Mishnah. More likely is the circulation of written versions of the Mishnah, probably in the form of individual tractates in scroll-format that were sometimes stored or bound together. Whether and to what extent individual amoraim had access to copies of the written Mishnah or at least to individual written tractates remains uncertain. Occasional access to individual written tractates seems likely. According to a tradition in *y. Ket.* 2:4, 26c, something was taught 'in [the tractate of] Ketuvot of the house of the teacher', probably referring to a scroll of Mishnah Ketuvot that was stored in the (study) house of a particular rabbi who could afford to own such a scroll. The rabbi would have borrowed the tractate from a colleague-friend, paid for parchment and ink, and employed a scribe to copy the text for him. Some written aggadic collections

---

[19] On pre-redactional story collections in the Neziqin tractates of the Yerushalmi see Catherine Hezser, *Form, Function, and Historical Significance of the Rabbinic Story in Yerushalmi Neziqin* (Tübingen: Mohr Siebeck, 1993), 269–82.

[20] Jeffrey L. Rubenstein, *The Culture of the Babylonian Talmud* (London: The Johns Hopkins University Press, 2003), 118.

[21] Saul Lieberman, *Hellenism in Jewish Palestine*, 2nd ed. (New York: The Jewish Theological Seminary of America, 1962), 83–99.

[22] See Catherine Hezser, 'The Mishnah and Ancient Book Production', in *The Mishnah in Contemporary Perspective, Part One*, ed. A. J. Avery-Peck and J. Neusner (Leiden: Brill, 2002), 167–92, especially 183.

(with stories or biblical commentaries?) also seem to have existed in amoraic times. R. Yehoshua b. Levi and R. Hiyya b. Ba allegedly 'saw a book of aggadah' (*y. Shab.* 16:1, 15c). What it contained is not specified.

References to written rabbinic texts are very sparse and do not suggest that amoraic rabbis and their students used them in their oral discussions.[23] Even if written student notes, collections of particular rabbis' teachings, story collections, commentaries on particular biblical passages, and even copies of specific Mishnah and Tosefta tractates existed, the written versions were not considered superior to orally transmitted traditions. On the contrary, as Martin Jaffee has already pointed out, 'both the Mishnah and Tosefta depend for their intelligibility as written texts on an oral-performative tradition that supplied, through repeated performative versions, the interpretive context needed for the proper reception of the written version's meaning'.[24] A similar need for a performative context applies to the Talmud Yerushalmi and amoraic Midrashim. Even when these compendia existed in book form, the emphasis continued to be on the oral discussion of the texts.

One of the main differences between the situation then and nowadays is that in late Roman and early Byzantine times the number of written texts a rabbi could gain access to would have been very low. Individual tractates of the Mishnah may have been stored in the houses of some wealthy urban rabbis.[25] Whether the owners were willing to let others peruse their texts depended on their relationship to them. They would probably have allowed only the small circles of their colleague-friends and advanced students to look at the texts. If one lacked a friend or master who owned a tractate or needed a tractate that was unavailable locally, one would have to locate the desired scroll and travel there oneself to consult it. To check a certain passage in the written version of the Mishnah would therefore require a lot of effort, especially if one lived in a village rather than a city where more people were wealthy enough to possess written texts. Whether local study houses (*batei midrash*), of which we know so little, had Mishnah scrolls and made them available to attendees remains uncertain and is rather unlikely. One or the other study house may have been frequented by a wealthy rabbi who owned scrolls of one or more tractates and brought them with him to study sessions. Yet there is no evidence that such a situation was customary and that study houses were book repositories.

It seems, then, that in general in amoraic times rabbinic discussions were conducted orally, without access to written tannaitic traditions or lists of halakhot of rabbis who were not present.[26] We must assume that rabbis only rarely checked written versions of the Mishnah, if at all. Mostly, they quoted from memory. Since an individual's memory is limited – even if ancient scholars were trained more in memorizing than we are nowadays – the knowledge an individual rabbi incorporated would have been

---

[23] For a discussion of the references, see Hezser, *Jewish Literacy*, 142–3.
[24] Jaffee, *Torah in the Mouth*, 112.
[25] See especially George W. Houston, *Inside Roman Libraries: Book Collections and Their Management in Antiquity* (Chapel Hill: The University of North Carolina Press, 2014), 12–38, on individual copying of books, assembling of private libraries, and lending of books to friends.
[26] See also Elizabeth Shanks Alexander, 'The Orality of Rabbinic Writing', in *The Cambridge Companion to the Talmud and Rabbinic Literature*, ed. C. E. Fonrobert and M. S. Jaffee (Cambridge: Cambridge University Press, 2007), 49.

circumscribed, probably leading to specializations. These areas of specialization were, perhaps, sometimes related to these rabbis' worldly professions.[27] The advantage of study sessions, whether among rabbinic colleague-friends or teachers and their students, was that each person contributed to and supplemented the other attendees' knowledge. Yet we must assume that only once the larger documents existed and were studied in written form did scholars become aware of the sheer mass of rabbinic knowledge that had accumulated over centuries and of the diversity of opinions their predecessors – and contemporaries – held on any given topic. Only the use of a written Talmud allowed a rabbinic disciple to look beyond the boundaries of his own master's teaching and to gain access to the halakhic views and practices of the Palestinian (and later also the Babylonian) rabbinic movement as a whole.

Yet even in the high Middle Ages, the Babylonian Talmud continued to be studied orally in some communities, as Talya Fishman has emphasized: 'Over the course of the Middle Ages, some Jews read the text of Talmud, but others truly encountered it as Oral Torah, mediated by living masters through face-to-face instruction.'[28] The continued focus on orality would have been linked to the Talmud's purpose: to enable later generations of scholars to embody halakhah and to apply halakhah for new situations. 'The oral transmission of Talmud was not geared simply to memorization of the corpus; students hoped to so thoroughly internalize its content that they would be able to summon the apt Talmudic tradition for application in any life situation.'[29]

4. The Rabbinic Use of the Biblical Tradition: From Memorized Prooftexts to Written Commentaries

Amoraic Midrashim are composed as commentaries on specific books of the Torah. They quote, paraphrase, cross-reference, and use keywords from the Torah and other books of the Hebrew Bible.[30] In the Talmud biblical prooftexts feature in disputes and are used to support or question particular rabbis' views. Especially in the Babylonian Talmud, biblical stories appear as the basis of theological and ethical commentaries.[31] In rabbinic Midrash, the literary form of the parable or *mashal* often has a biblical prooftext secondarily attached to make the parable fit its literary, exegetical context.[32]

---

[27] For example, rabbis who worked as physicians would have been especially knowledgeable of halakhic issues concerning the human and animal body; rabbinic scribes knew halakhot concerning the material aspects of writing documents and/or Torah scrolls; farmers were experts in halakhot concerning crops and farm animals; priestly rabbis specialized in Temple-related matters and holy things.

[28] Talya Fishman, *Becoming the People of the Talmud: Oral Torah as Written Tradition in Medieval Jewish Cultures* (Philadelphia: University of Pennsylvania Press, 2011), viii.

[29] Ibid.

[30] For a specific example of how a biblical story is used in Midrash, see Lieve M. Teugels, *Bible and Midrash: The Story of 'The Wooing of Rebeccah' (Gen. 24)* (Leuven: Peeters, 2004).

[31] Eliezer Segal, *From Sermon to Commentary: Expounding the Bible in Talmudic Babylonia* (Waterloo: Wilfrid Laurier University Press, 2005), examines the use of biblical traditions in selected aggadic texts of the Bavli.

[32] On the use of biblical verses in connection with parables, see especially David Stern, *Parables in Midrash: Narrative and Exegesis in Rabbinic Literature*, 2nd ed. (London: Harvard University Press, 1994), with many examples. Discrepancies in meaning between the parable and the verse may

It is immediately obvious that the Hebrew Bible, and the Torah in particular, constituted the major base text used by the editors of late antique Midrashim. For the editors of the Talmud, on the other hand, the Torah had an important albeit secondary role, for the focus is on the Mishnah and rabbinic traditions.[33] Studies of the use of the Bible in amoraic texts can tell us a lot about the role of the Bible at the later stages of literary composition and editing of these documents in the fifth and following centuries CE. It is methodologically impossible, however, to draw direct conclusions from this later literary stage to the preceding oral cultural environment of amoraic times.

Although Torah study constituted the focus of rabbinic scholarship, we know little about rabbis' actual access to the Hebrew Bible in the first five centuries CE. Those who decided to become disciples of rabbis would have been expected to be able to read Torah scrolls and to have memorized large portions of the legal rules of the Pentateuch. This Jewish primary education, which was also provided by scribes from the third century CE onwards, was primarily seen as a duty of (learned) fathers toward their sons. It was a prerequisite for rabbinic Torah study that constituted a higher – or secondary – form of learning.[34] Accordingly, when a disciple approached a rabbi and asked him to study with him, he would already possess a certain amount of memorized Torah knowledge that would enable him to understand his master's allusions, interpretations, and applications to new circumstances. On this basis, he could ask learned questions and supply prooftexts from memory.

While one or the other wealthy rabbi may have owned a Torah scroll, most rabbis probably did not. Due to the material used and the time-consuming production process, Torah scrolls were very expensive objects that could be owned by wealthy individuals or communities only. The requirement that the Torah be handwritten with ink on parchment, special precautions to avoid errors, and the limited availability of Torah scribes would have determined the scrolls' price. In Hellenistic and Roman times, at least until the fourth century CE, Egyptians, Greeks, and Romans generally used papyrus for writing literary works.[35] Initially, these works were produced on papyrus rolls. In the second century CE, however, the codex came to replace the roll and was early adopted by Christians.[36] Initially, codices were produced from papyrus, but from the fourth century onwards, parchment was used for codices, probably because papyrus could not be folded and stitched together easily.[37]

---

indicate a secondary combination of the two. In the context of the literary genre Midrash parables often have an exegetical function that may have been different from the rhetorical function they had in an oral context.

[33] On the role of the Mishnah, which rarely uses prooftexts, in the Talmuds, see Karin Hadner Zetterholm, *Jewish Interpretation of the Bible: Ancient and Contemporary* (Minneapolis: Fortress, 2012), esp. chapter 2.

[34] On primary education, see Hezser, *Jewish Literacy*, 40–89.

[35] Cornelia Roemer, 'The Papyrus Role in Egypt, Greece, and Rome', in *A Companion to the History of the Book*, ed. S. Eliot and J. Rose (Oxford: Wiley Blackwell, 2009), 84.

[36] On the Christian adoption of the codex format, see Larry W. Hurtado, *The Earliest Christian Artifacts: Manuscripts and Christian Origins* (Grand Rapids: Eerdmans, 2006), 53–82, where he discusses the various possible reasons why Christians might have preferred the codex. While the answer to the 'why' question remains difficult, Hurtado stresses the great significance of the Christian adoption of this format in the second century already.

[37] Parchment codices were produced from the second century CE onwards, but only a few examples from before the fourth century CE are known. See Eric G. Turner, *The Typology of the Early Codex*

On this background, the Jewish production of parchment Torah scrolls would have been an anomaly in late Hellenistic and Roman-Byzantine times. Haran has suggested that the use of skins (of kosher animals) 'was the outcome of particular circumstances which gained in force in the Second Temple period and were connected with the canonization of biblical literature'.[38] Different types of parchment were used for the text fragments that were found at Qumran.[39] According to Jodi Magness, 87 percent of the Dead Sea Scrolls are made of parchment, only 13 percent of papyrus, with no codices found.[40] This 'intentional collection of selected works' may represent a 'religious library' kept by the sectarians.[41] Steven Fraade's description of the Essenes as a 'studying community' seems to fit this evidence well.[42] No other Jewish libraries of this kind are known to us from antiquity, except for the Jerusalem Temple perhaps.[43]

Why did rabbis not keep similar libraries? How did they gain access to and use Torah texts without such libraries? In answer to the first question, it is necessary to point out that the social structure of the rabbinic network was much looser and more widespread geographically than the community of the Qumran Essenes. It seems that there were only a few rabbis at any one location at a given period of time.[44] Even in cities such as Caesarea in the late third and fourth centuries rabbis seem to have been unable – and perhaps unwilling – to pool resources toward the creation of a Torah library that could be accessed by any scholar or any local able to read the texts.

One could argue that in late antiquity local study houses and/or synagogues would house Torah scrolls and remove the necessity of individual ownership. Yet these institutions seem to have mostly or even exclusively existed in larger towns and cities, leaving small towns and villages without access to scrolls. Very little is known about local study houses. No archaeological evidence of buildings that could be identified as study houses exists.[45] Sometimes they may have been connected to synagogues, with separate entrances.[46] That study houses served Torah study does not necessarily

---

(Eugene: Wipf & Stock, 1977), 37: 'It is not till the fourth century that the parchment codex begins to be at all common in Egypt'. Even after the fourth century, papyrus codices continued to be produced, however, alongside parchment codices. See T. C. Skeat, 'Early Christian Book Production: Papyri and Manuscripts', in *The Cambridge History of the Bible*, vol. 2, ed. G. W. H. Lampe (Cambridge: Cambridge University Press, 1969), 76.

[38] Menahem Haran, 'Book-Scrolls in Israel in Pre-Exilic Times', *JJS* (1982): 162; see also idem, 'Bible Scrolls in the Early Second Temple Period – The Transition from Papyrus to Skins', *Eretz Israel* 16 (1982): 86–92 (Hebrew).

[39] Ira Rabin, 'Material Analysis of the Fragments', in *Gleanings from the Caves: Dead Sea Scrolls and Artefacts from the Schøyen Collection*, ed. T. Elgvin et al. (London: T&T Clark, 2016), 63.

[40] Jodi Magness, *The Archaeology of Qumran and the Dead Sea Scrolls* (Grand Rapids: Eerdmans, 2003), 33.

[41] Ibid., 34.

[42] Steven D. Fraade, 'Interpretive Authority in the Studying Community at Qumran', *JJS* 44 (1993): 46–69.

[43] There may have been some archive – or a biblical scroll library? – in the Temple in Jerusalem. See the discussion in Sidnie White Crawford, 'The Qumran Collection as a Scribal Library', in *The Dead Sea Scrolls at Qumran and the Concept of a Library*, ed. S. W. Crawford and C. Wassen (Leiden: Brill, 2016), 116–17.

[44] Hezser, *Social Structure*, 180–4.

[45] See the discussion in ibid., 202–5.

[46] Zvi Ilan, 'The Synagogue and Study House at Meroth', in *Ancient Synagogues: Historical Analysis and Archaeological Discovery*, ed. D. Urman and P. V. M. Flesher, 2nd ed. (Leiden: Brill, 1998), 256–88, shows that there were separate entrances and argues that the two institutions were separate.

imply that they housed Torah scrolls. As in the case of synagogues, which seem to have had permanent Torah shrines from the fifth century CE onwards only,[47] Torah scrolls may have been brought in from outside when needed. The Talmud Yerushalmi distinguishes between Torah scrolls that belonged to individuals and were privately owned and those that were owned by 'the many' (*y. Ned.* 5:5, 39b), that is, the local community. According to *m. Ned.* 5:5, Torah scrolls usually belonged to 'the town' (*ha-ir*) and were publicly owned. Where such publicly owned Torah scrolls were kept when they were not in use remains unclear. We may assume that the one or other wealthy representative of a local community owned a scroll and granted access to it on particular occasions.

The main – and perhaps only – occasion when the presence of Torah scrolls would have been required was the Torah-reading ceremony in synagogues on the Sabbath. The rabbinic expounding of Scripture (*derash*) in public, which is associated with some amoraim,[48] seems to have happened outside of the synagogue service proper, on Sabbath evenings. It was probably related to the scriptural portions that were read out in synagogues in the mornings.[49] Since the sermons happened on the same day as the readings, rabbis and their audiences would have been familiar with the portions. The presence of a Torah scroll was unnecessary for the delivery of a sermon. On the contrary, we must assume that people gathered around rabbis because they considered them to be thoroughly familiar with the text and able to go beyond its literal meaning.

In the literary genre of rabbinic Midrash, the biblical texts that are commented upon are divided into numerous small parts, often consisting of parts of single verses only. For example, at the very beginning of Genesis Rabbah, 'At the beginning God created…' (Gen. 1:1) is quoted (*Gen. Rab.* 1:1). The readers would have known the continuation of the verse. The Torah quote is followed by the quotation of a verse from Proverbs (Prov. 8:30), attributed to R. Oshaiah, and its relation to Gen. 1:1 remains unclear. What follows are various explanations of the Hebrew consonants that appear in *amon* (which means 'infant', 'nursling') in Prov. 8:30, with further biblical prooftexts to support the suggested meanings. Eventually, the meaning of *uman*, 'craftsman' is suggested, and this interpretation connects the *petichtah* (lit. 'opening') verse to the *seder* ('order' of Torah reading) verse (Gen. 1:1), where God is presented as a craftsman who created the world. Another suggested connection is the Torah, which rabbis assumed to be personified as a child, speaking in the first person in Prov.

---

[47] Rachel Hachlili, 'The State of Ancient Synagogue Studies', in *Ancient Synagogues in Israel: Third-Seventh Century C.E.*, ed. R. Hachlili et al. (Oxford: British Archaeological Review, 1989), 3.

[48] See Hezser, *Social Structure*, 371–2, for references.

[49] See also Gary Porton, 'Midrash and the Rabbinic Sermon', in *When Judaism and Christianity Began: Essays in Memory of Anthony B. Saldarini*, ed. A. J. Avery-Peck et al. (Leiden: Brill, 2004), 461–482, who also argues that rabbinic sermons were not common parts of synagogue services in antiquity; Günter Stemberger, 'The Derashah in Rabbinic Times', in *Preaching in Judaism and Christianity: Encounters and Developments from Biblical Times to Modernity*, ed. A. Deeg et al. (Berlin: de Gruyter, 2008), 7–21. On p. 13 he writes: 'I fully agree with Porton that Rabbinic literature offers much less evidence for rabbis preaching in the synagogue to a general public than is usually thought. Most frequently they are presented in an inner-rabbinic setting, even if it is in a synagogue'. But see Richard Hidary, *Rabbis and Classical Rhetoric: Sophistic Education and Oratory in the Talmud and Midrash* (Cambridge and New York: Cambridge University Press, 2018), 43–6, who reckons with widespread rabbinic public preaching.

8:30 ('Then I was beside him like a little child [*amon*], and I was daily his delight...'). Linking Prov. 8:30 to Gen. 1:1, the midrashic editor suggests that God used the Torah as his work plan in his creation. 'At the Beginning' (*bereshit*) is related to the Torah that was allegedly present at the time of creation already.

Obviously, the beginning of Midrash *Genesis Rabbah* is a careful literary construction that artistically connects verses from the Torah and other parts of the Hebrew Bible and plays with the meanings of Hebrew roots, to arrive at theological ideas important to rabbis. We cannot draw a direct connection between this literary form and amoraic rabbis' actual activity of expounding Scripture in various settings in Roman Palestine.[50] Nevertheless, the following characteristic is crucial: Scripture is segmented into numerous small parts. This also applies to the base text (Genesis) that is commented upon. The traditional material used by the editors consists of individual comments on specific verses or parts of verses as well as connections that are made between verses of the Torah and other parts of Scripture on the basis of word play, Hebrew roots, and other, sometimes elusive, reasons. The editors combined this received material and constructed midrashic proems out of them.

Comments on particular scriptural verses and the suggestion of connections between verses from different parts of the Bible constitute the basis of rabbinic scriptural exposition.[51] Such comments can be of variable length and have various literary forms such as parables, as in *Gen. Rab.* 1:1, where a short king parable is quoted. These component parts of the literary Midrashim were probably part of oral transmission in amoraic times.[52] What is striking is that we do not find more detailed comments or sermons on extended biblical passages. A rabbi who commented on a particular verse or came up with another verse to highlight some aspect of the first one did not need written Torah scrolls in front of him. On the contrary, the elusive connections that are drawn between verses suggest that verses were quoted from memory. Connections based on the roots of Hebrew words also suggest oral associations: it is not the literary context that matters or the specific pronunciation or meaning of a word but the very phenomenon of the multivalence of the roots that mattered most.

Even if Torah scrolls were present at the places where rabbis expounded Scripture, it is unlikely that they would have unrolled them to find the verses they wanted to comment upon. The scrolls consisted of many pieces of parchment that were sewn together and rolled up into one large scroll.[53] This scroll would have been heavy to lift and difficult to unroll to find a particular verse. The fact that there was no punctuation and readers were confronted by a consecutive text would have increased the difficulty

---

[50] See also Stemberger, 'The Derashah in Rabbinic Times', 20.

[51] A discussion of various definitions of Midrash as a literary genre and midrash as an exegetical approach can be found in Carol Bakhos, 'Method(ological) Matters in the Study of Midrash', in *Current Trends in the Study of Midrash*, ed. C. Bakhos (Leiden: Brill, 2006), 161–87, esp. 162–7.

[52] See also Reuven Hammer, *The Classic Midrash: Tannaitic Commentaries on the Bible* (Mahwah: Paulist, 1995), 22: 'Thus midrash is an oral form that found its way into writing when it was no longer practical to keep it oral'.

[53] On this process see Michael Avi-Yonah, *Ancient Scrolls: Introduction to Archaeology* (Jerusalem: Jerusalem Publishing, 1994), 21. On the making of a Torah scroll, see also Leila Avrin, *Scribes, Script and Books: The Book Arts from Antiquity to the Renaissance* (London: The British Library, 1991), 115–16.

of finding the verse or passage one was looking for. Reading was usually loud reading in antiquity rather than the silent visual identification of words and phrases we are used to nowadays.[54] Therefore finding a verse would have involved pronouncing – or murmuring – portions of the preceding text. Another important issue to take into consideration is the fact that Torah scrolls were deemed holy objects to which specific rules for handling them applied.[55] They could not be touched and checked like any other books but required adherence to specific purity rituals.[56] Damaging them would have constituted a serious religious offence. Therefore, rabbis and synagogue functionaries would have hesitated handling them in the public sphere for any other then the most necessary purposes.[57]

While rabbis' exegetical discourse did not require direct access to Torah scrolls but seems to have mostly relied on memorized scriptural knowledge, legal disputes were even less dependent on access to the Torah, since the specific issue and logic of rabbinic argumentation mattered most. In halakhic argumentation biblical verses are sometimes employed as prooftexts but, in general, had secondary significance only. In the Bavot tractates of the Talmud Yerushalmi, which are sometimes considered to represent an earlier stratum of Talmud,[58] entire *sugyot* often lack biblical quotations or references, consisting of sequences constructed of tannaitic and amoraic material with anonymous framing statements only. This is, for example, the case in the *sugya* that discusses who one's main teacher is, for whom one should tear one's garment upon hearing of his death (*y. B. Mes.* 2:11, 8d).[59]

The phenomenon is not limited to the Bavot tractates. The shortage of biblical quotations is also characteristic of other tractates and parts of the Talmud. For example, at the very beginning of Yerushalmi Berakhot, where the recitation of the evening *Shema* is discussed (*y. Ber.* 1:1, 2a), there is an allusion to Temple priests eating the heave offering (*terumah*) at a particular time of the day. This analogy between reciting the evening *Shema* and Temple priests' eating of the heave offering is already part of the Mishnah (*m. Ber.* 1:1) and alludes to Lev. 22:6-7. Leviticus 22 deals with the case of the 'sons of Aaron', who had contracted uncleanness. They remain unclean

---

[54] On loud reading, see Jocelyn Penny Small, *Wax Tablets of the Mind: Cognitive Studies of Memory and Literacy in Classical Antiquity* (London: Routledge, 1997), who argues that silent reading became customary in the Middle Ages only. 'Scholars now agree that reading silently to oneself did not occur in antiquity' (p. 22). If books were generally read aloud, they may have been read "*sotto voce*" to find the passage one was looking for.

[55] See *m. Yad.* 4:6 and Martin Goodman, 'Sacred Scripture and "Defiling the Hands"', *JTS* 41 (1990): 99–107.

[56] Jodi Magness, *Stone and Dung, Oil and Spit: Jewish Daily Life in the Time of Jesus* (Grand Rapids: Eerdmans, 2011), 27, assumes that Qumran sectarians would not have shared rabbinic concerns 'that touching Torah scrolls conveys impurity'.

[57] On Torah scrolls in synagogues, see Steven Fine, *Art, History and Historiography of Judaism in Roman Antiquity* (Leiden: Brill, 2014), 153: 'Objects that are closer to the scroll are considered more holy. Thus, the cloth wrappers in which a Torah scroll is wrapped are holier than the chest (*teva*) in which the scrolls are stored, and the scrolls cabinet is more holy than the synagogue building'.

[58] See Hezser, *Form, Function*, 360, confirming Saul Lieberman's thesis that Yerushalmi Neziqin was edited earlier than the rest of the Yerushalmi in *The Talmud of Caesarea* (Jerusalem: Supplement to *Tarbiz*, 1931 [Hebrew]). The main part of Lieberman's study consists of a synopsis of parallel *sugyot* with brief comments.

[59] The text is discussed in Hezser, *Form, Function*, 83–94.

until the evening, when they are supposed to take a bath and purify themselves before eating from the heave offering in their homes. When the sun has gone down, they are considered pure again (Lev. 22:7). In the context of the Yerushalmi (and the Tosefta, cf. *t. Ber.* 1:1), the allusion to the time of the priests' eating of heave offering is only one aspect of the argumentation, an aspect that has been taken over from the Mishnah and is immediately replaced by a more contemporary alternative example. A tannaitic statement attributed to R. Hiyya (probably the fifth-generation tanna by that name) refers to the time when people customarily return home on Sabbath eves to eat dinner (cf. *t. Ber.* 1:1, where this example is attributed to R. Meir). In the following anonymous (and probably editorial) part of the *sugya*, the two examples (priests and common people) are contrasted with each other: they allegedly refer to different time periods, the priests entering their houses to eat from the heave offering while it is still day, whereas ordinary people eat the Sabbath evening meal one or two hours after night break only. A statement attributed to R. Yose subsequently harmonizes between the two views: R. Hiyya allegedly referred to the specific case of the villagers who returned to their houses early in the evening because of their fear of wild animals. The discussion whether the evening *Shema* may be recited before or only after the appearance of the first evening stars continues without further reference to biblical examples.

What is important here is that the biblical allusion does not seem to have more value than the rabbinic reference to ordinary people's practices. Leviticus 22:6-7 is not used as a prooftext to support a particular view. It is not quoted but merely alluded to in the Mishnah and associated with Temple times: different terminology is used ('priests' instead of 'sons of Aaron'; 'heave offering' [*terumah*, cf. Num. 18:28] instead of 'holy things' [*qedushim*]); all of the details of the biblical text (references to the various impurities, the purification ritual) are left out; the eating of heave offering in the houses of Aaron is replaced by the institutional setting of the Temple court. The Mishnah's elliptic phrase, 'from the time when the priests enter [the Temple court] to eat heave offering', requires the audience and readership to be knowledgeable of the biblical rule but not the details of the biblical text. In the Yerushalmi's discussion, the *mishnah* (Temple priests) and *baraita* ('R. Hiyya taught': ordinary people) have equal value.[60] The inconsistency between them concerning the envisioned time of the evening requires an explanation, which is offered through R. Yose's limitation of R. Hiyya's statement (limiting it to villagers, not all people). The allusion to the eating of the heave offering is entirely subservient to the rabbinic discussion about the correct time for the recitation of the evening *Shema* here. The way in which the Yerushalmi uses the Mishnah's example also shows that linking prayer times to pre-70 Temple rituals was less important in late antiquity.

In the following *sugya*, a biblical verse is used as a prooftext. According to a statement attributed to R. Zeira in the name of R. Jeremiah, someone who is in doubt whether he has recited the Grace after Meals is required to recite it. This view is

---

[60] In the Tosefta (*t. Ber.* 1:1), where the two examples are juxtaposed as well, the order is reversed: R. Meir's statement referring to ordinary people precedes sages' allusion to the priests. Both the order of the statements and the fact that 'sages' may represent the majority of rabbis in the minds of the editors seem to give precedence to the biblical allusion here.

supported by the quotation of Deut. 8:10: 'for it is written: "And [when] you have eaten, and you are full, you shall bless [the Lord your God for the good land he has given you]"'. Since the recitation of the Grace after Meals is a biblical obligation, one needs to make sure that one has fulfilled this obligation, even if one might recite it a second time. The quotation of Deut. 8:10 serves to indicate the stringency of the obligation to recite the blessing. The necessity to make sure that one has recited the Grace after Meals is subsequently contrasted with the Prayer (*Tefillah*, *Amidah*). Since the recitation of this prayer is a rabbinic imposition, if one is in doubt whether one has recited it, one need not recite it (again).

These examples from the beginning of Yerushalmi Berakhot point to some of the uses of the Torah in the Talmud. They show that the Torah is always subordinated to the flow of rabbinic argumentation, even if used as a prooftext. Biblical rules can be merely alluded to or (parts of) verses literally quoted. Neither of these approaches suggests that written Torah scrolls were checked even by the editors of the written *sugyot*. As in the case of *midrash*, the Talmudic *sugyot* are literary constructs rather than transcripts of rabbinic oral discussions. The allusion to Leviticus was already part of the Mishnah that the editors probably knew in written form. Whether they received the prooftext from Deuteronomy as part of R. Zeira's statement or added it themselves to support the statement remains uncertain. Nevertheless, one may assume that in amoraic oral discussions biblical texts would have been used and alluded to in similar ways, to support, contradict, or problematize rabbinic views on topics that were relevant to rabbis in their own times and circumstances. The topics and arguments were not derived directly from biblical texts. In halakhic discussions the Torah was not primary, but it had an important supporting and correcting function in rabbinic disputes and arguments.

5. Conclusions

Whether and to what extent rabbis used written biblical or rabbinic texts depends on the time period we are talking about. We need to distinguish between three periods that constitute distinct stages in the use of written material: the amoraic period, the time when the Talmud and Midrash were edited, and the post-Talmudic stage that leads to the Middle Ages. Only at the time when the large written documents existed, and when rabbinic academies for the study of the Talmud emerged, did a culture of rabbinic study develop that focused on the reading and interpretation of the written text. As David Stern has pointed out correctly, the eventual Jewish adoption of the codex form facilitated this study of Jewish 'books'.[61] Only from the time of the wider use and distribution of the codex in Jewish scholarly culture, that is, from the tenth and eleventh centuries onwards, can one – still hesitatingly – talk about 'bookish' circles in Jewish culture. Yet even at this stage the focus would have been on oral discussion, a phenomenon that continues in traditional *yeshivot* until today.

---

[61] See Stern, 'The First Jewish Books', 163.

When moving backwards from this later stage to the time of the editing of rabbinic documents between the late fourth and early seventh centuries and continuing into early Gaonic times until the tenth/eleventh century CE, we have to reckon with a mixed use of oral and written sources, memorized written sources, and only occasional access to written Torah scrolls. It remains uncertain whether and to what extent the editors of the Talmud and Midrash had written rabbinic and biblical texts available and made use of them. They may have used written tractates of the Mishnah alongside orally transmitted *baraitot*, memorized amoraic traditions alongside occasional collections of stories. The editors of amoraic Midrashim are more likely to have used written Torah scrolls than the editors of Talmudic *sugyot*, but even midrashic proems seem to quote biblical verses by memory, based on keyword associations. There is still no evidence at this stage that written sources were valued higher than orally transmitted material. The reason why anonymous editors decided to create written compilations would have been the realization that oral transmission was risky and might lead to the eventual loss of rabbinic knowledge of previous generations. In a context in which Byzantine Christians were producing more and more books, rabbinic Jews probably realized that the written preservation of rabbinic knowledge was necessary for its survival and transmission to future generations.

In the few hundred years after the editing of the Talmud and Midrash, various manuscript versions circulated and few copies would have been available. Taking the huge volume of the Talmud, and especially the Babylonian Talmud, into account, very few full collections of its orders and tractates would have circulated. Eli Yassif has argued that at least until the tenth century the shortage of written Talmud corpora would have increased the authority of Babylonian Geonim: 'Anyone anywhere in the Jewish world who was in need of an accurate version of the Mishnah or Talmud…had no alternative but to turn to the Babylonian *yeshivot*'.[62] The earliest extant manuscripts of the Babylonian Talmud date to the twelfth century and the first printed edition (Daniel Bomberg in Venice) to the early sixteenth.[63] Only once printed editions circulated and the written Talmud became more widely available, the use of the term 'bookish' can be considered an appropriate denominator for Talmud scholarship.[64] The 'bookish' scholarship of the last five hundred years was based on a standardized text, fixed orders of reading, and easier access to written commentaries.[65]

In earlier amoraic times (third to fourth centuries CE), the situation would have been very different. There is scarce evidence of a rabbinic use of written texts, whether rabbinic or biblical. Individual wealthy rabbis might have owned a Mishnah tractate

---

[62] Eli Yassif, 'Oral Traditions in a Literate Society: The Hebrew Literature of the Middle Ages', in *Medieval Oral Literature*, ed. K. Reichl (Berlin: de Gruyter, 2012), 501.

[63] For a summary of the manuscripts and printed editions of the Bavli, see Richard Kalmin, *Migrating Tales: The Talmud's Narratives and Their Historical Contexts* (Berkeley: University of California Press, 2014), xv. On designing the printed Talmud, see also Marvin J. Heller, *Studies in the Making of the Early Hebrew Book* (Leiden: Brill, 2008), 92–105.

[64] On the ways in which printing the Talmud changed Jewish Talmud, study see Sharon Liberman Mintz et al., eds., *Printing the Talmud: From Bomberg to Schottenstein* (New York: Yeshiva University Museum, 2005).

[65] See Heller, *Studies in the Making*, 109.

and brought it to a study session. Some disciples may have taken notes of some rabbis' views or practices. A few written collections of rabbinic stories may have circulated. Some Jewish communities would have owned Torah scrolls. Yet there is no evidence that such written texts were used regularly in rabbinic study sessions or that they were considered more authoritative than orally transmitted traditions and memorized Torah verses. As embodied repositories of the Written and Oral Torah, rabbis would not have needed to consult written texts. On the contrary, they seem to have valued memory and oral transmission more. Amoraic rabbis and their students would have memorized vast portions of Torah during primary education. They would hear Torah read out in synagogues on the Sabbath and some of them offered public sermons. They were so much immersed in Torah that they did not need to check written texts. The very purpose of rabbinic study was to make Torah relevant in new, contemporary situations and circumstances. This endeavour was based on the Torah but went far beyond it, creating a new and continuing (Oral) Torah to which each generation of scholars contributed.

6

Sympotic Learning: Symposia Literature and Cultural Education

Sean A. Adams

For the ancients, the best pieces of literature were both entertaining and instructional.[1] In this investigation of ancient *symposia* we witness a similar pairing, although in these texts the theme of education and learning is much more prominent than in many other genres. This paper evaluates the narrative worlds constructed by the authors with a specific focus on the ways that learning is represented in ancient *symposia*. I explore the themes of who should learn, what they should learn, and when they should learn, highlighting common features and distinctive elements. In the last section, I evaluate the *symposia* genre to see how reading traditions influenced the ways that the literary form developed over time and how previous works were seen to instruct later authors in their writing or were intentionally inverted to make a point.

Symposia Texts

The first requirement of this study is to differentiate between symposia, as in drinking parties, and *symposia*, as in literary works.[2] The former were common events in antiquity in which a group of people, typically men, gathered together to eat and drink, but also, more importantly, form and reinforce bonds of friendship.[3] The latter are literary works that depict drinking parties, focusing on the debates and discussions

---

[1] Cf. Horace, *Ars* 333–346; Plutarch, *Mor.* 614b.
[2] For clarity, I use 'symposia' to refer to drinking parties and '*symposia*' to refer to sympotic works in general.
[3] Plutarch claims that the purpose of drinking parties was to develop friendships among the participants: 'The drinking party is the passing of time over wine which, guided by gracious behaviour, ends in friendship' (*Mor.* 621c; cf. *Mor.* 612d; 644a; 645b; 660a; *Cat. Maj.* 25.1-3). The foundational text for discussing friendship in antiquity is books 8 and 9 of Aristotle's *Nicomachean Ethics*. On

that occurred. Although in the narrative world the latter are said to be representative of the former, the ancient reality of these events was surely much less neatly ordered.[4] The works that have survived are intricate literary writings that amuse the reader whilst educating them. Indeed, in these works the blending of historicity and narrative, alongside autobiography and philosophy create complex works that beguile simplistic categorisations and readings.

Almost all of the texts we are investigating present the narrative as reported speech; someone hears from someone what happened at a particular dinner party. For Plutarch and Athenaeus these works are more autobiographical, although one must not be too quick to conflate reported action with historical reality.[5] No doubt elements of personal experience will be included within the text, but we must also be aware that the elements included are there because the author wished them to be; the text is the creative output of the author and therefore not necessarily autobiographical. In light of this reality, caution must be used when seeking to determine the historical nature of each work. Although determining historicity is not the focus of this investigation, elements and values found in the narrative world reflect views held by certain people within society.

The sympotic works provide a window into the world of elite, free men, not what we might consider a depiction of events by those in the rest of society. Athenaeus, in fact, highlights this difference in one of his comments (*Deipn.* 3.97a-b). Providing a near quotation of Plato's *Protagoras* 347c-d as a critique of the Cynics, the narrator claims that,

> Arguing about poetry is like the symposia of common, agora people (τοῖς συμποσίοις τοῖς τῶν φαύλων καὶ ἀγοραίων ἀνθρώπων). For their lack of education (ἀπαιδευσίας) makes them unable to enjoy one another's company over wine by relying on their own voices; they therefore put a premium on pipe-girls... But whenever educated men from good backgrounds drink together, pipe-girls, dancing-girls, and harp-girls are nowhere to be seen; they have sufficient resources of their own.

In this passage we have a negative depiction of symposia held by τῶν φαύλων καὶ ἀγοραίων ἀνθρώπων,[6] one that is contrasted with those depicted in Athenaeus' narrative.[7] Because the presentations of symposia that have survived are from a specific

---

the purpose of eating together in antiquity, see R. S. Ascough, 'Forms of Commensality in Greco-Roman Associations', *CW* 102 (2008): 33–45.

[4] C. B. R. Pelling, *Plutarch: Life of Antony* (Cambridge: Cambridge University Press, 1988), 36.

[5] Cf. F. E. Brenk, '"In learned conversation": Plutarch's Symposiac Literature and the Elusive Authorial Voice', in *Symposion and philanthropia in Plutarch*, ed. J. R. Ferreira (Coimbra: Classica Digitalia, 2009), 51–61.

[6] One way to render this phrase is 'low, working-class people' (so Olson, Loeb), but this creates a possible tension with the concept of them arguing about poetry. Although I would agree that Athenaeus is elevating his group over the former, it would be a mistake to view these individuals as being of low class, especially when the semantic range of ἀγοραῖος extends to include orators or advocates (e.g. Plutarch, *Per.* 11.1), both of which are associated with arguing.

[7] A. Lukinovich, 'The Play of Reflection between Literary Form and the Sympotic Theme in the *Deipnosophistae*', in *Sympotica: A Symposium on the Symposion*, ed. O. Murray (Oxford: Oxford University Press, 1990), 263–71.

social and literary stratum, they embody select ideas and do not represent the full range of such events in antiquity, nor the beliefs held by other classes, ethnicities, or even other members of elite society. Recognising this perspective is important because it shapes the way that learning is discussed within the texts, the expectations of what is valued by the characters, and the type of culture that is prioritised. Accordingly, what we see in Athenaeus, as well as in other *symposia*, is a depiction of an event that was widely practiced in antiquity but curated and presented in literary form to promote a specific worldview, one that prioritises education and literary culture.

According to Athenaeus (*Deipn.* 11.505b), who cites Nicias of Nicaea and Sotion, Alexamenus of Teos was the first to create a work of dialogue. Although Plato is credited with the prototypical *Symposium* work, some ancients claimed that Xenophon was the first to write the *Symposium* genre (e.g. Athenaeus, *Deipn.* 11.506c).[8] Others, such as Diogenes Laertius (3.34), claim that both Plato and Xenophon wrote similar narratives 'as if out of rivalry with each other'. In his work, Plato provides a report of a drinking party at the poet Agathon's house that is given fourth-hand by Apollodorus (173b). The primary topic of the event is Love ("Ερος) and six speeches are given by the participants on the topic (by Phaedrus, Pausanias, Eryximachus, Aristophanes, Agathon, Socrates), with a final speech by Alcibiades in praise of Socrates. Plato excels in his ability to write from the perspective of the different speakers (e.g. Eryximachus as a medical professional), an idea made explicit by Agathon (196d; 198a), who, in a desire to honour his craft (τέχνην), speaks in poetic verse (197c) in the style of Gorgias (198c).[9]

Like Plato, Xenophon recounts a drinking party at which Socrates and a number of other prominent, learned, and/or wealthy people attend (*Sym.* 1.2-3).[10] A majority of the text is dedicated to each person's declaration and explanation of what they are most proud of (3.1–4.64). All of these answers show a high degree of humour and learning as each speaker is able to turn what might at first appear to be a negative characteristic into something positive, or each might choose to poke fun at himself for something that might appear detrimental.[11] After a round of entertainment, Socrates proposes the topic of Love ("Ερος) for discussion (8.1-43), and, following this debate, the dinner party breaks up and the guests go home.

---

[8] This issue is still debated today. Cf. E. C. Marchant and O. J. Dodd, *Xenophon: Memorabilia, Oeconomicus, Symposium, Apology*, LCL, rev. J. Henderson (Cambridge, MA: Harvard University Press, 2013), 560.

[9] For an introduction to Plato's *Symposium*, see K. Corrigan and E. Glazov-Corrigan, *Plato's Dialectic at Play: Argument, Structure, and Myth in the Symposium* (University Park: Pennsylvania State University Press, 2004), 147–62.

[10] For the artistic structure of Xenophon's *Symposium*, see G. Danzig, 'Xenophon's *Symposium*', in *The Cambridge Companion to Xenophon*, ed. M. A. Flower (Cambridge: Cambridge University Press, 2017), 134–5. Both Plato's and Xenophon's *Symposia* are written at least a couple decades after the supposed event. This distance reinforces the view that the setting, characters, and contents of both works were intentionally selected, likely because of the aura and tradition surrounding them. For a discussion of dating and an argument for the priority of Xenophon's work, see H. Thesleff, 'The Interrelation and Date of the *Symposia* of Plato and Xenophon', *BICS* 25 (1978): 157–70; G. Danzig, 'Intra-Socratic Polemics: The *Symposia* of Plato and Xenophon', *GRBS* 43 (2005): 331–57.

[11] For example, Antisthenes' 'wealth' (*Sym.* 4.34-45) or Kritoboulos' beauty (4.10-17).

We know of a number of *symposia* composed in the Hellenistic era, especially from Peripatetic authors, but none of the extant works are sufficiently complete to provide a detailed discussion.[12] Two sympotic works survive from Plutarch: *The Dinner of the Seven Wise Men* and *Table Talk*.[13] The former is a short work similar to those of Plato and Xenophon in which the diners solve riddles and give advice to the envoy of the King of Egypt. The latter work consists of nine books, each with ten questions, of selected discussions that took place at dinner parties Plutarch had attended (*Mor.* 612e).[14] Unlike the works of Plato and Xenophon, Plutarch's text does not follow a larger narrative arc, nor are all of the questions taken from a single dinner party. Rather, *Table Talk* is a collection of questions, appearing often to lack thematic or temporal order, in which Plutarch provides a carefully shaped version of his life, embedding autobiographical statements within philosophical discussions.[15]

The final work evaluated in depth is Athenaeus' *Learned Banqueters*, a fifteen-volume treatise of an account given by an individual named Athenaeus to his friend Timocrates of a banquet held at Larensius' house.[16] Similar to Plato's work, *Learned Banqueters* is a dialogue within a dialogue, though it is substantially longer, is disproportionately focused on food, and has many citations from other authors.

Theme of Learning

Arguably the most common aspect of symposia is the regular display of learning and cultural knowledge by the characters within the text. Although some ancient symposia certainly had such learned attendees, the examples that we have from surviving literature are of famous or important individuals. In all of the surviving compositions, learned men take turns giving speeches or discoursing on a particular topic. Oftentimes the conversation would develop organically, moving from one topic to a related one based on the progression of the narrative (e.g. Xenophon, Plutarch).[17]

---

[12] These include works by Speusippus, Epicurus, Prytanis, Hieronymus, and Dio of the Academy. Cf. Diogenes Laertius 3.2; 4.5; 7.174.

[13] On the former, see D. E. Aune, 'Septem Sapientium Convivium', in *Plutarch's Theological Writings and Early Christians Literature*, ed. H. D. Betz (Leiden: Brill, 1972), 51–105; J. M. Mossman, *Plutarch and His Intellectual World* (London: Duckworth, 1997), 119–40.

[14] 'The *Table Talk* stands at the crossroads of three important Greek literary traditions, namely, the *symposium*, the literature of *problems*, and miscellanistic writing. Its experimentation with genre is typical of the Second Sophistic's predilection for hybridity, and it parallels the innovative form of other key Plutarchan works'. F. Klotz and K. Oikonomopoulou, 'Introduction', in *The Philosopher's Banquet: Plutarch's Table Talk in the Intellectual Culture of the Roman Empire*, ed. F. Klotz and K. Oikonomopoulou (Oxford: Oxford University Press, 2011), 12.

[15] Although some have assumed that there is a strong correlation between the text and Plutarch's historical experience, this perspective minimises the nature of text production, in which Plutarch actively selected, arranged, and polished texts to fit his literary purpose. For an ancient view of Plutarch's autobiographical statements, see Eunapius, *Lives* 454. Cf. D. A. Russell, *Plutarch: Selected Essays and Dialogues* (Oxford: Oxford University Press, 1993), xiii.

[16] Athenaeus (*Deipn.* 1.1b) claims a clear organizational principle to his work. Cf. J. Wilkins, 'Dialogue and Comedy: The Structure of the *Deipnosophistiae*', in *Athenaeus and his World: Reading Greek Culture in the Roman Empire*, ed. D. Braund and J. Wilkins (Exeter: Exeter University Press, 2000), 23–37.

[17] In Plato's *Symposium*, the change in speaker corresponds with Aristophanes' hiccoughing (e.g. 185d-e, 188e).

In other texts, the topic is set by one of the diners and each person has a turn to contribute to the discussion (e.g. Plato, Xenophon, *Letter of Aristeas*), and still some texts display a strong mixture of planned and organic discussions (e.g. Athenaeus).[18] The range of topics can be focused (Plato) or broad (Plutarch, *Mor.* 629d; Athenaeus, *Deipn.* 1.1a-b), although the consistent feature is that every surviving discussion functions at a high level of literary and cultural awareness.

The theme of learning is prominent even among those characters who are thoroughly steeped in literary knowledge.[19] This perspective is entrenched in the purpose or goal of symposia, namely to allow the attendee to feast both physically and intellectually, leaving with both a full stomach and mind (Plutarch, *Mor.* 645c; 660b).[20] Conversations take place, not only to show off and display one's intellectual prowess,[21] but because all those who attend share a love of learning (Plutarch, *Mor.* 628b). In fact, within the narratives, individual characters regularly express a desire to learn or declare that he is going to teach the rest of the company something.[22] For instance, in Plato's *Symposium*, Socrates is the prominent character and models the attitude and posture that the reader should adopt. Accordingly, Socrates is both an ideal learner and teacher – ready to share his knowledge, but also willing to learn from his fellow symposiasts. In *Sym.* 207c, Plato's Socrates expresses his need for an instructor (διδασκάλων) in love matters, though at the same time he is re-teaching his listeners what they should take from the conversation. Although he is teaching in the text, Socrates is the ideal learner in that he is willing to express ignorance and need for instruction. As a result, as Socrates learns so also does the reader.

Although the focus in these texts is clearly on those in the upper echelons of society, some of the authors also recognize that not all who attend will have the same level of learning. For example, Plutarch (*Mor.* 618e) claims that when he invites someone who is eager to learn he will have him sit next to a learned man so that the latter might be

---

[18] In certain sections in Athenaeus the texts proceed in a way to catalogue all the known types of a particular food, animals, or dishware (e.g. *Deipn.* 1.13c; 11.782d–11.509e).

[19] The theme of teaching and learning is most explicit in Plutarch's *Dinner of the Seven Wise Men* as each of the seven take turns giving advice and tutelage to Neiloxenus to take back to the King of Egypt. E.g. *Mor.* 152a-b (how best to rule); 154e-f (what makes the best government of the people); 154f–155e (how best to manage one's house).

[20] The goal of the dinner party is to renew the best part of the soul with the help of literature and learning (Plutarch, *Mor.* 645c).

[21] The standard way to show off was to display one's deep knowledge of Homer or other authorities on the subject (e.g. Xenophon, *Sym.* 3.5; Plutarch, *Mor.* 676e; 677a; Athenaeus, *Deipn.* 10.458a-d). For a negative example, see Athenaeus, *Deipn.* 1.4c. Concealment of ignorance is also mentioned by Plutarch, *Mor.* 644f. Although performative displays of *paideia*, intellectual competitiveness, and rhetorical self-fashioning are a central part of the symposium, Plutarch asserts that the event was not to degenerate to a sophistic contest in which one speaker attempts to outdo the previous one in rhetorical flair (so Plutarch, *Mor.* 615b; 713f). Similarly, previous competition and rivalry were to be dissipated through the sharing of the common cup (cf. Homer, *Il.* 23.810), though on occasion the conflict continued at the dinner party and became a source of strife (*Mor.* 736e). Cf. G. Roskam, 'Educating the young…over wine? Plutarch, Calvenus Taurus, and Favorinus as Convivial Teachers', in *Symposion and Philanthropia in Plutarch*, ed. J. R. Ferreira et al. (Coimbra: Classica Digitalia, 2009), 369–83.

[22] On statements for desiring to learn, see Plato, *Sym.* 206b; Xenophon, *Sym.* 2.16; Athenaeus, *Deipn.* 3.97d. For statements about teaching, see Plato, *Sym.* 189d; Athenaeus, *Deipn.* 3.127a; 9.366b; 9.398c; 9.407d.

able to impart some of his knowledge to the former.[23] Similarly, there is an expectation that unlearned (ἰδιῶται) people, although they may be few in numbers (ὀλίγοι), are to be welcomed to participate in the discussion (*Mor.* 613e).[24] At the same time, Plutarch makes it clear that the symposium is not to become a classroom in which individuals are taught aspects that they would typically learn at school (e.g. *Mor.* 621b; 712a; 737d-e);[25] these are educated people and so it is probably better to interpret ἰδιῶται as not having specific expertise.[26] As a result, Plutarch creates a distinction between the educated and intellectually curious and those who are only interested in self-promotion (i.e. sophists).[27] This requires that the topic of conversation be well chosen and the investigation suitably comprehensible so that less knowledgeable guests will not be stifled or turned away (614d; 630a). If the learned members do delve into difficult and obscure topics, however, they will likely lose to dance and foolish stories those with a desire to learn (614f), and for Plutarch this would constitute a failure.[28] This idea is potentially subversive as it restricts those with advanced accumulation of knowledge from displaying it. However, it prioritises the philosophical outlook that those who attend the dinner party are enriched and leave in a more elevated state than when they arrived. For Plutarch, the ideal model of engagement for those who are philosophically minded is found in Plato's *Symposium* (201d-215a), specifically Socrates' desire to learn and his ability to express deep ideas with simple premises and corresponding examples.[29]

The above discussion raises the question: What is one to learn at/from a symposium? So far, we have discussed learning as a general item, but it is clear from the sympotic works that not all learning was equal.[30] As the *symposium* is widely viewed as a Greek genre and essentially all sympotic literature before the third century CE is composed in Greek, it is unsurprising that Greek literature and authors were thought to be the primary, if not the only, acceptable form of culture.[31] One would expect this restricted

---

[23] Even common, unlearned folk (οἱ φορτικοὶ καὶ ἀφιλόλογοι) engage in mental pursuits. The reason for this is that in each person there is a thirst for knowledge in the soul (φιλόσοφον τῆς ψυχῆς) that seeks gratification once the body is satisfied (*Mor.* 673a–b).

[24] Cf. Plutarch, *Mor.* 710b; Plato, *Protag.* 347c; *Symp.* 176e; Isocrates, *Paneg.* 11.

[25] In Athenaeus' work, characters who give standard answers they were taught in school are met with disdain as a premium was placed on providing new material not found in the standard curriculum. For example, in *Deipn.* 15.676f, the speaker is interrupted and told, 'Do not offer us material drawn from Aelius Asclepiades' work entitled *Garlands*, as if we had never heard of it'. Athenaeus also criticizes Epicurus' *Symposium* because it had a classroom feel (*Deipn.* 5.186e).

[26] For a recent discussion, see E. Dickey, 'What Does a Linguistic Expert Know? The Conflict Between Analogy and Atticism?', in *Scholastic Culture in the Hellenistic and Roman Eras: Greek, Latin, and Jewish*, ed. S. A. Adams (Berlin: de Gruyter, 2019), 103–18.

[27] Also explicitly distinguished in Philo's *Contempl.* 31.

[28] According to Plutarch, music should not replace philosophical discussion, but can be used effectively if conversation has deteriorated to quarrels, as this is not conducive to friend-making or learning (*Mor.* 713e-f; cf. Athenaeus, *Deipn.* 3.97c).

[29] Cf. Macrobius, *Sat.* 1.1.3.

[30] For a thorough discussion of the dimensions of moral pedagogy in Plutarch's *Table Talk*, see S. Xenophontos, *Ethical Education in Plutarch: Moralising Agents and Contexts*, BZA 349 (Berlin: de Gruyter, 2016), 173–94.

[31] Other cultures also employed dialogue or speech as a prominent means of teaching. Indeed, ancient wisdom literature, such as the book of Job or the Egyptian text, *A Man's Argument with his*

focus in the works of Plato and Xenophon; however, a similar pattern is found in Roman-era authors (e.g. Plutarch, Lucian, and Athenaeus).[32] In none of the surviving *symposia* are non-Greek authors mentioned or quoted, let alone engaged with in any depth.[33] Rather, all of the quotations in Plato,[34] Xenophon,[35] Plutarch,[36] Lucian,[37] and Athenaeus[38] are from Greek-speaking authors. In fact, references to other cultures are almost completely absent.[39] The notable exception to this is the extended discussion of Jewish eating and worship practices by Plutarch (*Mor.* 669e-672c). On other occasions, when the conversation veered towards other cultures, one of the members of the drinking party would return the discussion to Greek matters. For example, there are a couple instances in Plutarch where the origin of a word was thought to be derived from Latin, but some argued for a Greek original (*Mor.* 726e). This practice went so far as to try to provide a Greek etymological answer for the Hebrew word 'Levite' (*Mor.* 671e).[40] Overall, the command by one of the guests (Florus) 'to leave the Egyptians out of it, and to find a Greek answer to our own question' (*Mor.* 684f) accurately depicts the nature of the sympotic dialogues and their passionate adherence to the supremacy of Greek culture.[41]

Ba, as well as early rabbinic midrashic texts explore philosophical and theological issues through debate. These are important similarities and speak to wider educational practices in antiquity. However, these texts do not participate in the genre of *symposia* and so are not central to our discussion.

[32] In contrast, symposia presented by Jewish authors (*Letter of Aristeas* and Philo's *Contemplativa*) are not centred on Greek authors, but on their Scriptural texts.

[33] The person of Cicero is mentioned in Plutarch, *Mor.* 631d, though there is no mention of his writings. This is also true of other Latin authors, such as Livy, Virgil, Seneca, and Pliny the Younger.

[34] Quotations in Plato's *Symposium*: Homer (174b, 179b, 180a, 183e, 190b, 195b, d, 214b, 220c); Euripides (177a, 196e); Hesiod (178b); Acusilaus (178b); Parmenides (178b); Aeschylus (180a); Heraclitus (178a); Alcidamas (196c); Sophocles (196c); Aristophanes (221b).

[35] Quotations in Xenophon's *Symposium*: Theognis (2.4); Homer (4.6, 45; 8.30).

[36] Examples of each author quoted in Plutarch's *Symposium*: Homer (*Mor.* 613d; 614c; 615e; 616a; 617b, c); Plato (614a); Euripides (615d; 622a); Pindar (617c); Empedocles (618b); Hesiod (618f); Sophocles (619a); Aeschylus (619e); Philoxenus (622c); Aristotle (627a); Theocritus (631e); Alexander the Epicurean (635e); Orpheus (636e); Herodotus (636e); Aesop (645b); Sappho (646f); Alcaeus (647e); Menander (654d); Archilochus (658b); Alcman (659b); Eupolis (662d); Menander (666f); Phanocles (670c); Euphorion (677a); Callimachus (677b); Timon (705d); Phrynichus (732f); and many unknown Greek poets (e.g. 700e; 707e). Plutarch includes no Latin quotations.

[37] Quotations in Lucian's *Symposium*: unknown Greek author (3); Homer (12, 17, 25, 44); Pindar (17); Hesiod (17); Anacreon (17); Euripides (25, 48); Sophocles (25); Plato (37); Histiaeus (41).

[38] There are far too many authors and texts quoted in Athenaeus to mention. For a list of these texts, see the index, 'Authors, Texts, and Persons', in S. D. Olson, *Athenaeus: The Learned Banqueters*, LCL, vol. 8 (Cambridge, MA: Harvard University Press, 2012), 220–360.

[39] Plutarch's *Sympotic Questions* is a unique composition as it places Greeks and Romans (i.e. Sossios Senecio, Mestrius Florus) at the same table. Not every Greek genre was interested in other cultures, although historiography, ethnography, biography, and others gave more attention to the contributions and records of other people groups. Cf. Gaëlle Coqueugniot, 'Scholastic Research in the Archive? Hellenistic Historians and Ancient Archival Records', in *Scholastic Culture in the Hellenistic and Roman Eras: Greek, Latin, and Jewish*, ed. S. A. Adams (Berlin: de Gruyter, 2019), 7–30.

[40] For Philo's etymology of Levi, see L. L. Grabbe, *Etymology in Early Jewish Interpretation: The Hebrew Names in Philo*, BJS 115 (Atlanta: Scholars, 1988), 179.

[41] On the importance of Greek culture, see T. Whitmarsh, *Greek Literature and the Roman Empire: The Politics of Imitation* (Oxford: Oxford University Press, 2001), 5.

Who Should Learn and When Should They Do So?

Although the theme of learning is prominent in the symposia, there is an underlying assumption within the texts that the people who are learning already have some education and that they began this journey in their youth.[42] The theme of when one is supposed to learn is rarely discussed within the texts, but it is taken as a given that a person could not fully succeed in their intellectual endeavours if they started learning late in life.[43] The best example of this discussion is found in Athenaeus, *Deipn.* 3.127b, in which one symposiast offhandedly comments that he is not able to progress in his discussion because he is constantly bombarded by others who failed to get an education when they were young. This negative comment emphasizes the disdain that certain educated elite had for people who were uneducated or had gained insufficient learning in their youth.[44] A comparable scene occurs in Plutarch's *Mor.* 634c, in which a harpist rebuked King Philip II of Macedon because of his late-won knowledge (ὀψιμαθίαν) in playing music.[45] Overall, one who learns late in life was not thought to be able to progress very far and so would not excel in their area of study (cf. Lucian, *Merc. cond.* 23).[46]

On the other hand, within the *symposia*, a different standard appears to be used for evaluating women who sought an education during their adult life. Athenaeus (*Deipn.* 13.579e-581a, 584b-585b) tells a series of stories about how a courtesan named Gnathaena attracted a lot of attention and gained a substantial clientele because of her ability to entertain educated men by her quick, witty comments.[47] She was said to be so sophisticated in her employment of literature and elite culture that she composed a set of dinner regulations in imitation of similar documents created by contemporary philosophers (13.585b). Other courtesans, seeing her success and wishing to emulate it, decided to get an education and dedicated a lot of time to their lessons (*Deipn.* 13.583f). As a result, they too learned how to entertain men with witty remarks and gained a greater number of wealthy patrons.[48] In this case, learning late in life was not viewed as a detriment, possibly because such learning was not expected of

---

[42] See Athenaeus, *Deipn.* 13.588a-b, for a speaker congratulating (sarcastically?) a person coming to philosophy without having any education.
[43] For the argument that education should start as early as possible, see Plato, *Resp.* 2.377a; Quintilian, *Inst.* 1.1.4-24; Plutarch, *Mor.* 3e-f.
[44] Cf. Herodotus, *Hist.* 2.154; Diogenes Laertius 4.36; Philo, *Ebr.* 51; Plutarch, *Dem.* 2.3.
[45] Cf. Plutarch, *Mor.* 334c. For a positive example of late learning, see Plato, *Resp.* 409b; *Soph.* 251b.
[46] Suetonius (*Nero* 20.1; 41.1) offers a similar example of Nero's inability to learn to sign and play the lyre well late in life, although Suetonius makes it clear that he was not naturally suited to these endeavours. On music education in antiquity, see H. I. Marrou, *A History of Education in Antiquity*, trans. G. R. Lamb (London: Sheed & Ward, 1956), 134–41, 181–2.
[47] She is not the only one to do this. Athenaeus tells similar stories about courtesans named Lamia (*Deipn.* 13.577e-f) and Mania (*Deipn.* 13.578a-579d). Leontion was also rumoured to have continued being a prostitute despite starting to study philosophy with Epicurus (13.588b) and Nicarete of Megara, who was well-born, reputedly studied philosophy with Stilpo (13.596e). Cf. L. McClure, *Courtesans at Table: Gender and Greek Literary Culture in Athenaeus* (London: Routledge, 2003).
[48] These courtesans showcased their wit through the composition of riddles, often with double entendre (e.g. *Deipn.* 10.449d-e; 10.450e-451b; Plutarch, *Mor.* 150e-f). Cf. McClure, *Courtesans*, 80–83.

women.[49] That these women successfully gained a level of literary education was seen as something positive – an idea supported by Athenaeus' quotation of Agathon, 'The fact that a woman does no physical labour does not mean that she has a lazy mind inside her' (*Deipn.* 13.584a-b).

The idea of a women learning is also brought up in Xenophon's *Symposium*, but this discussion is less complimentary. Socrates, viewing a female dancing and noting her skill, said, 'women's nature is really not at all inferior to man's, except in its lack of judgment and physical strength. So if any one of you has a wife, let him confidently set about teaching her whatever he would like to have her know' (2.9).[50] This backhanded compliment provides a window into the world of domestic education. First, it indicates, at least to Xenophon's Socrates, that women had the ability to learn. Second, it demonstrates a woman's ability to learn was not limited to her early years, but continued through her married life.[51] Third, that a husband had some input and influence in his wife's education. Although it is difficult to know the extent to which these ideas were accepted and implemented within antiquity, we have evidence that at least one ancient author created space for women to learn, even if that place was elsewhere and not at a symposium.[52]

The common presentation by almost all of our ancient authors was that a symposium was primarily a male event and that they alone had access to the learning and teaching held within.[53] The primary exception to this female exclusion is the entertainment, namely pipe/flute girls and acrobats, who would perform for the male guests.[54] In these cases, the women are to be appreciated, not for their intellectual ability, but for their physical beauty and their talents.[55] Accordingly, despite being present in the building, it is clear that they were not partakers in the learned dialogue, and it is also fair to assume that they would not have been encouraged to listen and learn from the discussion.

---

[49] Diogenes Laertius 1.91; Stobaeus, *Flor.* III.6.58. Cf. R. Cribiore, *Gymnastics of the Mind: Greek Education in Hellenistic and Roman Egypt* (Princeton: Princeton University Press, 2001), 74–101; T. Morgan, *Literate Education in the Hellenistic and Roman Worlds* (Cambridge: Cambridge University Press, 1998), 48–9.

[50] Cf. *Let. Aris.* 250. Socrates also expresses a bit later that courage must also be teachable, because the female dancer danced amongst swords without showing fear (Xenophon, *Sym.* 2.11-12). A funerary inscription for the freedwoman Eucharis highlights her education by the muses (*CIL*² 1.1214).

[51] Quintilian (*Inst.* 1.1.6) claimed that it would be ideal if mothers were also educated in order that they might be able to contribute to, or at least not hinder, the development of her sons in their pursuit of being an orator.

[52] Cf. R. S. Bagnall and R. Cribiore, *Women's Letters from Ancient Egypt: 300 BC–AD 800* (Ann Arbor: University of Michigan Press, 2006), 48–9; M. Deslauriers, 'Women, Education, and Philosophy', in *A Companion to Women in the Ancient World*, ed. S. L. James and S. Dillon (Oxford: Blackwell, 2012), 343–53.

[53] On the other hand, Lucian indicates that there were women present in his symposium (*Sym.* 35) and so too does Theocritus present a woman at a dinner party (*Id.* 14), although here she is struck by a jilted lover. However, they are not given any speaking roles and are only mentioned when something inappropriate happened (e.g. when one of the philosophers urinated in front of them). For evidence of women at symposia based on Corinthian votive offerings, see N. Bookidis, 'Ritual Dining in the Sanctuary of Demeter and Kore at Corinth: Some Questions', in Murray, ed., *Sympotica*, 86–94.

[54] For Nicanor's fear of flute-girls, see Hippocrates, *Epidemics* 5.81.

[55] E.g. Plato, *Sym.* 176e; Xenophon, *Sym.* 2.1; Plutarch, *Mor.* 147f; 710b-d; Athenaeus, *Deipn.* 3.97a; 4.129a, d.

The notable exception to this absence of female characters in Greek *symposia* is Plutarch's *Dinner of the Seven Wise Men*, in which two girls, Melissa and Eumetis, are included in the activities (*Mor.* 148c-e; 150b; 155e). However, within the narrative world there is conflict at the idea of Eumetis' involvement, with Cleodorus making snide remarks and not acknowledging her ability to create suitably challenging riddles (154b-c). Eumetis is defended by Aesop, who compliments her wit, but still she does not get to speak.[56] Rather, Aesop speaks for her, repeating a riddle she gave before dinner. Both girls leave when the drinking cup is brought out (155e) without making any further contribution to the narrative. As a result, although Plutarch includes two girls within his narrative, they are limited to non-speaking roles. Nevertheless, they are shown to be listening participants of the learned dialogue and it is clear in the narrative that Eumetis is thought to be sufficiently capable to learn from her inclusion.

Although women were physically absent in Plato's *Symposium*, the knowledge held by one is discussed at a strategic point in the narrative. At the beginning of his speech, Socrates recalls a discourse on love he heard from the priestess Diotima, a Mantinean woman, whom he describes as skilled in many topics and his teacher in matters of love (σοφὴ ἦν καὶ ἄλλα πολλά...ἣ δὴ καὶ ἐμὲ τὰ ἐρωτικὰ ἐδίδαξεν, *Symp.* 201d).[57] Socrates' signalling of a dialogue-within-dialogue mitigates Diotima's physical absence and affords an opportunity for a female perspective, even if her insight is offered through a male voice.[58]

An even more inclusive depiction is the sympotic event by the Therapeutae and Therapeutrides recounted by the Jewish author Philo of Alexandria (*Contempl.* 64–90).[59] Here, Philo compares (συγκρίνειν) the content, activities, and perceived function of symposia, explicitly contrasting Jewish practices with those of the other nations (ἀντιτάξας τὰ τῶν ἄλλων συμπόσια, *Contempl.* 40; cf. §§48–56). Unlike the Greek examples found in Plato and Xenophon, both men and women share in the communal meal as well as the teaching (*Contempl.* 68),[60] although for propriety's sake they are kept separate and their view of each other is obstructed by a dividing wall (cf. *Contempl.* 33).[61] Both sexes are thought capable of bettering their soul through learning and take part in hymns and prayers to God (*Contempl.* 88–89). As a result, although he does not report a woman speaking, women are placed on a much more even footing by Philo than by other Greek and Jewish authors.

---

[56] Her restraint is attributed to her (appropriate) modesty, as indicated by her blushes (*Mor.* 154b).
[57] For the claim that Pythagoras received his ethical doctrines from Themistoclea, a priestess at Delphi, see Diogenes Laertius, 8.8, 21.
[58] Cf. A. Nye, 'Irigaray and Diotima at Plato's Symposium', in *Feminist Interpretations of Plato*, ed. N. Tuana (University Park: Pennsylvania State University Press, 1994), 197–215.
[59] Cf. S. A. Adams, *Greek Genres and Jewish Authors: Negotiating Literary Culture in the Greco-Roman Era* (Waco: Baylor University Press, 2020), 139–47.
[60] For a more thorough discussion, see J. E. Taylor, 'Spiritual Mothers: Philo on the Women Therapeutae', *JSP* 23 (2002): 37–63.
[61] Cf. J. E. Taylor and D. Hay, *On the Contemplative Life*, PACS (Leiden: Brill, 2020), *ad locum*.

How Does One Learn?

The above discussions highlight the fact that learning in symposia occurred through dialogue and discourse. Literary *symposia*, unsurprisingly, are often structured on the asking and answering of questions and, although collections of questions are recognized as a type of literary work (i.e. ζητημάτων),[62] they are not limited to ζητημάτων literature, but are regularly found in symposia. For example, Plutarch explicitly references ζητημάτων in his *Table Talks*, highlighting their appropriateness for dinner conversation.[63] Similarly, the symposium described in the Jewish work, *Letter of Aristeas* (§§187–300), is entirely focused on the asking and answering of questions. Here, King Ptolemy II holds seven symposia during which he asks all 72 Jewish translators a different question about kingship, ruling, and a variety of other political matters. The questions are answered by pithy, pious sayings and there is no extensive speech by any one individual.[64]

In contrast to the use of dialogue, the symposium of the Therapeutae described by Philo only has one person speaking and answering questions, the senior member of the community (*Contempl.* 31).[65] This singular individual is the only/primary one to answer questions because he is thought to be the most learned of the community. However, he shares his knowledge because he recognizes that all those in attendance share with him a deep desire to learn (*Contempl.* 75). This centring of knowledge in a singular individual is in sharp opposition to the essence of Greek symposia expressed above, namely that it was expected that all would share their knowledge and so all would learn.[66] The localising of knowledge within an individual is distinctive, but does not represent normative Jewish practice in literary depictions.[67] Furthermore,

---

[62] Cf. Adams, *Greek Genres and Jewish Authors*, 111–17.

[63] E.g. *Mor.* 644e; 645c; 660d; 736c; cf. Athenaeus, *Deipn.* 5.186e. For rhetorical discussions of appropriateness, see Aristotle, *Rhet.* 3.7, 1408a-b; Quintilian, *Inst.* 11.1.1; for brevity of speech, see Demetrius, *Eloc.* 197–198, Cicero, *Inv.* 1.28; Quintilian, *Inst.* 4.2.31.

[64] Similarly, in Josephus, *Ant.* 12.210-214, Hyrcanus impresses King Ptolemy with his courtly wit at a dinner party. For a larger discussion of *Letter of Aristeas*' participation in *symposia* as well as other genres, see Adams, *Greek Genres and Jewish Authors*, 119–34.

[65] Although no record of any specific questions or answers is provided in the text, it could be presumed that multiple individuals (including women?) asked questions (*Contempl.* 75).

[66] Although not in the format of a symposium, we also find works from the Qumran community that focus on the teachings of a singular individual, the *Maskil*, for the benefit of the larger community. For examples of the *Maskil*, see 1QS III 13; IV 22–23; IX 12–25 (and parallels). Cf. C. Hempel, 'Maskil(im) and Rabbim: From Daniel to Qumran', in *Biblical Traditions in Transmission: Essays in Honour of Michael A. Knibb*, ed. C. Hempel and J. Lieu, JSJSup 111 (Leiden: Brill, 2006), 133–56. For the role of the *Maskil* in liturgical settings, especially *Songs of the Maskil* (4Q510–511), see J. L. Angel, 'Maskil, Community, and Religious Experience in the *Songs of the Sage* (4Q510–511)', *DSD* 19 (2012): 1–27. For the Teacher of Righteousness, see CD 1:8-11; 1QpHab 7:3-6.

[67] See *Letter of Aristeas* above and Sir 31:12–32:13, which is another Jewish work that speaks to banquet etiquette (cf. Prov. 23:1-8). Although Sirach does not directly describe a particular sympotic event, some of the advice given, such as brevity of speech (32:7-9) is thought to be universal in its application. Cf. J. K. Aitken, 'Ben Sira's Table Manners and the Social Setting of His Book', in *Perspectives on Israelite Wisdom: Proceedings from the Oxford Old Testament Seminar*, ed. J. Jarick, LHBOTS 618 (London: T&T Clark, 2015), 418–38. See also U. Rapp, 'You Are How You Eat: How Eating and Drinking Behaviour Identifies the Wise According to Jesus Ben Sirach', in *Decisive Meals: Table Politics in Biblical Literature*, ed. K. Ehrensperger, N. MacDonald, and L. Sutter Rehman, LNTS 449

if, as mentioned above, one of the purposes of ancient symposia was to form and reinforce friendships, Philo's depiction of the symposium in the Therapeutae community does not encourage this practice. Admittedly, Philo has already shown that the Therapeutae had strong bonds of unity (e.g. *Contempl.* 32), but affirming this connection was not depicted as an important element within the symposium. Not only is discussion limited by apportioning the speaking to one individual, but males and females are physically separated in order to minimise interaction. These distinctive features suggest that Philo's depiction of the Therapeutae intentionally contrasts Greek sympotic practices and should be read as directly engaged with that literature.

Dialogue was not the only way that people learned new information, although it is the prominent way in the *symposia*.[68] In antiquity, as in today, people undertook research in order to solve a particular problem or answer a pressing question. We see in a comment in Athenaeus (*Deipn.* 15.675f) that, in addition to questioning people who might know, a common way of pursing an answer was to read a range of books.[69] The importance of books is not prominent in early *symposia* and is not the practice adopted by Socrates. However, as this genre develops, references to literary works and scholastic activity increases. Examples of book learning are found in nearly every section of Athenaeus' work, although it is explicitly noted in certain passages. For example, the idea that books were a source of information is highlighted by the inquiry in Athenaeus' narrative by the grammarian Aristarchus into the type of flower used in a Naucratean garland. According to the speaker, traditions and ceremonial actions have their roots in ancient events and so their origins can be identified and explained. In some cases, it is difficult to find the information desired, and so the discovery can be displayed with great boasting (e.g. *Deipn.* 15.673d-e).[70] Plutarch also supports this position, as he resists using well-worn examples from school (ὑπὸ τῶν γραμματικῶν) to support his proposal that poetry was not a late

(London: Bloomsbury, 2012), 42–61, who rightly sees the Greek/Roman sympotic elements of Ben Sira as secondary to the biblical image of the wise banquet. Little is said about communal meals at Qumran, but 1QS VI 2-5 suggests that, should there be ten or more men, they would require the presence of a priest, be seated according to rank, and each give their opinions on different matters. When discussing the procedure of any ten-men gathering, 1QS VI 6-8 says that someone must be engaged in the study of the Law and that all members of the *Yahad*, in order of rank, would have an opportunity to give their thoughts on the topic under discussion.

[68] Cf. J. König, *Saints and Symposiasts: The Literature of Food and the Symposium in Greco-Roman and Early Christian Culture* (Cambridge: Cambridge University Press, 2012), 69–70.

[69] The securing of information, especially about specific events, is a prominent concern in historiography that led to the importance of conversing with eyewitnesses (e.g. Josephus, *C. Ap.* 1.46, 53-55; 2.37, 62; *Vita* 357-360; Thucydides, *Hist.* 1.22.2-3; Polybius, *Hist.* 4.2.2-3; 12.4c.3-5; 12.25g.1-5; Lucian, *Hist.* 29, 47). Gellius (*Noct. Att.* 5.18.1-6) differentiates between histories and annals by their author's level of participation in events and time period in focus (cf. Polybius, *Hist.* 12.25e.1-7; Dionysius, *Ant. Rom.* 1.7.3). Cf. J. Marincola, *Authority and Tradition in Ancient Historiography* (Cambridge: Cambridge University Press, 1997), 63–86; S. A. Adams, 'Luke's Preface (1.1-4) and its Relationship to Greek Historical Prefaces: A Response to Loveday Alexander', *JGRChJ* 3 (2006): 187–90. For the Jewish practice, see Adams, *Greek Genres and Jewish Authors*, 201–56. Historians writing about distant history must rely on reports, which is viewed as a hindrance (e.g. Polybius, *Hist.* 4.1.1-4; Plutarch, *Per.* 13.12).

[70] Cf. *Deipn.* 15.678f: 'For you are the person who not only collects the obscure passages in his books but actively roots them up'. In *Deipn.* 15.671c, the speaker, Cynylcus, accuses Ulpian of picking the most thorny, difficult passages for discussion, while others select those that are useful and worth hearing.

arrival to religious festivals, but rather provides an example from a book that was not widely read (Acesander's *Libya*) so as both to educate and to entertain his fellow diners (*Mor.* 675a).

More examples could be offered, but it is clear from later *symposia* that a deep knowledge of a wide range of literature was desirable.[71] The sharing of knowledge among comparatively learned individuals, all of whom engage in the reciprocal giving and receiving of literary culture, not only results in mutual learning, but also in the reinforcement of in-groups that can be expressed through the terminology of friendship.

Who Read *Symposia*?

Plutarch introduces his *Table Talk* by placing it within a larger literary history through references to previous sympotic authors: Plato, Xenophon, Aristotle,[72] Speusippus, Epicurus, Prytanis, Hieronymus, Dio of the Academy (*Mor.* 612d-e).[73] This list, arranged in chronological order, shows Plutarch's genre awareness and indicates his intention to follow a literary practice, one with which he assumes his reader(s) is familiar. A later, comparable example is offered by Macrobius (*Sat.* 7.3.23), who identifies Plutarch as now being part of this tradition: 'I advise you at your feasts… either to propound or yourselves to resolve questions suitable to the occasion. This kind of thing the ancients were so far from thinking ridiculous that both Aristotle and Plutarch and your Apuleius wrote on such questions.'[74] Plutarch (*Mor.* 612d) identifies these authors as 'philosophers', implying that symposium literature was thought to be philosophic in nature.[75] The mention of Aristotle, Plutarch, and Apuleius by Macrobius further supports the association between philosophy and *symposia*, helping both ancient and modern readers see *symposia* as participating in certain genre categories. Furthermore, the fact that almost all of the authors mentioned by Plutarch are Peripatetics suggests that *symposia* literature was important to their school and might have been part of their philosophical curriculum.

One of the unique aspects of the quotation by Macrobius is the inclusion of a Latin author alongside Greek ones. Plutarch only mentions Greek authors and, as we have discussed above, Greek authors were almost exclusively mentioned in all of the

---

[71] This would also include the ability to cite *scholia*. Cf. Plutarch, *Mor.* 676e; Lucian, *Sym.* 34.

[72] There are very few references to Aristotle's *Symposium*; however, a number of scholars equate this with his work *On Drunkenness*. If this is the case, there are a few more fragments, but very little survives. Cf. V. Rose, *Aristotelis qui ferebantur librorum fragmenta* (Leipzig: Teubner, 1886), frs. 100–111.

[73] On this point, cf. Klotz and Oikonomopoulou, 'Introduction', 13–18. For a similar practice among biography writers, see S. A. Adams, 'What are Bioi/Vitae? Generic Self-Consciousness in Ancient Biography', in *The Oxford Handbook of Ancient Biography*, ed. K. De Temmerman (Oxford: Oxford University Press, 2020), 19–31.

[74] These are not the only *Symposium* works in antiquity. For example, Athenaeus, *Deipn.* 2.64a, e-f; 2.67e; 3.79e-80a references a little-known *Symposium* by Heraclides of Tarentum. It is interesting that all of the references to Heraclides occur at the beginning of Athenaeus' work and are not mentioned in later passages in which other *Symposia* are discussed.

[75] An idea further supported by his positive answer to the works opening question: is philosophy a fitting topic for conversation at a drinking party? (*Mor.* 612e–615c).

sympotic works, an association that is understandable in light of the strong preference for philosophy in Greek literary culture.[76] The mention of Apuleius by Macrobius indicates that not only Greek authors were participating in this genre, but that at least one Latin author had done so. Furthermore, the pairing of Apuleius with Aristotle and Plutarch indicates that Macrobius understood Latin authors as continuing the literary practice of Greek writers, a tradition started by Plato and Xenophon, and that Apuleius was viewed as prototypical.

The works by Plato and Xenophon were thought to be the pinnacle or prototypical expressions of this genre form, and became precedent-setting for later authors who wished to compose similar literary works.[77] This is best recognized by the number of times either *Symposium* is referenced, discussed, alluded to, or imitated by later authors.[78] An explicit example of their influence is found in Athenaeus' *Deipn.* 5.179d. Here Athenaeus identifies elements of good literary practice in the depictions of Plato and Xenophon, namely that the former, after dinner, made libations and sang a paean to god (Plato, *Sym.* 176a) and the latter did something similar (Xenophon, *Sym.* 2.1). Epicurus, however, fails to give customary honours to the deity in his *Symposium* and so receives a censure by Athenaeus. Another example follows in *Deipn.* 5.186e, in which the author claims that Plato and Xenophon, again drawing on Homeric precedent, provide a clear introduction to the characters who will be taking part in the symposium.[79] According to Athenaeus, the omission of this practice in Epicurus' *Symposium* is a fault and detracts from the quality of the work.[80] Ironically, Athenaeus is also guilty of this omission, failing to follow his own advice to model his work on Homer, Plato, or Xenophon by introducing the people at the dinner party. Plutarch follows the established pattern of introducing characters in his *Dinner* (e.g. *Mor.* 148d, f; 150a), but he does not do so in his *Table Talk*. In this text the characters are not stable, nor is Plutarch recounting a single event.

Plato and Xenophon are not without their faults and Athenaeus spends a portion of his text identifying where they fall short (e.g. *Deipn.* 5.182a, 187b-188d). This critical evaluation highlights the way that genres are discussed in antiquity, but also establishes that, at the time of Athenaeus, there has already been substantial debate on the nature of the *symposium* genre and the strengths and weaknesses of key authors. Such discussions are not found in early works (e.g. Plato, Xenophon, etc.) and for good reason: the literary form had not been sufficiently established to warrant critique or

---

[76] Quintilian, *Inst.* 10.1.123; cf. S. A. Adams, *The Genre of Acts and Collected Biography*, SNTSMS 156 (Cambridge: Cambridge University Press, 2013), 52–3.

[77] Plutarch, *Mor.* 686d; Philo, *Contempl.* 57–58. Apuleius also drew upon previous *symposia* for some parts of his *Metamorphoses*. Cf. S. J. Harrison, *Apuleius: A Latin Sophist* (Oxford: Oxford University Press, 2004), 224–5. Petronius also has an extended dinner sequence, the well-known *cena trimalchionis* (*Sat.* 26–78), that shows literary parallels to Plato and others. Cf. Aulus Gellius, *Noct. att.* 1.2.1-13; 7.13.1-12; 17.8.1-17.

[78] For example, Plutarch quotes Plato's *Symposium* (*Mor.* 622c) and references characters (i.e. the buffoon) in Xenophon's *Symposium* (*Mor.* 629c).

[79] Cf. Plutarch, *Mor.* 613d, in which Plutarch lists the people who attended Plato's *Symposium* and Xenophon's *Symposium*.

[80] According to Athenaeus (*Deipn.* 5.187b), Epicurus also erred because he did not mix his guests like the model works of Plato and Xenophon, but only has atomists attend. For Athenaeus' modelling on Plato's *Symposium*, see *Deipn.* 1.1f.

extended comparison. It is only in the work of authors in the Hellenistic and Roman eras that such conversations can take place as they look back to see the lasting quality of certain works.

These discussions allow us to witness the chain of learning that traced its way from Plato and Xenophon regarding the nature of sympotic literature and the type of questions that were typical. In them we see the repetition and expansion of certain themes and topics, as well as the desire to advance discussions and uncover new fields of inquiry. A good example of this is the topic of love, which occupies a prominent position in both Plato and Xenophon's works.[81] Subsequent authors also considered love to be a suitable topic for conversation, but it is clear that they do not limit their discussions to those covered by Plato and Xenophon, but expand it to deal with courtesans, prostitutes, and homosexuality in deeper and often new ways.[82] As a result, what we see is the development of literary form to encompass additional topics and ideas.

Another example of the development of the genre is Lucian's parody, *Symposium* (also known as *The Carousel* or *The Lapiths*), a second-century CE composition full of critique and mockery. In this work, Lucian includes select standard genre features, such as introducing each guest (*Sym.* 6–7), identifying where they are sitting (*Sym.* 8–9), and the cliché of an uninvited guest showing up and making the commonplace joke about Menelaus (*Sym.* 12; cf. Homer, *Il.* 2.408). However, although Lucian sets up an expectation in his readers about what the symposium should be like (i.e. well-behaved, orderly, and with high levels of conversation),[83] he undermines the traditional assumptions of the reader by inverting the roles of the attendees: the unlettered people were acting with great decorum, simply laughing and passing judgment on the learned men, who were abusing each other, gorging themselves, and coming to blows (*Sym.* 35). Lucian makes his implicit critique explicit near the end of the work through a reference to Plato's *Symposium* as a model for how to have a dinner party (*Sym.* 37), indicating to the reader his literary point of departure. The ability to successfully satirise a work requires a high level of education as well as a wide awareness among readers of the literary form to know when it is being subverted. In this case, the genre of symposium had been sufficiently established so as to allow Lucian to invert major tropes and to critique the philosophers of his day by comparing them to their more dignified predecessors.

One question we do not have an answer to is how widely these symposium texts were read.[84] The genre of *symposia* was not as popular or well-known as other works

---

[81] Plato, *Sym.* 177a–201c; Xenophon, *Sym.* 8.1-41. Cf. Philo, *Contempl.* 59.

[82] Courtesans and prostitutes: Athenaeus, *Deipn.* 13.555b-612f; homosexuality: Plato, *Sym.* 181d, 184d; 192a-b; 218c; Plutarch, *Mor.* 619a; 691c; 712c; Athenaeus, *Deipn.* 13.563e-565f; 13.601e-605b; cf. Philo, *Contempl.* 60–1.

[83] 'It's a learned academy, this dinner party you are telling me of. Philosophers almost to a man' (*Sym.* 10).

[84] For evidence of library collections in antiquity, with specific reference to *symposia*, see G. W. Houston, 'Papyrological Evidence for Book Collections and Libraries in the Roman Empire', in *Ancient Literacies: The Culture of Reading in Greece and Rome*, ed. W. A. Johnson and H. N. Parker (Oxford: Oxford University Press, 2009), 233–67, esp. 235. On the popularity of miscellany, see T. Morgan, *Popular Morality in the Early Roman Empire* (Cambridge: Cambridge University Press, 2007), esp. 257–74.

or genres in antiquity (e.g. epic, tragedy, history). Even in Plutarch's dining circles he notes that some in attendance did not have a sufficient familiarity with the contents of previous *symposia*: 'Certain young men with no long experience in the ancient literature were attacking Epicurus on the ground that he had introduced in his *Symposium* an unseemly and unnecessary discussion about the proper time for sexual intercourse' (*Mor.* 653b). This comment provoked a response by Zopyrus the physician, who, being very well acquainted with the works of Epicurus, claims that 'they had not read Epicurus' *Symposium* with attention' (653c). In response to this lack of understanding, some diners brought forward examples from Xenophon and Zopyrus took the young men for a walk after dinner to further instruct them. This example indicates that these young men, who did not have a lot of experience with literature, were at least aware of its existence and familiar enough with Epicurus' *Symposium* to critique it. However, their understanding of it suggests that they had read it superficially and had not processed it with sufficient depth. On the other hand, even Zopyrus expresses that he cannot remember all the details accurately (653f).

These examples indicate that *symposia* were part of Greek cultural heritage and that highly educated people would have been familiar with them. We also witness in the discussions of genre and the development of the literary form that previous works were used as models and were the subject of praise and critique. These discussions imply that *symposia* were themselves part of the education processes for future authors wishing to write a *Symposium* and that their literary conventions and prototypical characteristics would need to be learned in order to participate successful in this genre. In addition to these authors, other ancients read *symposia* and saw elements of value within them. The texts are rich with literary anecdotes and exempla that not only help the reader learn a breadth of literary culture, but they also model the idealised form of dialogue in which skills in speaking can be displayed.[85] The essence of the works, including the positing of questions and riddles, draws the reader into the world of the symposiasts and challenges them to engage with the texts' contents and to cultivate a philosophical understanding of the world. As a result, the learning within the text becomes the model of teaching, the didactic element gained by the reader to be implemented at future parties.

Conclusion

This study has highlighted how *symposia* promote the value of learning and demonstrate learnedness in action. The characters within the text, even though many of them were extremely well educated, are presented as eager to learn and actively doing so. For them, learning was a lifelong process and their fellow symposiasts were their teachers as well as their co-learners. The reader, who, through the act of reading, participates

---

[85] The repetitive process of exposure to common patterns of argumentation allows for a greater understanding of the nature of the *symposia* and provide for the reader a way of learning dialogic repartee. Cf. König, *Saints and Symposiasts*, 73. On rhetorical speaking by Socrates in Plato's *Symposium*, see Quintilian, *Inst.* 8.4.23. L. Gonzàlez Julià, 'Plutarch's *techne rhetorike* for the Symposium in *Quaestiones Convivales*: The Importance of Speaking Well to Cultivate Friendship', in *Symposion and philanthropia in Plutarch*, ed. J. R. Ferreira et al. (Coimbra: Classica Digitalia, 2009), 63–74.

(albeit silently) within the symposium, also learns along with the characters and in so doing gains access to elite conversation. The sympotic discussion is to be orderly, with each participant having the opportunity to contribute and share their accumulated knowledge. However, the ancient authors distinguish between sophistry and genuine intellectual strength, dismissing the former as out of place and prizing the latter for its authenticity.

The depicted symposia afforded their authors the means by which to reinforce the centrality of Greek culture and show how one can advance within it. Although the narrative world was limited to the elite, the characters recognized that learning was inherently important, even for those who were lower in society. The ideal learner, according to our texts, is that of a free, Greek male, who started young, but even women and late-learning adults could embark on gaining an education, though they will never reach the highest heights. Women's access to and participation in education was raised in a number of texts, usually positively, but exclusively from a male perspective. When women are represented in *symposia*, which is rare, they are silent and only speak through the mouth of male characters.

Moving beyond the world within the texts, we see that symposia literature itself was part of the education that the writers had. We witness in the prefaces and characters' explicit discussions of previous works that it was necessary for the authors to have a detailed knowledge of sympotic texts in order to produce new examples of that literary form. Explicit signalling of other *symposia* could be a way of marketing the text, emphasizing the author's familiarity with his literary predecessors and his participation in the genre. At the same time, the references encourage an intertextual reading approach. This is seen in Lucian's parody and the inverting of characters' actions and Philo's explicit contrasting of an idealised Jewish dinner ritual with those of his Greek antecedents. Philo's *Contemplativa* and the symposia in *Letter of Aristeas* also function to facilitate cultural negotiation by showing how a Jewish community exceeds the practices of their neighbours and how Jewish wisdom can be of benefit to a Greek king. Although these texts could be read and enjoyed by those who are unfamiliar with the *symposia* of Plato and Xenophon, the full impact of them would only be appreciated by those with knowledge of sympotic prototypes. In time, these sympotic texts could come to be viewed as prototypical, as is evidenced by Macrobius' discussion, and so continue to shape how literary *symposia* are crafted.

7

Teaching and Learning in Philosophical Schools of the Second Century AD: Arrian's Epictetus and Aulus Gellius's Calvenus Taurus

Michael Trapp

The classic parody of the earnest student of philosophy from the early centuries CE is Lucian's Hermotimus, in the dialogue that bears his name.[1] Hermotimus's interlocutor, Lycinus, observes that for about the last twenty years – after a late start at the age of forty – he has spent his every minute 'attending classes with your teachers, for the most part hunched over a book and writing out your lecture notes';[2] and at the precise moment of their encounter, the book he is clutching, his purposeful stride, and the way he is muttering to himself and sawing the air with his hand betrays the fact that he is on his way to yet another day's lessons.[3] But we never actually discover what goes on inside the classroom. Because, as Lycinus gleefully informs him, Hermotimus's revered teacher – not surprisingly for a philosopher in Lucian – has proved unable to live up to his own principles of sobriety and abstinence, and is suffering from a crippling hangover: there's a notice hanging on his door saying 'no philosophy class today' (τήμερον οὐ συμφιλοσοφεῖν).[4] We never get inside; Hermotimus and the conversation are diverted instead into a discussion of how he chose his teacher in the first

---

[1] For discussion of the structure, themes and humour of *Hermotimus*, see H.-G. Nesselrath, 'Kaiserzeitliche Skeptizismus in platonischen Gewand: Lukian's "Hermotimos"', *ANRW* 2.36.5 (1992): 3451–82; M. Edwards, 'Lucian and the Rhetoric of Philosophy: The *Hermotimus*', *AC* 62 (1993): 195–202; P. von Möllendorff, *Lukian, Hermotimos oder, Lohnt es sich, Philosophie zu studieren* (Darmstadt: Wissenschaftliche Buchgesellschaft, 2000); C. García Ehrenfeld, 'Lucian's *Hermotimus*, Essays about Philosophy and Satire in Greek: Literature of the Roman Empire' (PhD diss., King's College London, 2017).
[2] Lucian, *Hermot.* 2.
[3] Lucian, *Hermot.* 1.
[4] Lucian, *Hermot.* 11.

place, and where he hopes to get to with him, and eventually into a devastating – and paradoxically salvational – demonstration by Lycinus that his philosophical ambitions are in fact built on sand. Hermotimus ends the conversation swearing that henceforth he will avoid philosophers as he would mad dogs.[5]

Nor is much help to be had from Lucian's apparently more reverential depiction of the Platonist Nigrinus (again in a dialogue named after him). The narrator of the dialogue visits Nigrinus at his residence in Rome and discovers him

> with a book in his hand, surrounded by various statues of the ancient philosophers. Before him lay a tablet, with geometrical figures described on it, and a globe of reeds, designed apparently to represent the universe. He greeted me cordially and asked after my welfare. I satisfied his inquiries, and demanded, in my turn, how he did, and whether he had decided on another trip to Greece. Once on that subject, he gave free expression to his sentiments; and, I assure you, it was a veritable feast of ambrosia to me. The spells of the Sirens (if ever there were any such creatures), of the Pindaric 'Charmers', of the Homeric lotus, are things to be forgotten, after his truly divine eloquence.[6]

There are certainly some intriguing details here, hinting at a variety of possible didactic activities, from the exegesis of classic philosophical texts (the works of the past greats commemorated in the statuary) to the use of visual aids to work through problems in geometry, cosmology, and astronomy (the tablet and the sphere); and the range seems exactly right for a Platonist such as Nigrinus. But we are not allowed to see these implied didactic processes in operation in a classroom setting. This is a private visit, and the philosopher is encountered alone, by a single enquirer, who has the sole benefit of his attentions, and in the sequel reels away dizzy and drunk on the uplift of his words. In a kind of inversion of the ending of the *Hermotimus*, this Lucianic character ends up being compared to someone bitten by a rabid dog, who promptly passes the infection on to yet another victim.[7] And what both old and new convert clearly want is simply to sit at the feet of the master, so as to let his inspiring eloquence wash over them; no more intricate forms of interaction are either hinted at or desired.

---

[5] Lucian, *Hermot.* 86.
[6] Lucian, *Nigr.* 2–3: καὶ παρελθὼν εἴσω καταλαμβάνω τὸν μὲν ἐν χερσὶ βιβλίον ἔχοντα, πολλὰς δὲ εἰκόνας παλαιῶν φιλοσόφων ἐν κύκλῳ κειμένας. προὔκειτο δὲ ἐν μέσῳ καὶ πινάκιόν τισι τῶν ἀπὸ γεωμετρίας σχημάτων καταγεγραμμένον καὶ σφαῖρα καλάμου πρὸς τὸ τοῦ παντὸς μίμημα ὡς ἐδόκει πεποιημένη. σφόδρα οὖν με φιλοφρόνως ἀσπασάμενος ἠρώτα ὅ τι πράττοιμι. κἀγὼ πάντα διηγησάμην αὐτῷ, καὶ δῆτα ἐν μέρει καὶ αὐτὸς ἠξίουν εἰδέναι ὅ τι τε πράττοι καὶ εἰ αὖθις αὐτῷ ἐγνωσμένον εἴη στέλλεσθαι τὴν ἐπὶ τῆς Ἑλλάδος. Ὁ δὲ ἀπ' ἀρχῆς ἀρξάμενος, ὦ ἑταῖρε, περὶ τούτων λέγειν καὶ τὴν ἑαυτοῦ γνώμην διηγεῖσθαι τοσαύτην τινά μου λόγων ἀμβροσίαν κατεσκέδασεν, ὥστε καὶ τὰς Σειρῆνας ἐκείνας, εἴ τινες ἄρα ἐγένοντο, καὶ τὰς ἀηδόνας καὶ τὸν Ὁμήρου λωτὸν ἀρχαῖον ἀποδεῖξαι· οὕτω θεσπέσια ἐφθέγξατο. On *Nigrinus*, see D. Clay, 'Lucian of Samosata, Four Philosophical Lives: Nigrinus, Demonax, Peregrinus, Alexander Pseudomantis', *ANRW* 2.36.5 (1992): 3406–50; K. Schlapbach, 'The Logoi of Philosophers in Lucian of Samosata', *CA* 29 (2010) : 250–77; M. B. Trapp, 'Lucianus's *Nigrinus* and the Anxieties of Philosophical Communication', in *International Symposium on Lucianus of Samosata, 17-19 October 2008*, ed. M. Cevik (Adiyaman: Adiyaman Universitesi, 2009), 113–24.
[7] Lucian, *Nigr.* 37–38.

At all events, we need to look elsewhere for accounts of what was expected to go on when the door of the second-century philosophical classroom was open, the teacher himself not disabled by over-indulgence, and a regular class of pupils was in attendance. Two documents that might seem – and have indeed often been taken – to offer particularly detailed accounts of classroom procedures, both of them texts in which an admired and charismatic instructor is recalled by a former pupil, are Arrian's account of the discourses of the Stoic Epictetus, of which four books survive from an original eight, and the recollections of the Platonist Calvenus Taurus distributed at intervals by Aulus Gellius through his *Noctes Atticae (Attic Nights)*.[8] In the former we find ourselves ushered into a provincial, but celebrated classroom on the northwest coast of Greece in the decades between 95 and 135 CE;[9] the latter takes us to the old homeland of philosophy, Athens, in the mid-to-late 140s.

It is worth pausing briefly here to underline at the outset an important shared characteristic of these two bodies of evidence because it is at least a shade more troublesome than might initially be supposed: both of the philosophers they present are mediated figures. Although no one who has written on these matters is in any doubt that we see Taurus through the selective and warmly reminiscent gaze of the middle-aged Gellius, looking back on his student youth, it is surprisingly common to speak of Epictetus in other terms, as a self-standing figure owing little or nothing to Arrian's presentation of him. The very fact that translations tend to announce themselves as translations of Epictetus, not of Arrian's *Discourses of Epictetus* or the like,[10] speaks volumes. Philosophical commentators – Dobbin and Long are the star recent examples – want a genuine, unmediated Stoic to grapple with and admire, and correspondingly play down Arrian's contribution, relying in part on the prefatory epistle attached to the *Discourses* in which he characterizes them as a set of private notes not originally intended for publication.[11] But Arrian and his writerly ambitions may not be as easily effaceable as that. The prefatory epistle, to begin with, is probably not composed by Arrian himself, and on any authorship is most plausibly read as an attempt to steer reader reactions to the text, rather than a dispassionate factual account of its origins.[12] And in any case, quite apart from the prefatory letter, why should we take Arrian's Epictetus as unmediated and unspun reporting when no-one would think to do the same for Arrian's model in this venture, Xenophon's Socrates in the

---

[8] Arrian and Gellius's accounts are both exploited by M. L. Clarke in his discussion of the philosopher's classroom in Chapter 3 of Clarke, *Higher Education in the Ancient World* (London: Routledge, 1971). For Arrian's Epictetus, see also P. A. Brunt, 'From Epictetus to Arrian', *Athenaeum* 55 (1977): 19–48; P. A. Stadter, *Arrian of Nicomedia* (Chapel Hill: University of North Carolina Press, 1980), 19–31; R. Dobbin, *Epictetus. Discourses, Book 1* (Oxford: Oxford University Press, 1998); and A. A. Long, *Epictetus, A Stoic and Socratic Guide to Life* (Oxford: Oxford University Press, 2002). For Gellius's depiction of Taurus, see also J. Dillon, *The Middle Platonists* (London: Duckworth, 1977), 237–47; L. Holford-Strevens, *Aulis Gellius* (London: Duckworth, 1988), 66–71.
[9] Long, *Epictetus*, 10–12; Dobbin, *Epictetus*, xi–viv.
[10] E.g. the Everyman translation, revised from Elizabeth Carter's version by Robin Hard: Epictetus, *The Discourses: The Handbook, Fragments* (London: Dent, 1995). Or the Penguin Classic by Robert Dobbin: Epictetus, *Discourses and Selected Writings* (London: Penguin, 2008).
[11] Long, *Epictetus*, 38–43; cf. Dobbin, *Epictetus*, xx–xxiii.
[12] Cf. T. Wirth, 'Arrians Errinerungen an Epiktet', *Museum Helveticum* 24 (1967): 148–61.

Memorabilia?¹³ This may seem to be a point that is more important for assessing the content of Epictetus's thought and his persuasive strategies than his value as evidence for the basic details of classroom routine, but I shall suggest later on that it has a little more bite than that.

Let us begin, then, with Gellius's Taurus, in the Athens of the 140s CE. As is often observed, although he looks (in Gellius's lens at least) like the leading Platonist in town at this time, it is as a private instructor, a καθηγητής,¹⁴ that he operates, not as a head of institution in the style that had been current previously in fourth-century and Hellenistic Athens, and was due to return in later antiquity with the Neo-Platonists. Indeed, it seems that at this period there was no Platonic Academy – just the old gymnasium without a school, and in its place a scatter of individual Platonists like Taurus.¹⁵ He teaches, to all appearances, at his own modest home address – like Hermotimus's Stoic, indeed – receiving his pupils at relatively set times, and for something like a set programme, but as we shall see with some flexibility and fringe activity as well.

Unsurprisingly, reading and exposition of classic philosophical texts seems to have a central place in Taurus's didactic routines. *Noctes* 17.20 tells of an instructive exchange arising out of a reading of the *Symposium*:

> The *Symposium* of Plato was being read before the philosopher Taurus. Those words of Pausanias in which, taking his turn among the banqueters, he eulogizes love, I admired so much that I even resolved to commit them to memory. And the words, if I remember rightly, are as follows: 'Every action is of this nature: in and of itself, when done, it is neither good nor bad; for example, what we are now doing, drinking, or singing, or arguing. Not one of these things is in itself good, but it may become so by the way in which it is done. Well and rightly done, it becomes a good action; wrongly done, it becomes shameful. It is the same with love; for not all love is honourable or worthy of raise, but only that which leads us to love worthily.'
>
> When these words had been read, thereupon Taurus said to me: 'Ho! you young rhetorician' – for so he used to call me in the beginning, when I was first admitted to his class, supposing that I had come to Athens only to work up eloquence – 'do you see this syllogism, full of meaning, brilliant,

---

¹³ The case for supposing a high degree of creative authorial input from Arrian was made most fully by Wirth, 'Arrians'. Long's response (*Epictetus*, 40–1, cf. 64) is perfunctory and confused. (He speaks, oddly, of 'the gist [sic]' of Arrian's record being 'completely [sic] authentic to Epictetus' own style and language' – how can a 'gist' be '*completely* authentic'?) Dobbin, *Epictetus*, xxi, simply appeals to 'the majority of scholars' in rejecting Wirth in favour of something more like H. W. F. Stellwag's contention (*Epictetus: Het Eerste Boek der Diatriben* [Amsterdam: H. J. Paris, 1933]) that Epictetus himself is effectively the author. Stadter, *Arrian*, 26, opts for a middle position, but without exploring the detail of how this might work out.

¹⁴ For the figure of the καθηγητής and his importance in the history of philosophical teaching in the Hellenistic and Roman periods, see J. Glucker, *Antiochus and the Late Academy* (Göttingen: Vandenhoeck & Ruprecht, 1978), 127–34.

¹⁵ Dillon, *Middle Platonists*, 239; Glucker, *Antiochus*, 142–3.

well rounded and constructed in brief and smooth numbers with a kind of symmetrical turn? Can you quote us so apt and so melodiously formed a passage from the works of your rhetoricians? But yet I advise you to look upon this rhythm as an incidental feature; for one must penetrate to the inmost depths of Plato's mind and feel the weight and dignity of his subject matter, not be diverted to the charm of his diction or the grace of his expression.'[16]

The passage is worth quoting at some length because there are a number of features in it that will claim our attention again later. For the moment, its importance is the glimpse it gives of a reading out loud (it is implied by someone other than Taurus) interspersed by comments from the master, which may at least sometimes be personalised to a particular member of the group, rather than being a more abstract, impersonal progress through points calling for comment. (It also, incidentally, offers a nice sidelight on the old issue of the ongoing 'conflict' between philosophy and rhetoric, suggesting that this could at least sometimes work itself out in relatively good-humoured classroom banter, rather than anything more vitriolic or pointed.)

Noctes 19.6 again has Taurus and Gellius reading a text together (it is not clear how many others, if any, are also present), but this time it is the pupil who takes the lead in raising an issue:

> In the *Problems* of the philosopher Aristotle is the following passage: 'Why do men who are ashamed turn red and those who fear grow pale; although these emotions are similar? Because the blood of those who feel shame flows from the heart to all parts of the body, and therefore comes to the surface; but the blood of those who fear rushes to the heart, and consequently leaves all the other parts of the body.'
>
> When I had read this at Athens with our friend Taurus and had asked him what he thought about that reason which had been assigned, he answered: 'He has told us properly and truly what happens when the blood is diffused or concentrated, but he has not told us why this takes place. For the question

---

[16] Symposium Platonis apud philosophum Taurum legebatur. Verba illa Pausaniae inter convivas amorem vice sua laudantis, ea verba ita prorsum amavimus, ut meminisse etiam studuerimus. [3] Sunt adeo, quae meminimus, verba haec πᾶσα γὰρ πρᾶξις ὧδε ἔχει· αὐτὴ ἐφ' αὑτῆς πραττομένη οὔτε καλὴ οὔτε αἰσχρά· οἷον ὃ νῦν ἡμεῖς ποιοῦμεν, ἢ πίνειν ἢ ᾄδειν ἢ διαλέγεσθαι. οὐκ ἔστι τούτων αὐτὸ καθ' αὑτὸ καλὸν οὐδέν, ἀλλ' ἐν τῇ πράξει, ὡς ἂν πραχθῇ, τοιοῦτον ἀπέβη· καλῶς μὲν γὰρ πραττόμενον καὶ ὀρθῶς καλὸν γίγνεται, μὴ ὀρθῶς δὲ αἰσχρόν· οὕτω δὴ καὶ τὸ ἐρᾶν, καὶ ὁ ἔρως οὐ πᾶς ἐστὶν καλὸς οὐδὲ ἄξιος ἐγκωμιάζεσθαι, ἀλλ' ὁ καλῶς προτρέπων ἐρᾶν.
[4] Haec verba ubi lecta sunt, atque ibi Taurus mihi 'heus' inquit 'tu, rhetorisce', – sic enim me in principio recens in diatribam acceptum appellitabat existimans eloquentiae unius extundendae gratia Athenas venisse – 'videsne' inquit 'enthymema crebrum et coruscum et convexum brevibusque et rotundis numeris cum quadam aequabili circumactione devinctum? [5] habesne nobis dicere in libris rhetorum vestrorum tam apte tamque modulate compositam orationem? sed hos' inquit 'tamen numeros censeo videas ὁδοῦ πάρεργον. [6] Ad ipsa enim Platonis penetralia ipsarumque rerum pondera et dignitates pergendum est, non ad vocularum eius amoenitatem nec ad verborum venustates deversitandum'.

may still be asked why it is that shame diffuses the blood and fear contracts it, when shame is a kind of fear and is defined by the philosophers as 'the fear of just censure'. For they say: αἰσχύνη ἐστὶν φόβος δικαίου ψόγου.[17]

We thus have at least one piece of evidence for some kind of text reading and exegesis, extending over Aristotle as well as Plato. Elsewhere, in *Noctes* 7.14, Gellius also mentions a commentary by Taurus on Plato's *Gorgias*, and although the explicit reference is to a written text ('has bequeathed to us in written form', *scriptas reliquit*, he says) it is perhaps safe to assume that Taurus's oral performance in class sometimes took this more systematic form of exposition.

The sense of a larger didactic routine comes across from *Noctes* 1.26:

> I once asked Taurus in his lecture room whether a wise man got angry. For after his daily *lectiones* he often gave everyone the opportunity of asking whatever questions he wished. On this occasion he first discussed the disease or passion of anger seriously and at length, setting forth what is to be found in the books of the ancients and in his own commentaries; then, turning to me who had asked the question, he said: 'This is what I think about getting angry, but it will not be out of place for you to hear also the opinion of our fellow Platonist Plutarch, a man of great learning and wisdom...'[18]

The word *lectiones* here is worth underlining, since it tells us that the main fixed point of Taurus's instruction was indeed the reading and exposition of classic texts, rather than independent discourse from his own chosen starting points. But the picture given here of the daily routine also signals the regular availability of a change of gear, from essentially one-way exposition to question and answer. In this case, Gellius's question seems to be one from general curiosity, rather than necessarily arising out of the preceding exposition; and Taurus's answer involves both going over authoritative written materials (the classics and their commentators) and adding anecdotal matter from his own experience.

But profitable interaction, with Taurus still on duty as a philosopher, even if not in full didactic mode, can be seen happening in less formal settings too. *Noctes* 2.2 shows us Taurus receiving a distinguished visitor – the provincial governor of Crete – and

---

[17] In *Problematis* Aristotelis philosophi ita scriptum est: διὰ τί οἱ μὲν αἰσχυνόμενοι ἐρυθριῶσιν, οἱ δὲ φοβούμενοι ὠχριῶσιν, παραπλησίων τῶν παθῶν ὄντων; ὅτι τῶν μὲν αἰσχυνομένων διαχεῖται τὸ αἷμα ἐκ τῆς καρδίας εἰς ἅπαντα τὰ μέρη τοῦ σώματος, ὥστε ἐπιπολάζειν· τοῖς δὲ φοβηθεῖσιν συντρέχει εἰς τὴν καρδίαν, ὥστε ἐκλείπειν ἐκ τῶν ἄλλων μερῶν. [2] Hoc ego Athenis cum Tauro nostro legissem percontatusque essem quid de ratione ista reddita sentiret, 'Dixit quidem', inquit, 'probe et vere quid accideret diffuso sanguine aut contracto, sed cur ita fieret non dixit. [3] Adhuc enim quaeri potest quam ob causam pudor sanguinem diffundat, timor contrahat, cum sit pudor species timoris atque ita definiatur: "timor iustae reprehensionis". Ita enim philosophi definiunt: αἰσχύνη ἐστὶν φόβος δικαίου ψόγου.'

[18] Interrogavi in diatriba Taurum, an sapiens irasceretur. [2] Dabat enim saepe post cotidianas lectiones quaerendi quod quis vellet potestatem. [3] Is cum graviter, copiose de morbo affectuve irae disseruisset, quae et in veterum libris et in ipsius commentariis exposita sunt, convertit ad me, qui interrogaveram, et: 'haec ego' inquit 'super irascendo sentio; sed, quid et Plutarchus noster, vir doctissimus ac prudentissimus, senserit, non ab re est, ut id quoque audias...'

discussing with him the proper balance of honours and obligations between fathers and sons. He does this, Gellius says, when he had just dismissed his pupils (*sectatores*, regular attenders) and was sitting outside his bedchamber chatting with Gellius and a few others. A few special associates, it seems, remain behind when the bulk of the class have gone. The philosopher can now be interrupted by a social call, but is always likely to turn even that conversation in an improving direction. In the same way, when members of the inner circle are invited to dinner with the master, they are expected to bring suitable topics of dinner time conversation with them: nothing too heavy, but profitable all the same. So, at *Noctes* 7.13:

> This custom was practised and observed at Athens by those who were on intimate terms with the philosopher Taurus; when he invited us to his home, in order that we might not come wholly tax-free, as the saying is, and without a contribution, we brought to the simple meal, not dainty foods, but ingenious topics for discussion. Accordingly, each one of us came with a question which he had thought up and prepared, and when the eating ended, conversation began. The questions, however, were neither weighty nor serious, but certain neat but trifling ἐνθυμημάτια, or problems, which would pique a mind enlivened with wine; for instance, the examples of playful subtlety which I shall quote.
>
> The question was asked, when a dying man died – when he was already in the grasp of death, or while he still lived? And when did a rising man rise – when he was already standing, or while he was still seated? And when did one who was learning an art become an artist – when he already was one, or when he was still learning? For whichever answer you make, your statement will be absurd and laughable, and it will seem much more absurd, if you say that it is in either case, or in neither.
>
> But when some declared that all these questions were pointless and idle sophisms, Taurus said: 'Do not despise such problems, as if they were mere trifling. The most respected thinkers have investigated this subject in all seriousness...'[19]

Similarly, *Noctes* 17.8 finds Taurus and his guests, at his instigation, discussing why oil congeals in cold surroundings more readily than wine does. The world

---

[19] Factitatum observatumque hoc Athenis est ab his qui erant philosopho Tauro iunctiores; [2] cum domum suam nos vocaret, ne omnino, ut dicitur, immunes et asymboli veniremus, coniectabamus ad cenulam non cuppedias ciborum, sed argutias quaestionum. [3] Unusquisque igitur nostrum commentus paratusque ibat quod quaereret, eratque initium loquendi edundi finis. [4] Quaerebantur autem non gravia nec reverenda, sed ἐνθυμημάτια quaedam lepida et minuta et florentem vino animum lacessentia, quale hoc ferme est subtilitatis ludicrae, quod dicam. [5] Quaesitum est quando moriens moreretur? cum iam in morte esset, an cum etiamtum in vita foret; et quando surgens surgeret? cum iam staret, an cum etiamtum sederet; et qui artem disceret, quando artifex fieret? cum iam esset, an cum etiamtum non esset. [6] Utrum enim horum dices, absurde atque ridicule dixeris, multoque absurdius videbitur, si aut utrumque esse dicas aut neutrum. [7] Sed ea omnia cum captiones esse quidam futtiles atque inanes dicerent, 'Nolite', inquit Taurus, 'haec quasi nugarum aliquem ludum aspernari. Gravissimi philosophorum super hac re serio quaesiverunt'.

described by Gellius here joins hands – no doubt quite intentionally – with that of Plutarch's *Table Talk* (*Quaestiones convivales*), with the same understanding that philosophical talk of the appropriate kind could and should be fostered in informal, convivial settings as well as in the classroom.[20] A final illustration, stretching the range of possible venues still further, would be *Noctes* 12.5: on the way to see the Pythian Games at Delphi, Taurus and his entourage stop off at Lebadia to visit a Stoic friend of his, who is suffering from a painful stomach complaint. The walk back from this man's house to the waiting carriages after the visit provides the space for an earnest discussion of the Stoic theory of *dolor*, fuelled by a question from 'a young man from among Taurus's pupils who was no slouch in his grasp of philosophical doctrine' (*in disciplinis philosophiae non ignavus*).

Through this whole range of forms of interaction, philosophical texts are clearly central; it is in the authoritative works of the classic thinkers that the answers are to be found, and through commentaries that these answers are to be clarified and expounded. In the passages already surveyed, we have encountered Taurus's own commentary on the *Gorgias*, and his own and others' commentaries on unspecified earlier works taking up the topic of anger, plus the possibility (though not the certainty) of commentaries on the *Symposium* and Aristotle's *Problems*. From other sources (Philoponus, the *Suda*, Iamblichus) we know of a further commentary, on the *Timaeus*, and a work on the differences between Plato and Aristotle.[21] The perceived authority and efficacy of classic writing is also acknowledged when in *Noctes* 20.4, Taurus attempts to wean one of his rich pupils away from an excessive enthusiasm for actors and musicians by sending him a well-chosen excerpt from Aristotle's *Problems in the Curriculum* ('Ἐγκύκλια Προβλήματα').[22] But we have also seen – in the passage relating to the *Symposium* that I flagged earlier – an alertness to a possible problem with at least some of these written authorities: the problem of inappropriate modes of reading. Taurus invites Gellius, as a rhetorical connoisseur, to admire the stylistic elegance of Plato's writing, but warns him that he should not be diverted away by this from the real point, which is the depth of Plato's thought about the subject matter in hand. In a similar vein, he is also found in *Noctes* 1.9.8–10 expostulating at the frivolity of novices who think they can pick their starting places in philosophy according to personal taste, on the basis of an enthusiasm for such purple passages as the drunken entry of Alcibiades in the *Symposium*, or the speech of Lysias in the *Phaedrus*. Classic texts – particularly those with a high literary finish – can seduce the unwary into the wrong sort of reading, and into missing the point even as one thinks one is actually engaging with the author. And some people come to philosophical texts with just the sort of training that makes it easy for them to fall into this snare.

---

[20] *Quaest. conv.* 1.1, 612e-615c: εἰ δεῖ φιλοσοφεῖν παρὰ πότον, 'Whether philosophy is a fitting topic for conversation at a drinking-party'; cf. F. Klotz and K. Oikonomopoulou, eds., *The Philosopher's Banquet: Plutarch's* Table Talk *in the Intellectual Culture of the Roman Empire* (Oxford: Oxford University Press, 2011).

[21] Philoponus, *De aeternitate mundi*, 520.20-23 Rabe; Iamblichus, *De anima, ap.* Stob. 1.378.25ff. Wachsmuth; Suda T 166.

[22] Fr. 209 Rose = *Problem.* 956b.

Gellius records what he does in the *Noctes* as an admirer of Taurus, but avowedly not a full insider: although he participates in a wide range of activities, and is entirely at ease on a social level, he is not one of the *sectatores*, the regular pupils, and can be teased albeit affectionately by Taurus as a moonlighting rhetorician. And Taurus himself is just one of a much larger group of contacts and mentors on whom Gellius looks back. When we move from this to Arrian's account of Epictetus, there is an obvious contrast. Even though Arrian edits himself out of the picture entirely as participant, we get both a more thoroughgoing focus on the voice of the philosopher, and more of a sense of immersion in the world of the committed pupil – even though there is evidently plenty of space for temporary visitors as well as long-term habitués. In Long's appreciative formulation, Arrian's account gives us 'the best record we have of a professional Stoic teacher's (or indeed any ancient professor's) advisory sessions with his students, covering their life in and outside the school, and ranging over consolidation and interpretation of Stoic theory, students' urgent need to rethink their intellectual and everyday priorities, exemplification of what their training is designed to equip them for, and much more'.[23] Strong words, though it is as well to note straightaway, for later reference, that Long here speaks of 'a professional Stoic's *advisory* sessions', not of the whole range of his didactic activities.

With Epictetus, then, we are no longer in the Athens of the 140s CE, but across on the other side of the Greek mainland, some thirty to forty years earlier, say around 110 CE, in the port of Nicopolis in Epirus. The city had been founded by Octavian (Augustus) in celebration of his victory at the Battle of Actium, and by this stage, some century and a half later, it was a major administrative and commercial centre, well connected both westwards to Italy and eastwards to the rest of Greece. It is plausibly conjectured that Epictetus, former slave and former pupil of the Rome-based Stoic Musonius Rufus, set up here as a teacher when the Emperor Domitian expelled philosophers from the capital in the first half of the 90s CE.[24] Whether, like Taurus, he taught in a part of his own home, or rented a separate schoolroom, we do not know; just as we do not know, but have to guess, that he supported himself on an income deriving from a substantial stable of regular, long-term pupils. But it is on the other hand abundantly clear from Arrian's record that, quite apart from the regular pupils, some at least of this teacher's sessions were open as well to more casual, shorter-term visitors, dropping in with a particular issue to consult over, or simply wishing to expose themselves to a celebrated authority's bracing words. In *Discourses* 3.9.14 Epictetus imagines a hypothetical visitor saying, 'We're passing through, and while we charter our ship, we can have a look at Epictetus too; let's see what he has to say', but then departing afterwards with the words 'Epictetus was rubbish – bad grammar and bad Greek'. The reference to passing through, and to chartering a ship, remind us of how Epictetus's location in Nicopolis must have facilitated this kind of casual, walk-in trade. But we can also look to *Discourses* 2.14, which hangs on a visit from a well-connected Roman who 'comes in with his son' and, as he is listening to a single

---

[23] Long, *Epictetus*, 48.
[24] Brunt, 'From Epictetus'; F. G. B. Millar, 'Epictetus and the Imperial Court', *JRS* 55 (1965): 141–8; Stadter, *Arrian*, 19–20.

anagnôsma, is disconcerted when Epictetus falls silent with the words 'This is how I teach'. '*Anagnôsma*', like '*lectiones*' with Taurus, seems to indicate exposition of some classic philosophical text; but the main message, explicated in the remainder of the discourse, is that Epictetus, pointedly sensitive to the capacities of his audience of the moment, breaks off something that would normally have gone on longer, on the grounds that a casual lay visitor, lacking expert appreciation, will not understand the detail of what a professional at work is doing, and will simply be bored by it.

Peter Brunt's 1977 *Athenaeum* article 'From Epictetus to Arrian', from which I have borrowed these two examples, constructs a list of a dozen and more such casual visitors who are identified by name, or by official status, or both (*correctores, praefecti annonae*, and the like). Brunt also neatly corrals and catalogues the hard evidence in the *Discourses* for what one would in any case have been tempted to assume about the profile of the longer-term students, as opposed to the incidental visitors. They emerge as mainly young adults, for the most part not natives of Nicopolis, but foreigners residing there precisely for their education, and financially comfortable enough to have had nursemaid and tutors and to have been on sightseeing tours of Greece, and to be looking forward to careers in public life. In contemporary social terms, these are definitely members of the class of *honestiores*, not that of the *humiliores*. A neat illustration, one of many that might be used, is provided by *Discourse* 2.16 ('That we fail to practise the application of our judgements about good and evil'), in which the familiar experiences that Epictetus appeals to in his efforts to connect with his audience include education in oratory, attending musical recitals, practising incubation in temples, having nursemaids, frequenting gymnasia and baths, going on sea voyages, and visiting Athens – a set which cumulatively, even if not individually, indicates a decidedly comfortably social level.

It is not, of course, any part of the main purpose of the *Discourses* to give us this information about the clientèle. It simply comes up incidentally to the main purpose, which is to highlight the distinctive didactic style, methods and central message of their chief character, Epictetus. Perhaps more surprisingly, the same is also true of large parts of the day-to-day procedures of this teacher's classroom. The real focus of the *Discourses* is on three things. First, on the priority Epictetus assigns to the need to achieve autonomy by freeing of oneself from the external tyranny of false impressions, with all the effort and rigorous self-scrutiny that this demands.[25] Secondly, on the 'Socratic' teaching strategy, so well and admiringly studied by Long, which seeks to pick up each interlocutor individually from where they are, find the barb that will stick in them, and challenge them to undertake their own improvement.[26] And thirdly – something perhaps not so well studied so far – the *Discourses* concentrate consistently on reproducing (or should that be 'on creating'?) Epictetus's distinctively challenging – aggressively frank – tone of voice, blended as it is from a whole series of interlocking stylistic choices.[27] In this frame, giving a clear picture of what a whole day, or a whole

---

[25] Long, *Epictetus*, 27–31 and 207–30.
[26] Long, *Epictetus*, 67–96.
[27] Namely, the choices for which 'diatribe' used to be the accepted stylistic/generic label – exclamation and abrupt apostrophe, everyday and even 'coarse' or 'low' analogies and images, calling-out of imagined interlocutors, and so on. Standard general discussions of 'diatribe' style and its principal

week or month, studying with Epictetus will have been like in its mundane, routine detail, is not a priority. We may still be able to use the *Discourses* to build up such a picture, but this will involve more than a little reading against the grain.

As I have already suggested, I think Arrian's role in determining this very partial and particular focus should not be underestimated. At the very least, it is his selection from the totality of what passed between Epictetus and his pupils and other interlocutors that brings this about. But I think in fact we should go further, and credit Arrian with a greater degree of creativity than is involved in mere selection of what to transcribe. It might in the end be too much to say that the Epictetus of the *Discourses* is simply a character of Arrian's creation, but thinking about them in this way might still be an effective heuristic tool (just as it is good at least some of the time to think of the Socrates of the Platonic dialogues – or of Xenophon's *Socratica* – as a fictional Platonic or Xenophontic creation).

But what is it that even Arrian's selective vision allows us to glimpse of the bread and butter of Epictetus's classroom? Not perhaps after all quite as much, in some respects, as we might have been hoping for, or as much as that line from Long about 'the best record we have' might at first hearing lead us to expect.

Classic Stoic texts must have been read, just as we have seen classic Platonic texts being read with Taurus. The bare fact seems guaranteed by the regular references to the authority, and even in some cases to specific works, of Chrysippus, Zeno, Cleanthes, Antipater, and others, and in general terms to the activity of reading them. This is not experience that Epictetus's pupils can have been expected to bring with them on entry; it must have been part of what they received once signed up with him.[28] But there is no explicit acknowledgement of this, or glimpses of any kind of commentator-like activity on Epictetus's part; indeed, the voice of Arrian's character does not obviously sound like a commentator's at all. Did the real Epictetus, one wonders, have two distinct voices, or acts, one for textual study and one for free form exhortation and exchange, and did Arrian select just the one of them for imitation, or what?

Epictetus must also have lectured. In *Discourses* 3.21 and 23 he berates those who lecture 'epideictically', that is, with an eye to showing off their rhetorical fluency and stylistic polish rather than to the real moral enlightenment and improvement of their hearers. The implication that he himself is not like this is unmistakable, and is reinforced by the story about the time-killing visitors who left complaining of Epictetus's bad grammar and bad Greek – these are complaints more suited to

---

components include A. Oltramare, *Les origines de la diatribe romaine* (Lausanne: Payot, 1926), 9–17; W. Capelle, 'Diatribe', *RAC* 3 (1957): 990–7; E. Schmidt 'Diatribai', *Kleine Pauly* 2 (1967): 1577–8, all of which need, however, to be taken together with the demonstrations by H. D. Jocelyn, 'Diatribes and Sermons', *Liverpool Classical Monthly* 7 (1982): 3–7, and A. E. Douglas, 'Form and Content in the *Tusculan Disputations*', in *Cicero the Philosopher*, ed. J. G. F. Powell (Oxford: Oxford University Press, 1995), 197–218, that 'diatribe' has to be understood as a stylistic register rather than a self-standing genre (let alone one with particular connections to Cynicism or Stoicism). In connection specifically with Epictetus, the best discussion is Halbauer, *De diatribis Epicteti* (Leipzig: R. Noske, 1911), 19–36.

[28] This seems to be the implication of Epictetus's words at *Disc.* 1.4.9: being able to read Chrysippus for oneself is held up by an imagined interlocutor as mark of progress (i.e. it is not a novice's capability, most people have to have him read for them). See also 1.4.14, where a teacher(?) is invited to test how well a pupil has read *On Impulse*.

connected, oratorical discourse rather than to conversational style. Or again, in *Discourses* 2.6.23, Epictetus imagines a disappointed student complaining the 'it was not worthwhile for this to have listened so much and written so much and to have sat for so long with an old man of no exceptional worth'. But it is remarkably difficult to find any direct reflection of this lecturing activity in the text of the *Discourses*. Even the long and structured discourse in 3.22, on the nature of the ideal Cynic, is presented as the answer to an enquiry, not a pre-planned element in some course of instruction. ('When one of his pupils, who seemed inclined to the Cynic philosophy, asked him what sort of a man a Cynic should be...Epictetus replied...') And in general each successive element in the collection making up the *Discourses* is cast as a response to an encounter or an enquiry, a miscellaneous remark, or a short self-contained set of reflections (whether or not enlivened by the show of an exchange with an imagined interlocutor); they do not come across as extracts from longer, more formalised addresses, let alone any such thing in its full length. In the light of this it looks well advised of Long to praise the collection for the insight it gives into a philosopher's 'advisory sessions', rather than into the full range of his didactic routines. Against the background provided by Gellius's account of Taurus, the entire performance recorded by Arrian seems to fit best – even if not perfectly – with Taurus's habit, after his *cottidianae lectiones*, of allowing his pupils to ask any questions they wished.[29]

One thing we do however hear something more of – to a degree that takes us away from the pattern set by Gellius's Taurus – is exercises in logic. In a celebrated passage looking back to his own student days in Rome with Musonius Rufus, Epictetus is made to recall how he himself was witheringly reproached for a botched task:

> This is the very thing that I myself said to Rufus, when he reproved me for not finding the single missing step in some syllogism. 'Why', said I, 'have I burned down the Capitol, then?' 'Slave', he answered, 'what was missed out here *is* the Capitol!' (*Discourses* 1.7.32)[30]

And it is evident that in his own instruction Epictetus maintained this emphasis. *Discourses* 1.17.4–12 argue, in good Stoic vein, that logic is foundational to proper understanding, even if not sufficient in itself for a well-lived life (the title 'That Logic is Indispensable' is given by the manuscripts to the whole of 1.17, but this is one case among many where the title – which may well be editorial rather than going all the way back to Arrian – is manifestly appropriate to part of the discourse only, not the whole). *Discourses* 1.7, in which Musonius's remark about the Capitol comes, is more consistently devoted, right through, to the proposition that logic is relevant to morals, and that a skilled acquaintance with 'arguments which have equivocal or hypothetical premises, and those which are developed by questioning' must be acquired by the serious student. In both 2.13.21 and 2.17.27, where Epictetus is addressing individuals implied to have finished their schooling and to be out in the big bad world, 'syllogisms

---

[29] The connection is noted by Halbauer, *De diatribis*, 55.
[30] ἐπεί τοι τοῦτ' αὐτὸ καὶ ἐγὼ Ῥούφῳ εἶπον ἐπιτιμῶντί μοι ὅτι τὸ παραλειπόμενον ἕν ἐν συλλογισμῷ τινι οὐχ εὕρισκον. 'Οὐχ οἷον μέν', φημί, 'εἰ τὸ Καπιτώλιον κατέκαυσα', ὁ δ' 'Ἀνδράποδον', ἔφη, 'ἐνθάδε τὸ παραλειπόμενον Καπιτώλιόν ἐστιν'.

and equivocal arguments' (συλλογισμοὶ καὶ μεταπίπτοντες) are pointedly highlighted as elements of the instruction they ought to look back on. Most concretely of all, 1.26.13 records a specific classroom moment:

> Once, when he had thrown into confusion the student who was reading out the hypothetical arguments, and the man who had set that student to read laughed, Epictetus said, 'You are laughing at yourself; you did not give the young man any preliminary training, nor find out if he is capable of following these arguments, but simply used him as a reader'.[31]

The roles here are not completely transparent, but perhaps what we see is (as Dobbin suggests) a set-up in which there was 'an assistant, perhaps a senior student, who took charge of assigning the readings in logic'.[32] It's also implied that the reading out is in some way an interactive process, in which a student can show greater or lesser grasp of what he is reading, and be interrogated along the way by the master, and that it should standardly be preceded by some kind of preparatory explanation and exercise.

Along with the strong defence of logic, however, and the evidence for the amount of time and effort given to it in Epictetus's immediate environment, there is also an emphasis on its ultimately subordinate role. *Discourses* 1.26, from which the case of the misfiring reading exercise comes, begins with the warning that, however important it may be to recognize and acknowledge what follows logically from a hypothesis, it is still more important to acknowledge the 'law of life' that we must do what follows from nature. Logic is a tool, a means to an end, and it is misused, indeed positively dangerous, if mistaken for an end in itself.:

> ...some people are captivated by these very things and remain where they are, one captivated by the style, another by syllogisms, another by arguments with equivocal premises (μεταπίπτοντες again), and another by some other hostelry (πανδοκεῖον) of this kind, and there they remain and moulder away, as though amongst the Sirens. (2.23.41)[33]

Logic is indeed captivating; but for that very reason, it also has to be warned against. We should pause to appreciate the way Epictetus's warning here figures false turns in learning as both listening to Siren voices (with all the suggestions that brings with it), and opting for the pub over more serious and constructive activity.

Nor are logical exercises in fact the only part of the curriculum that hold this kind of danger. Arrian's Epictetus, like Gellius's Taurus, has firm views also on the potential snares in the reading of authoritative texts, indeed rather more firm and more frequently and insistently enunciated. When he refers to the writings of Chrysippus,

---

[31] Ταράξας δὲ τὸν ἀναγιγνώσκοντα τοὺς ὑποθετικοὺς καὶ γελάσαντος τοῦ ὑποθεμένου αὐτῷ τὴν ἀνάγνωσιν Σεαυτοῦ, ἔφη, καταγελᾷς· οὐ προεγύμνασας τὸν νεανίσκον οὐδ' ἔγνως εἰ δύναται τούτοις παρακολουθεῖν, ἀλλ' ὡς ἀναγνώστῃ αὐτῷ χρῇ.

[32] Dobbin, *Epictetus*, 213.

[33] ὑπ' αὐτῶν τινες τούτων ἁλισκόμενοι καταμένουσιν αὐτοῦ, ὁ μὲν ὑπὸ τῆς λέξεως, ὁ δ' ὑπὸ συλλοισμῶν, ὁ δ' ὑπὸ μεταπιπτόντων, ὁ δ' ὑπ' ἄλλου τινὸς τοιούτου πανδοκείου, καὶ προσμείναντες κατασήπονται ὡς παρὰ ταῖς Σειρῆσιν.

Zeno, Cleanthes, Antipater, and others (especially Chrysippus) – references which were mentioned earlier as an indication that text-reading and exegesis were part of the full Epictetan curriculum – he tends to do so with a warning about the folly, indeed the self-defeating perversity, of mistaking mere book-learning and theoretical competence for success in living a virtuous life. *Discourse* 1.4, entitled *On Progress* in the manuscripts (περὶ προκοπῆς), will do as an example pretty much on its own.

> Who is making progress, then? The person who has read many treatises by Chrysippus? Why, does virtue consist in this, in having gathered a thorough knowledge of Chrysippus? For if that is the case, we must agree that progress is nothing other than knowing many works by Chrysippus!... 'This man here', someone says, 'is already able to read Chrysippus, even by himself' – By the gods, that is good progress you are making, man. What progress! 'Why do you make fun of him?' – And why do *you* distract him from an awareness of his deficiencies?... 'Take the treatise *On Impulse*, and see how thoroughly I have read it'. That is not what I am looking for, slave, but how you exercise your impulse to act and not to act...[34]

Compare, for instance, 2.16.34, 2.17.34–35, 2.19.10, 3.2.13–15, or the brief and dismissive sideswipe in 1.29.56, 'books are stuffed with Stoic quibbles (λογάρια)'. Arrian's Epictetus is happy to concede that reading books can do you good (e.g. 3.23.20–21), and that it is good to have your mind well stocked with recollections of them (e.g. 1.25.6), but only if it is done in the right spirit, as means to a practical end, not as end in itself; and on balance, it is the abrasive warnings about the dangers, not the assertions of the value, that stick in the reader's mind.

Like Gellius's record of Calvenus Taurus, Arrian's of Epictetus turns out to give us only a very partial set of glimpses of classroom procedure, more glimpsed *en passant* in the pursuit of other ends than described as an object of attention in itself. In particular, Arrian's keenness to give us an Epictetus constantly concerned to stress the vital importance of keeping book learning and technical expertise firmly subordinate to the business of moral self-improvement has imposed a kind of double filter. It has turned the spotlight away from the more formal and structured aspects of philosophical instruction and towards the philosopher's less structured and more opportunistic interactions with his pupils; and it has if only by default encouraged a perception that the more formal side did not matter so very much, or absorb so very much of the teacher's energy and attention, certainly in Epictetus's case, and perhaps more generally. We are entirely free to doubt how far this is indeed an accurate representation of the real state of affairs.[35]

---

[34] τίς οὖν προκόπτει; ὁ πολλὰς Χρυσίππου συντάξεις ἀνεγνωκώς; μὴ γὰρ ἡ ἀρετὴ τοῦτ' ἔστι Χρύσιππον νενοηκέναι; εἰ γὰρ τοῦτ' ἔστιν, ὁμολογουμένως ἡ προκοπὴ οὐδὲν ἄλλο ἐστὶν ἢ τὸ πολλὰ τῶν Χρυσίππου νοεῖν ... 'οὗτος', φησίν, 'ἤδη καὶ δι' αὑτοῦ δύναται Χρύσιππον ἀναγιγνώσκειν'. εὖ, νὴ τοὺς θεούς, προκόπτεις, ἄνθρωπε· ποίαν προκοπήν. τί ἐμπαίζεις αὐτῷ;' τί δ' ἀπάγεις αὐτὸν τῆς συναισθήσεως τῶν αὑτοῦ κακῶν; ... 'λάβε τὴν περὶ ὁρμῆς σύνταξιν καὶ γνῶθι πῶς αὐτὴν ἀνέγνωκα'. ἀνδράποδον, οὐ τοῦτο ζητῶ, ἀλλὰ πῶς ὁρμᾷς καὶ ἀφορμᾷς...

[35] On this point, cf. Halbauer, *De diatribes*, 56, in the concluding remarks to his study: Iam perspicimus, quid sint quemque locum teneant Epicteti diatribai. Non sunt proprius scholae cursus,

Our hopes of using Taurus and Epictetus to get further into the philosopher's school than either of Lucian's representations – in the *Hermotimus* and the *Nigrinus* – allowed us, have thus only been realized in a very qualified sense. From one point of view this may look like a disappointment, but rather than concluding on that downbeat note, I should like instead to propose a couple of ways in which this situation of continuing exclusion might be viewed more positively.

In the first place, I think it is a gain rather than a loss to be reminded in this quite specific and focused way of the fact – which I have gently been trying to underline throughout – that Epictetus and Taurus are indeed not freestanding historical characters to whom we have independent access, or at least access as close to direct as would be provided by substantial documents from their own hands. To a more considerable degree than some students of ancient philosophy might like to think, they are shaped by the authors who record them. Taurus is shaped to suit Gellius's agenda of self-presentation in the *Noctes*, as part of a gallery of past sages and mentors who helped to form him; their remembered eminence and the easy relations he enjoyed with them establish his credentials too as a member of the right sort of club.[36] Epictetus is shaped as a neo-Socrates with a distinctively direct and anti-pretentious personal style in order to meet Arrian's agenda of self-presentation as a Xenophon of the modern world, and also as a master of the different stylistic levels required for the different subject matters of his varied prose output (he can do Socratic philosopher-speak every bit as well as he can do prose historian and technical manual).[37] These are agendas on Arrian's and Gellius's part which allow a degree of representative background detail, which must be broadly faithful to the kinds of context and procedure with which their subjects worked, and they thus furnish us with some kind of overview of classroom modes and procedures. But they are also agendas which encourage some selectivity of vision and emphasis, in which precision, detail, and balance in documenting didactic routines are not high priorities. We ought in short to be reading these accounts more for what they tell us about Gellius's and Arrian's expectations of a philosophical teacher's ethos and impact than for accurate factual information about specific individuals and contexts.

My second concluding positive follows on from the first, to the extent that the emphasis on the potential seductiveness of some standard learning tools – the literary power of Platonic dialogue, the mesmerising possibilities of Stoic technical treatises,

---

non pars eius modi cursus. Immo scholae cursus continetur lectionibus librorum Stoicorum; diatribae autem hunc cursum quasi comitantur, eis utique in rebus morantur, quas Epicteti maximi ponderis esse iudicat, imprimis facultatem ei dant familiariter discipulis utendi benigneque de ipsorum rebus cum eis colloquendi ('We can now see clearly what Epictetus's *Diatribae* are and what place they occupy. They are not the school curriculum proper, nor any part of a curriculum of that kind. On the contrary, the school curriculum consists of readings from Stoic books; the *Diatribae* for their part so to speak accompany this curriculum, dwelling on those topics which Epictetus regards as particularly important, and above all giving him an opportunity for associating with his pupils on friendly terms and talking with them benevolently about their own concerns'). Cf. W. A. Oldfather, ed. and trans., *Epictetus: The Discourses as Reported by Arrian, the Manual, and Fragments* (London: Heinemann, 1925), xiv–xv.

[36] Holford-Strevens, *Aulis Gellius*, Chapters 5–8.
[37] On Arrian's literary ambitions and self-fashioning, see Stadter, *Arrian*, 1, 5, 14, 27–28 and 31, and idem, 'Flavius Arrianus: The New Xenophon', *GRBS* 8 (1967): 155–61.

and of the intricacies of logic – is part of what both these selective presentations choose to highlight. Here too I see a handy reminder of something larger. Worries about the dangers of mis-weighting the importance of technical grasp, and of approaching philosophical texts, and philosophical discourse more generally, in the wrong spirit as reader or hearer, are by no means confined to just these two representations (of Taurus and Epictetus), and are indeed more pervasive in the latter than I have so far been letting on. Besides worrying about logical exercises and the reading of classic Stoic texts, Arrian's Epictetus also inveighs against both the producers of oral discourse – lectures – who care more for stylistic finish, large audiences and applause than for the beneficial moral impact of their words, and against listeners who are likewise on the lookout for, and apt to applaud, the style rather than the substance, and thus deflect or sidestep that same moral medicine:

> Men, the lecture-room of the philosopher is a hospital; you ought not to walk out of it in pleasure, but in pain. For you are not well when you come; one man has a dislocated shoulder, another an abscess, another a fistula, another a headache. And then am I to sit down and recite to you dainty little notions and clever little mottoes, so that you will go out with words of praise on your lips, one man carrying away his shoulder just as it was when he came in, another his head in the same state, another his fistula, another his abscess? And so it's for this, is it, that young men are to travel from home, and leave their parents, their friends, their relatives, and their bit of property, merely to cry 'Bravo!' as you recite your clever little mottoes? Was this what Socrates used to do, or Zeno, or Cleanthes? (*Discourses* 3.23.30–32)[38]

In all this I see a telling reminder of the position of philosophy and of philosophical engagement in the Hellenistic and Roman periods, as it is, if not torn, at least stretched between different aspects of its identity: between, on the one hand, its role as the 'art of life', fundamentally oriented towards moral self-improvement and defiantly away from the allegiances of conventional social life and values, and on the other hand its institutionalization as a body of knowledge, technical procedures and canonical literature; and again, as an element in an essentially rhetorical – or 'oratorical' – culture that has both to use crafted prose as a vehicle and to try to ensure that the attraction of the vehicle does not deflect attention too far from what it is carrying.[39] Against this background, the warnings that Plato's stylistic elegance should not be a reason for neglecting his meaning, that it is missing the point to want to start your reading of Plato with the arrival of the drunken Alcibiades at Agathon's party, that there is nothing to boast of in merely having read reams of Chrysippus, or in knowing one

---

[38] ἰατρεῖόν ἐστιν, ἄνδρες, τὸ τοῦ φιλοσόφου σχολεῖον· οὐ δεῖ ἡσθέντας ἐξελθεῖν, ἀλλ' ἀλγήσαντας. ἔρχεσθε γὰρ οὐχ ὑγιεῖς, ἀλλ' ὁ μὲν ὦμον ἐκβεβληκώς, ὁ δ' ἀπόστημα ἔχων, ὁ δὲ σύριγγα, ὁ δὲ κεφαλαλγῶν. εἶτ' ἐγὼ καθίσας ὑμῖν λέγω νοημάτια καὶ ἐπιφωνημάτια, ἵν' ὑμεῖς ἐπαινέσαντές με ἐξέλθητε, ὁ μὲν τὸν ὦμον ἐκφέρων οἷον εἰσήνεγκεν, ὁ δὲ τὴν κεφαλὴν ὡσαύτως ἔχουσαν, ὁ δὲ τὴν σύριγγα, ὁ δὲ τὸ ἀπόστημα; εἶτα τούτου ἕνεκα ἀποδημήσωσιν ἄνθρωποι νεώτεροι καὶ τοὺς γονεῖς τοὺς αὑτῶν ἀπολίπωσιν καὶ τοὺς φίλους καὶ τοὺς συγγενεῖς καὶ τὸ κτησίδιον, ἵνα σοι 'οὐὰ' φῶσιν ἐπιφωνημάτια λέγοντι; τοῦτο Σωκράτης ἐποίει, τοῦτο Ζήνων, τοῦτο Κλεάνθης;

[39] Cf. M. B. Trapp, *Philosophy in the Roman Empire* (Aldershot: Ashgate, 2007), Chapters 1 and 9.

end of a fallacious argument from another, ring true to the period and to the perceived predicament of the philosophy that both Arrian's Epictetus and Gellius's Taurus are represented as professing. Certainly in this respect Gellius and Arrian give us a real sense of the professional problematics of their age, even if they sidestep the task of filling in the mundane procedural detail.

8

The Lone Genius and the Docile Literati: How Bookish Were Paul's Churches?

Jonathan D. H. Norton

In several of his letters Paul makes extensive reference to the Jewish scriptures in Greek. Commentators have long recognized that such reference is neither incidental nor merely decorative. Paul is evidently an erudite interpreter of the Jewish writings, highly trained in the skills of first-century Jewish exegesis. Moreover, it is evident that Paul's interpretation of Jewish scripture profoundly informs what he thinks and what he writes. These observations found a widely held intuition: gaining insight into Paul's exegesis enhances understanding of his thought.[1] Naturally this has implications for Paul's *readership*. That is, Paul's ideal reader must be sufficiently erudite to cope with the complexity and subtlety of Paul's exegesis. Such a reader must not only be well versed in the sacred writings Paul interprets but also skilled enough to parse the exegetical methods Paul employs. Anyone lacking the requisite erudition could not hope to follow Paul's exegetical manoeuvres or, consequently, his *arguments*.

This assessment of Paul's ideal reader did not raise any eyebrows through most of the twentieth century. Indeed, it was assumed without further ado. After all, serious students of Paul's exegesis were generally university professors pursuing academic theology and biblical studies. These academics – to whom the eyebrows belonged – generally considered themselves worthy readers of Paul. If some of the earliest readers found Paul's letters hard to understand (2 Pet. 3:16), modern interpreters have taken

---

[1] Thus, Hanson could declare his interest 'in divining Paul's mind on the subject of Scripture', A. T. Hanson, *Studies in Paul's Technique and Theology* (Grand Rapids: Eerdmans, 1974), 183, and Richard B. Hays could state his confidence that literary-critical study of Paul's reference to scripture 'can disclose important elements of Paul's thought that have been left unexplored by other critical methods', Richard B. Hays, *Echoes of Scripture in the Letters of Paul* (New Haven: Yale University Press, 1989), xii.

a certain 'donnish'[2] delight in possessing the learning and skill to engage the subtleties of Paul's exegetical 'genius'.[3] It is above all for this reason that, prior to 1989, critics had not given serious consideration to the question of how Paul's *first* audiences were supposed to follow his exegetical procedures.

Richard Hays' 1989 monograph, *Echoes of Scripture in the Letters of Paul*, was the first to make Paul's *original* audiences an overt factor in analysis of Paul's exegesis. And yet, as I argue in this essay, Hays' famous study has left a generation of commentators with the unfortunate impression that Paul's early Christian audiences can be (indeed *need* to be) credited with the exegetical skills of modern biblical critics. While some commentators have offered historical arguments against this widespread conflation, they tend to accept the same assumption: that audiences with insufficient literary and exegetical skill could not properly grasp Paul's arguments. I shall argue that both sides of the argument are predicated on a particular – and questionable – idea of how Paul's communication with his audiences worked. That is, we habitually treat each of Paul's letters as though it were a kind of monologic lecture by means of which Paul, an active expositor, seeks to convey his own complex exegetical ideas – which he has developed in private – to passive auditors. This model means that, to follow Paul's argument, his audiences must exhibit an historically very unlikely combination of advanced literacy (rote familiarity with the content of large swathes of text), on the one hand, and doctrinal blankness (an earnest desire for Paul to *provide them* with convictions about the meaning of those texts), on the other. I shall argue that this is not only historically unlikely in a general sense but also conflicts with the impression New Testament texts give about the communal nature of early Christian exegetical activity. I suggest that many of the exegetical manoeuvres we like to attribute to Paul's own coinage actually belong to a shared stock of early Christian exegesis, upon which Paul drew precisely because many Christians were already familiar with it through Christian preaching and ethical instruction. While most early Christians were illiterate, they had joined a movement with an overt ethos of exegetical aspiration. Rather than envisaging a lone genius dispensing his own arcane literary riddles to strangely docile literati, then, we should envisage Paul engaging with his audiences in widely shared exegetical conversations. We should also take into account the social and educational differentiation within early Christian groups that this ethos will have entailed.

Echoes of Audience in the Letters of Paul

Richard Hays' *Echoes of Scripture in the Letters of Paul* was the first enquiry into Paul's exegesis to make the *original* audiences an overt factor in analysis. In stark contrast with previous enquiries into Paul's use of scripture, the frequency with which Paul's

---

[2] See Leslie Houlden's observation on the study of Paul: 'It is a donnish conceit to want scriptural writers to be plainly of the dons' club, or a relic of older doctrines of inspiration'. 'Review of Heikki Räisänen's Paul and the Law', *Theology* 87 (1984): 384.

[3] Heikki Räisänen, *Paul and the Law*, 2nd ed. (Tübingen: Mohr Siebeck 1987), 1–15, notes commentators' desire to discover the genius of Paul's thinking.

'reader(s)' or 'audience(s)' appear in this monograph is striking. Why did Paul's audiences make their debut in this particular monograph? It was precisely Hays' commitment to a literary-critical method that explains the ground-breaking intrusion of *audience* at this moment. One might say, of course, that by the late 1980s it was only a matter of time before the question of audience should figure in a study of Paul's exegesis. After all, scholars had since the 1970s shown increasing interest in Paul's historical audiences.[4] But in fact this trend had hardly encroached into the sub-discipline devoted to Paul's use of scripture. Indeed, Hays stated that, while he was broadly *indebted* to such historical-critical developments in New Testament studies, his own concern was to apply *literary*-critical methods to the study of Paul's use of scripture.[5] Hays sought to apply the category of 'intertextual echo' developed by literary critics.[6] Such critics avoid recourse to 'real author' or 'real audience', concentrating instead on the literary effects *within* texts.[7] Accordingly Hays proposed a way of 'reading the letters as literary texts shaped by complex intertextual relations with scripture',[8] that is, 'a style of interpretation that focuses neither on the poet's psyche nor on the historical presuppositions of poetic allusions but on their rhetorical and semantic effects'.[9] Hays stated his awareness that we encounter the 'ideal reader' of Paul's letters primarily as an hypothetical construction of the text itself. It was, then, Hays' commitment to literary criticism that ushered the concept of 'the reader' into the discourse concerned with Paul's exegesis.

Yet, although Hays duly acknowledges that the 'reader' is a literary-critical construct, his study effectively conflates this 'reader' with Paul's historical audiences.[10] 'The task of this book', says Hays in his opening pages, 'is to retrace some of Paul's readings, seeking to grasp their novelty and to follow the intricate hermeneutical paths along which he led his readers'.[11] Hays asks whether his own perception of a biblical 'intertextual echo' in Paul's writing can reveal anything about Paul's authorial intent or whether Paul's 'original readers' (at Philippi, for instance) 'would have perceived the intertextual trope'.[12] Initially, Hays' answer is framed cautiously in terms of implied

---

[4] E.g., Gerd Theissen, *The Social Setting of Pauline Christianity: Essays on Corinth* (Philadelphia: Fortress, 1982); Karl P. Donfried, *The Romans Debate*, rev. ed. (Edinburgh: T. & T. Clark, 1991); Wayne A. Meeks, *The First Urban Christians: The Social World of the Apostle Paul* (New Haven: Yale University Press, 1983); John M. G. Barclay, 'Mirror-Reading a Polemical Letter: Galatians as a Test Case', *JSNT* 31 (1987): 73–93.
[5] 'To the trained eye, my debt to historical-critical scholarship is evident on every page. Nonetheless, I employ, for heuristic purposes, a set of analytical instruments different from those traditionally employed by Pauline scholars', Hays, *Echoes*, xi.
[6] Ibid., 15. Hays drew particularly on Harold Bloom's *Anxiety of Influence* (New York: Oxford University Press, 1973), and John Hollander's *The Figure of Echo: A Mode of Allusion in Milton and After* (Berkley: University of California Press, 1984).
[7] Hollander's 'concern is neither to investigate 'problems of actual or putative audience' nor to specuu late on the poet's 'degree of self-awareness, of conscious design' in echoing an earlier text' (ibid., 19).
[8] Ibid., xi.
[9] Ibid., 19.
[10] See nn. 20–2 below and also Christopher D. Stanley, *Arguing with Scripture: The Rhetoric of Quotations in the Letters of Paul* (London: T&T Clark, 2004), 38–9, 47.
[11] Hays, *Echoes*, 5.
[12] Ibid., 26; similarly, p. 25.

audience: 'Since Paul's audience is known to us only hypothetically, it is hard to speak confidently about their capacity to recognize Paul's evocations of scriptural language'.[13] Nevertheless, Hays has a stake in equating the abilities of implied and historical audiences as closely as possible, since 'claims about intertextual meaning effects are strongest where it can credibly be demonstrated that they occur within the literary structure of the text and that they can plausibly be ascribed to the intention of the author and the competence of the original readers'.[14] Hays' literary-critical project serves his interest in showing that Paul meant his *historical* audiences to detect the same intertextual effects that Hays does.[15]

To an extent there is justification for such an aspiration to social historical insights. As Hays rightly says, 'we know Paul and his original readers primarily as characters in these literary texts, but what we learn about them as the implied author and implied readers can inform our reconstructions of the history behind the texts, though that is not the goal of this book'.[16] This is reasonable. Indeed, much of the historical work we do in the field of New Testament studies is only possible because we infer things about the past from the people implied in texts. But, as subsequent critics have insisted, the process must be tempered with considerable care. The problem is that, although Hays declared that such specific historical work 'is not the goal of this book', his study then proceeds as though it *were* in fact based on such an historical foundation. Yet in lieu of any historical groundwork Hays offers only a (famous) preliminary disclaimer: 'If I, having learned something about Paul's historical circumstances and having read the same Scripture that Paul lived in so deeply, discern in his language echoes of that Scripture, it is not improbable that I am overhearing the same echoes that he and his earliest readers might have been able to hear'.[17] This is as close as Hays gets to any discussion of historical method. How 'probable' it might be that a modern academic experience of Paul's texts should resemble an early Christian one is a serious question which should not be brushed over with superficial ease. Nevertheless, the rest of the monograph – and the prolific industry[18] of echo-hunting which the monograph has inspired – is founded on this casual intuition. Since 'the implied readers of these letters appear to be primarily Gentile Christians with an extensive knowledge of the LXX and an urgent interest in its interpretation',[19] Hays' study proceeds as though Paul's historical audiences really did fit this description.

---

[13] Ibid., 29.
[14] Ibid., 28.
[15] Hays states this a number of times, e.g.: ibid., xii, 9–10, 18, 21, 28, 31.
[16] Ibid., 29.
[17] Ibid.
[18] Matthew Scott, *The Hermeneutics of Christological Psalmody in Paul: An Intertextual Enquiry*, SNTSMS 158 (Cambridge: Cambridge University Press, 2014), 2 and Paul Foster, 'Echoes without Resonance: Critiquing Aspects of Recent Scholarly Trends in the Study of the Jewish Scripture in the New Testament', *JSNT* 38 (2015): 96–111, describe the quest for echoes as an 'industry' and also as 'a mechanical production line' (Foster, 'Echoes', 99). Now see Hays' citation (*Echoes*, 65) of Harold Bloom concerning 'the wearisome industry of source-hunting, of allusion-counting' (*Anxiety*, 31).
[19] Hays, *Echoes*, 29. It is 'not implausible' this characterization fits 'Paul's actual readers' (*Echoes*, 201).

So, despite some judicious notes of methodological caution,[20] *at the level of analysis* Hays' study effectively conflates the exegetical skills of 'the implied reader'[21] with Paul's historical audiences.[22] Indeed, the study ultimately attributes Hays' own exegetical skills to this conflated *ideal reader/historical audience*. To be sure, Hays does occasionally acknowledge that the exegetical skills of the modern critic, the 'ideal reader' and Paul's historical audiences may not be identical.[23] But these infrequent remarks do not alter the presupposition pervading the monograph that Paul wrote letters which *require* erudite audiences to apply themselves to following his exegesis with determination. This presupposition is affirmed by page after page of analysis. Only the 'reader' who properly grasps the subtleties of Paul's exegesis can fully understand Paul's thought and the arguments by means of which Paul develops and expresses that thought.[24] As we shall see, this assumption is repeated again and again in numerous subsequent studies which have taken up Hays' method.

All this means that this seminal monograph achieved something rather peculiar. At the very moment Hays introduced the category of 'Paul's historical audiences' to this sub-discipline, these audiences were credited with a donnishly high level of exegetical acumen. Paul's audiences appeared on the scene as a novel analytical category without prompting any change in the way Paul's exegesis was to be analyzed. Although it was natural for 'the *reader*' to receive an invitation to Hays' literary-critical study, Paul's *historical* audiences slipped in through the door almost unnoticed

---

[20] Initially Hays questions the extent to which the *historical* audiences 'could have grasped' Paul's subtler echoes. A cluster of cautionary statements appears in Chapter 1 (ibid., 25, 26, 30, 32). Occasionally Hays expresses the same caution about the capacity of 'readers' (i.e., *any* 'reader', not specifically Paul's *historical* audiences) to detect very subtle echoes (e.g., pp. 29, 79). But in the main Hays' discussion proceeds as though audiences should detect Paul's subtle references.

[21] Hays' frequent references to 'the reader' blur the distinction between 'implied reader' and Paul's 'historical audiences'. The reader who 'perceives' (or 'hears', 'overhears', 'listens', 'attends carefully to', 'discerns', 'appreciates', 'recognizes', 'follows') the intertextual echoes will be able to 'grasp' Paul's arguments. Numerous examples in ibid., 21-3, 29, 38, 44, 49, 55, 63, 66, 86-8, 90, 95, 107, 127, 112, 115-16, 123, 127-8, 142, 145-8, 151, 153, 165, 167, 175, 177, 191.

[22] Hays often explicitly proposes that Paul expected audiences to follow his exegesis (e.g., ibid., 1, 29, 30, 86, 87, 91, 60, 92, 97, 105). At other times Hays strongly implies this (e.g., pp. 55, 58, 131, 132, 168). Hays often states that Paul expected his audiences to discover their own situation prefigured in scripture (e.g., pp. 55, 58, 60, 97, 105). Hays believes his approach gains validity when the original audiences' perception of Paul's intertextual exegesis 'can credibly be demonstrated' (pp. 26, 28), which requires a 'test, historical in character', 'of what might have been intended and grasped by particular first-century figures' (p. 30).

[23] Hays occasionally suggests that an historical audience's acumen might exceed that of the modern academic who lacks the intuitive immersion in the scriptures that the first Christians enjoyed. For example, we are 'belated roofless readers' (ibid., 43); 'ignorant and unstable belated readers' (p. 123). On the other hand, Hays occasionally acknowledges that his own exegetical acumen and that of the 'ideal reader' likely exceeds the capacities of Paul's historical audiences (see n. 20 above).

[24] This assumption, evident throughout Hays' book, is often stated explicitly. For example: Paul's reference to scripture 'can disclose important elements of Paul's thought that have been left unexplored by other critical methods' (ibid., xii); 'I seek to explore the evidence more carefully and to present an account of the role of Scripture in Paul's thought' (p. 8); 'the question of how Paul read Scripture is of great importance for grasping the logic and purpose of his arguments' (p. 10); Hays wants to know 'how scripture functions within Paul's argument' (p. 126); 'the intertextual echoes often anticipate the subsequent unfoldings of his dialectic, unifying the argument subliminally' (p. 158).

– and yet, once through the door, their presence was instantly unremarkable because scholars outside this sub-discipline had been thinking hard about the first recipients of Paul's letters for over a decade. Without sufficient historical scrutiny, Paul's original audiences were ushered into a sub-discipline on which Hays' book was to have a profound influence.

Equipped with the literary-critical tools Hays provided, a generation of scholars has enthusiastically set out to discover numerous 'intertextual echoes' of the Jewish scriptures embedded within Paul's letters. These echo-hunters often hold that the discovery of new intertextual echoes will further illuminate the theological truth of Paul's letters. This is a perfectly reasonable position to hold within the field of biblical theology in which any part of the corpus may legitimately illuminate the theological qualities of any other part. It is with this in mind, I think, that Paul Foster has described the method as 'a radical form of modern reader-response'.[25] However, Foster's term conveys his criticism of echo-hunters who blur the distinction between intertextual meaning effects that arise within texts, on the one hand, and what Paul and his audiences thought they were talking about, on the other. When the two are blurred, then creative biblical theology can be too easily passed off as social historical work. For instance, with no significant reference to Paul's audiences, N. T. Wright applies Hays' intertextual method extensively in work that purports to be historical.[26] The result is a lively portrait of Paul's thought which weaves together intertextual echoes resonating across several letters sent to different communities, but which no single historical audience could have inferred from they letter that they received.

Although many commentators have discussed Hays' *Echoes* over the past thirty years, I have discussed the book at some length here for three reasons. First, since the present volume bridges three subject areas – classical, Jewish, and Early Christian studies – I hope that this survey will be helpful to readers not particularly acquainted with New Testament debates about the 'Haysian' intertextual method.[27] Second, within New Testament studies Hays is famous for introducing the category of the 'intertextual echo' to the study of Paul's exegesis. It is not usually observed, however, that Hays effectively introduced the category of historical *audience* into the sub-discipline. From a social-historical perspective, I consider this to be the aspect of Hays' *Echoes* which has had the most profound but also the most unfortunate impact on the study of Paul's exegesis: *Echoes* introduced the complex question of audience while in the same stroke *appearing to* dispense with the social-historical complexities of that question, but only through a superficial equation of historical audience, implied reader, and modern critic.

---

[25] Foster, 'Echoes', 109 (cf. 96, 107).
[26] To take one of many examples, Wright discovers 'echoes' of Ezek. 36:20 in Paul's citation of Isa. 52:5 (Rom. 2:24) which informs Wright about what was going on in 'Paul's mind' more clearly than anything Paul says explicitly. The words 'echoes' and 'adumbrates' recall Hays' distinctive language in *Echoes*. N. T. Wright, *Paul and the Faithfulness of God* (London: SPCK, 2013), 810–15. Wright's reading of Romans is very creative. But I think it owes more to the almost infinite web of intertextual insinuations that Wright assembles than anything that can be attributed to Paul with any confidence.
[27] On 'Haysian method', see Foster, 'Echoes', 108.

'Familiarity' with Scripture

In the same year that Hays' *Echoes* introduced Paul's audiences into discussion of Paul's exegesis, William A. Harris demonstrated that levels of literacy were very low in the Roman Empire.[28] Harry Y. Gamble's 1994 study of literacy among early Christians reached similar conclusions.[29] These low estimations of literacy quickly gave rise to doubts about both the ability of Paul's audiences to follow the intricacies of his exegesis and, consequently, the likelihood that Paul expected them to. In large part, the debate has concerned the extent to which illiterate people could be sufficiently *well-acquainted with* the sizeable range of Jewish texts Paul routinely interprets in his letters.

Most prominently Christopher D. Stanley has called for historical correctives.[30] First, he warns against complacent conflation of the ideal reader with Paul's first-century audiences. If they discuss the matter at all, Haysian scholars tend to attribute early Christian audiences with extensive knowledge of Jewish scriptures and the skill to follow Paul's complex exegetical manoeuvres. On historical grounds, however, Stanley insists that the demographic of Paul's audiences would generally lack the immersion in Judaism, the education, the literacy, and the access to scrolls to have been able to follow Paul's exegesis properly. Against common Haysian assumptions Stanley insists that Paul's audiences could not 'routinely supply for themselves the background and context of Paul's many quotations, allusions, and other references to the Jewish Scripture'[31] and 'would have been incapable of recognizing and appreciating his many unmarked references', that is, 'allusions' and 'echoes'.[32]

Second, Stanley emphasizes that the historical audiences were not homogenous.[33] While some early Christians were literate and educated in the Jewish literary heritage (acumen which probably earned them leadership positions),[34] most cannot have been. The early Christians to whom Paul wrote were largely urban traders and artisans inhabiting the *poleis* of Asia Minor, Greece, and Italy. Members came neither from the most destitute strata of society nor from elite equestrian or senatorial ranks where advanced literacy was the norm. Non-Jews in this period, even those with an interest in Judaism, tended to be ignorant of the literary contents of the Jewish

---

[28] William A. Harris, *Ancient Literacy* (Cambridge, MA: Harvard University Press, 1989).
[29] Harry Y. Gamble, *Books and Readers in the Early Church: A History of Early Christian Texts* (New Haven: Yale University Press, 1995), 5: 'We must assume, then, that the large majority of Christians in the early centuries of the church were illiterate, not because they were unique but because they were in this respect typical'.
[30] Stanley, *Arguing*; idem, '"Pearls Before Swine": Did Paul's Audiences Understand His Biblical Citations?', *NovT* 41 (1999): 124–44; idem, 'The Social Environment of "Free" Biblical Quotations in the New Testament', in *Early Christian Interpretation of the Scriptures of Israel*, ed. C. A. Evans and J. A. Sanders (Sheffield: Sheffield Academic, 1997), 18–27; idem, 'The Rhetoric of Quotations: An Essay in Method', 44–58, in the same volume.
[31] Stanley, 'Pearls', 133–8; followed by Christopher M. Tuckett, 'Paul, Scripture and Ethics: Some Reflections', *NTS* 46 (2000): 403–24.
[32] Stanley, 'Pearls', 139.
[33] This may respond to Tuckett, 'Paul', 410.
[34] 'In a community in which texts had a constitutive importance and only a few persons were literate, it was inevitable that those who were able to explicate texts would acquire authority for that reason alone' (Gamble, *Books*, 9–10).

scriptures.³⁵ Most members of Paul's assemblies were non-Jews. So 'while there may have been individuals in Paul's churches (mostly educated Jews and an occasional educated Gentile) who were capable of appreciating these references, most of Paul's allusions and echoes (along with his unmarked citations) would have gone unnoticed by the bulk of his first-century audience'.³⁶ We should 'assume no more audience knowledge of Scripture than would be required to make minimal sense of Paul's explicit biblical quotations'.³⁷

In response to these historical concerns about the 'author-centred' approach to studying Paul's exegesis, Stanley has developed a 'reader-centred', rhetorical approach, set out most fully in his 2004 monograph.³⁸ Stanley emphasizes that interpretation of scripture was one of Paul's rhetorical tools – that is, a means by which Paul sought to *affect* audiences (not merely a means by which to work out some 'truth' for himself in a detached piece of theological writing). Stanley has sought to show that Paul generally pitched his interpretations of scripture at the competence level he judged the majority of his audiences to possess. Thus many of Paul's 'competent' readers – those with a fair 'familiarity' with some of the key biblical narratives – would have got the gist of Paul's exegetical points. The 'minimal' readers would sometimes get the gist, too, but would often have been unable to follow Paul's scripture-based arguments. Only the 'informed' audience – those with literary and exegetical skills as advanced as Paul's – would grasp the full complexity and significance of Paul's exegesis (although in some cases their erudition might allow them to perceive exegetical weaknesses in Paul's interpretations, especially when Paul had pitched such interpretations at a merely competent audience, or when Paul forced his exegesis to meet the more compelling interpretations of rivals).³⁹ In offering these nuanced arguments Stanley has shone a welcome light onto a neglected question – how Paul meant his appeals to scripture to affect the people he was actually writing to. But one thing is important to note: Stanley's scale of hearer competence ultimately *affirms* the same pre-supposition that runs through Hays' *Echoes*: that is, full appreciation of Paul's exegesis is reserved for those who know their scripture.

Like most studies in the Haysian tradition, Ross Wagner's 2002 monograph focuses primarily on '*Paul's* reading' and 'not, in most cases, on what the first hearers of Paul's letter might have picked up' from Paul's intertextual references.⁴⁰ Nevertheless, taking seriously Stanley's historical concerns about literacy, Wagner concludes his first chapter with a discussion of how he thinks Paul meant the Roman audience to engage with his use of intertextual references.⁴¹ Although Wagner acknowledges that Paul's

---

[35] Menahem Stern, ed., *Greek and Latin Authors on Jews and Judaism*, 3 vols. (Jerusalem: Israel Academy of Sciences and Humanities, 1974–84); Louis H. Feldman, *Jew and Gentile in the Ancient World* (Princeton: Princeton University Press, 1993).
[36] Stanley, 'Pearls', 132–3.
[37] Ibid., 136.
[38] Stanley, *Arguing*.
[39] Ibid., 66–8, defines 'informed', 'competent', and 'minimal' audiences. The reactions of these hypothetical audiences to Paul's exegesis are measured against test cases in the Corinthian correspondence (pp. 75–113), Galatians (pp. 114–35), and Romans (pp. 136–70).
[40] J. Ross Wagner, *Heralds of the Good News: Isaiah and Paul 'in Concert' in the Letter to the Romans*, NovTSup 101 (Leiden: Brill, 2002), 18–19 (italics his).
[41] Ibid., 33–9.

largely Gentile audience in Rome 'probably represented *varying degrees* of familiarity with Israel's scriptures and with Jewish interpretive traditions'.[42] Wagner believes that to grasp Paul's exegesis fully, an audience must be sufficiently 'familiar' with the scriptures Paul interprets.[43] So Wagner faces the problem which Hays brushes over and Stanley confronts: the exegetical competence of the *implied* audience of Romans far exceeds what we can reasonably attribute to most of his actual audience.

Wagner's solution is to envisage the house churches in Rome functioning not only as religious meeting places but also as schools for training adult literacy. Accordingly, Paul wrote a letter whose exegetical nuance, he knew, would initially confound most of the recipients in Rome. However, he intended the letter as *a means of* schooling the recipients in exegetical methods. That is, by means of this letter – which was to be frequently 'reread, discussed, or debated' in Rome – Paul was presenting his exegesis as a 'model' for his Roman audience to emulate. In this way, under the tutelage of Christian leaders, illiterate Christians could be schooled to '*acquire* the familiarity with [the] sources necessary to grasp his argument fully' and finally 'become interpreters capable' of following Paul's exegesis.[44] Having sketched how Paul's earliest readers could develop their exegetical competence, Wagner can proceed with his classically Haysian intertextual study of Romans. Wagner's proposal has proved attractive to those enamoured of Hays' intertextual method because it appears to sure up the methodological fudge at the heart of Hays' *Echoes* and answer historical concerns about early Christian literacy levels.[45]

What Kind of Literacy?

The debate hinges on audiences' *familiarity* with scripture. Although Hays,[46] Wagner,[47] Stanley,[48] and others[49] reach diverging conclusions about audiences' actual levels of

---

[42] Ibid., 34 (italics his).
[43] Wagner considers 'familiarity' with the scriptures a prerequisite for an audiences' ability to follow for Paul's arguments. See especially ibid., 37.
[44] Ibid., italics his.
[45] For example, Brian J. Abasciano, 'Diamonds in the Rough: A Reply to Christopher Stanley concerning the Reader Competency of Paul's Original Audiences', *NovT* 49 (2007): 53–183, cites Wagner extensively.
[46] Examples: Paul's 'implied readers' are 'Gentile Christians with an extensive knowledge of the LXX' (Hays, *Echoes*, 29); 'a reader nurtured on the LXX' (p. 21) is 'a reader standing within the same "cave of resonant signification" where Paul stood' (p. 44). Such a 'reader' will be 'able...not only to discern the echo but also to locate the source of the original' (p. 29). 'The reader, signalled by the echoes, is required to grasp together old text and new' (p. 38). 'No reader familiar with the psalter could possibly fail to hear the resonance of the psalm's unquoted verses with the theme of Romans 3' (p. 49). 'This pronouncement is fraught with poignancy for the reader who has already heard the echoes of Psalm 51 in Rom. 3:4' (p. 55). 'Paul's readers presumably knew what he was alluding to' (p. 117). 'Paul assumes his readers' familiarity with the story, on which he comments in an allusive manner' (p. 132).
[47] Wagner, *Heralds*, 37.
[48] Stanley, *Arguing*, often discusses Christian audiences' 'familiarity with (the content of) scripture'; 'knowledge of the biblical text'; 'biblical knowledge'; 'biblical literacy'; and similar appelations. See the numerous examples on pp. 1–4, 29, 31, 38–9, 43, 46–8, 50–7 and throughout.
[49] For example, Abasciano believes Paul expected audiences to: be 'familiar with Scripture' ('Diamonds', 161); have 'knowledge of the Scriptures' (p. 172); 'know Scripture well' (p. 169); possess 'biblical knowledge' (p. 169); be 'well versed in Scripture' (p. 169).

literacy, they share the idea that Paul's audiences would *need* to be 'well acquainted' with key texts *to follow* his exegesis. Some kind of literacy is in view. But what kind?

The envisaged 'familiarity' amounts to rote memorization of Greek text. This text must encompass large parts of those Septuagint books which Paul most frequently interprets, that is, at least: Genesis, Exodus, Deuteronomy, Numbers, Psalms, Isaiah, and the Minor Prophets. This is a bookish kind of literacy. It does not matter whether the text is learned visually by people reading it or aurally by people listening to it. The act of memorization transfers written text to memory.[50] That scholars have an essentially *bookish* notion in mind is shown not only by the common debate about what 'access' early Christians had to 'scrolls',[51] but also commentators' routine supposition that early Christians' 'biblical knowledge' was acquired in a context of school-like education and formal literary study. Following Wagner's portrayal, cited above, Abasciano proposes that mid-first-century Christian congregations ordinarily received 'scriptural training' from 'church leaders' whose 'main function…was to teach the Scriptures'.[52] For Abasciano, book teaching and book learning were baked into the hierarchy of early church offices. These teachers, who 'had significant knowledge of the Scriptures',[53] 'would have studied [Paul's] scriptural allusions and shared their understanding with their Christian community'[54] in a context of 'reading, discussion, or study'.[55] It should be noted that, although Stanley credits most early Christians with only modest levels of 'biblical knowledge',[56] he too imagines that this 'knowledge' *would* be attained through bookish forms of education, amounting to a combination of scripture 'instruction' that Paul had given during his initial missionary tour of a city,[57] group Bible 'study' conducted within house churches after Paul's departure,[58] or 'teaching' received in local synagogues.[59]

The implication, once again, is that early Christians must have a certain amount of text fixed in their minds *in order to* engage with Paul's exegesis. Hays established this image with his famous statement that Paul presupposes 'Gentile Christians with an extensive knowledge of the LXX and an urgent interest in its interpretation'.[60] To follow Paul's exegesis fully, these audiences must know a certain quantity of *lexical content*, more or less by rote, such that they can recognize Paul's references to particular passages, recall the wider literary context, and perceive what Paul has done with the wording at an interpretive level. For example, Abasciano writes: 'Paul would probably have expected his original audiences to (1) be sufficiently familiar with Scripture so as to benefit from his scriptural quotations and allusions, and (2) possess the ability

---

[50] See J. D. H. Norton, *Contours in the Text: Textual Variant in the Writing of Paul, Josephus, and the Yaḥad* (London: T&T Clark, 2011), 25–30.
[51] Stanley, 'Pearls', 126–30; idem, *Arguing*, 41–3; Abasciano, 'Diamonds', 158–60.
[52] Abasciano, 'Diamonds', 168–9.
[53] Ibid., 172.
[54] Ibid., 170.
[55] Ibid., 172.
[56] E.g., Stanley, *Arguing*, 65, 176.
[57] E.g., ibid., 68–9, 75, 91, 114, 135, 141, 175, 178.
[58] E.g., Ibid., 64, 65, 114, 141, 178.
[59] E.g., Ibid., 64, 67, 69, 138.
[60] Hays, *Echoes*, 29.

to reflect on them further in their original contexts if they so chose'.⁶¹ This portrait implies that Paul's audiences committed themselves to a considerable amount of book study, either *prior* to receiving a letter or *in order to* follow a letter they had not yet fully digested. Here we have a picture of early Christians who have learned a vast quantity of raw lexical content and are now eager for Paul to tell them what to make of it. Since they have such an 'urgent interest in its interpretation', they attend to Paul's letter with receptive alertness.

It is important to note the roles into which this portrait casts Paul and his audiences. Paul is cast as an active expositor, his audiences as passive auditors. Commentators typically portray Paul as a lone thinker who developed his convictions – that is, his *Thought*⁶² – through sustained intellectual effort and intensive private reflection on the Jewish scriptures.⁶³ The letters are widely understood to express Paul's own exegetical 'struggle' to reconcile the message of Christ with Israel's scriptures.⁶⁴ As such, the letters are usually read as though Paul were effectively inviting recipients to audit his efforts to set his *own* thoughts in order.⁶⁵ At the same time critics speak as though Paul meant his letters to *instruct* audiences.⁶⁶ Thus, each letter is typically treated as though it were a kind of monologue or lecture by means of which Paul seeks to convey his 'Thought' to an audience. This is particularly how Romans is viewed, since the body of this letter is generally read as Paul's attempt to set out his thought in the form of a coherent and self-contained theological exposition.⁶⁷ Verse-by-verse commentary

---

⁶¹ Abasciano, 'Diamonds', 161.
⁶² See the citations from Hays, *Echoes*, in n. 24 above. Wagner says: 'Romans represents Paul's most explicit reflection on his own mission and its relation to God's promises to Israel' (*Heralds*, 3); 'Romans represents a stage in Paul's thinking about his mission and about the fate of Israel' (p. 3).
⁶³ 'In Paul we encounter a first-century Jewish thinker who, while undergoing a profound disjuncture with his own religious tradition grappled his way through to a vigorous and theologically generative reappropriation of Israel's Scriptures' (Hays, *Echoes*, 2). 'The convictions Paul expresses [in Romans 9–11] have been molded and shaped by his wrestling with Israel's scriptures' (Wagner, *Heralds*, 5). 'Paul's use of the figure of echo reveals the extent to which his thought is permeated and shaped by Israel's scriptures' (Wagner, *Heralds*, 10). Romans 'represent[s] the fruit of many years of deliberate and intense theological reflection' (Wagner, *Heralds*, 3). Paul was a 'Jewish thinker' whose thought is elucidated by attending to his subtle use of scripture (Wright, *Paul*, 611); Paul's 'thinking' (Wright, *Paul*, 613, 616, 617 and often).
⁶⁴ For Hays, Paul 'grapples' (e.g., *Echoes*, 2, 10, 35, 59, 158–9), 'wrestles' (e.g., pp. 14, 64); 'seek[s] to come to terms with' (p. xii) with Israel's scriptures. For Wagner, Paul's 'wrestling with Israel's scriptures' has shaped his convictions (*Heralds*, 4–5). Wright often makes such statements; e.g., Israel's rejection of God's messiah 'is the massive paradox with which Paul is wrestling' (Wright, *Paul*, 1180). So, too, Stanley: Paul 'grappled' with theological problems and 'struggled' and to formulate his arguments (*Arguing*, 144). See also D.-A. Koch, *Die Schrift als Zeuge des Evangeliums: Untersuchungen zur Wendung und zum Verständis der Schrift bei Paulus* (Tübingen: Mohr, 1986), 257–85; Christopher D. Stanley, *Paul and the Language of Scripture* (Cambridge: Cambridge University Press, 1992), 78.
⁶⁵ It is very common to think *both* that Romans is an exposition of Paul's own private reflection *and* that Paul's thought itself develops *as Paul writes the letter*. See, e.g., E. P. Sanders, *Paul, the Law and the Jewish People* (Minneapolis: Fortress, 1983); Räisänen, *Paul*; Hays, *Echoes*, 35; Wagner, *Heralds*, 3.
⁶⁶ Paul 'was writing pastoral letters to fledgling churches, interpreting Scripture…to guide these struggling communities as they sought to understand the implications of the gospel' (Hays, *Echoes*, 5). Paul meant his letter as a teaching tool (a *correspondence course*, as it were) for training the Roman Christians in exegesis (Wagner, *Heralds*, 37).
⁶⁷ In fact, most modern commentary on Romans exhibits a deep tension in this respect. *If* Paul is working out his position as he writes, he can hardly intend the letter to convince others of a position he is still struggling to formulate to his *own* satisfaction, and *vice versa*.

routinely presupposes that Paul depended on audiences' willingness to reflect on his arguments with open-minded patience and expected them to attend to his complex intertextual exegesis with a considerable degree of intellectual commitment.[68]

This portrait (a lone thinker expounding to passive auditors) explains why the debate revolves around a particular question, that is, how *entire* congregations – and thus every *individual* within a congregation – might come to be edified by Paul's exegesis. Once Paul is cast as a lone expositor instructing mutely attentive audiences, it is virtually inevitable that the debate will move in this direction. If Paul wrote to instruct whole congregations, and his audiences accepted that this was their goal in auditing a letter, then the ability of the least literate individuals to follow Paul's exegesis is inevitably a matter of priority for a congregation – the lowest common denominator must be raised to a level of considerable sophistication. This is why commentators debate the existence of widespread programmes of education in first-century churches. It is the only conceivable means by which whole congregations could parse Paul's exegesis with anything like the competence that most modern critics think Paul's writing demands.

It is, of course, *conceivable* that the first-century Christian network was characterized by programmes of scholastic book study. But the notion smacks of anachronism. Acquainting oneself with a text in anticipation of receiving instruction on how to interpret it is familiar to modern university students, who are often asked to read a whole book 'before next week's class'. Such an approach was also familiar to Augustine, who lived in a scholastic community in which broad familiarity with the scriptures was an important prerequisite to the tuition that formed part of his and fellow scholastics' routine.[69] But, as we shall see, the New Testament evidence does not suggest anything comparable. In fact, when exponents of Hays' intertextual method express their certainty that early Christians prioritised the schooling of entire congregations in advanced exegetical discourse, I think these scholars are really only expressing their own conviction that Bible study is an essential aspect of Protestant devotion. The idea that each believer should directly encounter and personally reflect on the biblical text

---

[68] For example, Hays refers to: 'the reader who has attended carefully to the echoes of Scripture' (*Echoes*, 63), 'the reader who recognizes the allusion' (p. 66), 'the reader who follows these echoes' (p. 127), 'the reader who perceives the convergence of metaphorical significations' (p. 146), 'the reader [who] grasps anew the purpose of the veil as metaphor' (p. 147). For Stanley, committed book study is what *equips* Paul's 'informed audience' to parse Paul's exegesis; and this is what the 'competent' and 'minimal' audiences *lack* in proportion to their *inability* to follow Paul's exegesis (see n. 39, above).

[69] Augustine, *Doctr. chr.* 2.9.14. Wagner (*Heralds*, 26–7) cites this passage to claim that Augustine is 'not addressing an elite guild scholars' (p. 27) but 'those with the wit and will to learn' (*Doctr. chr.* preface, 1). But Augustine *does* seem to be addressing people with distinctly scholastic skills, aspirations and leisure, that is, 'earnest students of the word' who read others' books on scripture interpretation in pursuit of their own close exegetical studies (*Doctr. chr.* preface 1); learn other languages, 'if we have the leisure', in order to compare different translations of scripture (*Doctr. chr.* 2.14.21); and 'use their skill to correct' faulty copies of scripture (*Doctr. chr.* 2.14.21). Similarly, William A. Johnson, *Readers and Reading Culture in the High Roman Empire: A Study of Elite Communities* (Oxford: Oxford University Press, 2010), 14–19, points to the scholastic context which explains Augustine's surprise (*Conf.* 6.3.3) that Bishop Ambrose continued reading silently *although* he was aware of the presence of students who expected him to teach them (they expected him to read aloud). Johnson holds that the passage's scholastic context has usually been ignored to draw unwarrantedly *general* conclusions about ancient reading.

is a central tenet of Reformation religion. This is, to be sure, a noble conviction which has played a profound and precious role in the emergence of widespread literacy and education in the modern West. But the question we must pursue is whether the leaders of mid-first-century churches shared the same conviction.

I shall shortly argue that they did not, at least, not in the way Haysian scholars propose. But first a general social-historical observation is in order. According to the common bookish portrait of first-century house churches, sketched above, social activity is conducted *in the service of* scholastic outcomes: Christian congregations receive schooling such that they might engage with their leaders' exegetical discourse at a suitably expert level. On this view, early Christians are understood to have conducted their activities in pursuit of scholastic ends.[70] From a social-historical perspective, this seems back-to-front. Research shows that reading and book culture in the high Roman Empire always served social goals, that is, the negotiation of social relations, the consolidation of status, and the preservation of community values and boundaries. The bookish circles that William A. Johnson has studied comprise 'great men' of equestrian elite. As such, the literary activities of 'tastemakers and gatekeepers', like Pliny, Galen, or Fronto, focus on conserving the exclusive boundaries of elite communities and carefully regulating the extent to which they were permeable, if at all, by persons of lower rank. As Johnson shows, these men trod a fine line between making certain kinds of literary pursuit accessible to those of lower social status while at the same time reserving the highest levels of literary acumen for themselves as the exclusive mark of their own unattainably elite status. Although Pliny and his ilk valued the highest levels of literary acumen, their literary pursuits were never ends in themselves. Rather, these pursuits constituted 'a complex sociocultural construction that is tied, *essentially*, to particular contexts'[71] and, most importantly, *served* the social values embedded in those contexts. Book 'study' was such a fundamentally social activity that, when such men did 'study' alone or read silently, it was only because no *amici* – who as house guests were free to come and go as they pleased – *happened* to be present and participating on a given occasion.[72] Literary activity within these elite circles was never a purely scholastic end in itself but was rather deployed to demark existing distinctions in social status – both within and beyond the exclusive social stratum these men inhabited – and, just as importantly, to indicate kinds of value and behaviour men like Pliny wanted to promote as desirable within their class.[73]

Early Christians inhabited different social strata and had distinct goals. Yet, while the conservation of elite social boundaries was not their concern, the *negotiation* of community boundaries most certainly was their concern, as was the negotiation of community values, and defining relations within and beyond those boundaries. Just as different *kinds* of literary pursuit played distinct roles in Pliny's life, so various kinds of literacy played distinct roles various Christian contexts. New Testament scholars tend

---

[70] Of course, the ultimate goal of early Christians' literary activity was determined by an eschatological religious ideology – the cataclysmic transformation of the world and the transfer of believers to an eternal heavenly state. But in concrete daily terms, scholastic ends determined their social activities.
[71] Johnson, *Readers*, 20; his italics.
[72] E.g., ibid., 50–1.
[73] E.g., ibid., 46–52.

to debate whether or not a very static and undifferentiated model of literacy pertained in first century churches, that is, whether early Christian assemblies functioned as institutions of book learning. Johnson's work shows, however, that we need to distinguish different kinds of literacy, what roles they served in various early Christian contexts, and where Paul's correspondence fits into all this.

The New Testament materials certainly show that different kinds of literary activity served distinct functions in first-century contexts. Some literary events were *exclusive* in the sense that their participants were *by necessity* literary experts who neither expected nor required Christian laity[74] to engage at an expert level. Other kinds of literary events were specifically designed for the edification of whole congregations with particular religious outcomes in mind. It seems to me that the New Testament literature, including Paul's letters, reflect elements of both kinds of literary event. It remains to sketch what kinds of event are reflected, what social purposes they served, and under what circumstances.

Literary Events Reflected in the New Testament

Expert Exegetical Investigations

Within a few years of the crucifixion,[75] some of the earliest followers of Jesus began intensive exegetical activity. This activity might be called 'scribal' in the sense that it can only be conducted by literary experts trained in particular exegetical traditions.[76] As is often noted, examples of such work preserved in New Testament texts resemble the kinds of expert activity evinced in many of the Judaean manuscripts.[77] What can be known about Pharisees and Sadducees, too, indicates that members of these groups developed and maintained particular exegetical traditions. Whoever the earliest Christian exegetes were, they engaged in activities characteristic of other expert literary Jewish groups of the period. My guess is that this work must have been conducted within, and at the behest of, the earliest circles of Christian leadership. It is impossible to say how many of Jesus' earliest followers possessed exegetical expertise. But some within the circle around James in Jerusalem evidently did and he may have numbered among them. A short time later, the leadership in Antioch probably also included such a circle of exegetes.

These exegetical endeavours, which were apparently motivated by principally christological concerns, amount to what I would call a kind of bibliomancy. The exegetes set out to uncover, through close lexical-grammatical investigation, truths encrypted within traditional sacred writings. To be sure, this was no merely hypothetical

---

[74] In the following I use 'lay' and 'laity' to mean early Christian people whose community roles were neither as religious experts nor religious leaders.
[75] C. H. Dodd, *According to the Scriptures: The Sub-Structure of New Testament Theology* (London: Nisbet & Co., 1952), 23; Larry W. Hurtado, *How on Earth did Jesus Become a God? Historical Questions about Earliest Devotion to Jesus* (Grand Rapids: Eerdmans, 2005), 25–30.
[76] With 'scribal' I mean that these early Christian exegetes reveal a high level of literary training, not that they were necessarily professional writers.
[77] See, e.g., George J. Brooke, *Exegesis at Qumran: 4QFlorilegium in its Jewish Context* (Sheffield: Society of Biblical Literature, 1985); Norton, *Contours*, 82–103.

exercise. They sought to make sense of events and experiences they considered urgently important. That they did so through *exegetical* enterprise shows that at least some of them were already trained in literary methods current among Jewish scholastic groups of the day. Within a few short years of Jesus' death, then, a core of recollections circulating among his earliest followers came to be understood in light of key prophetic writings. Recollections were framed exegetically. In part, these exegetes applied common Jewish exegetical traditions to Jesus. For example, traditions relating to an awaited-royal messiah, which are found in sectarian Dead Sea scrolls and 'Enochic' literature written between perhaps 200 BCE and 70 CE, were employed to demonstrate the claim that Jesus was a messianic descendant of David.[78] Other traditions concerning heavenly angelic figures were employed to identify Jesus as a heavenly redeemer now exulted to God's right hand.[79] In part, these early Christian exegetes generated their own exegetical innovations. For example, the discovery of suffering, trial, crucifixion, and resurrection motifs[80] in the Psalms and Isaiah form the basis of the passion narratives found in the four canonical Gospels, the underlying exegetical work for which may have been conducted very early. The distinct infancy narratives found in Matthew and Luke seem to represent the continuation of this kind of exegetical work into the late first century.

Traces of these anonymous Christian exegetes' work (apparently done in the 30s) are preserved in Paul's letters (written in the 50s) and other New Testament texts (written from the late 60s onwards). For example, the early Christian hymn preserved in Paul's letter to the Philippians appears to preserve a very early piece of christological exegesis on Isaiah 45.[81] Early Jewish Christian exegetes, intrigued by a lexical oddity (now preserved) in the Septuagint text of Isa. 45:23, discovered there a reference to Christ which is only visible to exegetes on the lookout for encrypted references to Jesus' divinity. Directing exegetical attention to tiny syntactical or semantic oddities in the received text, and discovering there divine elucidation of contemporary events, is typical of various Jewish exegetical movements in this period.[82] Again, prompted by an oddity in the text, early Christian exegetes discovered a reference to Christ in Psalm 110. This exegetical discovery must have been made early since Paul refers to it in 1 Corinthians 15 and further references appear in later first-century Christian writings.[83] These christological discoveries, which can only be appreciated through

---

[78] See, e.g., William A. Horbury, 'The Messianic Associations of "the Son of Man"', *JSNT* (1986): 503–27; idem, *Jewish Messianism and the Cult of Christ* (London: SCM, 1998); John J. Collins, *The Scepter and the Star: The Messiahs of the Dead Sea Scrolls and Other Ancient Literature* (London: Doubleday, 1995); J. Thomas Hewitt, 'Ancient Messiah Discourse and Paul's Expression ἄχρις οὗ ἔλθῃ τὸ σπέρμα in Galatians 3:19', *NTS* 65 (2019): 398–411.

[79] See John Ashton, *Understanding the Fourth Gospel*, 2nd ed. (Oxford: Oxford University Press, 2007), 281–98, for examples in Jewish literature where the distinction between God and his heavenly messenger are blurred.

[80] These innovations may draw on the martyr cycles of the Maccabean literature.

[81] Hurtado, *How*, 83–107.

[82] For example, the interpretation of Amos 5:26-27 in CD A VII 14–15 (Norton, *Contours*, 91–2).

[83] Citations: Acts 2:34-35; Mk 12:36; Heb. 1:13. Allusions: Mk 14:63; Acts 7:55; Rom. 8:34; Eph. 1:20; Col. 3:1; Heb. 1:3; 8:1; 10:12; 12:2; 1 Pet. 3:22. Dodd, *According*, 34–5; Larry W. Hurtado, *Lord Jesus Christ: Devotion to Jesus in Earliest Christianity* (Grand Rapids: Eerdmans, 2005), 105, 179, 183, 299, 499, 501.

extremely close attention to syntax, are the work of literate people trained in highly specialized Jewish exegetical traditions.

Other christological insights were derived through combining passages drawn from different places in the Jewish literary corpus. An exegetical tradition which associates the 'stone' of Isa. 8:14 and 28:16 with Christ occurs in Rom. 9:33 and then later in 1 Pet. 2:6-8.[84] Another early Christian exegetical tradition associated the 'subjugation' of the Davidic king's 'enemies' in Psalms 8 and 110 with the risen Jesus now identified as God's heavenly messiah. Paul appeals to this traditional composite citation in 1 Corinthians 15, as do later authors.[85] A combination of Gen. 12:3 and 22:18 which identifies Christ as Abraham's 'seed', and which links Christ to the Gentile mission, appears in Gal. 3:8 and Acts 3:25.[86] The combination of these passages by means of key-word and thematic linkage is the work of literate people, and the techniques used belong to a stock of exegetical techniques which the earliest Christian exegetes shared with various expert Jewish groups active in the Hellenistic and Roman periods.

These early investigations were surely group activities. Our evidence for other Jewish groups conducting such exegetical investigations indicate group activity.[87] Just as these activities helped Jewish voluntary associations like the *yaḥad* and the Damascus Covenanters to distinguish themselves along ideological (and therefore social) lines from non-members, so the earliest Christian exegetes also distinguished themselves from other Jewish religious movements. Profoundly important religious convictions were in play for such groups and literacy comprised one of the modes by which they negotiated their boundaries and their relations. This is a negotiation among experts, where literati seek to distinguish themselves from literati by means of common repertoires of exegetical techniques applied to a common stock of Jewish writings. Although they held much literary tradition in common, the significant thing is what Johnson calls the 'sociocultural encumbrance' they placed upon texts.[88] We have already seen that early christological exegesis often involved close attention to lexical minutiae. It also seems to have involved the comparison of variant textual traditions. Early Christian exegetes evidently made use of Septuagint and Hebraising forms of Isaiah.[89] Likewise, the exegetes who composed and edited several *yaḥad* texts made exegetical use of textual variants they found in various text forms, for example, of

---

[84] Dodd, *According*, 41–3; Frank Thielman, 'Paul's View of Israel's Misstep in Rom 9.32–33: Its Origin and Meaning', *NTS* 64 (2018): 362–77.

[85] Psalm 8:4-6 is cited in Heb. 2:6-8 and Ps. 110:1 in Heb. 1:3. Psalms 8:4-6 and 110:1 are cited in several other New Testament books; see Dodd, *According*, 32–5.

[86] Ibid., 43–4. Paul and Luke conflate the passages differently, so they do not appear to be using a testimonium.

[87] Sectarian scrolls indicate group exegetical activities conducted within the *yaḥad* and the Damascus Covenant. See, e.g., Mladen Popović, 'Reading, Writing, and Memorizing Together: Reading Culture in Ancient Judaism and the Dead Sea Scrolls in a Mediterranean Context', *DSD* 24 (2017): 447–70.

[88] Johnson, *Readers*, 190.

[89] The composite citations which Paul inherits and reuses in his letters show that early Christian exegetes combined readings from Septuagint and Hebraising forms of Isaiah. Hosea 13:14 LXX is combined with a Hebraising reading of Isa. 25:8 in 1 Cor. 15. Isaiah 28:16 LXX is combined with a Hebraising reading of Isa. 8:14 in Rom. 9. The early Christian hymn preserved in Phil. 2 relies on the LXX reading of Isa. 45:23, while a traditional identification of Jesus as the suffering servant of Isa. 53, which surfaces in Rom. 5:19, relies on a Hebraising form of Isaiah.

Genesis, Habakkuk, and Amos.[90] This is one of the ways in which groups of religious experts distinguished themselves from the less expert. In similar fashion, when elite Roman literati gathered, they liked to discuss the variant readings they had found because the activity showcased their enviable access to the libraries which housed the copies and elite connections within Rome's highest social circles this access entailed.[91] Of course, the 'sociocultural encumbrance' which religious voluntary associations like the *yaḥad* or the early Christians placed on their texts was quite different from that which Roman statesmen like Galen placed on theirs. What is comparable, however, is that these are sociocultural contexts where the highest levels of expertise are deployed to mark the social boundaries.

The examples of early Christian exegetical work that I have sketched, then, amount to expert literary activity which must have been more or less confined to the educated circles of early Christian leadership. I do not mean to suggest that these exegetical processes were *withheld* from lay members of the earliest Christian groups. I mean only that the earliest christological endeavours were inherently so expert that laity could not easily be involved at the level of exegesis.

Lay Encounters: The Kerygma

So how *did* Christian laity encounter this expert exegesis? The answer is, in the *kerygma*. At some point during the 30s the christological insights gleaned from the earliest Christian exegesis were purposefully distilled into a stock of missionary declarations which could be presented to widening circles of potential converts and lay believers throughout the expanding Christian network. As the *content* of preaching – that is, *what is preached* – the *kerygma* amounted to a core of propositions about Jesus Christ, the outlines of which can be recovered from Paul's letters and Acts:

> Jesus' life, death, and resurrection fulfil ancient Israelite prophecies and inaugurate a new age; as the Christ, he was descended from the line of David; he died 'in accordance with the scriptures' in order to deliver humans from the present evil age; he was buried and then, after three days, he rose from the dead 'in accordance with the scriptures'; he is exulted at the right hand of God as Son of God and as resurrected Lord of both the living and the dead; he will come again as cosmic judge and as the heavenly saviour of all who put their faith in him.[92]

---

[90] See Norton, *Contours*, 82–103, and references to literature there.

[91] E.g., Galen, Cicero, Lucullus, Aulus Gellius, or Fonto. See William A. Johnson, 'Libraries and Reading Culture in the High Empire', in *Ancient Libraries*, ed. J. König, K. Oikonomopoulou, and G. Woolf (Cambridge: Cambridge University Press, 2013), 350–63, and, in the same volume, Fabio Tutrone, 'Libraries and Intellectual Debate in the Late Republic: The Case of the Aristotelian Corpus', 157–9, and Pier L. Tucci, 'Flavian Libraries in the City of Rome', 301.

[92] I have paraphrased C. H. Dodd's classic formulation in *The Apostolic Preaching and its Developments: Three Lectures with an Appendix on Eschatology and History* (London: Hodder & Stoughton, 1936), 17. See also David E. Aune, *The New Testament in Its Literary Environment* (Cambridge: James Clark, 1987), 23–5. Principal passages are Acts 2:14-39; 3:12-26; 4:8-12; 5:29-32; 10:34-43; 13:16-41; Rom. 1:1-4; 1 Cor. 15:3-8; 1 Thess. 1:10; 2:8.

Paul and Acts show that early Christian missionaries presented each element of this *kerygma* as being 'according to the scriptures', that is, in fulfilment of the ancestral Israelite prophetic writings. Early Christian missionaries did not merely offer their audiences reports of events that had taken place in Judaea during the late 20s and early 30s. They made claims about the eschatological significance of these events, explicitly emphasizing that it was an *exegetical* enterprise that established the veracity of their claims. That is, missionaries declared that an inner circle of the early Christian leadership had, through scholastic study, discovered Jesus' divine significance prefigured in Judaism's holy writings. If Paul and Acts are anything to go by, many missionaries also claimed such exegetical expertise themselves. In other words, the *idea* of exegesis was 'on display' *during preaching*. This does not mean, however, that missionaries required audiences to follow exegetical intricacies at the lexical-grammatical level. These displays were designed to *show* that the Christian *kerygma* was rooted in authentic Judaean religious expertise, not to initiate all and sundry into the exegetical arts in which some Christian missionaries specialized.[93]

It is in *this* context that potential converts will have encountered the scriptures in the initial missionary contexts of conversion – in direct association with specific points of the *kerygma*. For most of these Greco-Roman folk, there will not have been a time when they knew these sections of scripture *apart from* the *kerygma*. For example, there will have been no time when they knew the words 'The Lord said to my Lord, Sit thou on my right hand, until I make thine enemies thy footstool' (Ps. 110:1 LXX) but did not know that these words depict God addressing the heavenly Jesus Christ. Words and Christological interpretation went together.

Later, after conversion, lay believers will have continued to encounter extracts of scripture in the context of ethical instruction. In this paraenetic context, Christian leaders and teachers selected scripture passages beyond the specifically christological repertoire of the *kerygma*. For example, the extracts applied paraenetically in 2 Cor. 9:9-10 or 1 Pet. 1:24–2:3 have no obvious christological application. These passages serve as material for ethical instruction aimed at conforming believers' behaviour to the standards of holiness required of the elect at the end of days.

Lay Christians, then, never encountered the Mosaic and prophetic scriptures in a doctrinal vacuum. They encountered extracts from scripture either in the missionary context of christological preaching or in the subsequent context of ethical instruction. There is no indication that book learning was considered an essential part of Christian devotion or a prerequisite for salvation. Yet commentators often assert that lay Christians *did* routinely receive bookish training. Abasciano says that 'the main function of early church leaders was to teach the Scriptures (Acts 6:2, 4;

---

[93] As Heidi Wendt, 'Galatians 3:1 as an Allusion to Textual Prophecy', *JBL* 135 (2016): 369–89, argues, Paul's statement that Christ was prophetically 'forewritten' before the Galatians eyes (Ἰησοῦς Χριστὸς προεγράφη ἐσταυρωμένος) indicates Paul's role as Judaean freelance expert whose authority as Christian missionary derived substantially from his ability to interpret the 'oracles of God' (τὰ λόγια τοῦ θεοῦ, Rom. 3:2) for Gentile congregations. See also Stanley, *Arguing*, 58: 'Paul's facility in interpreting the holy Scriptures would have cast him in the role of a hierophant dispensing the sacred mysteries of God'.

Gal. 6:6; 1 Tim. 3:2; 4:13-16; 5:17; 2 Tim. 3:14-4:3; Heb. 13:7; 1 Pet. 1:24-2:3; 5:1-2)',[94] citing Beale in support, who says that 'we know from Acts and elsewhere in the NT that Jewish and Gentile believers were trained in their new faith on the basis of the OT, the Bible of the early church (e.g. Acts 17:10-12; 18:24-28; 2 Tim 2:2, 15; 3:16-17)'.[95]

As far as I can see, none of these thirteen passages[96] shows that lay Christians received exegetical training or were required to memorise entire texts in preparation for such training. Indeed, these passages show more or less the opposite, that is, that exegetical instruction was aimed at community leaders. The author of Acts assumes that those who engaged in christological exegesis were literate people of comparatively high social standing within their communities. In keeping with Luke's interests, the examples in his narrative reflect missionary contexts. So, Acts 17:10-12 narrates how, after Jewish leaders in Thessalonica had responded badly to Christian preaching:

> The brethren immediately sent Paul and Silas away by night to Beroea; and when they arrived, they went into the synagogue of the Jews (εἰς τὴν συναγωγὴν τῶν Ἰουδαίων). Now these (Jewish people) were more noble-born than those in Thessalonica (οὗτοι δὲ ἦσαν εὐγενέστεροι τῶν ἐν Θεσσαλονίκῃ); they received the word with all eagerness, examining the scriptures daily to see if these things were so (ἀνακρίνοντες τὰς γραφὰς εἰ ἔχοι ταῦτα οὕτως). Many of these (Jews) and (many) Greek women of high standing believed, therefore, and not a few (Greek) men (τῶν Ἑλληνίδων γυναικῶν τῶν εὐσχημόνων καὶ ἀνδρῶν οὐκ ὀλίγοι) (Acts 17:10-12)

The RSV translates εὐγενέστεροι as 'more noble', which implies that they had a more open-minded and commendable attitude. But Luke attributes this capacity for open-mindedness to their social standing and attendant level of education, which allows them to engage in an exegetical investigation that evidently had them pouring over synagogue scrolls for several days. In the same vein Luke observes that, like these 'noble born' Jewish Beroeans, so also the Greeks who 'believed' were 'of high standing' (εὐσχημόνων). When we think of Pliny, Cicero, or Galen – for whom an 'excellent character' is inseparable from key social activities among which literary pursuits are indispensable – then it becomes evident that Luke is simply thinking like an educated Roman: the connection between 'nobleness' of character, high social standing, and literacy is obvious to him.

Luke's assumption that it was literate people of high social standing who engaged in christological exegesis surfaces elsewhere. Acts 18:24-28 recounts how Priscilla and Aquila improved Apollos' partial understanding of the *kerygma*. This 'native Jew of Alexandria', whom Luke describes as 'an eloquent man (ἀνὴρ λόγιος) well

---

[94] Abasciano, 'Diamonds', 169.
[95] G. K. Beale, *The Book of Revelation* (Grand Rapids: Eerdmans, 1999), 83, cited in Abasciano, 'Diamonds', 168-9.
[96] Acts 6:2-4; 17:10-12; 18:24-28; Gal. 6:6; 1 Tim. 3:2; 4:13-16; 5:17-18; 2 Tim. 2:1-2, 14-15; 3:14-4:3; Heb. 13:7; 1 Pet. 1:24-2:3; 5:1-2.

versed in the scriptures (δυνατὸς ὢν ἐν ταῖς γραφαῖς)', is evidently highly educated and (tellingly) comes from the famous North African centre of learning. He is able to address synagogue congregations – suggesting that he moved within Achaian synagogue leadership circles – and publicly conducts intellectual debates (διακατελέγχομαι) with synagogue leaders and Jewish notables, 'showing by the scriptures (ἐπιδεικνὺς διὰ τῶν γραφῶν) that the Christ was Jesus'. Luke presents these events as somewhere between quasi-legal disputations, of the kind that Romans like Pliny and Cicero might pursue in their public careers, and the sort of intellectual investigations that one would expect in a philosophical school. So Luke conceives of these events as inherently erudite.

On the basis of such passages from Acts, Dodd concluded that 'in addition to what is called 'preaching' (κηρύσσειν), early Christian missionaries also employed the method of discussion, in which certain questions were propounded – questions arising unavoidably out of the kerygma – and answers sought by a study of the Old Testament'.[97] The points which Paul raises in his defence before Agrippa and Festus are introduced by the particle εἰ used interrogatively: '*whether* the Christ suffers and *whether* rising from the dead he will proclaim...' (Acts 26:22-23). As Dodd noted, this 'interrogative form is eminently appropriate to a method of teaching which is described by the verb διαλέγεσθαι'. That is, seeking to persuade Jewish leaders in a Thessalonian synagogue, Paul is said to have been '*arguing* with them from the scriptures, *explaining* and *proving* that it was necessary for the Christ to suffer and to rise from the dead' (διελέξατο αὐτοῖς ἀπὸ τῶν γραφῶν, διανοίγων καὶ παρατιθέμενος ὅτι τὸν χριστὸν ἔδει παθεῖν καὶ ἀναστῆναι ἐκ νεκρῶν, Acts 17:2-3). I also note that Luke depicts: the educated synagogue leaders in Beroea eagerly '*investigating* the scriptures daily to see *if* these things were so' (ἀνακρίνοντες τὰς γραφὰς εἰ ἔχοι ταῦτα οὕτως, Acts 17:10-12); Apollos *conducting* public 'enquiries' (διακατελέγχομαι) and exegetical 'demonstrations' (ἐπιδεικνὺς διὰ τῶν γραφῶν, Acts 18:24-28); and Paul '*disputing*' (διελέγετο) in Corinthian synagogues every sabbath (Acts 18:4). That is, Luke's language registers bookish events belonging to quasi-legal contexts and philosophical spheres.

Dodd did not consider what kind of people might principally have comprised the audiences Luke depicts in these missionary narratives. Reason for this, perhaps, is that Luke often describes Christian missionaries addressing 'the Jews' (οἱ Ἰουδαῖοι) in synagogues, a broad ethnic term (that reflects Luke's theological gripe with the Jewish people as a whole and) which can easily be taken to indicate entire congregations, including laity, or even whole communities. Indeed, there is no reason to doubt that entire congregations were *privy* to Christian preaching in the synagogues of Asia Minor and Greece. But Luke evidently assumes that the Christian missionaries' principal task was to persuade the leadership. After all, whatever positions leadership adopted would likely also be adopted by the laity.

---

[97] Dodd, *According*, 17.

Lay Encounters: Ethical Instruction

Of the thirteen passages that Abasciano takes to show that early Christian congregations received exegetical training,[98] two have proved to show that Luke, writing in the 90s, thought the opposite (Acts 17:10-12; 18:24-28). The remaining eleven passages refer to Christian preaching[99] and ethical instruction,[100] not to general exegetical schooling. To be sure, some of these passages refer to ethical instruction using cognates of διδάσκειν[101] (the passages from 1 and 2 Timothy) or κατηχέω (Gal. 6:6).[102] But, as Dodd observed, references to 'teaching' (διδάσκειν) in the New Testament are generally references to ethical instruction.[103] None of these passages suggests that lay Christians received exegetical training or that they were encouraged to memorise Mosaic and prophetic writings by rote in preparation for such training.

Three passages explicitly associate someone's ability to read the scriptures with ethical instruction (*paraenesis*), but none indicates that congregations as a whole were asked to engage in book study. The author of 1 Tim. 4:13-16 depicts Paul asking his deputy, Timothy, to 'attend to reading aloud, to preaching, to teaching' (πρόσεχε τῇ ἀναγνώσει, τῇ παρακλήσει, τῇ διδασκαλίᾳ) in Paul's absence. The RSV reasonably renders πρόσεχε τῇ ἀναγνώσει as 'attend to the public reading *of scripture*', but this 'reading' is explicitly associated with ethical instruction (τῇ παρακλήσει, τῇ διδασκαλίᾳ), not general exegetical training of laity. 2 Timothy 3:14–4:3 similarly envisages a Christian teacher appealing to scripture in the context of ethical instruction ('all scripture is inspired by God and profitable for teaching, for reproof, for correction, and for training in righteousness').[104] The text notes that Timothy is particularly well qualified to ground his ethical instruction in the scriptures because 'from childhood you have been acquainted with the sacred writings (ἱερὰ γράμματα οἶδας) which are able to instruct you for salvation through faith in Christ Jesus (τὰ δυνάμενά σε σοφίσαι εἰς σωτηρίαν διὰ πίστεως τῆς ἐν Χριστῷ Ἰησοῦ)'. The text does not imply that a teacher was expected to train laity in rote book-memorisation or exegetical techniques. Indeed, the emphasis on Timothy's life-long acquaintance with the texts implies that his book learning marks him *off* from the laity with respect to his ability to appeal to sacred writings. 1 Peter 1:24–2:2 appears to

---

[98] See n. 96, above.
[99] Acts 6:2-4 and Heb. 13:7 refer to missionary preaching: Acts 6:4 (τῇ διακονίᾳ τοῦ λόγου) (cf. 6:7, ὁ λόγος τοῦ θεοῦ); Heb. 13:7 (ἐλάλησαν ὑμῖν τὸν λόγον τοῦ θεοῦ).
[100] Galatians 6:6, 1 Pet. 1:24–2:3, and 5:1-2 refer to ethical instruction. The passages from 1 and 2 Timothy refer to a combination of preaching and ethical instruction (1 Tim. 3:2; 4:13-16; 5:17-18; 2 Tim. 2:1-2, 14-15; 3:14–4:3).
[101] 1 Timothy 5:17-18 (οἱ κοπιῶντες ἐν λόγῳ καὶ διδασκαλίᾳ); 3:2 (διδακτικόν); 4:13-16 (πρόσεχε τῇ ἀναγνώσει, τῇ παρακλήσει, τῇ διδασκαλίᾳ...ἔπεχε σεαυτῷ καὶ τῇ διδασκαλίᾳ); 2 Tim 2:1-2 (παράθου... διδάξαι); 3:14–4:3 (διδασκαλίαν...κήρυξον τὸν λόγον...διδαχῇ). 2 Timothy 2:14-15 appeals to leaders to 'avoid disputes' (μὴ λογομαχεῖν) and to 'handle the word of truth properly' (ὀρθοτομοῦντα τὸν λόγον τῆς ἀληθείας). I add that the cognates of διδάσκειν also indicate ethical instruction in Rom. 6:17; 12:7; 15:4; 16:17; 1 Cor. 4:17; 12:28-29; 14:6, 26.
[102] Galatians 6:6 (Κοινωνείτω δὲ ὁ κατηχούμενος τὸν λόγον τῷ κατηχοῦντι ἐν πᾶσιν ἀγαθοῖς).
[103] Dodd, *Apostolic*, 7.
[104] πᾶσα γραφὴ θεόπνευστος καὶ ὠφέλιμος πρὸς διδασκαλίαν, πρὸς ἐλεγμόν, πρὸς ἐπανόρθωσιν, πρὸς παιδείαν τὴν ἐν δικαιοσύνῃ.

offer an example of how a passage from scripture can be used to found ethical instruction. While flesh 'withers like' the 'grass' of Isa. 40:6-8, believers should 'grow up' to salvation like new grass fed by the enduring word of God. The example does not indicate that lay Christians were required to memorise entire texts as part of a programme of exegetical training. I think it more likely that the Christian laity knew this passage in inexchangeable relation to the ethical teaching derived from it in 1 Pet. 40:6-8.

Paul's Audiences

New Testament texts written during the latter half of the first century, then, give a consistent impression that lay Christians encountered passages from the scriptures in the immediate context of preaching and ethical instruction. These texts do not envisage anything like Bible study of the kind known in modern Protestant churches and certainly not the kind of book-learning and exegetical study required of anyone taking a Haysian intertextual approach to Paul's letters. This brings us back to Paul's audiences in the 50s. As we saw above, commentators debate the existence of widespread programmes of adult education in first-century churches because this is the only conceivable means by which whole congregations might come to parse Paul's exegesis. Unlike many modern Protestants, however, neither Paul nor his contemporaries considered improving the literary and exegetical competence of the Christian laity a priority. Their priorities revolved around what we might call eschatological ethics, that is, around maintaining the levels of holiness required for the pending divine judgement in the hope of entering the eternal heavenly life to follow. Unlike some later Christian Gnostic groups, early Christians do not seem to have made a person's salvation contingent on acquiring special knowledge. New Testament texts are remarkably united in asserting that membership of the elect is available to anyone who undertakes certain basic commitments, principally: receiving baptism; publicly confessing exclusive commitment to the one true God through faith in Christ; and maintaining the unnegotiable standard of holiness required of anyone seeking to enter God's heavenly kingdom. The latter principally involved eschewing idolatry and sexual miscreancy.

Paul is clear that he does not expect any believer to attain a particular standard in any sort of expertise, be that in wisdom, spiritual insight, charismatic power, or any other area. Paul famously insists that no skill – or lack thereof – has any bearing on a person's prospects for salvation. 'God has appointed in the church first apostles, second prophets, third teachers (διδασκάλους), then miracle-workers (δυνάμεις), then healers (χαρίσματα ἰαμάτων), helpers (ἀντιλήμψεις), administrators (κυβερνήσεις), speakers in various kinds of tongues (γένη γλωσσῶν). Are all apostles? Are all prophets? Are all teachers? Do all work miracles? Do all possess gifts of healing? Do all speak with tongues? Do all interpret (tongues[105])?' (1 Cor. 12:28-30). The answer is No, and – most importantly – the uneven distribution of these skills and appointments among

[105] That is, 'Do all interpret *utterances spoken in tongues*?'; cf. ἑρμηνεία γλωσσῶν, 1 Cor. 12:10.

his congregants has no bearing on salvation. Presumably no member of Paul's audience could aspire to the first office, apostle, and only some could aspire to the others. What matters is baptism, exclusive commitment to the Jewish God, and maintaining standards of holiness required within the community of Christ. Through baptism 'you *have been* washed, you *have been* sanctified, you *have been* made righteous in the name of the Lord Jesus Christ and in the Spirit of our God' (1 Cor. 6:11), and so, 'if you confess with your lips that Jesus is Lord and believe in your heart that God raised him from the dead, you will be saved' (Rom 10:9). However, those who drop the standard of holiness will infect the holy community with unholiness (like leaven spreads through dough) and may be expelled (1 Cor. 5).

Although many of the skills and appointments which Paul mentions in 1 Corinthians 12 are (what we might consider) extraordinary – such as making or interpreting ecstatic utterances, performing miraculous feats of healing, or discerning among spirits (12:9-10) – others involve more ordinary (ψυχικός) abilities, such as the ability to 'speak with wisdom' (λόγος σοφίας, 12:8), 'speak with knowledge' (λόγος γνώσεως, 12:8), 'teach' (12:28-29), 'lead' or 'administrate' (κυβερνήσεις, 12:28), and 'support' (ἀντιλήμψεις, 12:28). The ability to 'read' could have numbered among the more ordinary abilities in this list and indeed the 'teaching', 'administrating', and 'supporting' in Paul's mind may have involved some level of literacy on the part of some Christians. Paul considers all these abilities – the ordinary and the extraordinary – to be enabled by the Spirit of God (12:7-11), which believers only receive through the baptism which incorporates them into Christ (1 Cor. 6:12-21; Rom. 6). But he does not think that all believers will or should exhibit the same skills. In fact, he is adamant that they will not and should not seek to.

Take knowledge. There are things Paul *knows* which none of his audiences will *know* in this age. As *pneumatikos*, Paul is tutored by the Spirit in a way in which many of the Corinthian congregation are not (1 Cor. 2:10–3:1). Paul has seen the risen Lord, while none of the Corinthians has (1 Cor. 1:7; 9:1; 15:10). Paul has been shown things in the heavens which he cannot tell them (2 Corinthians 12). But they do not need to *know* these things to 'be saved'. They *have been* 'sanctified' (1 Cor. 6:11) and they *are* 'saved' (1 Cor. 15:2) 'from sin' (1 Cor. 15:17, 56-58), as long as they continue to follow Paul's guidance. What they need to do – beyond the sanctifying baptism they have already received – is to 'confess with your lips', 'believe in your heart', and continue to eschew unholy practices. These actions require lay Christians to attend to the christological preaching (*kerygma*) and ethical instruction (*paraenesis*) of leaders, not to undertake exegetical training or book learning.

So Paul requires no minimum standard of intellectual or charismatic competence from his believers. Indeed, when *some* Corinthian believers challenge Paul on intellectual and philosophical grounds, Paul moves to *curtail* their intellectual activities in order to bring them back under his authority and safeguard their place in the holy community. These challenges evidently come from people holding a relatively high social and educational status within the Corinthian congregation, those from among the few 'noble-born' (1 Cor. 1:26) who, among other things, denigrate Paul's philosophical and rhetorical abilities, and justify on philosophical grounds behaviours or beliefs which Paul considers antithetical to life 'in Christ'.[106] These critics, who seem to be leaders of factions hardening within the Corinthian church, have apparently compared Paul's intellectual abilities unfavourably with those of Apollos, an apostle known for his learning and erudition.[107] In response Paul insists that, as *pneumatikoi*, he and Apollos are united and that their insights have divine origin, whereas Paul's detractors are factious *psychikoi* squabbling over the irrelevant trappings of mundane education. Paul draws this section of the letter to a close saying: 'I have applied all this to myself and Apollos for your benefit, brothers, so that you may learn by us what "not beyond what is written" means, that none of you may be puffed up in favour of one against another' (1 Cor. 4:6). Apparently certain factious Corinthian leaders (claiming to share in the exegetical kudos they attribute to Apollos, their adopted apostle) are confronting Paul with their own biblical exegesis. Paul's rebuke seeks to put them firmly in their place: neither Paul nor Apollos will have any truck with this factionalism; *Paul* is their father in Christ and *Paul* will interpret the scriptures for them; they are not to bother him with their own sloppy counter-exegesis.[108]

Lone Genius and Docile Literati? A Proposed Revision

According to the common 'bookish' portrait of first-century Christian education, church leaders made sure that their congregations were sufficiently 'familiar' with Jewish writings to follow Paul's exegesis. But the kind of 'familiarity' commentators usually envisage is an historically implausible combination of advanced literacy and doctrinal blankness. The evidence I have reviewed suggests that, for the majority of Gentile Christians in Paul's audiences, 'what the scriptures say' amounted to what had been presented to them during preaching and paraenesis. Lay believers were *not* usually familiar with extensive tracts of literature, but they *were* confident about the meaning of the passages which had been interpreted for them during preaching and paraenesis.[109]

The implausibility of the common picture is only highlighted when we consider Paul's letter to the Romans. This letter is the most densely exegetical of Paul's surviving writings. It is widely held that this Gentile audience, most of whom Paul had neither converted nor taught,[110] would have required sustained schooling in order to follow

---

[106] For instance, some are justifying their participation in idol feasts on philosophical grounds in 1 Cor. 8:1-11. Gordon G. Fee, *The First Epistle to the Corinthians* (Grand Rapids: Eerdmans, 1987). Some are appealing to Aristotelian physics to deny that terrestrial bodies may enter the celestial realm in 15:1-58. So Jeffrey R. Asher, *Polarity and Change in 1 Corinthians 15: A Study of Metaphysics, Rhetoric, and Resurrection* (Tübingen: Mohr Siebeck, 2000).

[107] See Fee, *Corinthians*, e.g., 8–10, 49, 56–7, 121–3.

[108] This reading of 1 Cor. 4:6 follows that of Tuckett, 'Paul', who was modifying suggestions by J. Ross Wagner, '"Not Beyond the Things which are Written": A Call to Boast only in the Lord (1 Cor 4.6)', *NTS* 44 (1998): 279–87, and Morna D. Hooker, '"Beyond the Things Which Are Written": An Examination of 1 Cor. IV.6', *NTS* 10 (1963): 127–32. Wendt, 'Galatians', 389, hints at a similar reading of 1 Cor. 4:6, although with no reference to Tuckett.

[109] Pace Hays' famous statement (*Echoes*, 29) that Paul's audiences generally had 'an extensive knowledge of the LXX and an urgent interest in its interpretation'.

[110] Paul had never visited the Roman Christians (Rom. 1:10-13; 15:22-24) and so seems not to have known most of them. But there were members of Paul's missionary network in Rome, some of whom had apparently established house churches there (16:3-15).

this demanding letter. But it is *also* widely held that Paul's doctrines and exegesis were highly controversial. Hays, Wagner, and Wright, for example, observe very often how Paul's 'radical', 'audacious', and 'brazen' interpretations of Jewish scriptures must have 'shocked' and 'scandalised' his first audiences,[111] and none more than the *Roman* audience.[112] Here is a problem. If Paul's controversial ideas could offend his Christian audiences' doctrinal convictions, he can hardly have expected these audiences to attend to the intricacies of his exegesis with the patience commentators suppose.

Indeed, I suspect that lay Christians' convictions about the 'true' meaning of Bible passages will have been rather conservative because they learned them in a context that was adversarial in two particular respects. First, by the 50s Gentile Christians were often encountering considerable social stigmatisation for publicly abandoning the gods and pledging their exclusive allegiance to the Judaean god.[113] Second, they had been taught the 'true' meaning of Bible passages in that adversarial context in which early Christians were asserting novel christological interpretations in the face of more conventional Jewish readings. With its urgent eschatological outlook, the Christian movement was marked by a pious sense of voluntary social marginalisation and the bravura of shared suffering. In this context I think that the early Christian laity will have held rather fiercely onto the christological readings they had been taught.

Viewed in this light, the 'familiarity with scripture' often attributed to Paul's audience is most implausible. We are asked to envisage lay Christians in Rome who have carefully memorised swathes of text and yet apparently have so little doctrinal conviction that they are keen to grapple with the complexities of Paul's exposition. Yet they do this in order to follow arguments that offend the doctrinal sensibilities they have embraced at great social cost. We must imagine that Paul – who *knows* his interpretations of scripture are controversial within the wider Christian network but *urgently* desires to persuade sceptical audiences – inexplicably decides to encrypt his points within exegetical subtexts of abstruse complexity. We are required, in short, to imagine that Paul wrote for improbably *docile literati*.

---

[111] According to Hays (*Echoes*) Paul's exegesis was 'audacious' (e.g., pp. 4, 67, 112, 130, 170); 'shocking' (e.g., pp. 114, 168); 'scandalous' (e.g., pp. 2, 44, 67, 131, 190); 'startling' (e.g., pp. 1, 60, 91, 159, 163, 169); 'controversial' (e.g., pp. 31, 44, 136); 'radical' (e.g., pp. 44, 110, 123, 129, 149, 151, 185); 'revisionary' (e.g., pp. xiii, 1, 4, 31, 66, 81, 157, 172, 185, 186, 190); 'idiosyncratic' (e.g., pp. 2, 54, 152); also 'flagrantly revisionary' (p. 157), 'radically revisionary' (p. 185), 'scandalously revisionary' (p. 190); a 'counter-reading' which succeeded in 'leaving his audience agape' (e.g., p. 112). 'Virtually every citation of Scripture in the letter to the Romans' can be described as 'ironic reversal' (p. 169). Wagner (*Heralds*) makes similar claims: Paul's 'radical rereading' (e.g., pp. 5, 25, 82, 154, 271) and 'misreadings' (p. 25) of scripture in Romans are 'shocking' (pp. 10, 82), 'scandalous' (p. 10), 'tendentious' (pp. 185, 212), 'stunning' (p. 205), 'brazen' (pp. 159, 211). Stanley, *Arguing*, 56 agrees with Wagner that Paul 'radically' re-read scripture. Wright calls Paul's thinking 'radical' on numerous occasions, e.g., Paul's 'radical revisions' of Second Temple Jewish theology (Wright, *Paul*, 751–2).

[112] Hays' frequent observation that Paul's exegesis was 'audacious', 'shocking', etc., relates to Romans more than to all the other letters put together. Wagner applies the claim only to Romans.

[113] See Peter Oakes, *Philippians: From People to Letter* (Cambridge: Cambridge University Press, 2001), 77–102, esp. 89–91.

Such *docile literati* are hardly conceivable. We can only maintain that Paul's 'radical' exegesis 'shocked' the Roman Christians *if we also* credit them with doctrinal convictions firm enough to be offended in the first place. But we can only imagine an audience attending to Paul's exegesis with receptive alertness *if we also* credit them with a lack of doctrinal conviction that my review of the evidence has ruled out. These two central elements of the 'bookish' portrait of early Christian education exclude each other.

The problem of the *docile literati* stems, I propose, from our habit of treating Paul as a lone genius composing a written exposition of his 'Thought'.[114] This is how Romans in particular is usually treated.[115] On this view, the people addressed by the letter are effectively invited to audit passively as Paul sets his thoughts in order. But the evidence I have reviewed requires us to modify our view of the Roman audience in two important ways: we must take seriously their doctrinal convictions;[116] we may not credit them with an implausibly pristine familiarity with the uninterpreted lexical content of an extensive literature. These adjustments must lead us, I believe, to doubt that Paul filled his letter with content that was as shocking as generally supposed.

The solution, I suggest, is to acknowledge that many of the exegetical moves we usually attribute to Paul's own coinage actually belong to a common stock of early Christian exegesis, upon which Paul drew precisely because many Christians were already familiar with it through preaching and ethical instruction. That is, Paul was engaging with his audiences by means of a widely shared exegetical repertoire. When we look back to older studies, such as Dodd's *According to the Scriptures*, Otto Michel's *Paulus und seine Bibel*, or Hans Vollmer's *Die Altestamentlichen Citate bei Paulus*,[117] we realize that this is an old insight which has become obscured by the tendency – especially prominent in intertextual studies of the past thirty years – to treat more or less all the exegesis in Paul's letters as Paul's own 'radical' innovation. Dodd showed long ago that many of the passages that Paul cites are also cited in other New Testament texts and interpreted along similar christological lines. I have noted the example of Ps. 110:1. We may add Isa. 53:1,[118] Joel 2:28-32,[119] and Hab. 2:4.[120]

---

[114] See n. 24.
[115] 'Paul is writing to his contemporaries at Rome, and no doubt he has some practical purpose for doing so... Once the conversation begins, the *addressees recede curiously into the background*, and Paul finds himself engaged with...the voice of Scripture, that powerful ancestral presence *with which Paul grapples*' (Hays, *Echoes*, 35; my italics). Similarly, Wagner, *Heralds*, 3. Sanders, *Paul*, did much to establish the common view that Paul wrote Romans in order to set his own ideas in order.
[116] My argument suggests that they would have such convictions, and Paul affirms this. He acknowledges the non-Pauline 'doctrine which you have been taught' (τὴν διδαχὴν ἣν ὑμεῖς ἐμάθετε ποιοῦντας, 16:17) and praises their commitment to it: 'you have become obedient from the heart to the standard of teaching to which you were committed' (εἰς ὃν παρεδόθητε τύπον διδαχῆς, Rom 6:17); cf. 1:8, 'your faith' is widely admired within the Christian network.
[117] Otto Michel, *Paulus und seine Bibel* (Gütersloh: C. Bertelsmann, 1929); Hans Vollmer, *Die Altestamentlichen Citate bei Paulus: textkritisch und biblisch-theologisch gewürdigt nebst einem Anhang über das Verhältnis des Apostes zu Philo* (Freiburg: Mohr, 1895).
[118] Cited by Paul (Rom. 10:16) and in Jn 12:38; Dodd, *According*, 39.
[119] Cited by Paul (Rom. 10:13) and, in a different form, in Acts 2:17-21 (cf. 2:39); Dodd, *According*, 46-8.
[120] Cited by Paul (Rom. 1:17; Gal. 3:11) and, in a different form, by the author of Hebrews (10:37-38), Dodd, *According*, 49-51.

Paul cites a Hebraising form of Isa. 28:11 in 1 Cor. 14:21 which E. Earle Ellis thought belonged to common early Christian stock.[121] Paul also cites traditional combinations of passages. I have noted the combinations of Pss. 8:4-6 and 110:1, Isa. 8:14 and 28:16, and Gen. 12:3 and 22:18. It seems to me likely that the combination of (Hebraising) Isa. 25:8 and (LXX) Hos. 13:14 cited in 1 Cor. 15:54-55 was also traditional, since Paul expects the combination to clinch his dispute with the Corinthians over corporeal resurrection, which suggests that he expected them to recognize the citation. I suspect the same of the combinations of Isa. 59:20 and 27:9 (Rom. 11:26-27), and of Isa. 40:13 and Job 41:3 (Rom. 11:34-35), although an argument would be required to maintain this. Scholars have often voiced their sense that the thematic catena of passages on human sinfulness, cited in Romans 3, was already traditional when Paul inherited it.

If a number of the exegetical moves Paul makes in his letters drew on material already circulating in Christian preaching and teaching, then we need not imagine that he required his Roman or other audiences to contend with a deluge of his own exegetical *innovation*. Undoubtedly the interpretation of some biblical passages in the letters are Paul's own innovations. For instance, Hans Hübner, Richard Hays, Florian Wilk, and Ross Wagner have all offered compelling arguments that Paul interpreted his own mission especially in light of Isaiah 40-66.[122] But it seems unlikely that all of the exegesis in Paul's letters was novel. Regarding Paul's adaptation in Philippians 2 of the hymn containing the early Christian interpretation of Isa. 45:23, for example, Hurtado observes that 'Paul here is no christological innovator, at least as far as the contents of this passage and the devotional practice it reflects are concerned'.[123] If Paul was making significant use of *common* exegetical material, then lay audiences who had been exposed to the kind of preaching and ethical instruction I have outlined would be able to engage with a good deal of Paul's writing without having to commit to intensive programmes of adult education.

There is another thing to bear in mind, too. The scholars who imagine early Christian congregations committing scripture to memory all acknowledge the considerable effort required of semi-literate urban tradespeople[124] and the Christian leaders

---

[121] E. Earle Ellis, *Paul's Use of the Old Testament* (Edinburgh: Oliver & Boyd, 1957), 107-12 proposed that Paul drew on an early Christian collection of prophetic *logia* which diverge from the LXX and Masoretic Text through the addition of 'λέγει κύριος'. However, Koch, *Schrift*, 65, cf. 139 and Stanley, *Language*, 177 account for these forms differently. See the discussion in Norton, *Contours*, 155-8.

[122] The exegesis emerges particularly in Romans 9-11. See Hays, *Echoes*; Hans Hübner, *Gottes Ich und Israel: Zum Schriftgebrauch des Paulus in Römer 9-11* (Göttingen: Vandenhoeck & Ruprecht, 1984); idem, *Biblische Theologie des Neuen Testaments. Band. 2: Die Theologie des Paulus und ihre neutestamentliche Wirkungsgeschichte* (Göttingen: Vandenhoeck & Ruprecht, 1993); Florian Wilk, *Die Bedeutung des Jesajabuches für Paulus* (Göttingen: Vandenhoeck & Ruprecht, 1998); Wagner, *Heralds*.

[123] Hurtado, *Lord*, 112-13.

[124] Most early Christians would have no leisure to commit to book study. I think this is a far more important point than generally acknowledged (Stanley is unusual in noting this point several times, e.g., *Arguing*, 56, 68; cf. 41). The majority of early Christians in Asia Minor, Greece, and Rome were urban craftworkers and artisans, that is, low-level retainers who often lived quite close to the subsistence line. They may indeed have *wished* they could study the scriptures (as Abasciano, 'Diamonds', 158-60, contends) but could not fit this around long days of hard physical work. For the social level

teaching them. But, if all of the exegesis in the letters were Paul's innovation,[125] the 'bookish' view of early Christian churches would face a much more serious problem. It is not at all clear *which* Septuagint text these early Christians should learn in the first place. Although Paul's citations generally conform with the Alexandrian Old Greek, the frequent deviations from this text form raise a problem. If a congregation took the time to learn the Alexandrian text of, say, Isaiah by rote, then they would be wrong-footed[126] by Paul's citations from Hebraising Greek recensions of Isa. 8:14 (Rom. 9:33), 25:8 (1 Cor. 15:54), and 28:11 (1 Cor. 14:21) which diverge substantially in meaning from the Septuagint versions of these verses. There are other examples in Paul's citations from other biblical books, too.[127] Although aware of this (having reviewed Koch's 1986 book on the subject), Hays undertakes his entire study of Paul's scripture echoes using 'the Greek text of Alfred Rahlfs' Septuaginta'.[128] This is a serious fault in Hays' search for subtle echoes in Paul's letters, because echoes of Hebraising recensions may not produce the cadences that Hays discovers using Rahlfs. Debates about whether it would have been easy for churches to get hold of scrolls are rather eclipsed by this problem.[129] No church patron could hope to obtain a copy of Isaiah whose text matched the profile of Paul's Isaiah citations. So the laity could not learn a text that Paul was sure to cite or echo.

Further, if we envisage Paul participating in a common early Christian exegetical repertoire, then it becomes less likely that his Roman audience found his views as 'radical' and 'audacious' as often supposed. Indeed, Neil Elliott has argued that, according to the rhetorical logic of Romans 1–4, the doctrines of 'freedom from the law' and 'justification by faith' – doctrines usually considered the most radical of Paul's innovations – are tenets which both Paul and his Roman audience *already* held in common.[130] Elliott reads Romans 1–4 as an extended *insinuation* intended to prepare the audience for the point that Paul *expects* to be contentious, which comes in Romans 5–7. That is, whereas the Hellenistic Christian *kerygma* understands Jesus' death as atonement enabling the forgiveness of sins (a new moral beginning for the believer), Paul understands Jesus' death and resurrection to be a cataclysmic event that

---

of Christians, see Meeks, *Urban*; Abraham Malherbe, *Social Aspects of Early Christianity*, 2nd ed. (Philadelphia: Fortress, 1983); Theissen, *Social*; idem, 'The Social Structure of Pauline Communities: Some Critical Remarks on J. J. Meggitt, Paul, Poverty and Survival', *JSNT* 84 (2001): 65–84. See in particular Oakes' vivid and historically sharp portrayal of daily life for urban Christian artisans (*Philippians*, 77–102).

[125] See n. 63, above.

[126] Think of the uproar in a congregation at Oea when the bishop, adopting Jerome's Bible translation, substituted the unfamiliar word *hedera* ('ivy') in Jon. 4:6 for *cucurbita* ('gourd') which the congregation knew from the Old Latin. The congregants were outraged (Jerome, *Epist.* 75.7, 22, in 403 CE). See Andrew Cain, The *Letters of Jerome: Asceticism, Biblical Exegesis, and the Construction of Christian Authority in Late Antiquity* (Oxford: Oxford University Press, 2009), 65. It is true that by the fourth-century Septuagint texts had become more settled than in the first. But this congregation were surely used to the *copy* of Jonah belonging to their church before the copy of Jerome's translation intruded into their worship.

[127] See, e.g., Ellis, *Use*; Koch, *Schrift*; Stanley, *Language*.

[128] Hays, *Echoes*, xi.

[129] See n. 51, above.

[130] Neil Elliott, *The Rhetoric of Romans: Argumentative Constraint and Strategy and Paul's Dialogue with Judaism* (Minneapolis: Fortress, 1990), 146, 151, 159, 161–2, 203, 219, 235, 273.

results in the re-creation of the believer into a new person by overthrowing the great eschatological enemies, Sin and Death.[131]

This discussion must be pursued elsewhere. Here I want only to indicate a direction which might lead the discussion away from the problematic portrait of the lone genius and the docile literati which besets the study of Paul's exegesis. Although it will need to be developed elsewhere, I think that this solution – which is actually an old one – makes sense both of broad historical evidence and of internal rhetorical features of Paul's writing. It means that we do not need to consider large sections of Paul's audience excluded from engaging meaningfully with his exegesis. Nor do we need to conclude that Paul pitched his exegesis at a much less sophisticated level than is often supposed, in order to speak to the modest literary competence of the average lay Christian. The proposal does require us to modify our view of Paul, however, by considering the possibility that much of the exegesis and some of the doctrines we tend to attribute to Paul himself – to his own private reflection and radical religious genius – in fact belong to the common early Christian exegetical stock which Paul inherited and re-used in his letters. Paul is undoubtedly a very creative writer whose letters make considerable demands on any audience. I think there is merit in calling him a religious genius. But we do not need to suppose that everything he wrote was entirely novel. If it had been, I think his letters would have been incomprehensible to early Christians and we probably would not have them today.

[131] Ibid., 228–35.

9

READING THE NEW TESTAMENT
IN THE CONTEXT OF OTHER TEXTS:
A RELEVANCE THEORY PERSPECTIVE

Steve Smith

Reading is a fundamental way of acquiring new knowledge, and if we are to understand how people in the ancient world learned then it is important to think about how they read. As well as understanding the mechanics of reading in the ancient world – whether people read aloud, how many people were literate, whether people were more likely to be read to than read themselves – it is important to understand the intellectual processes involved in reading. How do people process information as they read? What cognitive processes do they go through? How do people add new knowledge to what they already know? How do ancient readers differ from modern readers as they do this?

This essay is concerned with this second set of questions, the cognitive processes that ancient readers engaged in reading. Ancient readers would have some prior knowledge to which they are adding, and a cultural/historical situation in which they belong (often loosely termed context), and new information will interact with them. So, I focus on how ancient readers would process quotations or allusions – specifically of the Old Testament (OT) in the New Testament (NT)[1] – because this is a well circumscribed area in which to evaluate how a person adds new information to what they already know. To do this, I engage relevance theory, a universal theory of human communication and cognition, to understand how readers process texts to find meaning.[2]

---

[1] Terminology here is difficult. 'Old Testament' can imply a sense of being superseded, though it is not meant in that way. 'Israel's Scriptures' is less defined and needs care over which texts are included or not, and, like 'Hebrew Bible', can suggest the Hebrew text and much of the NT utilized the LXX. Aware of the limitations, OT and NT are the terms used here.

[2] For a description of the psychological drive for readers to discern meaning, see Raymond W. Gibbs, *Intentions in the Experience of Meaning* (Cambridge: Cambridge University Press, 1999), 1–15.

The first section of this discussion offers an overview of the basics of the theory, drawing on examples from spoken communication where they more simply illustrate the point. The second section examines how relevance theory enables us to understand the process that ancient readers go through in evaluating new information in texts, and how they would add it to their current knowledge, particularly in allusion and quotation from the OT. A specific text with complex textual and cultural backgrounds will then be analyzed to demonstrate how the reader would process difficult texts in practice (Acts 17) before a final section will use relevance theory to address the important question of how much knowledge ancient readers would have of OT texts.

Relevance Theory

Relevance theory is based on the study of human cognition, and explains all communication whether spoken or written, ancient or modern.[3] It regards communication as more than a simple matter of encoding and decoding words;[4] words themselves do not contain meaning but they are cues which direct the reader in inferring meaning.[5] Inference is essential for communication, and readers infer meaning from the information which a writer conveys, through the interaction of the utterance with other information available to the recipient. So, if someone writes 'my car is green', the meaning of the utterance cannot be determined from the words alone, the context in which they are written matters: if writing about favourite colours it means one thing; in an article about fossil fuel pollution another. Relevance theory describes this in a particular way, focused around *relevance*, a technical term. A statement is *relevant* if it modifies the reader's *cognitive environment* to give new *cognitive effects*,[6] and there are three forms of these: strengthening prior assumptions, denying prior assumptions, or combining with prior assumptions to produce new *contextual implications*.[7] The reader's *cognitive environment* consists of anything which the reader is capable of representing mentally, and which the reader assumes to be true. This can include their physical environment; the previous content of the discourse; and *encyclopaedic*

---

[3] Originally described by Dan Sperber and Deirdre Wilson, *Relevance: Communication and Cognition*, 2nd ed. (Oxford: Blackwell, 1995), with the first edition in 1986; there is a helpful set of discussions in Wilson and Sperber, eds., *Meaning and Relevance* (Cambridge: Cambridge University Press, 2012); and an excellent overview in Wilson, 'Relevance and Understanding', in *Language and Understanding*, ed. G. Brown (Oxford: Oxford University Press, 1994), 37–58. A defence of the theory and the experimental evidence for it is beyond the present study, but for details see Robyn Carston, 'Lexical Pragmatics, Ad Hoc Concepts and Metaphor: A Relevance Theory Perspective', *Italian Journal of Linguistics* 22 (2010): 154–6; Jean-Baptiste van der Henst and Dan Sperber, 'Testing the Cognitive and Communicative Principles of Relevance', in Wilson and Sperber, eds., *Meaning and Relevance*, 279–306.

[4] A common way of understanding speech. See Claude Elwood Shannon and Warren Weaver, *The Mathematical Theory of Communication* (Urbana: University of Illinois Press, 1949): 6–7, 95–113; Sperber and Wilson, *Relevance*, 3–5.

[5] Gene L. Green, 'Relevance Theory and Biblical Interpretation', in *The Linguist as Pedagogue: Trends in the Teaching and Linguistic Analysis of the Greek New Testament*, ed. S. E. Porter and M. B. O'Donnell (Sheffield: Sheffield Phoenix, 2009), 236.

[6] Sperber and Wilson, *Relevance*, 48, 58, 108–9.

[7] Ibid., 118–23.

information, clusters or packets of information, including memories, beliefs, assumptions or knowledge associated with the topic.[8] The reader does not need to be aware of all of these aspects of their cognitive environment, just to be able to access them as *manifest* knowledge. The easier they are to access, the more manifest they are said to be.

In practice, the reader presumes that what they are reading is relevant and begins to search through their *cognitive environment* seeking where new contextual implications are formed, producing *relevance*. They begin with the aspects of their *cognitive environment* which are easiest to access (the most *manifest*) and analyse the new data there; if expectations of *relevance* are not met, they will continue to search for *contextual effects* elsewhere in less immediate parts of their *cognitive environment*. For example, if asked by a friend, 'do you have a pen?', the hearer would access the information available to them looking for where this statement is *relevant*. If the speaker is about to sign a document, *relevance* would be found as a request to borrow a pen, not a casual enquiry if they own one. If the speaker is managing to sign the document with their own pen, then the question would not achieve *relevance* as request to borrow pen, and the search for relevance would continue; if it is the hearer's birthday next week, then *relevance* would be found in the less immediate context of an enquiry about whether a pen would be a good gift.

It is vital to note that the reader will not continue processing in contexts exhaustively searching for as many *cognitive effects* as possible in order to gain maximum *relevance*, because communication is based on *optimal relevance*.[9] The extent of *relevance* is defined in terms of a balance between the magnitude of the *contextual effects* produced by the utterance, and the effort required to process them.[10] In order to limit the effort, a reader will search through available contexts beginning with the most manifest (often the immediate context of the discourse), looking for relevance.[11] When they obtain sufficient cognitive effects to satisfy their expectations of relevance they stop searching for relevance because accessing further contexts would expend extra processing effort. So, in the example involving a pen, relevance is achieved as a request to borrow a pen, even if it is also the hearer's birthday next week.

The hearer is able to treat utterances in this way because speakers design their utterance to be optimally relevant,[12] and they signal this to the hearer in making the

---

[8] See ibid., 138; see also Robyn Carston, *Thoughts and Utterances: The Pragmatics of Explicit Communication* (Oxford: Blackwell, 2002), 321; Agustín Rayo, 'A Plea for Semantic Localism', *Noûs* 47 (2013): 648.

[9] See the helpful discussion and examples in Billy Clark, *Relevance Theory* (New York: Cambridge University Press, 2013), 29–33.

[10] Sperber and Wilson, *Relevance*, 145, define this in two extent conditions: '*Extent condition 1*: an assumption is relevant to an individual to the extent that the contextual effects achieved when it is optimally processed are large. *Extent condition 2*: an assumption is relevant to an individual to the extent that the effort required to process it is small.'

[11] For successful communication, the speaker and hearer need to have the same facts or assumptions manifest to them for successful communication; the speaker also needs to be aware that the hearer has these things manifest to them (ibid., 38–46, 138).

[12] Of course, speakers and writers can be incompetent or deceptive in their communication, meaning that communication can fail according to these rules, but relevance theory is capable of explaining these events. See the explanation in Margaret A. Sim, *A Relevant Way to Read: A New Approach to Exegesis and Communication* (Cambridge: James Clark, 2016), 23–5.

utterance (communication is *ostensive*).¹³ Speakers judge which interpretive contexts are most accessible to the hearer, and construct the utterance to ensure that is relevant with the least processing effort. If the speaker is aware that their recipient is likely to misunderstand the utterance by finding relevance in a more immediate part of their cognitive environment, then the speaker will adapt the utterance, giving signals to direct the reader to the required context (e.g. in the second example above, waving the pen at the hearer to show they already have one to sign the document). The same applies in written communication, though writers are less certain of the immediate cognitive environment of their readers and will usually signal the contexts more carefully by using extra words.

While this process means that readers will look for optimal relevance, this does not require that optimal relevance is always a minimal reading. Frequently, optimal relevance will require a more detailed reading of the text, and to explain this it is necessary to discuss relevance theory's handling of implicature and metarepresentation.

Implicature

Relevance theory identifies *explicature* and *implicature*. Explicatures are assumptions developed from the logical form of the utterance itself,[14] and readers process explicatures using a pragmatic process governed by relevance in order to assign referents to lexemes or disambiguate difficult phrases. Implicatures are everything else, and they are derived solely by inference,[15] increasing the *cognitive effects*. To describe how implicatures work, it is helpful to consider indirect answers to questions. If someone is asked 'would you like chicken for supper?' and they reply, 'I'm still a vegetarian', then the answer 'no' is not explicit; it is an implicature derived from the explicature of the utterance (they are still vegetarian) and contextual information (chicken is meat). Saying this, they intend their hearer to realize that 'no' is their answer, but the indirect answer requires more processing effort of the hearer than a direct 'no', so it is not the best way to answer if 'no' is all it is conveying. The extra processing effort means that the hearer can expect further contextual effects through implicature. These may range in strength from strong ones that the speaker clearly intended to convey (they would not eat steak), or others that are quite probable (they are irritated that the speaker forgot they are vegetarian), to weaker implicatures that may or may not have been intended (e.g. they are concerned about their environmental impact).[16] Implicatures, therefore, fall on a spectrum of strength: the weaker they are, the less likely they are to form part of the communicative intent of the speaker, and the more responsibility the hearer must take for forming them.[17]

In this way, speech forms such as metaphors can lead to a range of implicatures. Some metaphors have a relatively fixed meaning that is commonly accepted by people, and these metaphors lead to one or two strong implicatures. Referring to someone

---

[13] Sperber and Wilson, *Relevance*, 260–79.
[14] Ibid., 182.
[15] Sperber and Wilson, *Relevance*, 182, 193–202; Carston, *Thoughts and Utterances*, 377.
[16] See an alternative example in Sperber and Wilson, *Relevance*, 196–99.
[17] Ibid., 199–200; Adrian Pilkington, *Poetic Effects: A Relevance Theory Perspective* (Amsterdam: John Benjamins, 2000), 36–8, 183–4.

who is healthy or energetic as 'fit as a fiddle' relies on an accepted meaning, a strong implicature where the author likely planned for relevance to be found;[18] despite potential riches the metaphor is not explored beyond this. Other metaphors are more innovative and characterized by a wide range of weak implicatures; here it is essential to optimal relevance that the reader finds several weak implicatures, but the precise implicatures are typically the decision of the interpreter (this happens in poetry where the metaphors can be sustained in several lines inviting the reader to examine them in detail).[19]

Metarepresentation

Relevance theory has a particular way of handling allusion or quotation to other texts.[20] Such reuse of material is regarded as a representation of these thoughts or words,[21] where the author typically adds their own thoughts to them (e.g. approval or disapproval). At other times, the writer uses representations of the representations (termed metarepresentations) where they attribute thoughts and opinions to others.[22] It is important to identify such representations, because they do not necessarily give the opinion of the author, instead they give the opinion of others that the author wishes to critique in some way. Such echoic language can be subtle, with the repetition of a small phrase or a conceptual echo. On noticing this similarity, the reader will subconsciously search for relevance according to the heuristic described above and will derive implications from the text they are reading that it shares with the prior text (the more implications the texts share then the closer their resemblance), stopping when expectations of relevance are attained.[23]

Relevance Theory and Reading Biblical Texts

With this overview of relevance theory in place it is now possible to examine how it is used subconsciously and automatically by a reader of a biblical text.[24] While the

---

[18] Adrian Pilkington, 'Poetic Effects', *Lingua* 87 (1992): 36.
[19] Sperber and Wilson, 'A Deflationary Account of Metaphors', in Wilson and Sperber, eds., *Meaning and Relevance*, 121–2.
[20] Deirdre Wilson, 'Metarepresentation in Linguistic Communication', in Wilson and Sperber, eds., *Meaning and Relevance*, 230–58.
[21] A representation is 'anything used in such a way that it can be construed as being *about* something (as having *meaning*) as opposed to just being itself; aboutness may be truth-based or resemblance-based' (from the glossary in Carston, *Thoughts and Utterances*, 380, italics original). See also Sim, *Relevant Way*, Vhapter 3.
[22] So 'metarepresentation is a representation of a representation: a higher-order representation with a lower-order representation embedded within it'. Wilson, 'Metarepresentation', 230.
[23] Ibid., 244.
[24] Much of the focus of relevance theory is on spoken utterances, and Keith Green, 'Relevance Theory and the Literary Text: Some Problems and Perspectives', *JLS* 22 (1993): 207–17, disputes the appropriateness of using it for texts because texts are less immediate or dialogical. However, there is no reason to regard texts as less applicable to the theory; see Tzvetan Todorov, *Genres in Discourse*, trans. C. Porter (Cambridge: Cambridge University Press, 1990), 1–12; Stephen W. Pattemore, *The People of God in the Apocalypse: Discourse, Structure and Exegesis*, SNTSMS 128 (Cambridge: Cambridge University Press, 2004), 23. Relevance has also been applied fruitfully to texts, see especially the recent volume dedicated to the topic: Terrance Cave and Deirdre Wilson,

theory explains all aspects of textual interpretation, the focus here will be on how the reader understands allusions to other texts, namely of the OT in the NT. There are two critical stages to this: first, the identification of the OT text itself; second, the process of searching the reader's cognitive environment in order to find relevance in the allusion. These two stages will be discussed separately. The interpretive process followed would be no different for the ancient reader or the modern reader, though there are differences in the cognitive environments of the two readers. While the discussion here follows the ancient reader in the details, crucial differences between ancient and modern readers will be discussed in a third point.

Underdeterminacy and the Identification of Context

For relevance theory, communication utilizes *underdeterminacy*: the writer gives just enough information for the reader to complete the gaps through their contextual knowledge.[25] In order to understand an allusion (in other words, find relevance in a part of the cognitive environment associated with that allusion) the reader will need to identify that allusion, thereby making cognitive environments associated with it more immediately available for finding relevance than any other context. Noticing the allusion will depend on the following four elements.[26]

(1) The presence of a *signal* in the text they are reading. A writer can use this to draw attention to an OT text, ensuring it is a more immediate place for finding relevance than any other. Signals can be overt like the introductory formula γέγραπται before the quotation of Lk. 2:23, or more subtle like a shift in style of writing. Having identified the signal, the reader will begin the search for relevance in potential OT texts.

(2) The *echoic strength* of the allusion reflects lexical similarity – both the degree of verbal similarity of the echoic phrase and the distinctiveness of the shared words. However, it also includes conceptual and thematic parallels, and if the allusion is to an

---

eds., *Reading Beyond the Code: Literature and Relevance Theory* (Oxford: Oxford University Press, 2018); but see also David Trotter, 'Analysing Literary Prose: The Relevance of Relevance Theory', *Lingua* 87 (1992): 11–27. In biblical studies there are many examples of exegesis involving relevance; see Joseph D. Fantin, *The Lord of the Entire World: Lord Jesus, a Challenge to Lord Caesar?* (Sheffield: Sheffield Phoenix, 2011); Benjamin J. Lappenga, *Paul's Language of Ζῆλος: Monosemy and the Rhetoric of Identity and Practice* (Leiden: Brill, 2015). Some have applied relevance to intertextual study: Pattemore, *People of God*; Steve Smith, *The Fate of the Jerusalem Temple in Luke-Acts: An Intertextual Approach to Jesus' Laments over Jerusalem and Stephen's Speech*, LNTS 553 (London: Bloomsbury, 2017); Nelson R. Morales, *Poor and Rich in James: A Relevance Theory Approach to James's Use of the Old Testament* (University Park: Eisenbrauns, 2018).

[25] See the fuller description in Sim, *Relevant Way*, 12–14.

[26] Much has been written about how scholars may identify intertextual allusions, but there has been some lack of methodological precision. For a critical view, see Paul Foster, 'Echoes without Resonance: Critiquing Certain Aspects of Recent Scholarly Trends in the Study of the Jewish Scriptures in the New Testament', *JSNT* 38 (2015): 96–111. Many rely of Richard Hays' so-called criteria in *Echoes of Scripture in the Letters of Paul* (London: Yale University Press, 1989), 29–32; however, David Allen has rightly critiqued the appropriateness of criteria in 'The Use of Criteria — the State of the Question', in *Methodology in the Use of the Old Testament in the New: Context and Criteria*, ed. D. Allen and S. Smith, LNTS 597 (London: T&T Clark, 2019), 129–41. For more detail on the four factors described here, see Steve Smith, 'The Use of Criteria — a Proposal from Relevance Theory', 142–54, in the same volume.

OT motif or story then such parallels are arguably more important.[27] An example of this is the raising of the son of a widow in Lk. 7:11-17. This narrative has significant parallels to Elijah raising the son of the widow of Zarephath (1 Kgs 17:17-24), and its link is through common themes, not verbal parallel.[28]

(3) The degree of *accessibility* of the OT text to the reader. This is not just a question of whether the text is available to the reader (as Hays' availability),[29] but whether it is the closest OT text in the reader's mind. This is a critical issue: no matter how strong the echoic strength is to a particular text, if sufficient relevance can be found in knowledge associated with something more immediate (a theme, a part of a biblical story, an event, or a motif shared by several texts) then that is the place where the reader will find relevance. A good example is the language of siege in Lk. 21:21:

τότε οἱ ἐν τῇ Ἰουδαίᾳ φευγέτωσαν εἰς τὰ ὄρη
καὶ οἱ ἐν μέσῳ αὐτῆς ἐκχωρείτωσαν
καὶ οἱ ἐν ταῖς χώραις μὴ εἰσερχέσθωσαν εἰς αὐτήν

Then those in Judea must flee to the mountains,
and those inside the city must leave it,
and those out in the country must not enter it

These three phrases have some parallel to a range of texts,[30] but none of these texts have more echoic strength than the others,[31] and none are more accessible than the theme of city destruction common to them all. It is in assumptions associated with this theme that a reader would find relevance.

(4) Finally, it is critical that there is some *interpretive benefit* to the intertext. The reader's search for relevance will stop at the most accessible context if that context satisfies expectations for optimal relevance;[32] if it does not, then the search for relevance will continue elsewhere.

Developing Encyclopaedic Information

Having identified the OT text, motif, or story, the reader accesses the encyclopaedic information associated with that text. Two things need to be noted about this encyclopaedic information. Firstly, it is composed of 'chunks' of memory, belief, and information which are accessed en masse when the topic is processed.[33] Relevance

---

[27] See the insightful comments of Ziony Zevit, 'Echoes of Texts Past', in *Subtle Citation, Allusion, and Translation in the Hebrew Bible*, ed. Z. Zevit (Sheffield: Equinox, 2017), 12.
[28] See the discussion in Richard Hays, *Echoes of Scripture in the Gospels* (Waco: Baylor University Press, 2016), 237-8.
[29] Hays, *Letters of Paul*, 29-30.
[30] From the LXX: Gen. 19:17, 19; Judg. 1:34; 6:2; 1 Kgdms 23:19; 26:1; 3 Kgdms 22:17; Isa. 15.5; Jer. 16:16; 21:8-10; 30:2; 27:6 (50:6; 49:8 ET); 41:21 (34:21 ET); 52:7; Lam. 4:19; Ezek. 7:16; Amos 5:19-20; Nah. 3:18; Zech. 14:5; 1 Macc. 2:28; 2 Macc. 5:27.
[31] Smith, *Fate of Jerusalem*, 84-5, and the references to other literature there.
[32] Pattemore, *People of God*, 40; Morales, *Poor and Rich*, 65.
[33] See Sperber and Wilson, *Relevance*, 138.

theory recognizes what has been proposed by evolutionary psychology that the mind is modular, and it works in an efficient manner with 'fast and frugal heuristics', employing efficient and quick approaches to difficult problems.[34] Part of this is dealing with information in batches. Secondly, even though many components of this encyclopaedic information will be common to other similarly situated interpreters, the contents of the encyclopaedic information for any one ancient reader would be individual. Needless to say, it is impossible to recreate its content with certainty, especially for ancient readers, though historical research may help to identify its likely contents.

Having accessed the encyclopaedic information associated with the OT text, the reader will begin forming cognitive effects: the new data in the text being read will either give new information or confirm or deny pre-existing knowledge in the encyclopaedic information. Essentially the reader is operating under a series of hypotheses about what the interpretation of the text may be, and by searching for relevance against different aspects of the cognitive environment these are tested out.[35] If expectations of relevance are satisfied in the first aspect of the cognitive environment examined then the reader will stop processing; if they are not, the reader will continue searching for relevance in other contexts.

If the search continues, the reader will search in other and broader contexts, whatever is now closest. At times this will move attention to a different proposed intertext for the material being considered, at other times it will be in material that was not accessible before but has now become assessable through considering the encyclopaedic information just accessed.[36] This could include the broader contexts of the OT text, such as the adjacent verses or whole section; it may include the narrative associated with the text, or a motif derived from the text; it may include emotional attachments made to a text which have a strong tradition of interpretation; it may include the liturgical use of the text, or anything else. This branching network of association would be explored almost instantaneously, until optimum relevance is found, or the reader gives up because the effort has become too great (when they may settle for a series of weak implicatures from the allusion awaiting more information if it becomes available later in the text).

This process helps to explain whether a prior text's wider context is considered by the reader when evaluating the echo, and what that context consists of (literary context, narrative context etc). In practical terms the context that is considered varies. Acts 1:20, for example, records a fulfilment of Ps. 108:8 LXX (τὴν ἐπισκοπὴν αὐτοῦ λαβέτω ἕτερος, 'Let another take his position of overseer'). This is clearly

---

[34] Using the term devised by Gigerenzer, Todd, and the ABC Research Group; see, for example, Gerd Gigerenzer and Peter M. Todd, 'Fast and Frugal Heuristics: The Adaptive Toolbox', in *Simple Heuristics That Make Us Smart*, ed. G. Gigerenzer, P. M. Todd, and ABC Research Group (New York: Oxford University Press, 1999), 3–36. For a brief overview, see Carston, 'Lexical Pragmatics', 154, and for detail, Sperber and Wilson, 'Pragmatics, Modularity and Mind-Reading', *Mind & Language* 17 (2002): 3–23.
[35] For more detail, see Carston, 'Lexical Pragmatics', 154.
[36] Some encyclopaedic information is only attainable indirectly by prior activation of other encyclopaedic information. Sperber and Wilson, *Relevance*, 137.

not something that requires the whole psalm's context, it is something restricted to the verse cited itself.³⁷ Luke 22:37 is different: here Jesus quotes Isa. 53:12 (τοῦτο τὸ γεγραμμένον δεῖ τελεσθῆναι ἐν ἐμοί, τό· καὶ μετὰ ἀνόμων ἐλογίσθη, 'this scripture must be fulfilled in me, "And he was counted among the lawless"'), but what scripture is he claiming is fulfilled here both when he says this and when he goes on to restate the fulfilment (καὶ γὰρ τὸ περὶ ἐμοῦ τέλος ἔχει, 'and indeed what is written about me is being fulfilled')? Most commentators think it is more than Isa. 53:12, and it includes the whole servant song.³⁸ That is surely correct: the reader is likely to understand it this way because the quotation is located in the narrative of the last supper where Jesus discusses the significance of his death (whatever encyclopaedic information is accessed would need to interact with that collection of data), and the common use of Isaiah 53 in the early Christian community demonstrates that the entire servant song is a readily available context for the reader.³⁹ An example of a more diverse exploration of context would be the statement, 'it is impossible for a prophet to be killed outside of Jerusalem' and the reference to Jerusalem as the city which kills prophets in Lk. 13:33-34. There are OT texts referring to the death of prophets in Jerusalem including Jer. 26:20-23; 45:4-6; and 2 Chron. 24:20-21. It is likely that an ancient reader would find relevance in the last text and the story of Zechariah, but not because anything in this text makes it stand out immediately. The route to the encyclopaedic information contained in this text is likely to be through the more immediate context of Lk. 11:49-51 and the reference to the blood of Abel and the blood of Zechariah shed in Jerusalem. This detail is closer at hand for the reader, and its content makes very accessible 2 Chronicles, where expectations of relevance would be found (that Jesus is a prophet like Zechariah, with potential parallels in terms of message as critical of some in Jerusalem, and in the context of the Jerusalem temple).⁴⁰

How far a reader explores is governed by their expectation of optimal relevance. As described above under the discussion of implicature, less direct forms of writing require more processing effort on the part of the reader, who will expect an increase in cognitive effects in order to achieve optimal relevance. As such, different types of allusion will give different expectations of optimal relevance. There are no hard and fast rules, but the following can serve as a guide. (1) Many texts have fixed meanings (as discussed with metaphors above) leading to easily processed implicatures;⁴¹ for example, quotations of Ps. 110:1 have relatively fixed meaning because of its use by Jesus (Lk. 20:42). In the absence of other signals suggesting the need to look further, the reader is going to be satisfied with these straightforward interpretations. (2) On occasions the writer directs attention to a specific aspect of the intertext, making

---

37 It has no regard for context, according to C. K. Barrett, *A Critical and Exegetical Commentary on the Acts of the Apostles*, ICC (Edinburgh: T. & T. Clark, 1994–98), 100. This is probably overstating things as it must be part of its implication that this comes from the Psalms; however, overall the point is true, the context of the psalm seems irrelevant.

38 Luke Timothy Johnson, *The Gospel of Luke*, SP 3 (Collegeville: Liturgical Press, 1991), 347. See the references in David W. Pao and Eckhard J. Schnabel, 'Luke', in *Commentary on the New Testament Use of the Old Testament*, ed. G. K. Beale and D. A. Carson (Grand Rapids: Baker, 2007), 385.

39 An idea supported by the use of Isa. 52–53 in Acts 8:32-33.

40 Smith, *Fate of Jerusalem*, 36–8.

41 Pilkington, 'Poetic Effects', 112–18.

certain encyclopaedic information very available for minimal effort and limiting expectations of contextual effects. The cognitive effect of the intertext may simply be just that an authoritative text agrees with the perspective of the writer (e.g. Acts 1:20). (3) A text may explicitly focus on the story behind a text, not the words of the text itself (Lk. 17:26-30 directs the reader to parts of the story of Noah and Lot). In these cases, the encyclopaedic information that is made available is that of the story – the reader may explore the story relatively extensively, but not anything more textual. (4) Where more effort is required, more cognitive effects are expected. All allusions require some effort, but there is particular effort required for allusions where a signal indicates the need to identify a text, but no text is immediately obvious. Un-signalled texts tend to need less effort because they are either found (because of sufficient echoic strength and availability) or the reader is unaware of them – there is little effort needed either way. (5) Certain intertexts function similarly to poetic metaphors, and the repeated examination of something from different perspectives invites the reader to create a wide range of weaker implicatures around a theme.[42] For example, the use of exilic language in the laments over Jerusalem have repeated allusions examining the exile from different perspectives,[43] and readers would use them to construct a complex representation of the exile as presented in the texts and use this as a basis for exploring the NT.[44]

Relevance theory describes a dynamic reading process, with understanding of the text developing as it progresses. The cognitive effects formed are capable of revision as new information becomes available.[45] As such, the reader's concepts develop as the text progresses, with some ideas held provisionally by the reader before being subsequently rejected or accepted.[46]

Ancient and Modern Readers

Relevance theory describes a process of reading which applies to any reader, and the cognitive processes above apply to modern readers as much as to ancient readers. However, readers differ from each other in two main ways. First, in the cognitive environment available to them. The original readers had a different set of encyclopaedic information to modern readers, meaning that they would find relevance in

---

[42] Pilkington, *Poetic Effects*, 42-3, 102-5. In fact, many writers give clues to the interpretation of metaphors even when they are less complicated. See Nam Sun Song, 'Metaphor and Metonymy', in *Relevance Theory: Applications and Implications*, ed. R. Carston and S. Uchida (Amsterdam: J. Benjamins, 1998), 94-5.
[43] As discussed in Smith, *Fate of Jerusalem*, 59-67, 82-93.
[44] There is some debate how such things work for complex metaphors, with Robyn Carston arguing for some process of metarepresentation similar to the above; see Carston, 'Lexical Pragmatics', 168-71. Others argue for the creation of *ad hoc* concepts in these complex metaphors, like Esther Romero and Belén Soria, 'Relevance Theory and Metaphor', *Linguagem em (dis)curso* 14 (2014): 489-509.
[45] Some describe *ad hoc* concepts, dynamic concepts which are created on the go, like Carston, *Thoughts and Utterances*, 322. These are often used to describe the broadening or narrowing definition of words as their referents are placed in the text, but their application can be wider than this. See Romero and Soria, 'Relevance Theory'.
[46] The process is described well in Clark, *Relevance Theory*, 249-51; Terrance Cave, 'Towards a Passing Theory of Understanding', in Cave and Wilson, eds., *Reading Beyond the Code*, 168-70.

places where modern readers would not. The cultural, linguistic, social and religious differences between the modern and ancient worlds are well documented, and the recreation of the ancient mindset is an important part of historical critical or social scientific interpretation of texts. What relevance theory adds is the importance of knowing which context would have been most available for the ancient reader, for it is here the reader begins the search for relevance. Because modern readers, including scholars, also follow the processes of relevance in looking at texts, a reading which may have been the most relevant for the ancient world may well *not* seem correct to the modern interpreter for whom relevance is found in a different more available collection of encyclopaedic information.[47]

The second difference is how far the reader goes in the search for relevance. Relevance theory is not a reader-centred approach which pays no attention to the author, but nor does it require recreation of a theoretical authorial intention. The text is seen as a form of communication from author to reader: the writer does all that is needed to ensure that the reader will arrive at relevance with minimal effort (optimal relevance); the reader trusts this and is cognitively wired to find optimal relevance. The reader has freedom to explore the text, but the principles of relevance lead the reader to self-enforce interpretive limits and look for relevance in what the author likely meant.[48] However, readers can read the text casually, stopping when relevance is first identified without exploring enough implicatures, thereby failing to achieve optimal relevance. Others can press beyond optimal relevance and explore maximal readings that are beyond the manifest communication of the author.[49]

So, modern scholars are likely to pursue a maximal reading because scholarly re-reading and study of the text raises their expectations of relevance. Some ancient readers are first-time readers looking for the simpler meaning of the text; others may be engaged in detailed study. It is not unreasonable to think that the authors of the NT texts designed them to be read in both ways: not only a document to be read out in church, but as one subject to re-readings,[50] with the elders of the church exploring the text in detail. As such, one may expect ancient readers of NT texts to study the text in greater detail, searching for more implicatures to enrich their cognitive effects.

With this in mind, it would help to explore a text to see how this is put into practice and Acts 17 is used as an example. Seeking to construct details about the original audience for Luke-Acts is not strictly necessary because relevance theory is capable of evaluating a range of different readings dependent on what a reader may know, but it is worth pausing to reflect on some of the characteristics of the original Lukan audience. It is a reasonable conclusion that Luke was writing for Christians because the speeches in Acts seem to be written for the education of believers rather than

---

[47] There is a helpful description of this in Morales, *Poor and Rich*, 46–7.
[48] See the discussion in Pilkington, *Poetic Effects*, 66.
[49] Anne Furlong, 'Relevance Theory and Literary Interpretation' (PhD diss., University College London, 1996), 189–204.
[50] If ideals in the wider culture are anything to go by, see William A. Johnson, *Readers and Reading Culture in the High Roman Empire: A Study of Elite Communities* (New York: Oxford University Press, 2010). See also Richard Bauckham, ed., *The Gospels for All Christians: Rethinking the Gospel Audiences* (Grand Rapids: Eerdmans, 1998), on the readership of the Gospels.

the persuasion of outsiders,[51] and it is possible that his audience was wealthy, and educated.[52] Being precise on such details is difficult though, because Luke probably wrote for a wide audience, not a single community.[53] Having said this, it is reasonable to assume that they would have understood biblical concepts and been able to engage in intelligent understanding of a text — or at least that the leaders and teachers in the community would have been able to do this. Whether this means that they were any more familiar with the Jewish scriptures than, say, recipients of Pauline epistles, is a matter of conjecture. The issue of biblical literacy will be picked up in the final section of this essay.

Reading Acts 17

Paul's sermon in Athens and the surrounding narrative in Acts 17:16-34 is an interesting text to investigate because it contains a complex interpretive background. With the Lukan Paul in the philosophical capital of the ancient world, many interpreters regard Paul as preaching the Gospel against a background of Greek philosophy.[54] Paul quotes Aratus ('in him we live and move and have our being', Acts 17:28), and he alludes to another Greek writer in the same verse ('for we too are his offspring').[55] In addition, there are portions of the speech which echo Stoic and Epicurean philosophers such as Pythagoras, Plato, Epictetus, and Zeno.[56] With these present, a reader would surely interpret the text against the encyclopaedic information concerning Greek philosophy.

However, Paul also echoes scripture, leading other interpreters to regard this is an attack on pagan idolatry based in scriptural anti-idolatry polemic.[57] While the Areopagus speech does not contain explicit OT quotations, NA[28] notes many echoes. For the purposes of this study it is enough to note that Paul seems to allude to at least the following texts from LXX.

---

[51] In addition, Lk. 1:1-4 makes an inclusive reference to 'us'. See David G. Peterson, 'The Motif of Fulfilment and the Purpose of Luke-Acts', in *The Book of Acts in Its First Century Setting. Vol. 1, the Book of Acts in Its Ancient Literary Setting*, ed. B. W. Winter and A. D. Clarke (Grand Rapids: Eerdmans; Carlisle: Paternoster, 1993), 83-104, 103.

[52] See the discussion in Craig S. Keener, *Acts: An Exegetical Commentary*, 4 vols. (Grand Rapids: Baker Academic, 2012-15), 1:424.

[53] Mikeal. C. Parsons, *Acts*, PCNT (Grand Rapids: Baker, 2008), 20, and the essays in R. Bauckham, ed., *The Gospels for All Christians: Rethinking the Gospel Audiences* (Grand Rapids: Eerdmans, 1998). Luke may have even had future readers in mind, see Charles H. Talbert, 'Reading Chance, Moessner and Parsons', in *Cadbury, Knox, and Talbert: American Contributions to the Study of Acts*, ed. M. C. Parsons and J. B. Tyson (Atlanta: Scholars Press, 1992), 229-40, here 229-30.

[54] Martin Dibelius, *Studies in the Acts of the Apostles* (London: SCM, 1956), 57-8, 71; Luke Timothy Johnson, *The Acts of the Apostles*, SP 5 (Collegeville: Liturgical Press, 1992); Joseph A. Fitzmyer, *The Acts of the Apostles: A New Translation with Introduction and Commentary*, AB 31 (New York: Doubleday, 1998).

[55] Possibly Epiminides according to Darrell L. Bock, *Acts*, BECNT (Grand Rapids: Baker 2007), 568, but this is not certain. See C. Kavin Rowe, 'The Grammar of Life: The Areopagus Speech and Pagan Tradition', *NTS* 57 (2010): 42.

[56] Joshua W. Jipp, 'Paul's Areopagus Speech of Acts 17:16-34 as Both Critique and Propaganda', *JBL* 131 (2012): 567-88.

[57] Bertil Gärtner, *The Areopagus Speech and Natural Revelation* (Uppsala: Gleerup, 1955); David W. Pao, *Acts and the Isaianic New Exodus* (Grand Rapids: Baker, 2000), 193-7.

Isaiah 42:5 in Acts 17:24-25: while not signalled, there is reasonable echoic strength here, with ὁ θεὸς ὁ ποιήσας (17:24) repeated from Isa. 42:5, and διδοὺς...πνοήν (17:25) also repeated. There are some differences in phrasing (probably adaptations to Isaiah in the service of echoing philosophers), but there remains a conceptual parallel.[58]

The Genesis origins story in Acts 17:26: the phrase, 'From one ancestor [ἐξ ἑνός] he made all nations to inhabit the whole earth', evokes Genesis 1–2, with ἐξ ἑνός likely to be masculine and refer to one man.[59] The creation account is so accessible to readers that a conceptual link to it is likely.[60]

The Isaianic anti-idol polemic in Acts 17:29: there are many texts which criticize idolatry in the LXX,[61] but they have neither the accessibility of the Isaianic text (because it has just been echoed), nor sufficient conceptual echoic strength, and the words in Acts (οὐκ ὀφείλομεν νομίζειν χρυσῷ ἢ ἀργύρῳ ἢ λίθῳ, χαράγματι τέχνης καὶ ἐνθυμήσεως ἀνθρώπου, τὸ θεῖον εἶναι ὅμοιον) bear considerable connection to passages like Isa. 40:18-20 and 46:5-7. These texts are all well-known in the Christian community, making them clearly accessible.[62] Like the other texts discussed, it is likely that an ancient reader would easily access the encyclopaedic information associated with these texts.

With this complex textual background, how is the reader to understand the text? Is the philosophical background dominant or is the biblical? Or is Kavin Rowe correct that both are required,[63] with the Lukan Paul arguing from philosophy, using the Christian message from creation to eschaton to frame this discussion?

Rowe makes a persuasive case for the role of both sets of texts. He notes the ambiguity of some of the terms: for characters in the text, σπερμολόγος (17:18) means Paul is someone without sophistication in his argument, but the readers of the text will not regard Paul this way.[64] In relevance theoretic terms, the readers process the narrative in two different sets of cognitive environments, and will form an *ad hoc* concept (σπερμολόγος*) that defines the meaning of σπερμολόγος as a narrowing of the word's meaning in critical judgement against Paul from the perspective of the hearers. They also read it from their own perspective, where the *ad hoc* concept σπερμολόγος* would be seen as a representation of the ideas of the hearers and viewed against the reader's own cognitive environment where Paul is a competent debater elsewhere in Acts; σπερμολόγος* is seen to be ironic and untrue. Readers then continue to read

---

[58] Noted by many commentators, including NA[28]; Bock, *Acts*, 565; David G. Peterson, *The Acts of the Apostles* (Grand Rapids Eerdmans, 2009), 495. For alternatives see I. Howard Marshall, 'Acts', in Beale and Carson, eds., *Commentary on the New Testament Use of the Old Testament*, 594.
[59] The western text adds αἵματος after ἑνός, and this is likely an expansion emphasizing that it is a man. See C. Kavin Rowe, *World Upside Down: Reading Acts in the Graeco-Roman Age* (Oxford: Oxford University Press, 2009), 199 n. 154.
[60] To this can be added Deut. 32:8 with its reference to boundaries. For details and alternatives, see Marshall, 'Acts', 595.
[61] See NA[28]; Peterson, *Acts*, 495. There are several specific possibilities, but Isa. 46:5-7 is most likely because of the reference to gold and silver.
[62] There are also some similarities between Acts 17:24 and Acts 7:48, with some conceptual overlap concerning idolatry.
[63] Rowe, *World Upside Down*, 27–41.
[64] Rowe, 'Grammar of Life', 36–7. See the examples of how this term was used in Rowe, *World Upside Down*, 28.

the text aware of the potential manifest assumptions of the *hearers* in Athens (to the philosophers), and of their own assumptions, as Luke's *readers* (attuned to the biblical text). Interpreting the text in this manner means that the ancient reader would find relevance in the following ways.

(1) Even though the narrative prepares the reader for the cognitive environment of the Athenian hearers by introducing them as Epicurean and Stoic philosophers who loved discussing philosophy (Acts 17:18, 21), the reader is quite likely to miss the allusions to philosophers in Paul's speech. This is for two reasons. First, the reader is not expecting Paul to discuss philosophy; second, the content of the philosophers' teaching is likely be outside the immediate cognitive environment of the reader (even when they imagine the context of the hearer). However, the formula that Luke's Paul uses in 17:28 ('as even some of your own poets have said') has an important role in ensuring that relevance will be located in the Greek writers by making the appropriate encyclopaedic information manifest.[65] With the philosophical quotations established for the readers, they are more likely to interpret the rest of the text through philosophical lenses on behalf of the hearers in Athens. Readers would not need to identify which philosopher spoke something – to do so would require too much processing effort – so it is more likely that relevance would be found in the idea that these are the sort of things Greek philosophers might say. This creates an overall implicature that Paul is engaging with Greek philosophy; it also confirms the reader's opinion of the use of σπερμολόγος by the Athenians – this is a false assessment of a skilful communicator.

(2) Readers would expect biblical allusions and quotations to be an important interpretive context because prior speeches in Acts are full of scriptural allusion. This, together with the availability of encyclopaedic information about these well-known texts, means that OT allusions are likely to be detected and appropriate cognitive effects formed. The reader would also be aware that the Athenian hearer is unlikely to access any encyclopaedic information concerning these texts because the Athenians do not have this information, and the texts are not signalled for these hearers. Because of this (and because the biblical allusions come both before and after the philosophical references) the reader will make the strong implicature that these texts form the foundation for Paul's theology and the structure for his speech, and that Paul has concealed this from the Athenians.

(3) The reader would also form implicatures that the OT texts relativize philosophy for the Lukan Paul. Paul is not constructing a natural theology, his understanding comes from scripture, and scriptural thoughts are then used to engage with the philosophy. This impression is reinforced by the use of καί in ὡς καί τινες τῶν καθ' ὑμᾶς ποιητῶν εἰρήκασιν (17:28), coming after the first biblical allusions.

(4) The allusiveness of the biblical texts means that they are a form of indirect language requiring more processing effort of the reader than direct language: in return they lead to more cognitive effects. As such, these references raise a series of implicatures associated with anti-idol polemic. This means that the use of scripture is not about giving a framework from creation to consummation (as Rowe argues), it

---

[65] That Luke *does* signal the poets this way is evidence for this. If this was the most manifest cognitive environment for the reader, then Luke would be requiring extra interpretive effort by this signal.

is constructing an argument about idolatry. This is the key theme on the agenda for the Lukan Paul as the speech is set, and the texts in the OT are arguing that direction too.[66] This also opens up the possibility of implicatures around the theme of worship, an important focus of the sermon.[67]

The Literacy of Luke's Audience

Relevance theory can also help address the issue raised in the discussion of the Lukan audience above: what was the textual awareness of the first readers of the NT, and Luke-Acts in particular? While it cannot show how aware the ancient readers were of OT texts, it does give an indication of how familiar the author expected the reader to be. Because the writer ostensibly communicates the optimal relevance of their communication, they will ensure that their writing does not require excess interpretive effort of the reader. So, if a writer is confident that encyclopaedic information associated with an OT text was the most manifest environment for the reader to find relevance in, they would not give any explicit signal to that intertext in their writing, because signals require further processing.[68] The converse is not true. The presence of a signal *may* mean that the writer was not confident the reader knew the text, and needed to signal it, but it can also direct readers to specific aspects of the OT context, direct readers away from a still more available context than the OT text that they are aware of, or signal that the reader needs to expend extra processing effort in attaining further implicatures. So, are there places where the writer does not signal an intertext essential to understanding the text? While not attempting to be comprehensive, there are several categories of text where Luke does not signal intertexts.

(1) Luke assumes that his readers are familiar with the biblical narrative. In the first two chapters of Luke's Gospel, he draws a number of parallels between the births of John or Jesus and the special births in the OT.[69] These births are an important context for the reader to understand the significance of Jesus and John. In addition, the retelling of the story of Israel in Acts 7 requires awareness of the underlying account because of its selectivity; the way the story is told does not signal each reference.

(2) Luke assumes an awareness of biblical themes. In the laments of Jesus over Jerusalem, there is a use of texts referring to the previous destruction of Jerusalem before the exile (see Lk. 19:41-44; 21:20-24). These are not signalled but it is essential that readers appreciate these echoes to understand the full import of the communication in these texts.[70] The same is true of the Isaianic New Exodus: even if prepared for by the hermeneutical lens of the quotation from Isa. 40:3-5 in Lk. 3:4-6, it requires an awareness of the motif of the New Exodus in Isaiah to detect it elsewhere.[71]

---

[66] There are also some verbal and conceptual similarities between Acts 17:24 and 7:48, and Stephen's speech is also a critique of idolatry in the prophetic mould. See Smith, *Fate of Jerusalem*, 167-8.
[67] This is significant if Bruce Winter is correct about the cultic background of the Areopagus address; see Winter, 'On Introducing Gods to Athens: An Alternative Reading of Acts 17:18-20', *TynBul* 47 (1996): 71-90.
[68] This approach is related to that taken by Fantin, *Entire World*, 215-18, in his demonstration of the referent for Lord language in the NT.
[69] Joel B. Green, 'The Problem of a Beginning: Israel's Scriptures in Luke 1-2', *BBR* 4 (1994): 61-86.
[70] Smith, *Fate of Jerusalem*, 59-67, 124-31.
[71] Pao, *Acts*, 111-248.

(3) Specific texts are alluded to with no signal. For example, the parable of the tenants in Lk. 20:9-19 requires an appreciation of Isa. 5:1-7;[72] the triumphal entry effectively enacts Zech. 9:9 without quoting it (as Mt. 21:5 and Jn 12:15 also do);[73] the quotation from Ps. 117:26 (LXX) on the lips of the crowd in Lk. 19:38 is not signalled as a quotation, but the meaning of the text requires the reader to identify it as a quotation.[74]

Of course, NT documents were not written for individuals, but for communities; they were typically reread, and it is likely that the leader of the community would explain allusions.[75] But at some level, Luke seems to anticipate a familiarity with the OT beyond story and motif; it requires knowledge of texts themselves. And this is a help in working out how much OT knowledge would be in the encyclopaedic information of the Christian communities; there is more than some assume.[76]

Conclusion

Relevance theory, in describing human communication and cognition, provides a helpful description of how readers read texts. In describing an almost instantaneous interaction in the reader's mind between the words on the page, and the interpretive context of the reader, it shows how the reader is active in constructing meaning in a process that is geared around relevance. In this way, ancient readers add new knowledge to what they already know. While this is a process common to all readers, it makes a particular contribution to understanding how ancient readers approach texts, especially those with complex contextual backgrounds, and it also explains how readers can read at more superficial and deeper levels. While the pre-existing encyclopaedic information may differ from reader to reader, the author of the ancient text takes care to ensure that the reader is likely to understand the text in a manner that will ensure accurate communication provided the reader reads in a manner that looks for optimal relevance. The encyclopaedic information is rich and elastic in its form, but the way that writers of the NT have written their texts (at least with Luke), suggests that they expected a good level of biblical competence in their readers.

---

[72] Robert L. Brawley, *Text to Text Pours Forth Speech: Voices of Scripture in Luke-Acts* (Bloomington: Indiana University Press, 1995), 28–41.
[73] Kim Huat Tan, *The Zion Traditions and the Aims of Jesus*, SNTSMS 91 (New York: Cambridge University Press, 1997), 151.
[74] Smith, *Fate of Jerusalem*, 57–9.
[75] See the discussion of expectations in Johnson, *Readers*.
[76] Against the ideas of Christopher D. Stanley, *Arguing with Scripture: The Rhetoric of Quotations in the Letters of Paul* (London: T&T Clark, 2004).

10

Divine Dissimulation and the Apostolic Visions of Acts

John Moxon

New Testament Audiences – Problems and Prospects

A running theme of this volume is audiences and what texts may imply about them. Whilst some use 'audience' to indicate *contemporary* readers,[1] here only the earliest context is in view. However, some care is needed. For rhetorically focused studies, the strategies of ancient authors are the principal focus and although their earliest readers' beliefs might be inferred by mirror reading, they may not be a scholar's fundamental concern.[2] Where they are of central interest, however, they can remain tantalisingly veiled.[3] Intra-textual groups may provide a range of model responses, but the text's immediate 'external' audience may not appear amongst them and almost always has

---

[1] Modern literary critics tend to speak interchangeably of audience and reader (cf. S. R. Suleiman and I. C. Wimmers, *The Reader in the Text: Essays on Audience and Interpretation* [Princeton: Princeton University Press, 1980]), and in such circles, audience criticism can become synonymous with reader-response criticism. In edited volumes on biblical interpretation, such as E. S. Malbon and E. V. McKnight, eds., *The New Literary Criticism and the New Testament* (Sheffield: Sheffield Academic, 1994), contributors use 'audience' for both ancient and contemporary readers.

[2] For a primarily ancient rhetorical construction of audience, cf. D. Patrick and A. Scult, *Rhetoric and Biblical Interpretation* (Sheffield: Sheffield Academic, 1990), 12. On the challenges of using 'mirror reading' for ethical issues amongst Pauline audiences, cf. N. K. Gupta, 'Mirror-Reading Moral Issues in Paul's Letters', *JSNT* 34 (2012) 361–81.

[3] Cf. J. A. Darr, *Herod the Fox: Audience Criticism and Lukan Characterization* (Sheffield: Sheffield Academic, 1998); D. S. Dodson, *Reading Dreams: An Audience-Critical Approach to the Dreams in the Gospel of Matthew* (London: T&T Clark, 2009), W. Carter, 'Recalling the Lord's Prayer: The Authorial Audience and Matthew's Prayer as Familiar Liturgical Experience', *CBQ* 57 (1995): 514–30; and S. Dowd and E. S. Malbon, 'The Significance of Jesus' Death in Mark: Narrative Context and Authorial Audience', *JBL* 125 (2006): 271–97.

to be inferred.⁴ In New Testament (NT) studies, this was traditionally pursued in a fairly crude manner, often only as far as deciding between Jewish and Gentile readers.⁵ More recently, however, this has involved much more detailed claims about audiences' contexts, histories and agendas.⁶

The limits of this speculative venture have been questioned. Thus, even where a readership seems to be implied quite clearly, this might not be able to be taken at face value.⁷ Completely different sorts of material can be enjoyed by the same people,⁸ and the preference in NT studies for tightly defined addressee groups facing specific contingencies has now been questioned.⁹ Indeed, some prefer the plural term *audiences*¹⁰ which can include divided or even opposed groups,¹¹ whilst others see

---

⁴ T. W. Manson, *The Teaching of Jesus: Studies of its Form and Content* (Cambridge: Cambridge University Press, 1967), and J. A. Baird, *Audience Criticism and the Historical Jesus* (Philadelphia: Westminster, 1969), were both interested in the 'stated' audiences of the Synoptic Gospels, dividing them into concentric levels of affiliation including the twelve, interested crowds, enemies and inimical crowds. Baird, *Audience Criticism*, 16, notes that although scholars have traditionally discounted these audience indicators as unreliable, they are relatively stable and are linked to material with variational characteristics. In addition, he argues that this audience segmentation assumes theological significance (e.g. as in Mk 4:11, 33-34).

⁵ As for instance in A. A. Das, '"Praise the Lord, All you Gentiles": The Encoded Audience of Romans 15.7-13', *JSNT* 34 (2011): 90–110.

⁶ Cf. R. L. Rohrbaugh, 'The Social Location of the Markan Audience', *Union Seminary Review* 47 (1993): 380–95, on Mark, and U. C. Von Wahlde, 'Community in Conflict: The History and Social Context of the Johannine Community', *Interpretation* 49 (1995): 379–89, on John.

⁷ Not only in the pseudepigrapha, as noted by D. Lincicum, 'Mirror-Reading a Pseudepigraphical Letter', *NovT* 59 (2017): 171–93, but also in apparently straightforward works; cf. Das, 'Praise the Lord'.

⁸ In classical studies, we are helpfully reminded that tragic and comedic drama were performed for the same audience (S. A. Nelson, *Aristophanes and his Tragic Muse: Comedy, Tragedy and the Polis in 5th Century Athens* [Leiden: Brill, 2016], 1–5) and that philosophical works and bawdy novels might also have been read by largely the same people (e.g. S. A. Stephens, 'Who Read Ancient Novels?', in *The Search for the Ancient Novel*, ed. J. Tatum [Baltimore: Johns Hopkins University Press, 1994], 405–18).

⁹ The consensus about 'tightly defined' audiences for the Gospels almost certainly arose via influence of studies in the Fourth Gospel, where talk of a Johannine 'school' (R. A. Culpepper, *The Johannine School: An Evaluation of the Johannine-School Hypothesis based on an Investigation of the Nature of Ancient Schools* [Missoula: Scholars Press, 1975]) or 'circle' (O. Cullmann, *The Johannine Circle: Its place in Judaism, among the Disciples of Jesus and in Early Christianity* [London: SCM, 1976]) soon gave way to the Johannine 'community' (R. E. Brown, *The Community of the Beloved Disciple* [New York: Paulist, 1979]). Although the earliest usages of the Synoptics were almost contemporaneous (cf. D. M. Sweetland, 'The Lord's Supper and the Lukan Community', *BTB* 13 [1983]: 23–7), this was always received circumspectly (e.g. by D. C. Allison, 'Was There a "Lukan Community?"', *IBS* 10 [1988]: 62–70) although has been resisted more comprehensively by R. J. Bauckham, *The Gospels for All Christians: Rethinking the Gospel Audiences* (Edinburgh: T. & T. Clark, 1998). Although it is still natural for social-scientific studies to speak of 'communities', Bauckham's caution has determined the tone of much subsequent debate (e.g. C. E. W. Vine, *The Audience of Matthew: An Appraisal of the Local Audience Thesis* [London: Bloomsbury, 2014]). For a recent Patristic critique of Bauckham, see M. M. Mitchell, 'Patristic Counter-Evidence to the Claim that "The Gospels Were Written for All Christians"', *NTS* 51 (2005): 36–79.

¹⁰ E.g. C. D. Stanley, '"Pearls before Swine": Did Paul's Audiences Understand His Biblical Quotations?', *NovT* 41 (1999): 124–44.

¹¹ E.g. B. Richardson, 'The Other Reader's Response: On Multiple, Divided, and Oppositional Audiences', *Criticism* 39 1997): 31–53.

authorial manipulation of readers' beliefs[12] as an attempt to 'create' an audience out of those engaging with a text.[13]

It is important to note that recipients may literally have been audiences in so far as texts were more often *heard* than they were read.[14] And in as much as gathered communities might be relatively diverse and not under anyone's absolute control,[15] authors would need to anticipate a variety of responses,[16] particularly at the emotional level, where individual differences might eclipse general group characteristics.[17] Nevertheless, scholars reasonably speak of the 'minimum competencies' required to negotiate a performance.[18] But disagreements arise even here as to the potential demands on the Lukan audience. How much knowledge of political, historical, and religious contexts, Greek philosophy, poetry, and literature is really required of them?[19] Which assumptions, pointers and parallels can safely go over readers' heads, and which must be recognized to ensure basic understanding?[20]

At this point, it is clear that labelling an audience in broad terms[21] may not be as useful as simply charting competencies the author presupposes for at least some readers as well as the interests, concerns, or anxieties they appear to display from time to time. This would not require that every single reader shared them all,[22] even if a rough centre of gravity could be identified. For instance, I suspect that the claimed Bacchic intertexture of Acts is intentional and visible to certain readers,[23] but am sure

---

[12] E.g. S. P. Ahearne-Kroll, 'Audience Inclusion and Exclusion as Rhetorical Technique in the Gospel of Mark', *JBL* 129 (2010): 717–35.

[13] R. A. Werline, 'Ritual, Order and the Construction of an Audience in 1 Enoch 1–36', *DSD* 22 (2015): 325–41. That in spite of the segmented address of Rom. 2:17 and 11:13, Paul's relentless use of 'we' for the audience as a whole (Rom. 1:5, 12 and throughout) seeks to unify the readers at every point. At a broader narrative level, audience 'creation' fits very well with the conciliatory reading of Acts.

[14] On the oral delivery of Mark, cf. J. Dewey. 'The Gospel of Mark as an Oral–Aural Event: Implications for Interpretation', in Malbon and McKnight, eds., *The New Literary Criticism and the New Testament*, 145–63. For the development of this idea in relation to Acts, cf. W. Shiell, *Reading Acts: The Lector and the Early Christian Audience* (Leiden: Brill, 200)

[15] By derivation, early Christian readers, as members of a community 'receiving' a text, were more a captive audience than a 'readership' in contemporary popular terms.

[16] A point made by Aristotle in *Rhet.* 2.12-17, and often portrayed in Gospel texts, e.g. in Mk 10:17-23; Lk. 3:10-14; 12:13-15.

[17] M. R. Whitenton, 'Feeling the Silence: A Moment-by-Moment Account of Emotions at the End of Mark (16:1–8)', *CBQ* 78 (2016): 272–89.

[18] B. J. Abasciano, 'Diamonds in the Rough: A Reply to Christopher Stanley Concerning the Reader Competency of Paul's Original Audiences', *NovT* 49 (2007): 153–83.

[19] Homer, tragedy and comedy, novels, didactic tales, and their character types.

[20] Stanley, 'Pearls before Swine'. This has sometimes involved a debate about the implications of the Lukan preface for our understanding of the 'centre of gravity' of the Lukan audience. Cf. L. Alexander, *The Preface to Luke's Gospel: Literary Convention and Social Context in Luke 1.1-4 and Acts 1.1* (Cambridge: Cambridge University Press, 1993).

[21] E.g. 'Christians with a Hellenistic-Jewish background in such and such a locale, favourable or otherwise to Paul etc.'. All are agreed Luke's composition points to a general familiarity with both the Graeco-Roman world and Jewish customs, but beyond this it would not make sense if more specialized knowledge were essential.

[22] H. Moxnes, 'The Social Context of Luke's Community', *Union Seminary Review* 48 (1994): 380 highlights this dilemma when he says we must 'draw a profile of the knowledge *required* of the readers and, on that basis, attempt to situate the empirical audience'.

[23] Cf. C. J. P. Friesen, *Reading Dionysus: Euripides' Bacchae and the Cultural Contestations of Greeks, Jews, Romans, and Christians* (Tübingen: Mohr Siebeck, 2015), 207 n. 3, 213–21.

that the text remains entirely functional if this is not picked up. The miraculous prison escapes, the great light from heaven, and the warning against fighting against God all work 'as is' even if their exact literary heritage is not appreciated by all.[24]

The ability of some audience members to appreciate such niceties, therefore, may not be very significant. Assuming a congregational profile similar to that noted by Paul, 'not many were…wise…powerful, [or] of noble birth' (1 Cor. 1:26), we might expect a few better educated readers to do so, but as suggested, without great import. But some aspects of Acts demand something more significant of the audience as a whole. The proposal here is that when distinctive features are visible in central or important parts of the book, then these should be noted, and particularly so when their normality might be questioned by other audiences.

Dialogue Pattern as Audience Marker

The issue I draw attention to here – something that might be unremarkable for modern readers, but potentially striking for Acts' original audience – is the pattern of divine–human dialogue in the visions of Paul and Peter in the central section of Acts.[25] In these encounters, the divine voice employs 'didactic dissimulation' to conceal its true intent. This includes the provocative question 'Why are you persecuting me?' (Acts 9:4) and the enigmatic command 'Rise, kill and eat' (Acts 10:13), both of which intend to cause confusion. These anonymous opening utterances, oddly unexpected and accompanied by feigned ignorance, ambiguity, and misdirection, arguably lead to the entrapment and humiliation of the recipients. Importantly, this pattern is not present in other Lukan examples of divine dialogue, which are handled more conventionally.

As the Old Testament (OT) and other ancient texts show, dissimulation and irony, as general pedagogic devices, are universal rather than uniquely Greek developments.[26] However Jewish and early Christian usage is almost certainly conditioned, if not entirely informed by its Graeco-Roman context. Thus, although several OT dialogues do contain examples of dissimulation,[27] these accounts in Acts would catch the reader's eye for their striking similarity to the perplexing challenges of Socratic–Cynic inquiry. I indicate the general nature of the resonance in this way, however, not because of

---

[24] Widely agreed to be Bacchic allusions, as tabulated by J. Moles, 'Jesus and Dionysus in "The Acts of the Apostles" and Early Christianity', *Hermathena* 180 (2006): 65–104.

[25] The Damascus road vision in Acts 9:1-19 and Peter's animal vision in Acts 10:9-16. In contemporary readings of these seminal events, it has become common to speak of them both as conversion-like experiences. See C. E. van Engen, 'Peter's Conversion: A Culinary Disaster Launches the Gentile Mission', in *Mission in Acts: Ancient Narratives in Contemporary Context*, ed. R. L. Gallagher and P. Hertig (New York: Orbis, 2004), 133–43.

[26] On irony in the OT, cf. C. J. Sharp, *Irony and Meaning in the Hebrew Bible* (Bloomington: Indiana University Press, 2009). At least some scholars seek to place the Socratic tradition and the world of the NT in this broader context; see, e.g., G. S. Holland, *Divine Irony* (Selinsgrove: Susquehanna University Press, 2000), who sets out a pan-Mediterranean understanding in pp. 59–81, before dealing with Socrates (82–118) and Paul (119–56) against this backdrop.

[27] E.g. 'Who will go for us?' God asks Isaiah (an audience of *one*) in Isa. 6:8 or 'Why are you robbing me?' asks God ironically in Mal. 3:8, lamenting uncollected tithes.

any claims of dependence on specific texts or named figures, but because the Socratic heritage ran very broadly into Greek philosophy and indirectly into its environs. Indeed, there is evidence of widespread awareness of and contact with Cynics by Jews and Christians in first-century Palestine and its diasporas, in spite of later conflict.[28] In so far as these two dialogues contain perplexing and distressing elements best located along a Socratic–Cynic trajectory, then it becomes reasonable to explore them on this basis and on the assumption that they could be recognized as such by at least some of Acts' earliest readers.

Engaging creatively with this style of exchange, however, may not have been second nature for all of Luke's audience. In terms of Jewish sensibilities, no doubt shared by some readers, there is evidence of discomfort with such devices, at least within divine speech. Thus, Philo denied that God used riddling or dissimulation in this way, seeing them as quintessentially pagan ploys. Whilst crossing this line might count as an ill-judged innovation on Luke's part, it could nevertheless be acting as a marker for at least part, perhaps a growing part of the audience.[29] This will involve discerning how far early Christian communities had been reflecting on this Socratic–Cynic idiom and how some, at least, felt able to use it in their storytelling about God.

In the following analysis, I shall first trace the development of Socratic–Cynic dialogue and its reception in Graeco-Roman, Jewish, and Christian circles. Then I shall offer detailed commentary on the two passages and their use of dissimulation. Finally, I will attempt to make sense of the appearance such motifs in Acts, the reason these appear in visionary rather than other contexts, and what this might say about the Lukan audience.

The Socratic Heritage and Cynic Development

The division of Greek philosophy into pre-Socratic, Classical, and Hellenistic periods testifies to the influence of a figure who, like Jesus, never wrote a book and is known only through the writings of his disciples.[30] Although clearly not the originator of the dialogue form,[31] Socrates is strongly linked to its rise in fifth-century Athens. In the

---

[28] Shortly after the NT, Justin is critical of Cynic beliefs and practices, particularly 'indifference' (*2 Apol.* 3; *Haer.* 2.14.5; 2.32.2), and disputed personally with the Cynic Philosopher, Crescens (*2 Apol.* 3).

[29] The pattern of speech thus fulfils both the criteria noted above, namely appearing in central or important passages, but also implying a particular presupposition that might not be shared by all.

[30] Socrates is thought to have lived c. 470–399 BCE, but his teachings are known primarily from the works of Xenophon and Plato, with smaller reminiscences from students, friends, and associates such as Antisthenes, Aristippus, Aeschines, and Aristophanes. Xenophon and Plato represent somewhat different pictures. The debate as to which is closer to the truth continues, with Plato more generally favoured today; see, e.g., L. A. Dorion, 'Xenophon's Socrates', in *A Companion to Socrates*, ed. S. Ahbel-Rappe and R. Kamtekar (Oxford: Blackwell, 2006), 93–109.

[31] Didactic dialogue with dissimulating elements clearly predates Socrates. Heraclitus and Pythagoras are often cited in this regard. On Heraclitus of Ephesus (c. 535–475 BCE), cf. C. H. Kahn, *The Art and Thought of Heraclitus: An Edition of the Fragments with Translation and Commentary* (Cambridge: Cambridge University Press, 1979). The Stoics honoured Heraclitus and were aware that their tradition could be viewed as going back to him rather than merely Socrates (ibid., 1). On Pythagoras of Samos (c. 570–495 BCE) and the first-century CE movement claiming to revive his

classic pattern,[32] a simple question, such as 'What is courage?' is posed to a student, and conversation ensues. After some initial response, a challenge, the ἔλεγχος, is pressed back, leading via further exchanges to apparent paradox (παράδοξος, ὀξύμωρο), and thence to impasse or ἀπορία[33] and the collapse of the student's position.[34] Because of Socrates' emphasis on the need for an examined life, the βίος ἔλεγχος, the student's integrity was as much the target as their logic per se, meaning the dénouement could assume a pointedly personal dimension.

So that the student would not see this coming, Socrates might embed a certain ambiguity in his initial challenge or throw out a bizarre, offensive or non-intuitive claim displaying a calculated strangeness or ἀτοπία.[35] Other tactics involved claiming not to know the answer,[36] remaining silent as the student made a fatal error, or worse, helping the victim along with polite encouragements. The cloaking of the exact intentions of the educator in this way was known as dissimulation, or εἰρωνεία,[37] and together with worries about the potential humiliation of students, provoked considerable ethical critique.[38]

---

teachings, cf. Kahn, *Pythagoras and the Pythagoreans: A Brief History* (Indianapolis: Hackett, 2001). Behind this, many have seen connections to the ancient Near Eastern sceptical wisdom tradition; cf. T. L. Holm, 'Literature', in *A Companion to the Ancient Near East*, ed. D. C. Snell (Oxford: Blackwell, 2005), 261–2.

[32] On the perennial problem of the mismatch between modern use of the 'Socratic' label and the pattern and technicalities of the 'original', see R. Reich, 'Confusion about the Socratic Method: Socratic Paradoxes and Contemporary Invocations of Socrates', *Philosophy of Education Archive* (1998): 68–78.

[33] Cf. C. H. Kahn, *Plato and the Socratic Dialogue: The Philosophical Use of a Literary Form* (Cambridge: Cambridge University Press, 1996), 95–101, 178–80.

[34] That this is a typically popular over-simplification is clear from the ongoing debates in G. A. Scott, ed., *Does Socrates Have a Method? Rethinking the Elenchus in Plato's Dialogues and Beyond* (University Park: Pennsylvania State University Press, 2002).

[35] It is widely agreed that much of this comes from Heraclitus, although M. L. McPherran, 'Elenctic Interpretation and the Delphic Oracle', in Scott, ed., *Does Socrates Have a Method?*, 114–44, argues that Socrates' love for the riddling ambiguity of oracular language is a major source for this.

[36] Small-scale claims to ignorance pepper the dialogues, but there is some debate as to how these relate to Socrates' grander claim to 'know nothing', the so-called disavowal of knowledge. Contrasting markedly with the Delphic acclamation of Socrates as 'the wisest man', J. H. Lesher, 'Socrates' Disavowal of Knowledge', *JHPh* 25 (1987): 275–88, suggests that besides making a serious point about the limits of philosophical inquiry, Socrates literally tried to turn himself into a living paradox.

[37] A. L. Damm, '"Speech Unhindered": A Study of Irony in the Acts of the Apostles' (Ph.D. diss., Wilfrid Laurier University, 1998), 57–9 speaks of εἰρωνεία as a form of pretended ignorance or 'pretension', otherwise referred to as προσποίησις or παραπροσποίησις. Later Church Fathers would allow this strategy to God only in so far as it amounted to 'accommodation' or συγκατάβασις (Lat. *condescendio*, cf. Julian's use in reference to Attis in *Or.* 5.171b). M. Lane, 'The Evolution of Eirôneia in Classical Greek Texts: Why Socratic Eirôneia Is Not Socratic Irony', *OSAPh* 31 (2006): 49–83, issues a helpful reminder that this original Aristophanic sense of concealment is what we should understand in relation to Socrates, and that this does not correspond to what many later critics understand by Socratic 'irony'.

[38] Thus whilst J. R. Labendz, *Socratic Torah: Non-Jews in Rabbinic Intellectual Culture* (New York: Oxford University Press, 2013), 41–2, claims that such scheming and obfuscation never belonged to elenchic dialogue proper, and P. Boghossian, 'Socratic Pedagogy: Perplexity, Humiliation, Shame and a Broken Egg', *Educational Philosophy and Theory* 44 (2012): 712–15, denies any intention to *hurt* a student (cf. Labendz, *Socratic Torah*, 44, 'not fundamentally hostile'), there is no doubt that Plato portrays Socrates defending himself from both of these charges.

With Socratic dialogue later falling out of favour with the academies,[39] it was primarily the Stoics and Cynics who brokered this tradition to the first-century world.[40] And in their hands its most concerning features were developed further. The Stoics continued the dialogue form, giving a heightened role to non-intuitive and ambiguous ideas,[41] leading to renewed concerns that the young might be misled by such language.[42] The Cynics became more extreme still;[43] relishing paradoxical forms and elevating ἀτοπία to the level of the bizarre, they moved beyond traditional Athenian 'frankness', or παρρησία, by causing deliberate offense.[44] Notionally intending a didactic provocation[45] and often deliberately off-putting, teachers might, for example, advocate incest or cannibalism, leaving the dead unburied or stealing from temples. This could spill over into action, including absurd gestures, such as offering a student a fish,[46] defacing a coin, urinating in public, or worse. Paradoxically, if these were not real commendations but didactic conceits, then Cynics' shocking presentations would constitute the very εἰρωνεία which traditional honesty or παρρησία always resisted.[47] Indeed, the difficulty of telling whether such statements or gestures were meant literally or figuratively lay at the heart of Diogenes' own story, at least according to legend (*Diog.* 6). There is no doubt that, however penetrating their critique of accepted norms, acting out such protests in full shamelessness (ἀναίδεια) and indifference (ἀδιαφορία) brought considerable censure.[48]

---

[39] V. Tejera, 'The Hellenistic Obliteration of Plato's Dialogism', in *Plato's Dialogues: New Studies and Interpretations*, ed. G. A. Press (Lanham: Rowman & Littlefield, 1993), 129–36, speaks of the Hellenistic 'obliteration'.

[40] In fact, Neo-Pythagoreans and other teachers showed considerable similarities of approach. Although viewed as 'Socratic' by modern scholars, they understood their origins to lie in Pythagoras (*Vit. Ap.* 6.11.132-135).

[41] On Cicero's *Paradoxa Stoicorum*, cf. R. Gorman, *The Socratic Method in the Dialogues of Cicero* (Stuttgart: Franz Steiner, 2005). On the Stoics' interest in Aristotle's work on linguistic ambiguity, cf. G. A. Kennedy, *Progymnasmata: Greek Textbooks of Prose Composition and Rhetoric* (Leiden: Brill, 2003), 1, 18–19, 31–2.

[42] E. Brown, 'Socrates in the Stoa', in Ahbel-Rappe and Kamtekar, eds., *A Companion to Socrates*, 283.

[43] Started in the fourth century BCE by Antisthenes, Diogenes of Sinopé et al. On their revival in the imperial period and Cynic lifestyle, see R. F. Hock, 'Cynics', *ABD* 1:1222–4.

[44] On the traditional Athenian virtue of frankness and its transformation in Cynicism, see K. Kennedy, 'Cynic Rhetoric: The Ethics and Tactics of Resistance', *RhetR* 18 (1999): 26–45, and on Cynic obscenities and verbal excesses, see J. F. Hultin, *The Ethics of Obscene Speech in Early Christianity and its Environment* (Leiden: Brill, 2008), 82–7. The traditional sense of παρρησία as the frankness proper to a concerned friend is certainly visible in the LXX, Philo, Josephus, and most of the NT, and Hellenistic and Roman authors continued to emphasize this meaning, e.g. in Plutarch's *How to Tell a Flatterer from a Friend* (*Quomodo adulator ab amico internoscatur*).

[45] L. E. Vaage, 'Cynic Epistles (Selections)', in *Ascetic Behavior in Greco-Roman Antiquity: A Sourcebook*, ed. V. L. Wimbush (Minneapolis: Fortress, 1990), 117–28. As noted, these patterns were visible in other contemporary teachers too. Philostratus reports that the neo-Pythagorean Apollonius of Tyana (first century CE) frequently reduced students' positions to 'absurdity' (ἀτοπία, cf. *Vit. Ap.* 1.19–3.58), delivered enigmatic rebukes to inquirers (*Vit. Ap.* 1.15.54-56; 1.16.24-26; 1.16.18-20 et sim), or engaged in riddling or dissimulating exchanges with strangers (*Vit. Ap.* 1.20.5-7), even kings and other dignitaries (*Vit. Ap.* 3.16-25; 3.34-37; 3.41-49).

[46] A σαπέρδης. The man was later dismissed when found without his 'gift' (*Diog.* 36.6-10).

[47] M. T. Riley, 'The Epicurean Criticism of Socrates', *Phoenix* (1980): 64–6.

[48] M. Griffin, 'Cynicism and the Romans: Attraction and Repulsion', in *The Cynics: The Cynic Movement in Antiquity and Its Legacy*, ed. R. B. Branham and M.-O. Goulet-Cazé (Berkeley: University of California Press, 1996), 192. Diogenes was happy to be dubbed 'Socrates gone mad', Σωκράτης μαινόμενος, D.L. *Diog.* 54.2.

It is perhaps surprising that first-century Jewish and Christian teachers may have had more contact with this itinerant, garish form of the tradition than its more moderate institutional forebears.[49] Thus, before surveying the general lines of criticism levelled at this heritage, I shall set out the evidence for Socratic and Cynic influence within first-century Judaism and Christianity.

Socratic and Cynic Elements in Jewish and Early Christian Teaching

It has been long acknowledged that some kind of relationship between the approaches of Jewish and Christian teachers and the Graeco-Roman tradition existed, even if due to a shared heritage. David Daube championed a picture of direct Greek influence on rabbinical discourse from the 1950s,[50] and the use of dialogue and searching questions has drawn forth Socratic comparisons for both Hillel and Jesus.[51] Although Stoicism as a philosophy is clearly present in the orbit of early Judaism and Christianity, particularly in Philo and Paul,[52] it is the itinerant and controversial Cynics, present in rural as well as urban Palestine, that have been particularly discussed in relation to teaching style. Fischel has suggested that the distinctive features of rabbinical chreiae are mediated from Cynicism,[53] and Boyarin finds a link from rabbinical humour to Menippean satire, itself a Cynic tradition.[54]

In early Christian sources, the numerous instances of provocative hyperbole in the Synoptic tradition have received much attention. Stories in which Jesus seeks to keep people out of the Kingdom by confusing them (Mk 4:10-12 and parallels), tells people to cut off their hands, pluck out their eyes, make themselves eunuchs or leave the dead unburied, have rightly led to discussion about possible contact with the Cynic movement. Although the Fourth Gospel is a very different text, it too displays a Socratic intertexture; its quizzical dialogues make extensive use of dissimulation and ambiguity[55] and provocative suggestions such as 'eating flesh' and 'drinking blood' again move into distinctively Cynic territory. And like the Cynics, both deeds and words hover tantalisingly between an apparently shocking radicalism and a veiled, but therefore dissimulating discourse that actively courts misunderstanding. Indeed, throughout, there is a studied indifference towards causing offence, as by turns

---

[49] Cf. F. G. Downing, 'Deeper Reflections on the Jewish Cynic Jesus', *JBL* 117 (1998): 102: 'Anyone learning Greek in Palestine would be likely to be introduced to Cynicism'.
[50] D. Daube, 'Socratic Interrogation', in *The New Testament and Rabbinic Judaism* (London: Athlone, 1956), 151–7.
[51] E.g. D. Flusser, 'Hillel and Jesus: Two Ways of Self-Awareness', in *Hillel and Jesus: Comparative Studies of Two Major Religious Leaders*, ed. J. H. Charlesworth and L. L. Johns (Minneapolis: Fortress, 1997), 74–6.
[52] E.g. T. Engberg-Pedersen, *Paul and the Stoics* (Edinburgh: T. & T. Clark, 2000).
[53] H. A. Fischel, 'Studies in Cynicism and the Ancient Near East: The Transformation of a Chria', in *Religions in Antiquity: Essays in Memory of Erwin Ramsdell Goodenough*, ed. J. Neusner (Leiden: Brill, 1968).
[54] D. Boyarin, *Socrates and the Fat Rabbis* (Chicago: University of Chicago Press, 2009), 193–280, not least because Menippus was a resident of Gadara.
[55] This apparently reflected in the disciples' relieved comment in John 16 that Jesus was capable of speaking 'plainly' (ἐν παρρησίᾳ) as well as in 'figures' (ἐν παροιμίαις).

Pharisees feel targeted by parables, inquirers are driven away by impossible demands, disciples balk at alarming imagery, and apostles are cut to the quick (e.g. Mk 10:22, 24; 12:12; Mt. 15:12; Jn 6:60, 66).

For the Gospel audiences, the surprise is how familiar all this seems. Thus, however perplexing or hurtful it might be for particular recipients (e.g. Mk 2:5-7; 10:25-26; Jn 3:4, 9), there is no suggestion that this mode of speech was *fundamentally unrecognizable*. Indeed, that reporting outrageous statements as *literally* intended could be exploited by political opponents, presupposes this (e.g. Jn 5:18; Mt. 26:61).

This does not mean, however, that pagans, Jews, and Christians remained entirely uncritical of Cynic preaching. In the following sections, their various responses will be explored before turning to the two texts in Acts. Whilst each group sensed the need for moderation, Jews and Christians developed their own points of sensitivity, and arguably developed distinct forms of critique.

Graeco-Roman Critique

It is widely agreed that by the Roman period Cynicism had undergone a process of moderation, and for many, blending with other traditions.[56] Many of the authors reporting and even commending Cynic views in this period betray a Stoicized or eclectic background.[57] These authors, whilst broadly appreciative, are able to join with more thoroughgoing opponents like the Epicureans in questioning the more extreme Cynic traits. This variously focused on their antisocial behaviour, provocative speech and didactic dissimulation. Concerns about behaviour are universal, but particularly strong from Roman commentators.[58] In relation to provocation, we hear frequent worries about speech that is *asperius*, λοίδορος, βλάσφημος, or ἄκαιρος,[59] with Dio warning against a παρρησία that strays into mere harshness (βάρος), commending a more considered form of admonition (νουθεσία), delivered in gentleness (ἠπιότης) and always at an appropriate moment (εὔκαιρος).[60] Others, however, specifically criticize dissimulation, which while not necessarily rude, still amounts to a form of deception, including the unannounced use of obscure, enigmatic, or ambiguous language.[61] Instead, they require sages to speak plainly (ἁπλῶς, ἐν εἰλικρινείᾳ) and not resort to

---

[56] R. B. Branham, 'The Cynics', in *REP* (1998), §4.
[57] Key figures include Musonius Rufus (c. 25–101 CE), Dio Chrysostom (c. 40–115 CE), Epictetus (c. 55–135 CE), Lucian of Samosata (c. 125–180 CE). Malherbe notes that their outlooks and their views of Cynicism are for the most part 'heavily Stoicised'. Other sources include the first-century pseudonymous 'Cynic Epistles'. See A. J. Malherbe, *The Cynic Epistles: A Study Edition* (Missoula: Scholars Press, 1977), 1–2. Cicero appears to imply two-way traffic when he speaks in *Off.* 1:128 of 'Stoics who are almost Cynics'.
[58] Cf. the numerous examples in Roman authors discussed by M. Griffin, 'Cynicism and the Romans: Attraction and Repulsion', in Branham and Goulet-Cazé, eds., *The Cynics*, 190–204.
[59] Cf. Cicero in *Tusc.* 1.43.104, who describes Diogenes's stated wish to remain unburied as harsh, or *asperius*. Lucian in *Fug.* 27.16 tells of a Cynic speaking roughly and abusively (τραχύφωνον, λοίδορον).
[60] Dio Chrysostom, *Or.* 32.11.
[61] M. Erler, 'Parrhesy and Irony: Plato's Socrates and the Epicurean Tradition', in *How Should One Live? Comparing Ethics in Ancient China and Greco-Roman Antiquity*, ed. R. A. H. King and D. Schilling (Berlin: de Gruyter, 2011), 155.

the cloaking of εἰρωνεία or the σχήματα of figured speech.[62] The key critics of dissimulation and deliberate obscurity were the Epicureans who deemed them incompatible with the older understanding of παρρησία as well-intentioned frankness.[63]

Jews and Christians were keen to associate themselves with any moderate voices in discussions about public propriety and language, but faced tensions too, not least in that some of their own teachers had shown distinctly Cynic traits. Whilst behaviour was rarely more than eccentric,[64] speech raised particular concerns, although differently in the two traditions. Jews were particularly worried about dissimulation in divine speech whilst Christians were apparently more sensitive about provocation in human teaching. These sensitivities will be examined in turn below, before exploring the distinctly Socratic intertexture of two of the apostolic vision accounts in Acts.

Jewish Sensitivities

Despite modern awareness that irony, dissimulation, and ambiguity were entirely natural within the world of biblical literature, including divine speech,[65] Jewish writers in the Hellenistic and Roman periods show considerable anxiety about countenancing any deliberate use of such ruses by God. Whilst they accept that prophets could use dissimulation when speaking in God's name,[66] they were more sensitive about *direct* divine speech, generally denying that God ever dissimulated or spoke ambiguously. This led to concern about statements in Genesis where God apparently feigned ignorance, worried about unforeseen consequences, expressed regret, and other issues.[67] In the Hellenistic and Roman periods, these attracted the attention of Pagan critics. Philo allowed this as a form of divine *accommodation*, or συγκαταβασις, such as parents might use with their children.[68] This image is taken up by Origen and the

---

[62] Cf. Chrysippus in *SVF* 3.161.3-6, Dio Chrysostom in *Or.* 51.1; 52.16. and others discussed by D. E. Fredrickson, 'Parrēsia in the Pauline Epistles', in *Friendship, Flattery, and Frankness of Speech: Studies on Friendship in the New Testament World*, ed. J. T. Fitzgerald (Leiden: Brill, 1996), 173-4.

[63] The theme can be seen particularly in the writings of Philodemus of Gadara; cf. C. E. Glad, *Paul and Philodemus: Adaptability in Epicurean and Early Christian Psychagogy* (Leiden: Brill, 1995), 104-24, who compares Philodemus and Paul on this point.

[64] In the Gospels, perhaps causing a disturbance in the temple (Mk 11:15-19 and parallels) and washing the disciples' feet (Jn 13:1-17) might have reminded an ancient audience of the Cynics.

[65] Cf. Holland, *Divine Irony*, 59-81.

[66] Cf. Nathan's parable about a rapacious neighbour designed to lure his hearer into a humiliating trap in 2 Sam. 11:27-12:6.

[67] On feigned ignorance, see Gen. 3:9-14 and 4:6, 9 and also the fact-finding missions in Gen. 11:5 ('The LORD came down to see the city and the tower, which mortals had built') and 18:21 on the sin of Sodom ('I must go down and see'). On unforeseen consequences, see Gen. 3:22-23 regarding regret (cf. Gen. 6:6, 'the LORD was sorry that he had made humankind'). Many of these divine utterances seem more unselfconscious than deliberately didactic, and several are private asides, accommodating more to the reader than to characters within the text.

[68] On accommodation as a theological problem, see D. Stern, 'Imitatio Hominis: Anthropomorphism and the Character(s) of God in Rabbinic Literature', *Prooftexts* 12 (1992): 151-74. On the questions in Gen. 3:10 and 4:9, cf. *QG* 1.45 and *QG* 1.68-69. On God's apparent worry in Gen. 3:22 about Adam's designs on the tree of life, Philo is quick to deny that God literally feels uncertainty or envy (*QG* 1.54-55). By adding that he speaks ὡς ἄνθρωπος παιδεύσει τὸν υἱὸν, he casts the utterance as a pedagogic dissimulation of a parental kind. It is likely, although not explicitly stated, that the thought comes to Philo via Deut. 1:31.

later and more relaxed rabbinical tradition,[69] where God might 'lose' an argument and gleefully exclaim 'My children have defeated me!'[70] However benign this parental play, some prophetic dialogue assumes more disturbingly Socratic characteristics, including feigned indifference when God is apparently oblivious to the ethical problem with the destruction of Sodom (Gen. 18:16-33), commands Abraham to sacrifice his son,[71] or presses shameful acts upon the prophets, such as Isaiah's nakedness, Ezekiel cooking over human dung, or Jeremiah's temptation of the Rechabites.

Another sensitive issue was ambiguous or riddling language. Although permissible when directed at foreign kings (e.g. Dan. 5:1-31) or errant Israelites (e.g. Isa. 6:9-10), it was routinely denied that God used this in ordinary circumstances. The key anxiety was its association with pagan oracles. Thus, whilst claiming the best of Greek philosophy for Judaism, Philo denigrates 'indistinctness and riddles' and distances God from them.[72] However, he is aware of places where the Bible lets slip its guard and notes that God speaks to most prophets in riddles.[73] Later, Josephus confesses that even Moses *sometimes* speaks 'in enigmas' (*A.J.* Praef 24) and compounds the problem when he suggests not only that Jewish leaders could misunderstand biblical prophecies, but that these were sometimes delivered 'ambiguously' (ἀμφιβόλως) at source (*B.J.* 3.325).

Christian Teaching

Many of these cautions came into early Christian thought. However, the appeal to divine accommodation for the cases of feigned ignorance noted by Philo became more or less routine in early Patristic thought, and more awkward texts were understood as mystical allegories.[74] As for ambiguity, Christians often had to be more flexible

---

[69] After the anxieties expressed by Philo, later rabbinic Judaism shows considerable relaxation about divine anthropomorphism which becomes an accepted device later midrash. See Stern, 'Imitatio Hominis'.

[70] So *b. B. Mes.* 59b. This tradition is seen in an even more playful form in the later idiom of the heavenly academy, populated by deceased or 'visiting' rabbis (cf. *b. Git.* 6b; *b. B. Metz* 86a). Here, God as anthropomorphized 'divine rabbinical master' engaged extensively in Socratic-style dissimulation, including feigned ignorance of the law, and even halakhic defeat in 'open' contests with his students.

[71] If this was intended as a test, then it must surely count as a cruel one. Scholars frequently point out the similarity with the classical episode of the divine command to Agamemnon to sacrifice his daughter, Iphigenia (Euripides, *Iph. aul.* 89-91), which is also resolved by the provision of an animal.

[72] He insists rather that God 'eradicates' ambiguity; cf. Philo, *Leg.* 3.226; *Plant.* 111; *QG* 1.34; *Migr.* 80; *Agr.* 16; 136; *Ebr.* 139.

[73] He works hard to ameliorate the implications of Num. 12:6-8 when it inadvertently suggests that, with the exception of Moses, God speaks to most prophets in dreams and riddles. Only to Moses does he speak 'clearly and *not* in riddles' (LXX, ἐν εἴδει καὶ οὐ δι' αἰνιγμάτων). The other prophets in this verse are not 'false' but are simply more ordinary. Philo, however, is very careful to rework this in terms of *relative directness* rather than of the nature of the speech as such. He thus paraphrases Num. 12:6-8 in *Her.* 262 and *Leg.* 3.103 and in both removes the LXX's λαλήσω αὐτῷ to make the contrast refer to the way God makes himself known (γνωσθήσομαι), thus removing the suggestion that this involved riddling speech as such.

[74] Cf. S. D. Benin, *The Footprints of God: Divine Accommodation in Jewish and Christian Thought* (Albany: SUNY Press, 1993), 1-30.

than their Jewish forebears as they made the figurative language of the psalms and prophets central to the identification of their messiah (e.g. Lk. 24:25-27). These tenuous readings became a major apologetic problem, and although Augustine argued that the figuration (*tropica locutio*) was reasonably transparent,[75] 'Christian' readings were nevertheless not obvious to Jewish opponents and had to be explained in terms of veiling and revelation (2 Cor. 3:14-16).

If milder cases of accommodating dissimulation had nevertheless ceased to be quite as controversial, we can, in the NT epistles and later patristic developments, see some anxiety about 'extreme speech'. As noted above, this might represent merely harsh, insensitive or inopportune teaching, but could constitute a more controversial kind of Cynic-style dissimulation where the deliberate shock of the literal form risked drowning out any intended figuration. Thus, for all Paul might owe to Cynic ideas and discursive forms, his manner is generally measured and opportune. We see numerous encouragements to gentleness (1 Thess. 2:7; Col. 3:21; Phlm 8-9; 1 Tim. 3:2; 2 Tim. 2:24-25; 4:2); indeed, Malherbe takes 1 Thess. 2:7's 'we were gentle' as a specifically anti-Cynic caution,[76] and when Paul urges fathers to avoid the incessant 'provocation' (ἐρέθισμα) of their children, he might be casting a glance in the same direction (Col. 3:21). Experienced teachers (διδακτικός) are encouraged to view all new believers as 'little ones' (Mt. 18:6, 10-14; cf. 1 Thess. 1:1; 2:7), guarding them from any σκανδάλον; in Church life, everyone must desist from demonstrations of personal freedom that might cause others to 'stumble' (1 Cor. 8:7-13) and in relations with outsiders, we must avoid giving offense (ἀπρόσκοπος, 1 Cor. 10:32). It is possible that we are witnessing here the creation of an ethos for later Christian *didache*, seen in a more developed form in Clement's *Paedagogos*.

Nevertheless, this caution curiously problematises Jesus' own provocative teaching style which cannot apparently be commended to later Christians. Later Stoic critics of Cynicism who nevertheless wished to acknowledge a great debt to earlier radicals like Socrates, honoured them as 'divine' exceptions,[77] and there is some evidence that Jesus' own function as a σκανδάλον was also understood in similar terms (Mt. 13:57; 15:12; Jn 6:61).

Thus, we observe a contrast. In the period of the NT, Jewish sages might use Cynic patterns in own their teaching whilst being cautious of admitting them of God. Christians, on the other hand, whilst clearly heirs to the 'Cynic Jesus', distance their own teaching from his style and yet continue to allow it for God and/or Jesus in at least *some* divine visions – as here in the two apostolic call narratives in Acts. Thus,

---

[75] Augustine, *C. mend.* 24. He certainly did not count it as dissimulation in any negative sense. He even believed that paradoxical forms such as *antiphrasis* could be understood by most readers, noting that 'a student is not hindered because [such truths] are shrouded…rather…they are more ardently desired and…more joyfully discovered'.

[76] A. J. Malherbe, '"Gentle as a Nurse": The Cynic Background to I Thess II', *NovT* 12 (1970): 216.

[77] Cf. Cicero, *Off.* 1.148: 'no one ought to…suppose that, because Socrates or Aristippus…did or said something contrary to…established customs…he has a right to do the same; it was only by reason of their great and superhuman virtues (*magnis illi et divinis bonis*) that those famous men acquired this special privilege. But the Cynics' whole system of philosophy must be rejected, for it is inimical to moral sensibility.' See the discussion in relation to Roman responses to Cynicism by Griffin, 'Cynicism', 192.

although the predominantly Jewish character of early Christianity is often emphasized in contemporary scholarship, there are hints here of a divergence of sensibilities within Luke's potential audience. We now turn to the text of the two visions to explore the Socratic–Cynic intertexture of their embedded dialogue.

Texts and Analysis

Paul in Acts 9:1-19

Although much studied in other regards, the rhetorical structure of the dialogue in Paul's conversion vision is relatively neglected. Although the connection between the initial question, 'Saul, Saul, why do you persecute me?' (Acts 9:4b), and Paul's campaign against the Christians seems self-evident, the withholding of the voice's identity and the teasing accusation constitutes unannounced enigmatic speech and thus a form of dissimulation, intending to probe Paul's behaviour.

The obscuring mechanisms display a nested structure where the lack of identification of the speaker constitutes an outer frame, within which logically lies an unstated maxim that 'to hurt what a man values is to hurt the man'.[78] At the outer level, Paul cannot answer the question if he does not know who is being persecuted. That the speaker does not appear to realize that their anonymity is a problem constitutes dissimulation. At the inner level, the maxim about how a person can be hurt *indirectly* has been removed altogether, and therefore cannot point to the solution of the riddling question. Semantically, this stratagem renders the riddle 'improper' in the sense that it is not soluble by analysis alone and requires privileged knowledge. Paul possesses the several parts but cannot make the connection deductively. But there is an additional cruelty. If he does solve the riddle, Paul will convict himself – a Socratic staple, and in folkloric terms, a 'neck riddle'.[79]

Paul is now in a double bind and stalls with a request for the speaker's identity. The famous reply 'I am Jesus, whom you are persecuting' (Acts 9:5) duly fills in this blank but now invites Paul to make the final connection via the concept of vicarious hurt, or risk another and more pathetic sounding question. In fact, he is spared this final humiliation. Paul's silence leaves the completion to the readers, and in the immediate switch to practicalities, the contest is conceded. Being led away blind for some days of seclusion is a fitting expression of the aporia just experienced and the reconstruction to come. Intriguingly, in the re-telling of this story in Acts 26:12-18,[80] the voice adds 'It hurts you to kick against the goads'. This second riddling aphorism, famously used in Euripides' *Bacchae*, reproduces the Socratic stratagem again as Pentheus is pressed to understand that by persecuting Dionysus' followers, the god 'suffers ill at his hands'.[81]

---

[78] This is not a Greek aphorism as such, but the essential thought is well known.
[79] R. Bauman, '"I'll Give You Three Guesses": The Dynamics of Genre in the Riddle Tale', in *Untying the Knot: On Riddles and Other Enigmatic Modes*, ed. G. Hasan-Rokem and D. D. Shulman (Oxford: Oxford University Press, 1996), 63–4.
[80] On the differences between the three accounts, cf. D. Marguerat, *The First Christian Historian: Writing the 'Acts of the Apostles'* (Cambridge: Cambridge University Press, 2002), 179–204.
[81] Euripides, *Bacch.* 778–795.

Peter in Acts 10:9-16

Although somewhat different from Paul's experience, Peter's vision in Acts 10:9-16 shares dissimulating and riddling elements and similarly precipitates a personal crisis. In comparison to Paul's divine light, the visual imagery of unclean animals is more fundamental to its sematic structure, and its dialogue is perhaps more perplexing. The unidentified voice provocatively invites Peter to 'rise, kill and eat', to which he rightly responds, 'By no means, Lord'.[82] The riddling riposte 'What God has made clean, you must not call profane' produces no further response, and unlike Paul, Peter does not ask for the speaker's identity. He thus remains at impasse, and after three repeats without progress, the vision ends.[83]

The Socratic elements however, are prominent. The initial brazen command to breach sacred law certainly has overtones of Cynic ἀναίδεια or ἀδιαφορία. And like Paul's vision, the speaker's anonymity counts as a form of dissimulation. Whilst not a formal part of the riddle, its radical proposal surely makes identification pressing. Although suitably horrified, by not querying the *intent* of the request Peter appears to be caught by the literal/figurative ambiguity central to such challenges. The divine riposte 'What God has cleansed etc.' (10:15) takes the form of an apparent or pseudo-aphorism.[84] The implication that it *should* be well-known is again a dissimulation, designed to unsettle the student before posing a secondary conundrum as to how it applies to the animals. By pointing forward to the as yet unanticipated Gentile reception of the Spirit, this again constitutes an improper or insoluble riddle. Whilst Paul comes to his shocking realization during the dialogue, Peter is left in ἀπορία for two days. Such gaps between challenge and solution are not unknown in Cynic exchanges,[85] so when Peter finally confesses that 'God has shown me' (Acts 10:28), he is reporting this delayed outcome.

For all their differences, these two accounts thus share common rhetorical features, including the dissimulating anonymity, unannounced riddling, stratagems aimed at trapping recipients into self-conviction, and disregard for their distress throughout. As with all Cynic teaching, the interlocutor's honesty and use of power can be called into question.

---

[82] This famously echoes Ezekiel's disgust at being asked to cook over human dung in Ezek. 4:14. Although not identically worded, the two refusals start with the same robust negative μηδαμῶς and go on to a denial of ever having eaten anything unclean. LXX Ezek. 4:14 has ἡ ψυχή μου οὐ μεμίανται ἐν ἀκαθαρσίᾳ and continues with examples of cases that are counted as unclean and Peter in Acts 10:14 has οὐδέποτε ἔφαγον πᾶν κοινὸν καὶ ἀκάθαρτον.

[83] The solution must wait for a moment of Aristotelian 'recognition' or ἀναγνώρισις in Cornelius' house. The term appears in Aristotle, *Poet.* 1452b.

[84] That is, something that sounds like an aphorism, but is not 'real' in the sense of the 'goads' saying of Acts 26:14. Aphorisms may be defined as pithy 'gnomic' sayings expressing a universal insight, common across the Semitic and Graeco-Roman worlds. See D. E. Aune, 'Prolegomena to the Study of Oral Tradition in the Hellenistic World', in *Jesus and the Oral Gospel Tradition*, ed. H. Wansbrough (Sheffield: Sheffield Academic, 1991), 93–5.

[85] As in the story when Diogenes inexplicably presents an inquirer with a fish. Finding him some days later (without it seems, his fish), he asks him why he has neglected his 'gift' (*Diog.* 36.6-10).

The Problem of Dissimulation in Divine Speech

Enigmatic utterance was a traditional feature of divine speech in the Graeco-Roman world, known particularly through the language of the oracles. As noted above, Jewish commentators like Philo saw it as a key difference from their own faith. Whilst Socratic dissimulation was a later and specifically pedagogic development, Socrates acknowledged the role of Delphi in his own story, and that enigmatic aspects of his teaching owed something to the gods (Plato, *Apol.* 33c). Nevertheless, by the first century, not only was his approach being challenged, but also the oracular idiom that undergirded it. The appearance of riddling elements in divine revelation, for instance, was questioned by Cicero (*Div.* 2.49, 101–102). If the gods could speak plainly, why should they risk being misunderstood? In their defence, Plutarch noted a preference for 'signifying' rather than merely revealing and Artemidorus added that the gods wanted people to work things out (*Oneir.* 4.71.11-13). An element of difficulty helped to deter lazy inquirers (*Oneir.* 4.22.36-45), and even for the diligent, intellectual challenge might engage the listener more powerfully than mere information. But Cicero presses the ethical point, asking if it would ever be fair to warn people about an imminent danger via a *coded* message.[86] Thus, while the value of such speech might be conceded on pedagogic grounds, there is no doubt that the deliberate introduction of impenetrable enigma, the Cynic-style delivery of shocking suggestions, and a dissimulating stratagem of entrapment raised ethical questions for Greeks, Jews, and Christians alike.

The classical defences of educational 'pain' made by Socrates had included images of stings, spurs, or goads on the one hand (Plato, *Apol.* 30e–31a), and unpleasant medicine, painful surgery, or robust midwifery on the other – analogies adopted in different ways by Stoics and Cynics (e.g. Plato, *Charm.* 157a.ff). In all of these, however, an ultimately benign purpose was claimed. For divine speech, this was not so easy, as deliberately added difficulty might suggest displeasure or punishment. In many oracle stories, the gods used ambiguity to entrap inquirers and, by dissimulation, point them to the *wrong* interpretation precisely to send them to their deaths. For lesser offenses, where there remained the intent that the message be understood and acted upon, ambiguous or riddling elements could be added simply for their ability to cause anxiety. This is seen in the story of Titus Latinius, who receives a riddling complaint three times before the senate understands the offense and makes suitable reparation.[87]

On the Jewish side, despite the protestations of Philo, for foreigners or errant Jews, enigmatic messages were still possible. Cicero's worries about warnings given in code are precisely reflected in the 'famine' dream of Pharaoh in Gen. 49:1-36, where a Jewish interpreter, Joseph, comes to his aid only after an anxious hiatus. This motif

---

[86] This made obscure speech in such circumstances, unnecessary, dangerous, and unworthy of the gods (Cicero, *Div.* 2.64.132–65.135). This lies at the heart of Philo's critique of pagan prophecy, when he makes the Jewish god's clear speech an issue of *character*.

[87] Recounted by Dionysius of Halicarnassus in *RA* 7.68.3–7.69.2, but known to several other Hellenistic historians.

appears again in Daniel with the dreams of Nebuchadnezzar and the riddle given to Belshazzar, all messages of judgment.[88] Whilst no such stories are related for Israelites, the image of incomprehensible speech symbolizes possible judgment[89] and dissimulating questions, such as 'Why are you robbing me?', express divine displeasure at missing gifts (Mal. 3:8). The engagements with the two apostles in Acts both contain strong notes of rebuke, and so can be located in general terms with this scriptural trajectory. The text's warning not to be found 'fighting against God' would certainly seem to suggest a painful rather than purely affirming encounter for the two protagonists (Acts 5:39; cf. 11:17).

Reflections on Luke's Audience

After highlighting the unusual nature of these accounts, I will briefly reflect on what Luke's boldness in framing them in this distinctive way reveals about his audience. In line with what was suggested about *significant* markers, unlike the more or less incidental Graeco-Roman motifs peppering other parts of the narrative, the two apostolic visions under consideration here tower over the central section of Acts. Repeated several times and helping to 'parallelise' the two apostles, the Socratic–Cynic cast of their dialogue is at least striking. Given the more or less controversial nature of this strategy, a number of possible inferences about the audience are explored and evaluated.

First, it could be suggested that the character of these dialogues might simply attest the readers' developing cultural assimilation to popular Roman expectations of divine speech. The enigmatic elements give the apostles a far greater role in working out what is really being said and aligns them with many of the protagonists of Hellenistic history and the novels.[90] With Luke's Greek-speaking audience showing a good degree of acculturation in other respects this might be reasonably expected. However, the question remains as to why he has been selective about this, with other Lukan visions depending on classical 'biblical' models.[91] Moving 'revelation' away from its older idiom of clear announcement towards perplexity and puzzle does not appear to be a wholesale or systematic change.

---

[88] Daniel 2, the dream of the great statue; Dan. 4, the dream of the huge tree (destroyed and cut down respectively); Dan. 5, the riddling message written on the wall at Belshazzar's feast, 'numbered, numbered, weighed, divided' (5:25).

[89] In Isa. 6:9-10, the ability of the people to understand is taken away, rendering the speech effectively incomprehensible, and in Isa. 28:11, speech in a 'foreign language' is used as a sign of judgment, a motif used to explain 'tongues' in 1 Cor. 14:21-22.

[90] Taking his cue from the Macedonian vision in Acts 16:6-10, J. B. F. Miller, *Convinced That God Had Called Us: Dreams, Visions, and the Perception of God's Will in Luke-Acts* (Leiden: Brill, 2007), contends that Luke conceives of an active role for the apostles in discerning the will of God throughout the narrative, and that this is precisely dependent on the way this is portrayed in Hellenistic history and fiction.

[91] For example, the annunciation visions to Zechariah and Mary respectively in Lk. 1:5-20 and 1:26-38 are both widely acknowledged to conform to typical biblical patterns. Although both recipients question the revelations, the messages as such are plainly delivered.

Second, by portraying the divine engagement with the visionaries in terms of a Graeco-Roman pedagogic motif, their 'conversions' are being located within a broader cultural narrative, where Christianity's role might otherwise be questioned. That Luke's readers might appreciate him enlisting the radically internationalising Cynics to help with this may constitute a significant audience marker, particularly since the protagonists suffer from an overly parochial view of the world. If this involves admitting that Christianity is a non-intuitive, almost bizarre candidate for such a role, then Luke's audience may oddly agree, helped at least by a view of providence that allows for the unexpected.[92]

However, it should also be noticed that the divine voice takes the recipients beyond mere surprise and into an experience of pain. They find themselves 'fighting' against God in a contest they are doomed to lose. Physical affliction and future suffering both result (Acts 9:8, 16), but the dialogues add a peculiarly intellectual trauma of their own. Not only do they dismantle long-cherished certainties, they do so in an anxiety-raising, enigmatic way, obtaining their humiliating confessions by guile. Such collisions may help articulate something of the audience's own experience, and what they might see again in the experience of future converts.

This note of trauma, however, may not be an entirely negative thing if a changing cultural narrative about heroism is at play. In his study of the dreams of Plutarch's lives in the context of trends and developments in Graeco-Roman biography, Brenk points out how perplexity, unwillingness and traumatic change feature at key turning points for several of his protagonists.[93] In some cases, this can lead to enigmatic exchanges with the divine realm, sometimes with disturbing or offensive elements. Caesar's famous 'incest' dream (Plutarch, *Caes.* 32.7-9) before crossing the Rubicon follows this pattern and resonates with the Petrine vision in Acts. If this is what Luke's audience is detecting here, then they may be acknowledging that the founding fathers of their new movement are 'new' men in this sense.

Finally, internal apologetics may yet be involved. Given the evident concerns of the central section of Acts, Luke's audience may still be entangled in the awkward afterlives of the Jew–Gentile problem, forever linked with the names of the two apostles. The idea that Acts is working to reconcile two factions by 'parallelising' Peter and Paul goes back to the Tübingen School but has been revived by Goulder.[94] Although largely abandoned in its original conception, the very similar agonistic quality of these encounters and their probing dialogue style beg important questions about their rhetorical purpose. Openly portraying dual fault and shared trauma here constitutes a remarkable if strikingly psychological 'foundation tale', particularly if this is understood to be of abiding significance for the church.

---

[92] Early Christianity has a particular apologetic problem if it is perceived to have a disruptive, global ambition, as per the accusation of Acts 17:6. The acknowledgement that the universalizing aspect of Christianity had not been anticipated by Christianity's earliest leaders, and that it could not be accused of having programmatic ambitions may be an important subtext to the way these visions are presented.

[93] F. E. Brenk, 'The Dreams of Plutarch's Lives', *Latomus: Revue d'Etudes Latines* 34 (1975): 336–49.

[94] M. D. Goulder, *A Tale of Two Missions* (London: SCM, 1994).

This brings me to a concluding thought about the agonistic quality just noted. If Luke's audience is able to pick up Cynic overtones here, then they know that they represent a spirit that could perplex, offend, even 'destroy' an individual in its mission to 'deface the currency' ('Why do you persecute me?'; 'Rise, kill, eat'). To recognize this and recover a due sense of nervousness is to un-domesticate 'God' and affirm that all, in the end, fail to comprehend his ways, even within the church. Whilst this Barthian sense of otherness and its necessary collision with the world has recently been emphasized in the context of Acts' understanding of mission,[95] that Luke here may be linking this apostolic abjection with the church's potentially ongoing experience, locates Luke's audience at a particularly significant juncture.

---

[95] Cf. C. K. Rowe, *World Upside Down: Reading Acts in the Graeco-Roman Age* (Oxford: Oxford University Press, 2009), 17–51, a chapter entitled 'Collision: Explicating Divine Identity'.

11

SCRIPTURAL LITERACY
WITHIN THE CORINTHIAN CHURCH:
FROM THE CORINTHIAN CORRESPONDENCE
TO 1 *CLEMENT*

H. H. Drake Williams, III

The reading levels of ancient people continue to gather critical attention.[1] This attentiveness has in turn influenced the study of early Christianity and the New Testament. What level of literacy did the earliest Christians have? Were they illiterate, somewhat literate, or able to read and write? Can reading levels be identified within the early churches?

Scriptural literacy is a related category. It concerns the amount of Scripture that early Christians knew and appreciated. Did they know the Scriptures well, partially, or hardly at all? Did they have an appreciation for the Scriptures or much less so due to their background? What did they read and understand?

Assumptions are usually made based on the Gentile or Jewish composition of the audiences. The normal, first-century Jewish experience involved exposure to Scripture at an early age in the home and in the synagogue (Josephus, *C. Ap.* 2.178, 204; Philo, *Leg.* 210). The goal of such instruction would have been accurate knowledge of the Scriptures (*4 Macc.* 18:10-19; Josephus, *C. Ap.* 2.175, 178).[2] Gentiles, however, would have not had such an experience. While some God fearers may have had some appreciation for Jewish Scripture, scriptural literacy would be expected to be far less. When

---

[1] E. g. Harry Y. Gamble, *Books and Readers in the Early Church: A History of Early Christian Texts* (New Haven: Yale University Press, 1995); Susan Niditch, *Oral World and Written Word: Ancient Israelite Literature* (Louisville: Westminster John Knox, 1996); David M. Carr, *Writing on the Tablet of the Heart: Origins of Scripture and Literature* (Oxford: Oxford University Press, 2008); William A. Johnson, *Ancient Literacies: The Culture of Reading in Greece and Rome* (Oxford: Oxford University Press, 2011).

[2] Brian S. Rosner, *Paul, Scripture, and Ethics: A Study of 1 Corinthians 5–7* (Leiden: Brill, 1994), 12.

this is applied to particular churches, some are designated as being more scripturally literate than others.

Focusing in on a specific church, this study evaluates the scriptural literacy levels of the congregation at Corinth in relation to Jewish Scripture. It will examine the scriptural literacy levels in three documents that have been preserved from this church in the first century, namely, 1 Corinthians, 2 Corinthians, and *1 Clement*. It will also evaluate how scriptural literacy developed. Paul visited Corinth and founded the church in 50 CE. The congregation was largely Gentile in composition. Some evidence for Jewish membership also exists, inferred from the discussion regarding the people of God in the wilderness wandering and the passage regarding idolatry (1 Cor. 10:1-11), but it is generally agreed that the congregation was largely composed of Gentiles and thus less scripturally literate.

Scriptural literacy will be inferred from documents written to the Corinthian church. Paul wrote several such letters, even though only the letters that came to be known as 1 and 2 Corinthians are extant. They witness to changes in scriptural literacy within a year or so of each other.[3] Approximately forty years later, *1 Clement* was written to the congregation at Corinth. This letter also provides a witness to scriptural literacy in the Corinthian community.

In what follows, the present study will examine the presence of scriptural texts in the form of citations and allusions within these writings. While early Jewish literature was circulating at the time of Paul's writing, influencing the Corinthian community, 'Scripture' will be limited to the law, the prophets, and the writings,[4] including the investigation of implied scriptural knowledge. At several points in these letters, Paul and the author of *1 Clement* indicate that the Corinthians know more Scripture than what is represented within their letters. These implied references will become an important consideration for scriptural literacy within the congregation. Besides references to Scripture, this essay will also examine any injunctions for reading and study and the Corinthian community. It will then draw conclusions for scriptural literacy within the Corinthian congregation from these first-century documents.

Categories for Literacy Within the Ancient World

In considering scriptural literacy in the Corinthian congregation, it is helpful to have categories related to ancient literacy in general in mind. These categories provide a framework for evaluating the subcategory of scriptural literacy more accurately.

---

[3] For further discussion regarding the history between 1 and 2 Corinthians and the integrity of 2 Corinthians, see Murray J. Harris, *The Second Epistle to the Corinthians* (Grand Rapids: Eerdmans, 2013), 1–66.

[4] This is customary for studies of Scripture in the Corinthian letters: e.g. Rosner, *Paul, Scripture,* and Harm-Jan Inkelaar, *Conflict over Wisdom: The Theme of 1 Corinthians 1–4 Rooted in Scripture* (Leuven: Peeters, 2011). Investigations of Paul's use of Scripture proceeds in this way, too. Cf. Dietrich-Alex Koch, *Die Schrift als Zeuge des Evangeliums: Untersuchungen zur Verwendung und zum Verständnis der Schrift bei Paulus* (Tübingen: Mohr Siebeck, 1986), 32–48, 123, and Christopher D. Stanley, ed., *Paul and Scripture: Extending the Conversation* (Atlanta: SBL, 2012). Note the fixed number of scriptural books that can be identified in the early first century. Cf. Josephus, *C. Ap.* 1.38-42 and *4 Ezra* 14:44-46.

This section will summarize the categories used in the evaluation of ancient literacy and then explore these in relation to expectation of literacy levels in the Corinthian congregation.

Various classifications have been used to describe the ability to read, write, and appreciate texts in ancient times. At the high end of the spectrum is scribal literacy. Such a category describes an educated reader who could read and write and also function as an interpreter of texts. A less proficient level is craftsman's literacy. This level describes 'a person who can write slowly or not at all and who can read without being able to read complex or lengthy texts'.[5] Finally, signature literacy designates someone who is able to write their name and could possibly read simple texts.[6] Illiterate indicates someone who is unable to read and write in any form. Thus, rather than thinking exclusively of the two extremities of literate and illiterate, semi-literate categories exist as well.

An important nuance that has also been proposed in the context of ancient literacy is textuality. Textuality refers to the knowledge, use, and appreciation of texts regardless of whether they can be produced by a certain person. Stock explains further that 'Literacy is not textuality. One can be literate without the overt use of texts, and one can use texts extensively without evidencing genuine literacy'.[7] This leaves open the possibility that one may not be able to read or write but can appreciate written texts. This is an important distinction in an ancient culture where there were many written texts.[8]

Greco-Roman society at Corinth displays evidence of high levels of literacy along with anticipated lower ones. Many within first-century society were illiterate due to the lack of institutionalised schooling, even though high levels of literacy were also found in Corinth. In his study on ancient literacy, Udo Schnelle concludes that between 30 to 50 per cent of those in cities such as Corinth could read and write at least at an elementary level.[9]

Several reasons exist for higher levels of literacy at Corinth. Cities were often hubs for literacy due to the number of social interactions needed for commerce as well as informal interactions. Associations were prevalent, and much of the urban population in ancient times was connected with these associations.[10] These groups were diverse and were connected with occupations such as barbers, builders, farmers, merchants,

---

[5] William V. Harris, *Ancient Literacy* (Cambridge, MA: Harvard University Press, 1989), 5.
[6] Cf. Raffaella Cribiore, *Writing, Teachers, and Students in Graeco-Roman Egypt* (Atlanta: Scholars Press, 1996), 10.
[7] Brian Stock, *The Implications of Literacy: Written Language and Models of Interpretation in the Eleventh and Twelfth Centuries* (Princeton: Princeton University Press, 1983), 7. While Stock writes this about the eleventh and twelfth centuries, Thomas Thatcher writes about this topic in regard to antiquity in Thatcher, 'Literacy, Textual Communities, and Josephus' *Jewish War*', *JSJ* 29 (1998): 87.
[8] Cf. Larry W. Hurtado, *The Earliest Christian Artifacts: Manuscripts and Christian Origins* (Grand Rapids: Eerdmans, 2006), 25.
[9] Udo Schnelle, 'Das frühe Christentum und die Bildung', *NTS* 61 (2015): 113–43.
[10] For the pervasiveness of these types of societies, see further Andrew D. Clarke, *Serve the Community of the Church: Christians as Leaders and Ministers* (Grand Rapids: Eerdmans, 2000), 59–78; Jean-Pierre Waltzing, *Étude historique sur les corporations professionnelles chez les Romains depuis les origins jusqu' à la chute de l'Empire de l'Occident*, 5 vols. (Hildesheim: Georg Olms, 1970). Waltzing indicates that there were some 2500 Roman *collegia*. Cf. Schnelle, 'Bildung', 113–43.

woodcutters, shipbuilders, wine dealers, carpenters, bankers, and many others.[11] Taken as a whole, the evidence suggests that every region, gender, age, profession, purpose, and socioeconomic strata is represented to some extent in regards to associations. Much of the population was connected with Greco-Roman associations and writing took place within these spaces.[12]

Another factor that would lead to a greater expectation of higher literacy in the Corinthian congregation would be the noticeable influence of παιδεία. Philosophers and wise men were present in the city. Dio Chrysostom records the presence of philosophers and sophists at the Isthmian Games and in other places within the city of Corinth (Dio Chrysostom, Or. 8.9-10). Epigraphical evidence in Corinth honoured those educated, such as Marcus Valerius Taurinus, who is described as 'a philosopher and a good orator, on account of his fine character'.[13] Several other Stoic philosophers named Lucius Peticius Propos and T. Flavius Arianus of Nicomedia are also honoured, and their memory has been preserved through epigraphical evidence at Corinth.[14]

In the examination of the Corinthian epistles and 1 Clement, aspects associated with παιδεία should be expected within the congregation. Greco-Roman education was associated with wisdom, power, status, riches, and boasting. While the word παιδεία is not used in 1 Corinthians, 1:26-29 addresses five associated characteristics with the idea. Issues surrounding status and boasting are repeated in 2 Cor. 10:12-18 and 11:16-33. Ideas connected with παιδεία extend into 1 Clement where the author resumes his confrontation with human wisdom, power, riches, and boasting (1 Clem. 13.1; 21.5; 32.4; 38.2). With παιδεία at Corinth and the values addressed within the three extant letters to Corinth, it suggests that the values of παιδεία as well as the benefits of higher literacy extended into the congregation.

Besides a high level of literacy, an appreciation of written texts can be deduced from public written texts in ancient Corinth. Conclusions from archaeological and epigraphic studies indicate that important written documents would be found within the public square. It would be expected that a wide number of people would be able to refer to these public writings whether they could be read or not. For example, the constitution of Julio Claudian Roman colonies was put on display within the Roman Empire in cities like Corinth. Corinth would have had such a document publicly displayed. While not everyone would be able to read it, the citizens would be expected to have a high appreciation of it. Citizens would be expected to interact with such a document that was prominently on display in the city.[15]

---

[11] Richard S. Ascough, Philip A. Harland, and John S. Kloppenborg, *Associations in the Greco-Roman World: A Sourcebook* (Waco: Baylor University Press, 2012), 1.
[12] Brian J. Wright, 'Ancient Literacy in New Testament Research: Incorporating a Few More Lines of Enquiry', *TJ* 36 (2015): 176.
[13] John H. Kent, *The Inscriptions, 1926–1950*, vol. 8 (Princeton: American School of Classical Studies at Athens, 1966), no. 268.
[14] Adam G. White, *Where Is the Wise Man: Graeco-Roman Education as a Background to the Divisions in 1 Corinthians 1–4*, LNTS 536 (London: T&T Clark, 2015), 69–70.
[15] Archaeologists have recently uncovered constitutions from the Spanish colonies of Urso, Salpensa, Malaca, and Irni. These appear to be similar to the one expected to be at Corinth. See the discussion in Bradley J. Bitner, *Paul's Political Strategy in 1 Corinthians 1–4: Constitution and Covenant*, SNTSMS 163 (Cambridge: Cambridge University Press, 2015), 52–83.

This summary indicates that a range of literary levels is present in ancient society from highly literate to semi-literate to illiterate. Textual appreciation is an important consideration for ancient literacy. A range of literary levels and an appreciation of texts can also be expected within Corinth due to it being an urban centre with παιδεία influencing the city. Textual appreciation was also important for citizens at Corinth. These may be expected within the Corinthian church with regard to Scripture. To be able to conclude further on scriptural literacy, the present study will turn to an examination of Scripture present in citations and allusions in these three letters to the Corinthian congregation as well as other indicators that witness to scriptural literacy.

1 Corinthians and the Corinthian Church's Scriptural Literacy

What evidence of the Corinthians' knowledge of Scripture can be ascertained in 1 Corinthians? It is important to begin with a history that Paul had with the church.[16] It is not the purpose of this section to provide a fresh perspective on this history but to set a foundation from which the examination of scriptural understanding at the time of 1 Corinthians can be measured.

Paul first visited Corinth in 49–50 CE during his second missionary journey. If one follows the account recorded within Acts 18:1-8, Paul's arrival at this time would agree with Claudius' expulsion of the Jews from Rome. The Acts account also records Paul's activities as a tentmaker and preacher. Paul remained with the Corinthians eighteen months. During this stay, Paul had plenty of time to teach the Scriptures. It would have been natural for his teaching to be filled with Scripture and knowledge concerning it. Beside his upbringing in a Jewish home, Paul was educated at the feet of Gamaliel (Acts 22:3). From his own testimony in Phil. 3:4b-6, Paul clearly implies that his family upheld distinctive Jewish characteristics: circumcised on the eighth day, a member of the people of Israel, and of the tribe of Benjamin, a Hebrew born of Hebrews (cf. 2 Cor. 11:22). It was his custom to teach in relation to the Scripture.

After the church was founded, Paul then left for Ephesus in 51 CE. Apollos and Cephas visited the church between 52–54 CE and likely taught the Scripture. After Paul left Corinth, he also wrote to the congregation in Corinth. He wrote one letter that is not extant, but evidence of it can be seen from 1 Cor. 5:9-13. That letter chided the Corinthians for their sexually immoral behaviour and forbade them from associating with immoral people. It is possible that this letter may have contained scriptural references.

After he wrote it, he received a report from Chloe's household at Corinth, saying that there was quarrelling and factions in the church (1 Cor. 1:11). At about the same time, Paul also received a letter from the Corinthians asking for him to give answers concerning marriage and divorce, weak and strong brothers, spiritual gifts, and collections. As a result of this report and these questions, Paul wrote 1 Corinthians in 55 CE from Ephesus. This letter contains eighteen references to Scripture that have been

---

[16] For a helpful summation, see Paul W. Barnett, *The Corinthians Question: Why Did the Church Oppose Paul?* (Nottingham: Apollos, 2011).

identified in major studies on Paul's use of Scripture.[17] In proportion to the rest of 1 Corinthians, this is approximately 4 per cent of the letter.[18]

When implied references to Scripture are considered in 1 Corinthians, there is further knowledge of Scripture that should be expected within the Corinthian congregation. Paul uses the phrase οὐκ οἴδατε ὅτι ten times in 1 Corinthians. It is a stylistic *crux* to the letter. Paul employs it only two other times within his letters in Rom. 6:16; 11:2 (cf. Rom. 6:3; 7:1).[19] With the use of this phrase, Paul assumes that the Corinthians had prior knowledge of Scripture. Apart from his reference to the Isthmian games found in 1 Cor. 9:24 when the οὐκ οἴδατε ὅτι wording is used, all other references to the formulaic phrase assume scriptural understanding.[20]

An understanding of Scripture is assumed when Paul uses this phrase with regard to the temple in Jerusalem in 1 Corinthians. This is particularly evident in the idea of the temple that is found within several places in 1 Corinthians. He uses οὐκ οἴδατε ὅτι in relation to the temple theme. The first occurrence is found within 1 Cor. 3:16-17, where he writes, 'Do you not know that you are God's temple and that God's Spirit dwells in you? If anyone destroys God's temple, God will destroy him. For God's temple is holy, and you are that temple.' He returns to the same idea in 1 Cor. 6:19-20, when he writes, 'Or do you not know that your body is a temple of the Holy Spirit within you, whom you have from God? You are not your own, for you were bought with a price. So glorify God in your body.' Finally, in 1 Cor. 9:13 he will return to temple imagery when he writes, 'Do you not know that those who are employed in the temple service get their food from the temple, and those who serve at the altar share in the sacrificial offerings?'

Temples existed in Corinth to Apollo, Poseidon, Hermes, Demeter, Aphrodite, Isis, and Asklepios. The way that Paul writes about temples in 1 Corinthians, however, favours a Jewish understanding of the idea rather than a Greco-Roman viewpoint. From his study on the temple motif in 1-2 Corinthians in relation to contemporary literature, Yulin Liu notes that purity was found in both Greco-Roman temples as well as the Jewish temple. The Jewish concept of temple, however, carries an ontological sense with regard to holiness. In contrast to the Greco-Roman perception, Liu explains that Paul's use of the temple idea indicates that the people in the congregation

---

[17] Cf. Koch, *Die Schrift*; Christopher D. Stanley, *Paul and the Language of Scripture: Citation Technique in the Pauline Epistles and Contemporary Literature*, SNTSMS 69 (Cambridge: Cambridge University Press, 1992); Roy E. Ciampa and Brian S. Rosner, '1 Corinthians', in *Commentary on the New Testament Use of the Old Testament*, ed. G. K. Beale and D. A. Carson (Grand Rapids: Baker, 2007), 695–752.

[18] References include: Isa. 29:14 in 1 Cor. 1:19; Jer. 9:23-24 in 1 Cor. 1:26-31; Isa. 64:4 and 65:17 in 1 Cor. 2:9; Isa. 40:13 in 1 Cor. 2:16; Job 5:13 in 1 Cor. 3:19; Ps. 94:11 in 1 Cor. 3:20; Deut. 17:7 in 1 Cor. 5:13; Gen. 2:24 in 1 Cor. 6:16; Deut. 25:4 in 1 Cor. 9:10; Exod. 32 in 1 Cor. 10:1–10; Deut. 32:17 in 1 Cor. 10:20; Ps 24:1 in 1 Cor. 10:25–26; Isa. 28:11-12 in 1 Cor. 14:21; Ps 110:1 in 1 Cor. 15:25 and Ps 8:6 in 1 Cor. 15:27; Isa. 22:13 in 1 Cor. 15:32; Gen. 2:7 in 1 Cor. 15:45; Isa. 25:8 in 1 Cor. 15:54; Hos. 13:14 in 1 Cor. 15:55. See also H. H. Drake Williams, III, 'Light Giving Sources: Examining the Extent of Scriptural Citation and Allusion Influence in 1 Corinthians', in *Paul: Jew, Greek, or Roman*, ed. S. E. Porter (Leiden: Brill, 2008), 7–38.

[19] Ben A. Edsall, 'Paul's Rhetoric of Knowledge', *NovT* 55 (2013): 252–71.

[20] Roy E. Ciampa and Brian S. Rosner, *The First Letter to the Corinthians* (Grand Rapids: Eerdmans, 2010), 159–60. The following examples are not examined in the present study but assume a Jewish understanding of leaven (1 Cor. 5:6) and entrance into the kingdom of God (1 Cor. 6:9).

comprise the temple and are to be holy. Rather than bringing an offering to achieve purity, Paul promotes a state of being compatible with the divine which is a condition for interaction with God.[21]

In their commentary on 1 Corinthians, Ciampa and Rosner also draw attention to the explicitly Jewish aspect of the temple as found in 1 Corinthians. Aside from the many Jewish texts on holiness in the Scripture, they point to the close association between God's dwelling place and warnings about the destruction of that place. God is not bound to a building, but he indwells his people (Exod. 25:8; 29:45; Lev. 26:11-12; Ps. 114:2; Ezek. 11:16; 37:26-28). The Peshitta of Jer. 7:9 states this clearly, 'the temple of the Lord, the temple of the Lord, you [plural] are the temple of the Lord'. It is this concept about the temple that comprises 1 Cor. 3:16-17 where God's holiness and Spirit indwells his people. From this particularly Jewish concept of the temple in 1 Cor. 3:16-17, they find Paul urging the expulsion of the incestuous man (1 Cor. 5), which is also based on a Jewish perspective.[22] 1 Corinthians 5 then finally culminates with the command to judge the insider as God's people were to judge their own. This is supported by the citation of Deut. 17:7 (cf. Deut. 13:5; 17:7; 19:19; 21:21; 22:21; 24:7). Paul's reason for excluding the incestuous man is based on a view from Deuteronomy, but it is in line with his understanding of the Jewish temple that he assumes that the Corinthians understood.[23]

Paul's Jewish temple metaphor then extends into 1 Cor. 6:19-20 in which he assumes scriptural knowledge again with the use of οὐκ οἴδατε ὅτι. Instead of allowing freedom with their bodies, Paul asks the Corinthians to recall the scriptural idea that their bodies are temples of the Holy Spirit. He appeals to the fact that the Corinthians do not solely belong to themselves, which also has a Jewish scriptural assumption. The idea has a strong parallel to Hos. 3:2-3. As Hosea ordered Gomer not to be a prostitute, Paul exhorts the Corinthians not to go to prostitutes (Hos. 3:3).[24] As in Hosea 3, when Hosea redeemed his wife, so now in 1 Corinthians 6, Paul recalls these same sentiments of Hosea 3.[25]

Besides the temple metaphor, Paul's explanation of eschatology assumes a Jewish understanding. In 1 Cor. 6:2-3, Paul writes, 'Or do you not know (οὐκ οἴδατε ὅτι) that the saints will judge the world? And if the world is to be judged by you, are you incompetent to try trivial cases? Do you not know that we are to judge angels? How much more, then, matters pertaining to this life!' This displays a Jewish hope which he asks the Corinthians to recall. The ideas are best expressed in Dan. 7:22, but it is also found within other sections of early Jewish literature which made the idea contemporary.[26]

---

[21] Yulin Liu, *Temple Purity in 1-2 Corinthians*, WUNT 2/343 (Tübingen: Mohr Siebeck, 2013), 47–70. E.g. See Tob. 1:4; 14:6-7; Jdt 9:8; *1 En.* 12:4-5; 14:22-25; 15:3-4; *Jub.* 1:27-29; 3:10-13; 4:26; 8:19-20; 1 Macc. 4:49; 2 Macc. 5:15, 13:10; 14:31; *T. Levi* 3:28; 5:1; 8:1-19; 9:9-10; 14:1-8; 15:1-2; 16:1-5; 18:6; *T. Benj.* 9:1-5; *Pr. Azar.* 1:16, 31; Sir. 49:12; *T. Mos.* 3:1-3; 5:3; *4 Ezra* 10:21-22 and many other ancient Jewish sources.
[22] Ciampa and Rosner, *Corinthians*, 210–11.
[23] Ciampa and Rosner, *Corinthians*, 213.
[24] Ibid., 265.
[25] Ibid., 264–5.
[26] See Dan. 7:22 expressed within other early Jewish texts: Wis. 3:7-8; *Jub.* 24:29; Sir. 4:11, 15; *1 En.* 1:9, 38; 38:5; 95:3; 96:1; 98:12; 108:12. These are picked up in Christian writings (Matt. 19:28; Luke 22:30; Jude 14–15; Rev. 2:26–27; 20:4). Ciampa and Rosner, *Corinthians*, 227; Hans Leitzmann, *An*

What do these indicators within 1 Corinthians reveal about Corinthian church's scriptural literacy at the time of approximately 55 CE? The number of texts as well as the number of implied references suggests a congregation that has textual appreciation. The use of particular citations favours scriptural literacy of the books of Deuteronomy, Isaiah, and the Psalter (1 Cor. 14:26),[27] but other texts and concepts from Scripture were expected to be understood by some within the congregation.[28] The predominantly Gentile congregation could have gained a textual understanding of the Scripture from Paul's teaching ministry among them, Paul's first letter to them that is no longer extant, Jewish members of the congregation, the visits from Apollos and Cephas, or a combination of these.

Would the Corinthians have been able to comprehend every single text of Scripture within the letter? It is unlikely that each one individually could do this, but some could. The expectation was that the letter would be read communally (1 Cor. 1:2). It would be the expectation that what he has written would be read within the entire church if he expects all of the commands to be followed (1 Cor. 4:6; 5:4-5; 16:11).[29] Some within the Corinthian church would need to be scripturally literate to follow through on the commands that Paul delivers in 1 Corinthians.

Second Corinthians and the Corinthian Church's Scriptural Literacy

The next document to evaluate regarding Corinthian congregation scriptural literacy is 2 Corinthians. Many question the unity of this letter, but the majority of it emerges from approximately 56 CE. Most of 2 Corinthians, then, provides a second point in the history of the Corinthian congregation to examine scriptural literacy of the Corinthian community.

The one section that may be dated substantially differently is 2 Cor. 6:14–7:1.[30] Scholars generally treat this section in two ways. Some believe that it may be penned by Paul.[31] Those who favour more partitions in 2 Corinthians consider it to be an earlier interpolation that is inserted into the letter.[32] If viewed in this way, it could be

---

die Korinther (Tübingen: Mohr Siebeck, 1949), 25. Cf. C. H. Dodd, *According to the Scriptures: The Sub-Structure of New Testament Theology* (London: Fontana, 1952), 68. For further implications of the presence of Scripture and the interpretation of 1 Corinthians from the perspective of a textually literate audience, see H. H. Drake Williams, III, 'From the Perspective of the Writer or the Perspective of the Reader: Coming to Grips with a Starting Point for Analyzing the Use of Scripture in 1 Corinthians', in *Paul and Scripture*, ed. S. E. Porter (Leiden: Brill, 2019), 153–72.

[27] Brian J. Wright, *Communal Reading in the Time of Jesus: A Window into Early Christian Reading Practices* (Minneapolis: Fortress, 2017), 159.

[28] Ciampa and Rosner, *Corinthians*, 28–32.

[29] Wright, *Communal Reading*, 157–60.

[30] For a history of interpretation of this passage, see William J. Webb, *Returning Home: New Covenant and Second Exodus as the Context for 2 Corinthians 6.14–7.1*, JSNTSup 85 (London: Continuum, 1993), 16–30.

[31] E.g. G. K. Beale, 'The Old Testament Background of Reconciliation in 2 Cor 5–7 and its Bearing on the Literary Problem of 2 Corinthians 6,14–7,1', *NTS* 35 (1989): 566–75.

[32] E.g. N. H. Taylor, 'The Composition and Chronology of Second Corinthians', *JSNT* 44 (1991): 67–87.

inserted by Paul into the letter. Due to the special character of this section, it will be treated separately.

The letter of 2 Corinthians contains a number of references to Scripture. Six quotations are found, even by those who assume minimal recognition of the presence of Scripture citations (Gen. 1:3 in 2 Cor. 4:6; Ps. 116:1 in 2 Cor. 4:13; Isa. 49:8 in 2 Cor. 6:2; Exod. 16:18 in 2 Cor. 8:15; Ps. 112:9 in 2 Cor. 9:9; Jer. 9:23 in 2 Cor. 10:17).[33] If NA[28] is consulted, however, other Scripture texts would be recognized as being present in the letter (Exod. 34:34 in 2 Cor. 3:16; Deut. 19:15 in 2 Cor. 13:1; Ps. 119:32 in 2 Cor. 6:11; Prov. 22:8a in 2 Cor. 9:7).[34] When added to the previous texts, Scripture comprises approximately 4 per cent of the letter. If the presence of Scripture in 2 Cor. 6:14–7:1 is added, more citations are evident, like a combined citation of Lev. 26:11-12; Isa. 52:4, 11, 55:10; Ezek. 20:34; 37:27 and 2 Sam. 7:8, 14 in 2 Cor. 6:16-18. If this is added to the other references in 2 Corinthians, Scripture comprises approximately 7 per cent of the letter. Less explicit references in 2 Corinthians could also be mentioned. Allusions from other sections of Scripture may be found as well which could number to over forty allusions.[35] If these citations and allusions are considered together, this would increase the percentage of scriptural presence within 2 Corinthians. It would be at a higher level than what is found within 1 Corinthians, possibly implying greater scriptural literacy.

Like 1 Corinthians, sections within 2 Corinthians assume scriptural knowledge. Unlike 1 Corinthians, however, these places that assume scriptural knowledge encompass larger sections of 2 Corinthians. For example, Paul bases his argument within 2 Corinthians on particular scriptural allusions. Paul refers to the new covenant (καινὴ διαθήκη) from Jer. 31:31-34 in 2 Cor. 3:6. His brief reference to this text without any explanation suggests that he expects that the Corinthians would have understood enough of it to make sense of his argument. For example, the discussion about letters carved in stone from Exodus 32–34 in 2 Cor. 3:7-11 only makes sense if the Corinthians understand knowledge of this section of Scripture. Paul does not elaborate on the reception of the law, Moses' fading glory, the inability to gaze upon Moses' face, and Moses' veil. Instead, he assumes their comprehension from an understanding of Exodus 32–34. Other passages such as Ezek. 36:26-27 and Jer. 31:31-34 have also been shown to influence 2 Corinthians 3 and are necessary for the understanding of the new covenant.[36] These may also be assumed scriptural knowledge.[37]

Paul also assumes scriptural knowledge of the Corinthian community by the way that he introduces the quotation of Jer. 9:24 in 2 Cor. 10:17. The wording that he uses

---

[33] Christopher D. Stanley, *Arguing with Scripture: The Rhetoric of Quotations in the Letters of Paul* (London: T&T Clark, 2004), 97–113.

[34] Stanley lists ten Scriptural references in Stanley, *Language of Scripture*, 215–34.

[35] See Scott J. Hafemann, 'Paul's Argument from the Old Testament and Christology in 2 Cor 1–9: The Salvation-History/Restoration Structure of Paul's Apologetic', in *The Corinthian Correspondence*, ed. R. Bieringer (Leuven: Leuven University Press, 1996), 283–6.

[36] See further Scott J. Hafemann, *Paul, Moses, and the History of Israel: The Letter/Spirit Contrast and the Argument from Scripture in 2 Corinthians 3*, WUNT 81 (Tübingen: Mohr Siebeck, 1995).

[37] Other sections from 2 Cor. 1–7 have been viewed to be formed by Scripture and may also indicate the congregation's understanding. See Beale, 'Background'.

for the quotation is identical to the citation found in 1 Cor. 1:31. In 2 Corinthians, however, Paul does not provide any introductory formula to the citation. It is likely that he assumes that the Corinthians would already recognize this citation. He is now extending the application of the Scripture text from the Christian's calling in 1 Corinthians to the apostle's field of service in 2 Corinthians.[38]

What does the witness of 2 Corinthians say about the scriptural literacy of the Corinthians? With the greater proportion of scriptural references and the assumption of the knowledge of Scripture in places within 2 Corinthians, it reveals a congregation that not only appreciates Scripture texts, but is likely increasing some in scriptural literacy. While the congregation may have appreciated Scripture to the same degree as when 1 Corinthians was written, 2 Corinthians reveals a congregation that understands more Scripture texts. Greater scriptural literacy is expected from the way that Paul refers to the old covenant ministry and also boasting. The increased literacy could have come from other opponents that entered the Corinthian congregation who claimed Jewish background or from Paul's painful visit that took place (2 Cor. 2:1-4; 11:22). It could have also arisen from further contact with the local synagogue.

1 Clement and the Corinthian Church's Scriptural Literacy

The final document to be examined within the study regarding the scriptural literacy of the Corinthian church is *1 Clement*. This letter is one of the earliest extant works of Christian literature outside from the New Testament. It is dated substantially later than 1 and 2 Corinthians.

This epistle has similar characteristics to the first two extant letters to the Corinthians. It is a letter that provides ethical commands. Like 1 and 2 Corinthians, *1 Clement* urges a spirit of peace and concord in the church at Corinth (*1 Clem.* 63:2) and aims to resolve problems of dissension (*1 Clem.* 1:1; 63:1). Jealousy is also a significant problem (*1 Clem.* 3:4–6:4) and warnings about poor behaviour are found as in 1 and 2 Corinthians (*1 Clem.* 46:7-9). Also like 1 and 2 Corinthians, *1 Clement* contains positive examples and encourages following these models (e.g. *1 Clem.* 16–19).

One notable difference between 1 and 2 Corinthians and *1 Clement* is the change in author. While the epistle is ascribed to Clement,[39] the authorship of *1 Clement* is uncertain. The letter begins by giving the impression that it is written from one church to another (*1 Clem.* 1:1), but a unity of style pervades the book. Furthermore, the book has been assigned to a single author from early manuscripts.[40] While early church tradition associates Clement's name with *1 Clement*, several other propositions for the authorship of this letter. These include: the Clement to whom Paul referred in

---

[38] Scott J. Hafemann, '"Self-commendation" and Apostolic Legitimacy in 2 Corinthians: A Pauline Dialectic?' *NTS* 36 (1990): 66–88.
[39] Cf. Irenaeus, *Adv. Haer.* 3.3; Eusebius, *Hist. eccl.* 4.22.1; 4.23.11.
[40] Andrew C. Gregory, '*1 Clement*: An Introduction', in *The Writings of the Apostolic Fathers*, ed. P. Foster (London: T&T Clark, 2007), 24.

Phil. 4:3,[41] the companion of Paul and the third bishop of Rome,[42] a freedman or the son of a freedman belonging to the house of Flavius Clemens,[43] or a Roman citizen of noble birth. All that can be definitely concluded is that the author was a Greek speaker whose residence was in Rome.

The traditional dating of the letter is in 95 or 96 CE.[44] While some see the date earlier in 70 CE,[45] and another dates *1 Clement* much later to 130 CE,[46] it is best to date *1 Clement* to 95 or 96 CE.[47] The deaths of Peter and Paul are well past (*1 Clem.* 5–7), and elders have been appointed following the deaths of the apostles (*1 Clem.* 44:2). The author also describes the church at Corinth as being 'well-established and ancient' in *1 Clem.* 47:6. In *1 Clem.* 63:3, the author also writes about men who were sent to Corinth who have lived from 'youth to old age'. Reading these texts in conjunction with each other, it is better to take the date as being after 70 CE but before the end of the first century. The traditional dating of 95 or 96 CE seems best. With this date, *1 Clement* provides an important witness to scriptural literacy at Corinth. It gives a picture of the church nearly forty years following 2 Corinthians.

1 Clement contains many references to Scripture and assumes more scriptural examples than 1 and 2 Corinthians. The letter has been noticed to be full of Scripture as well as other Christian texts. According to one scholar, Clement is a 'born quoter'.[48] Adolf von Harnack noted that 'der Brief selbst spricht die Sprache des Alten Testament; sie ist ihm religiöse Sprache'.[49] In his examination of Scripture citations within *1 Clement*, D. A. Hagner concludes that there are approximately 70 citations and an additional 17 allusions.[50] With this number of citations, *1 Clement* has more citations than any single New Testament book. In his examination of the presence of Scripture in *1 Clement*, A. C. Gregory concludes that approximately one quarter of *1 Clement* is given over to quotations from the Jewish Scriptures – about 75 in total – and there appear to be many allusions as well'.[51] When verses with citations are compared with the number of other verses within the epistle, approximately 17 per cent of the epistle contain references to Scripture. If one counts implicit references to Scripture, the influence of Scripture on this epistle would be far greater.[52]

---

[41] Origen, *Comm. Jo.* 6.36; cf. Eusebius, *Hist. eccl.* 3.15.1.
[42] Eusebius, *Hist. eccl.* 3.4.8-9; 3.15.1; 3.34.1.
[43] Joseph B. Lightfoot, *The Apostolic Fathers. Part I. S. Clement of Rome. A Revised Text with Introductions, Notes, Dissertations and Translations*, vol. 1 (London: Macmillan, 1890), 1, 61.
[44] See, e.g., Andreas Lindemann, *Die Clemensbriefe* (Tübingen: Mohr Siebeck, 1992), 12–13.
[45] E.g. George Edmundson, *The Church at Rome in the First Century: An Examination of Various Controverted Questions Relating to Its History, Chronology, Literature and Traditions* (London: Longman, Green & Co., 1913), 188–202.
[46] Christian Eggenberger, *Die Quellen der politischen Ethik des 1. Klemensbriefes: Die Quellen der politischen Ethik des 1. Klemensbriefes* (Zurich: Zwingli, 1951), 181–8.
[47] David G. Horrell, *The Social Ethos of the Corinthian Correspondence* (Edinburgh: T. & T. Clark, 1996), 240.
[48] Gerald H. Rendall, *The Epistle of James and Judaic Christianity* (Cambridge: Cambridge University Press, 1927), 102.
[49] Adolf von Harnack, *Einführung in die alte Kirchengeschichte: Das Schreiben der Römischen Kirche an die Korinthische aus der Zeit Domitians (I. Clemensbrief)* (Leipzig: Hinrichs'sche, 1929), 66 n. 2.
[50] Donald A. Hagner, *The Use of the Old and New Testaments in Clement of Rome*, NovTSup 34 (Leiden: Brill, 1973), 351–5, lists these 87 scriptural citations and allusions in *1 Clement*.
[51] Gregory, '*1 Clement*', 29.
[52] Hagner, *Use of the Old*, 21–2.

division from 1 Corinthians within the following verses (cf. 1 Cor. 1:12; 3:21-23; *1 Clem.* 47:2-3). Taking up carries the implication that the one who takes will also be able to read aloud (1 Esd. 9:45). It may also be possible that several letters were compiled together.[59] It is plain that the church had 1 Corinthians accessible as others had documents accessible for reading. The Corinthians appear to be collecting books from the New Testament, and they are being encouraged to refer back to them.

This is the first instance of public reading of Scripture within letters directed to the Corinthian congregation. Other letters to first-century congregations reveal that letters were being read (Col. 4:16; 1 Thess. 5:27; Rev. 1:3), and it is likely that the Corinthians were already reading letters aloud from the time of 1 Corinthians.[60] *1 Clement* 47:1 is the first reference to it taking place within the Corinthian congregation.[61]

In summary, from the evidence found within *1 Clement*, a greater scriptural literacy is apparent in the Corinthian church. This can be seen from the increasing number of Scripture texts, greater assumed knowledge of Scripture, the value placed on Scripture, the encouragement to read letters aloud which contain Scripture, and then the collecting of books with Scripture in them. The evidence in *1 Clement* reveals a noticeable increase in scriptural literacy from the time of 2 Corinthians. The greater interest in Scripture could have emerged from Paul's third visit to Corinth (2 Cor. 12:14; 13:1; cf. Acts 20:2-3), further contact with the local synagogue, the visit of other Christian leaders (*1 Clem.* 1:2), correspondence with other churches or church leaders, or other books circulating in the church at that time. While the rate of literacy throughout the entire congregation cannot be measured, a bookish ethos is developing.

Conclusion

This study has examined three documents written to the predominantly Gentile church in Corinth – 1 Corinthians, 2 Corinthians, and *1 Clement* with regard to scriptural literacy. As those living in Corinth, a number would have been able to read even if not all did read.[62] Using categories of ancient literacy that show a scale between illiterate and literate and also the appreciation of text as a separate designation, this study concludes that the Corinthian congregation was growing increasingly literate with regard to Scripture. They displayed textual appreciation from the time of 1 Corinthians and were scripturally literate with regard to the books of Deuteronomy and Isaiah in particular, but then some other texts and ideas at the time of 1 Corinthians. The amount of Scripture that Paul assumes in 2 Corinthians is similar, but he expects that the Corinthians will recognize Scripture with regard to boasting and understand sections of Scripture that refer to the new covenant. This displays an increase in scriptural literacy.

---

[59] Rudolph Knopf, *Das Nachapostolische Zeitalter. Geschichte der christliechen Gemeinden vom Beginn der Flavierdynastie bis zum Ende Hadrians* (Tübingen: Mohr Siebeck, 1905), 123. An analogous situation took place in 1 Esd. 9:45, when Ezra picked up the book of the Law. Lona, *Clemensbrief*, 506.
[60] Harris, *Second Epistle*, 157–63.
[61] See Gamble, *Books and Readers*, 232.
[62] Harris, *Second Epistle*, 187.

Rather than decreasing from the time of the writing of the Apostle Paul, the trend in textual appreciation increases and scriptural literacy grows at the time of *1 Clement*. This letter contains a high percentage of Scripture quotes. It also indicates that the Corinthians had knowledge of many scriptural examples. *1 Clement* refers reverently to the Scripture and states that the Corinthians have been studying it and collecting books with Scripture in them. A 'bookish ethos' had developed and was increasing in the predominantly Greco-Roman Corinthian congregation from the time of 1 Corinthians through the writing of *1 Clement*.

12

Libraries, Special Libraries, and John of Patmos

Garrick V. Allen

The tractate *De liberis educandis* (περὶ παίδων ἀγωγῆς), attributed to Plutarch, directly addresses the responsibility of fathers to educate their children. Applying to wealthy, free-born male children (*Lib. ed.* 1.1.1; 1.1.4f), the author sketches the important features that contribute to a well-educated and socially capable son, commenting on a range of topics including the proper selection of a spouse (she should be of equal social status to the son), conception (fathers should be sober during intercourse), sustenance in early life (children should be breastfed), and the hiring of a teacher (stinginess leads to ignorance), among other topics. However, the author only briefly mentions the use, or rather the collection, of textual artefacts, noting that

> it is useful, or rather it is necessary not to be indifferent about acquiring the works of earlier writers (παλαιῶν συγγραμμάτων), but to make a collection (συλλογήν) of these, like a set of tools in farming. For the corresponding tool of education is the use of books (βιβλίων), and by their means it has come to pass that we are able to study knowledge at its source. (*Lib. ed.* 1.1.8b)

For the author of this work, the use of textual artefacts is an assumed characteristic of education – they are as essential to learning as agricultural implements are to farming. Children are expected to both read and hear the works of previous writers, as other treatises attributed to Plutarch also indicate (e.g. *Quomodo adolescens poetas audire debeat* and *De recta ratione audiendi*).[1] Nonetheless, he fails to mention the context in

---

[1] Memory remains at the pinnacle of education according to our pseudo-Plutarch (*Lib. ed.* 1.1.9e-f), suggesting that textual artefacts were used as memory aids: books are to agricultural instruments what memory is to crops.

which these artefacts would have been available, who would have organized them, and how they would have been procured.

The use of textual objects that pseudo-Plutarch takes for granted is germane to questions that remain at the forefront of research on the New Testament's book of Revelation and the location of the New Testament within a much broader ancient Mediterranean textual culture. The author of this work ('John') is deeply embedded in the textual culture of the period, incessantly alluding to Jewish scriptural traditions and making use of literary devices that are hallmarks of the late Second Temple period and broader Greco-Roman traditions.[2] The book of Revelation's bookishness places it at the nexus of early Jewish, Christian, and classical traditions.

More specifically, the Apocalypse provides unique access into the educational and textual background of its author. John offers not only his name, but also a geographic location at which he purportedly experienced visions – Patmos, a small island off the coast of Asia Minor (Rev. 1:9), about 100 km west of Ephesus.[3] Although the question of authorship is a vexing one and intertwined with other Johannine traditions,[4] the identification of Patmos and the seven cities of western Asia Minor to which the book is addressed (1:4) provides a context (even if it is only a literary or fictive context) in which the author composed this work.

Additionally, it is probable that the author was a native of Judea, deduced from the fact that his native language was either Aramaic or Hebrew and, perhaps less conclusively, that he was familiar with the Jerusalem temple and cultic practices (Rev. 8:3-5; 11:1-3, 19).[5] John's status as an expatriate offers an opportunity to gauge the interplay

---

[2] This literature on John's use of scripture has increased dramatically since the 1980s and there is no need to rehearse the data here. For an overview, see Garrick V. Allen, *The Book of Revelation and Early Jewish Textual Culture* (Cambridge: Cambridge University Press, 2017).

[3] While the majority of commentators assume that the author of the Apocalypse was active on Asia Minor, including myself, Jan Dochhorn, 'Ist die Apokalypse des Johannes ein Text des Christentums der Asia?', in *The Rise and Expansion of Christianity in the First Three Centuries of the Common Era*, ed. C. K. Rothschild and J. Schröter (Tübingen: Mohr Siebeck, 2013), 299–322, has called this orthodoxy into question, indicating also that, at least in early Christian tradition, the author was also associated with Rome.

[4] Eusebius of Caesarea helpfully lays out the breadth of his knowledge of Johannine traditions in *Hist. eccl.* 3.20.9, 3.23.1–19, 3.24.1, 17–18, 3.25.4–6, 4.18.8, 6.25.9–10, 7.25.1–27. See Craig R. Koester, *Revelation*, AYB 38A (London: Yale University Press, 2014), 65–9, for a clear summary of the issue, and Jörg Frey, 'Das Corpus Johanneum und die Apokalypse des Johannes. Die Johanneslegende, die Probleme der johanneischen Verfasserschaft und die Frage der Pseudonymität der Apokalypse', in *Poetik und Intertextualität der Johannesapokalypse*, ed. S. Alkier, T. Hieke, and T. Nicklas (Tübingen: Mohr Siebeck, 2015), 71–133.

[5] R. H. Charles, *The Revelation of St. John*, 2 vols., ICC (Edinburgh: T. & T. Clark, 1920), 1:xxi; G. Mussies, *The Morphology of Koine Greek as Used in the Apocalypse of John: A Study in Bilingualism* (Leiden: Brill, 1971), 352–3; Hermann Lichtenberger, 'Die Schrift in der Offenbarung des Johannes', in *Die Septuaginta und das frühe Christentum*, ed. T. S. Caulley and H. Lichtenberger (Tübingen: Mohr Siebeck, 2011), 382–90. On use of Hebrew text forms see Garrick V. Allen, 'Textual Pluriformity and Allusion in the Book of Revelation: The Text of Zechariah 4 in the Apocalypse', *ZNW* 106 (2015): 136–45. On John's polyglossic ability, prophetic persona, and the distinction between his self-presentation and actual socio-historical standing, see Michael Labahn, 'Die Macht des Gedächtnisses: Überlegungen zu Möglichkeit und Grenzen des Einflusses hebräischer Texttradition auf die Johannesapokalypse', in *Von der Septuaginta zum Neuen Testament:*

between past education and access to documents in the context of literary composition. One might ask how John's past experiences in Palestinian Jewish educational contexts and his on-going scriptural encounters in the process of composition shaped the exegetical processes indicative of Revelation's substance.

In previous research, scholars have largely been silent on the details of John's textual access, simply noting that he knows Jewish scripture and knows it well. Many have argued that John had no access to manuscripts in the period in which the work was written, adopting the author's assertion that the work is largely a transcription of unprocessed visions experienced on Patmos.[6] And even those who highlight John's erudite engagement and knowledge of Jewish literary traditions, drawing close parallels between interpretive practices found at Qumran,[7] and attributing to him translation activities[8] and textual 'meditation',[9] fail to examine the textual culture of early Judaism within its broader context. These literary activities suggest at least sporadic access to textual artefacts, but in what locations would he have contact with such documents in first-century Asia Minor? I am interested in exploring this question to better comprehend the text-centred events that contributed to the writing of the Apocalypse and to explore how Revelation's bookishness might be situated in the Mediterranean literary world.[10] What social mechanisms allowed John to produce a text that is so relentlessly intertextual?

I answer these questions in two parts, beginning by surveying information relating to Jewish education in Roman Judea. Literary and documentary material create a likely scenario for the type of education that John may have experienced, however circumstantial the historical reconstruction. Second, I examine the likely points of access that John may have had to scriptural material in western Asia Minor, building a socio-historical situation that accounts for Revelation's intertextual relationships and complex literary shape. I highlight the role of textual objects (i.e. manuscripts) and text-based learning within in a culture that was minimally literate and orally/aurally organized.[11] I conclude by reflecting on the interrelationship of memory and reading in the literary culture of the late first century CE, arguing that they are co-dependent and inseparable processes.

Textgeschichtliche Erörterungen, ed. M. Karrer et al. (Berlin: de Gruyter, 2010), 387–90. Going back all the way to Charles, *Revelation*, 1:xxxix, the suggestion has been made that John was a refugee from Palestine.

[6] E.g. Leon Morris, *The Revelation of St. John* (Grand Rapids: Eerdmans, 1984), 30: 'Revelation was written in exile. The writer had no access to the tools of scholarship and apparently no opportunity for a leisurely scholarly approach.' Koester, *Revelation*, 124, also suggests that the author probably 'worked from memory, rather than a written source'.

[7] Pierre Prigent, *L'Apocalypse de Saint Jean*. 2nd ed. (Paris: Labor et Fides, 2000), 36.

[8] E.g. Charles, *Revelation*, 1:xxi–xxii.

[9] G. K. Beale, *John's Use of the Old Testament in Revelation* (Sheffield: Sheffield Academic, 1998), 76–99, here 84.

[10] Cf. William A. Johnson, 'Constructing Elite Reading Communities in the High Empire', in *Ancient Literacies: The Culture of Reading in Greece and Rome*, ed. W. A. Johnson and H. N. Parker (Oxford: Oxford University Press, 2009), 321, for a similar approach to Roman reading practices.

[11] Just as Philo insinuates that texts are teachers (*Cher.* 49), so too the author of Revelation used texts in the process of composition.

Jewish Education in the Roman Period and the Author of Revelation

In a previous generation, scholars posited an ingrained network of public elementary schools in the Tannaitic period, the precursor of which already existed in the time of the Second Temple.[12] In contrast, as Catherine Hezser has made abundantly clear, this

> argumentation is usually based on an uncritical understanding of later Talmudic texts which are not only anachronistic in associating the educational institutions of the amoraic period with pre-70 times, but also vastly exaggerate with regard to the number of educational establishments likely to have existed at either time.[13]

Instead of organized systems of public education, both in Judea and the Greco-Roman world generally, educational practices usually consisted of informal and opportunistic networks of patrons, teachers, and students, organized within a loose set of concentric circles consistent with varying levels of education.[14] As Sean Ryan has recently argued, Jewish educational practices were diverse and dependent on variables, including gender, wealth, social status, and location.[15] As an example, consider learning in the elite social classes represented by Flavius Josephus in Judea and Rome and Philo in Alexandria.[16] Much of this evidence has been rehearsed elsewhere, and I will not revisit these discussions in full.[17] But a few points are worth noting about the upper echelons of Jewish education.

First, education was privately available to those who could afford it in Greek and Hebrew/Aramaic.[18] Josephus, while aware of numerous non-Jewish traditions and sources, is well acquainted with Jewish scripture and its interpretive traditions as the first ten books of his *Antiquitates judaicae* demonstrate. Moreover, his ability to compose *Bellum judaicum* (81 CE) so soon after his arrival in Rome indicates a person already acquainted with Greek language and composition, although he admits that it is not ideal medium (*A.J.* 20.263-265).[19] In Judea, the opportunity to learn

---

[12] E.g. Emil Schürer, *The History of the Jewish People in the Age of Jesus Christ*, rev. ed., 3 vols. (London: Bloomsbury, 2014), 2:417-22.
[13] Catherine Hezser, *Jewish Literacy in Roman Palestine*, TSAJ 81 (Tübingen: Mohr Siebeck, 2001), 39.
[14] Hezser, *Jewish Literacy*, 39, notes, 'The financial and ideational support for primary teachers and schools seems to have come from private individuals only'. See also Raffaella Cribiore, *Gymnastics of the Mind: Greek Education in Hellenistic and Roman Egypt* (Princeton: Princeton University Press, 2011), and her work on educational practices in Hellenistic and Roman Egypt.
[15] Sean Michael Ryan, *Hearing at the Boundaries of Vision: Education Informing Cosmology in Revelation 9* (London: T&T Clark, 2012), 27-9. Cf. also Cribiore, *Gymnastics*, 174-244, for a similar typology of education.
[16] Cf. David M. Carr, *Writing on the Tablet of the Heart: Origins of Scripture and Literature* (Oxford: Oxford University Press, 2005), 244-51.
[17] Ryan, *Hearing*, 29-37.
[18] Hezser, *Jewish Literacy*, 90-4.
[19] Royce M. Victor, *Colonial Education and Class Formation in Early Judaism: A Postcolonial Reading* (London: T&T Clark, 2010), 87-108, points out that Greek language and culture were deeply entrenched in Judea by the first century CE.

The author quotes from diverse books in the Scripture. More than one-third of the citations come from the Psalms. A large number emerge from Isaiah, Job, Genesis, and Proverbs. Other books quoted in *1 Clement* include Exodus, Numbers, Deuteronomy, Joshua, 1 Samuel, Jeremiah, Ezekiel, Daniel, and Malachi.[53]

The presence of these citations exhibits a natural development from the time of 2 Corinthians. *1 Clement* refers to books that were not cited within either 1 or 2 Corinthians. These include: Numbers, Proverbs, Joshua, 1 Samuel, Ezekiel, Daniel, and Malachi. While scriptural knowledge of these books may have been assumed in 1 or 2 Corinthians, they are now cited in *1 Clement*. The writer of *1 Clement* also extensively uses Job and Proverbs. While Paul cites Job in 1 Cor. 3:19, the author of *1 Clement* cites Job eight times. Proverbs is cited six times, but it is not cited in 1 and 2 Corinthians and only six times throughout the rest of the New Testament. The presence of these texts in *1 Clement* may imply that the Corinthian church possessed a higher level of scriptural literacy to which the author can appeal.

Besides the number of texts from different books of Scripture that are found within *1 Clement*, the Epistle is also filled with Old Testament examples which imply knowledge of Scripture in the Corinthian community. From the beginning of the letter, the author appeals to scriptural examples that counter the problems of jealousy and division. In *1 Clement* 4 he appeals to Cain, Abel, Jacob, Esau, Joseph's brothers, Aaron, Miriam, Dathan, Abiram, Moses, Saul, and the Philistines. The references to each example are brief and assume that the Corinthians would have been able to complete their understanding with knowledge that they possessed from the Scripture.

The pattern continues in other places within *1 Clement* in which the author expects the Corinthians to complete their understanding of what he is writing from the broader witness of Scripture. In *1 Clem.* 7:6-7, the author refers to Noah and Jonah. He summarizes Genesis 7 in one verse (*1 Clem.* 7:6) and then Jonah 3 also in one verse (*1 Clem.* 7:7). In *1 Clement* 10, the author appeals to Abraham and his obedience. While he cites three times from Genesis (Gen. 12:1-3 in *1 Clem.* 10:3; Gen. 13:14-16 in *1 Clem.* 13:4-5; Gen. 15:5-6 in *1 Clem.* 13.6) and alludes to Abraham's willingness to offer Isaac (Gen. 22:1-19), the main aspects of the narrative of Abraham have been condensed into seven verses.

In *1 Clement* 17-19, the author continues to present examples from Scripture which he expects the Corinthians to understand so that they can follow. In ch. 17, Clement appeals to faithful ones from the people of God who are human models worthy of imitation. As he explains whom to imitate, he specifically refers to Elijah, Elisha, Ezekiel, Abraham, Job, and Moses, but he only speaks about them for one or two verses apiece. In ch. 18, the author focuses specifically on David, calling him 'illustrious'. Later in *1 Clement*, the author expects that the Corinthians will know enough about Abraham, Isaac, and Jacob (*1 Clem.* 31-32), Moses (*1 Clem.* 40-43), and Daniel, Ananias, Azarias, and Mishael (*1 Clem.* 45) so that he can hold them up as honourable people to follow (*1 Clem.* 45:8; 46:1, 4).

---

[53] Other Jewish sources that may be quoted include: Wisdom, *Apocryphal Ezekiel*, *Assumption of Moses*, and *Eldad and Modad*. Ibid., 351–2.

Besides the large amount of Scripture and the references to numerous scriptural examples within the letter, the author gives particular value to it. This is evident in *1 Clem.* 13:1 which reads:

> Let us therefore be humble, brothers, laying aside all arrogance and conceit and foolishness and anger, and let us do what is written. For the Holy Spirit says: 'Let not the wise man boast about his wisdom, nor the strong about his strength, nor the rich about his wealth; but let the one who boasts boast in the Lord, to seek him out and do justice and righteousness'.[54]

Clement has repeated what was cited in 1 Corinthians 1 and 2 Corinthians 10 from Jer. 9:23-24. Now he urges obedience to it and specifically attributes what was written to the Holy Spirit.[55] In *1 Clem.* 56:3-4, the author will once again display reverence for the Scripture. In *1 Clem.* 56:3 he will cite Prov. 3:12, but he will introduce it by calling it 'the holy word'.[56] *1 Clement* 62:3 also refers to Scripture as 'oracles of the teaching of God'.[57]

In addition to the increased presence of Scripture, the large number of scriptural examples, and the reverence for Scripture, *1 Clement* also indicates that the activities of reading and studying are taking place within the congregation. In *1 Clem.* 31:1, Clement urges the Corinthians, 'Let us therefore cling to his blessing, and let us investigate what are the pathways of blessing. Let us study the records of the things that have happened from the beginning.' From there he turns to the examples of Abraham, Isaac, and Jacob suggesting that the Corinthian church was familiar with them but their lives within the Scripture are to be examined again (*1 Clem.* 31:2-4). In *1 Clement* 62, the author returns to the importance of study. He writes in 62:3, 'And we have reminded you of these things all the more gladly, since we knew quite well that we were writing to people who are faithful and distinguished and have diligently studied the oracles of the teaching of God'. The perfect participle ἐγκεκυφόσιν indicates that such study has happened previously and now is a present reality (cf. *1 Clem.* 53:1; 56:1-2).[58] One verse later in 63:1, he affirms that the Corinthians have studied when he writes: 'therefore it is right for us, having studied so many and such great examples, to bow the neck and, adopting the attitude of obedience, to submit to those who are the leaders of our souls, so that by ceasing from this futile dissension we may attain the goal that is truly set before us, free from all blame'.

1 Clement also exhibits evidence of the Corinthian church reading aloud and collecting manuscripts. In 47:1, Clement urges the Corinthians to do the following, 'Take up the epistle of the blessed Paul the apostle'. The author is referring to 1 Corinthians or possibly 1 and 2 Corinthians together since Clement will refer to ideas about

---

[54] The translation is from Michael W. Holmes, *The Apostolic Fathers: Greek Texts and English Translations* (Grand Rapids: Baker, 2007), 59. All other quotations from *1 Clement* are from Holmes' translation.
[55] Cf. *1 Clem.* 16:2.
[56] Cf. *1 Clem.* 13.3; 57:3.
[57] Cf. *1 Clem.* 19:1. On each of these texts, see Hagner, *Use of the Old*, 110.
[58] Horacia E. Lona, *Der erste Clemensbrief* (Göttingen: Vandenhoeck & Ruprecht, 1998), 628. Lona mentions that the Corinthians are 'Erkenntnis besitzende'.

Greek language and literature was likely confined to the aristocracy and possibly also administration.[20] As a parallel example, Philo demonstrates an acute awareness of Jewish scripture (in Greek translation), coupled with knowledge of Greek texts that he often quotes (e.g. quotations of Homer in *Conf.* 4; *Abr.* 10; *Omn.* 31; *Cont.* 17; *Legat.* 80). Despite attention to Greco-Roman texts, the Torah and prophets remained at the centre of Jewish education in this period, a fact supported by the assertions of Josephus and Philo that Jewish records are far superior in their historicity and philosophical value to pagan sources (cf. Josephus, *C. Ap.* 1.38-41; 2.178; Philo, *Spec.* 2.64; *Legat.* 210).[21]

Second, those equipped with primary education were capable adult learners. In *A.J.* 20.262-263, for example, Josephus notes that his education in a Jewish context enabled him to perfect his knowledge of Greek grammar and poetry after a considerable time in Rome. Michael Tuval has also recently argued that Josephus greatly increased his understanding of Jewish scriptural traditions only after leaving Jerusalem and settling in Rome, due to the lack of explicit scriptural engagement in *Bellum judaicum* in comparison to the later *Antiquitates*.[22] In addition to the evidence of large Jewish communities in Rome and other urban centres, this conclusion signals that central Jewish works were available in the diaspora at the end of the first century CE.

Third, elite Jewish education was often associated with priestly status or closely connected to priestly circles. Josephus equates his own genealogy with priesthood and nobility, implicitly connecting these features of his background to his educational prowess:

> My family is no ignoble one, tracing its descent far back to priestly ancestors. Different races base their claim to nobility on various grounds; with us a connexion with the priesthood is the hallmark of an illustrious line. Not only were my ancestors priests, but they belonged to the first of the twenty-four courses…and to the most eminent of its constituent clans. Moreover, on my mother's side I am of royal blood; for the posterity of Asamonaeus, from whom she sprang, for a very considerable period were kings, as well as high-priests, of our nation. (*Vita* 1-2; LCL Thackeray)

Following a brief interlude, Josephus goes on to describe his progress in education (παιδείας), his excellent memory (μνήμη), his love of letters (φιλογράμματον), and

---

[20] Hezser, *Jewish Literacy*, 90. In the late first century BCE and early first century CE, the learning of Greek texts may have been closely connected to the Herodian dynasty and their collection of texts, for which there is anecdotal evidence. See Ben Zion Wacholder, 'Greek Authors in Herod's Library', *Studies in Bibliography and Booklore* (1961): 102–9, and Cribiore, *Gymnastics*.

[21] Cf. Carr, *Writing*, 260–1, who notes: 'Just as elite Hellenic identity appears to have been shaped by education and participation in a culture defined by Greek literature, the Hasmonean period saw the emergence and gradual diffusion of an emergent elite Jewish identity shaped by a sharply defined collection of Hebrew texts. Greek cultural forms were now opposed, balanced, and/or supplemented by a distinctively Jewish, purportedly pre-Hellenistic Hebrew form of *politeia* based – at least for elites – in a Hebrew *paideia*'. Cf. Cecilia Wassen, 'On the Education of Children in the Dead Sea Scrolls', *Studies in Religion* (2012): 350–63.

[22] Michael Tuval, *From Jerusalem Priest to Roman Jew: On Josephus and the Paradigms of Ancient Judaism* (Tübingen: Mohr Siebeck, 2013), esp. 283.

his decision to join the Pharisees (*Vita* 7–12).[23] Priests were also associated with leadership of communities in the diaspora. The description of Sceva in Acts 19:14 as a Jewish high priest (Ἰουδαίου ἀρχιερέως) in Ephesus intimates that priestly standing extended beyond Jerusalem.[24] A plethora of other texts, like *Aristeas* 310, *4 Macc.* 5:4 (cf. 2 Macc. 6:18), Philo (*Hypoth.* 7.13; *Contempl.* 82),[25] and some funerary inscriptions (e.g. IJO II 33 in Ephesus) demonstrate that priestly identity and communal leadership were enmeshed. Regardless of the function of priests in the diaspora, elite status and education were tied into the social standing and responsibilities of the priestly guild, although not exclusively.

In addition to these facets of elite education, Ryan identifies another layer of schooling defined by scribal proficiencies.[26] The use of the word 'scribe' in modern critical discourse is problematic since it has been used to describe composers of literature, craftsmen-like copyists, and administrative officials.[27] I refer here to the scholarly skills associated with this class of education, which included the ability to read and interpret texts, and also compose new compositions, although there certainly exists a wide spectrum of scribal skills.[28] This group likely lacked sufficient training in the contours of Greco-Roman literature, although this is true only in gradations. Though perhaps an idealized goal rather than a reality, this form of education equates closely to a description in the *Rule of the Congregation* (1QSa I 6–8): 'From [early ch]ildhood each boy [is to be in]structed in the Book of Meditation. As he grows older, they shall teach him the statutes of the Covenant, and he [will receive in]struction in their laws'.[29] Scribal activity was widespread in Jewish literary cultures of this period, witnessing a diversity of training practices, locations, and degrees of expertise.[30] The texts that eventually came to make up the Hebrew Bible and other 'parabiblical' Jewish literary sources played an outsized role in this form of education.[31]

---

[23] Numerous other statements of Josephus assume that priests were involved in education (e.g. *B.J.* 3.252). Hezser, *Jewish Literacy*, 422, notes that almost all Jewish literary production in this period was confined to priestly circles.
[24] See Tuval, *From Jerusalem*, 265–7.
[25] Ibid., 267.
[26] Ryan, *Hearing*, 27.
[27] For some aspects of the training for scribal craftsmen, see Philip S. Alexander, 'Literacy among Jews in Second Temple Palestine: Reflections on the Evidence from Qumran', in *Hamlet on a Hill: Semitic and Greek Studies Presented to Professor T. Muraoka on the Occasion of his Sixty-Fifth Birthday*, ed. M. F. J. Baasten and W. Th. Van Peursen (Leuven: Peeters 2003), 3–24. The social status of scribal craftsmen was probably relatively low, while the status of literary composers was more ample (p. 17).
[28] See Emanuel Tov, *Scribal Practices and Approaches Reflected in the Texts Found in the Judean Desert*, STDJ 54 (Leiden: Brill, 2004), 7–30.
[29] Cf. Wassen, 'Education of Children'. For rabbinic texts on education, see *b. B. Bat.* 21a and the texts noted in Schürer, *History*, 2:415–16.
[30] David Andrew Teeter, *Scribal Laws: Exegetical Variation in the Textual Transmission of Biblical Law in the Late Second Temple Period*, FAT 92 (Tübingen: Mohr Siebeck, 2014), 246–7; Alexander, 'Literacy', 14–15. Jewish scribes were active also in the diaspora, see, e.g., the funerary inscription IJO II 44 in Smyrna.
[31] Carr, *Writing*, 215–39. Tom Thatcher, 'Literacy, Textual Communities, and Josephus' *Jewish War*', *JSJ* 29 (1998): 128 notes that 'sacred writings formed the core of Jewish ideology in the at Second Temple period, whether or not individual Jews could read them and whether or not specific customs were actually based on them'. Cribiore, *Gymnastics*, 137–47, identifies the contexts in which books were used in Hellenistic Egyptian education.

Finally, situated at the border of the preceding levels of education stood the broader populace who possessed some minimal level of education, perhaps from parents, enabling them to read short passages and public texts (cf. Josephus, *C. Ap.* 2.204). Those with limited education could not write, or perhaps write only their name, even if they could read rudimentary texts; although, many scribal craftsmen could copy texts without comprehending their semantic sense as the documentary evidence from the Bar Kochba caves demonstrates.[32] The vast majority of the population in this period was not privy to advanced or even rudimentary literary or scribal education.

Where does John's literary educational fit into this scheme? The data internal to Revelation suggests that he was privy to a form of elite education and that Jewish scripture formed the core of his textual trajectory. First, as much of the research on John's reuse of scripture in the last thirty years has demonstrated, he was intimately familiar with the text of Jewish scripture in both Greek and Hebrew and adept at combining and interpreting these texts. His ability to function as a text-broker is alone indicative of exceptional training and social privilege.[33] Linguistically, the evidence from Revelation suggests that John was aware of multiple forms of Jewish scripture and ambient traditions associated with its interpretation. He also knows *dramatis personae* (Balaam and Balak [2:14]; Jezebel [2:20]) and significant geographic locations from Jewish scripture (Sodom and Egypt [11:8]; Babylon [14:8; 16:19; 17:5; 18:21]). His familiarity with these works likely goes back to education in Judea, perhaps connected to priestly circles. John's ability to read, write, and interact with scriptural texts in Greek indicates participation in a privileged level of Jewish education. His depiction of Jesus as the alpha and omega (1:8; 21:6; 22:13) and recording of numerous commands to write (γράφω: e.g. 1:11; 2:1, 8, 12, 18; 3:1, 7, 14; 10:4; 19:9), a trope shared with many other early Jewish prophetic and apocalyptic traditions, demonstrate his mastery not only of the Greek alphabet, but also the ability to transcribe visions and accurately record events, at least notionally. John as scribal transcriptionist is a literary veneer that is central to the integrity of his vision reports. As a character within the book, the seer acts primarily as a transcriber, not interpreter, of visions.[34]

Second, John is aware of priestly cultic duties. He depicts the risen Jesus (1:13) and the 24 elders in priest-like garb.[35] He also mentions numerous liturgical practices and items, including worship in the temple (7:15; λατρεύουσιν...τῷ ναῷ), the (heavenly) temple (11:19; 14:15, 17; 15:5, 8; 16:1), the grounds of the temple (11:1-2), altars (8:3; 9:13; 11:1; 14:18; 16:7, θυσιαστήριον), censers (8:3, 5; λιβανωτός), and the ark of the covenant (11:19; κιβωτὸς τῆς διαθήκης). This incessant reference to cultic items perhaps hints that John was somehow connected to a priestly milieu, or at least that he was familiar with literary traditions that depict cultic activity.

---

[32] Michael Owen Wise, *Language and Literacy in Roman Judaea: A Study of the Bar Kokhba Documents* (London: Yale University Press, 2015), 30, 50–3.
[33] Cf. Seth Schwarz, 'Hebrew and Imperialism in Palestine', in *Ancient Judaism and its Hellenistic Context*, ed. C. Bakhos (Leiden: Brill, 2005), 78–81.
[34] This is an important distinction to consider when examining questions relating to 'John': to what degree is the governing voice's self-presentation reflect the reality of the works literary production?
[35] There is some discussion on whether the long robe (ποδήρη) and belt (ζώνην) denote priestly vestments. Cf. David E. Aune, *Revelation*, 3 vols. (Nashville: Thomas Nelson 1997), 1:93–4.

Third, John is aware of Greco-Roman traditions. His knowledge of the Leto/Python or Isis/Seth-Tryphon combat myth (Rev. 12) and the *Nero redividus* legend (13:1, 3, 18; 17:8-12) may have also developed in Judea, but it is possible also that he was exposed to these traditions once in Asia Minor.[36]

Fourth, John has a developed cosmology. This is demonstrated first in the extended depiction of the heavenly throne room in chs. 4–5, which the seer describes after being taken up in the spirit (4:2; cf. *1 Enoch* 17–19).[37] The tripartite division of heaven, earth, and under the earth (5:3, 13; cf. Phil. 2:10) corresponds to other ancient Jewish (e.g. *T. Sol.* 16:3) and pagan cosmological conceptions (*ANET* 372–373). John's depiction in other places of a two-level cosmos (10:5, 6; 12:12; 14:6; 21:1), suggests that he is aware of various cosmological conceptions.[38]

Fifth, John transliterates and translates Hebrew words or is at least aware of transliterated traditions, suggesting again proximity to a bi-lingual context. In Rev 9:11, the Hebrew name of the king of the locusts in called Abaddon (אבדון), usually meaning 'underworld'.[39] John translates the word as Ἀπολλύων, 'destroyer', corresponding to some readings in the OG/LXX (Prov. 15:11; Job 26:6; 28:22; 31:12; Ps. 88:12). Additionally, in Rev. 16:16, John transliterates the Hebrew phrase הר מגדון, 'mountain of Megiddo', as Ἁρμαγεδών, although there is significant variance in the Greek manuscripts here. Both of these instances show his familiarity with Semitic languages and the latter example demonstrates his familiarity with a topographical feature of Judea.

Sixth, John asks his audience to partake in gematria, a form of paronomasia where graphemes represent a certain number value. In Rev. 13:18, the identity of the beast is coded in the number 666 (or 616 in some traditions). While one of the most debated interpretive issues in the Apocalypse,[40] it demonstrates that John is acquainted with forms of coded wordplay. Moreover, in 17:9, hearers are asked to identify yet another character – the whore of Babylon seated upon a seven-headed beast. Although gematria is not involved here, John asks his audience to decode his symbolic language, providing some hints along the way (17:10-14). Another example of bilingual paronomasia occurs in Rev. 21:17. John tells the reader that the wall of the New Jerusalem measured 144 cubits 'in the measure of men, which the angel was using' (NRSV) or 'which is also an angel's measurement' (ESV) (ὅ ἐστιν ἀγγέλου). The final three words of this phrase are syntactically difficult. However, the graphemes of the word ἄγγελος, when transliterated into Hebrew (אנגלס), equals 144 – the number of cubits of the wall.[41]

---

[36] Cf. Adela Yarbro Collins, *The Combat Myth in the Book of Revelation* (Missoula: Scholars Press, 1976), 57–85. I am not suggesting direct dependence, but simply pointing to the fact that the Apocalypse shows some awareness of Greco-Roman traditions.

[37] Cf. the diagram in Ryan, *Hearing*, 64.

[38] Aune, *Revelation*, 1:347–9.

[39] HALOT, 3.

[40] Cf. Aune, *Revelation*, 2:770–3; Garrick V. Allen, *Manuscripts of the Book of Revelation: New Philology, Paratexts, Reception* (Oxford: Oxford University Press, 2020), 121–55.

[41] 144 = 60 + 30 + 3 + 50 + 1 = ס + ל + ג + נ + א. Similar Greek–Hebrew word plays occur also in *3 Bar.* 4.7, 10. Cf. Gideon Bohak, 'Greek–Hebrew Gematrias in *3 Baruch* and in Revelation', *JSP* 7 (1990): 119–21.

The book of Revelation is the result of a complex literary process that showcases the author's various learned skills. John is closely connected with the substance of scriptural works, generally knowledgeable of contemporary Greco-Roman myths, adept in coded speech, multi-lingual, and cosmologically aware. His complex interweaving of traditions suggests not only that he is learned, but also that his education continued after he left Judea. Part of this on-going learning revolved around access to scriptural texts. Despite Revelation's silence on the processes of its composition (a feature shared with the majority of early Christian and Jewish literature), its detailed redeployments of scriptural idioms and images suggests that John continued to experience Jewish scripture as the book took shape. To explore his engagement with these traditions it is necessary to explore the social contexts in which he may have encountered these texts.

Book Collections in the Diaspora

The underlying tension of this section rests in the fact that the Apocalypse is a complicated work that belongs to a sub-group (nascent Christianity) with no well-defined point of cultural transaction and textual engagement. Most authors of early Christian works were not interested to show off the swish of their intellectual prowess or bookishness, even though a great amount of learning and literary design stands behind most of these works. We must reconstruct the social locations where continued learning occurred. In the case of Revelation, the initial confining of the search to Asia Minor brings into sharper focus the locus of his textual access.[42] I begin by considering the interaction between Greco-Roman libraries and early Christian reading culture.

Greco-Roman Libraries

When one thinks generally of access to literature in the diaspora, the great Greco-Roman libraries immediately come to mind. Among Greek and Latin authors from the third century BCE through to the Second Sophistic,[43] textuality, access to centres of learning, and the acquisition of obscure philological information was the pinnacle of elite reading cultures, particularly as Roman hegemony cemented itself in the eastern Mediterranean.[44] Writers like Galen portray their intellectual habits as closely intertwined with books, lucubration, and note taking,[45] although a noted affinity for the

---

[42] Most of these observations would also be valid if we posit an alternative location of composition, like Rome for example.
[43] On the importance of the book in the Second Sophistic, see Simon Goldhill, 'The Anecdote: Exploring the Boundaries between Oral and Literate Performance in the Second Sophistic', in Johnson and Parker, eds., *Ancient Literacies*, 96–113.
[44] Cf. Anthony Corbeill, 'Education in the Roman Republic: Creating Traditions', in *Education in Greek and Roman Antiquity*, ed. Y. L. Too (Leiden: Brill, 2001), 283, for the connection between Roman education elite status.
[45] See Matthew Nicholls, 'Galen and Libraries in the Peri Alupias', *JRS* 101 (2011): 124, 129, 138–40; Gregory H. Snyder, *Teachers and Texts in the Ancient World: Philosophers, Jews and Christians* (London: Routledge, 2000), 192–3.

spoken word remained (Galen, *Comp. med. sec. loc.* 6). The social cachet associated with abstruse knowledge was also connected to the production of complex Greek and Latin literary texts, both in Rome and in urban centres throughout the empire, including Asia Minor. Ephesus, for example, the first of John's seven cities (Rev. 2:1-7), was a text-driven city in the late first and early second centuries CE.[46] The Library of Celsus, constructed in the early second century,[47] became the focal point of this textual ideology, housing manuscripts of Greco-Roman authors and preserving a number of bilingual inscriptions on its still-standing façade.[48] Celsus' location adjacent to Ephesus' *tetragonos agora*, like the vast majority of other Greco-Roman libraries, was closely affiliated both geographically and in terms of social currency with temples, gymnasia, palaces, baths, or the villas of imperial fat cats, 'public' spaces where the elite transacted.[49] The irony of the ancient 'public' library is that the majority were 'founded by the cultural elite for the cultural elite'.[50]

Despite the broader social context of these libraries as locations of elite cultural interaction and education, authors also made liberal use of libraries' textual holdings. By the second century CE, lucubration was a dominant *topos* in Roman intellectual engagement, signifying that the author (be it Pliny, Galen, Cicero, Seneca or others) had expended an inordinate amount of effort.[51] Arduous personal study, including library usage, becomes 'a cultural construction of *otium* that carries with it essentialist notions of what it is to be "Roman"'.[52] In this way, access to literature and literary composition played a prominent role in organizing high society, functioning as an exclusionary device, an internal ordering scheme, and an ideological and aesthetic statement about what epitomized Romanness.[53]

In addition to Ephesus, another city addressed by John – Pergamum (Rev. 2:12-17) – was renowned in its pre-Roman context for its library (second century BCE) under the patronage of the Attalid dynasty and noted for its rivalry with the library of Alexandria (cf. Strabo, *Geo.* 13.1.54; 13.4.2).[54] Little is known of this library in comparison to its more famous Egyptian competitor, including its precise location, but

---

[46] Text here refers not only to complex literary works, but also public inscriptions and other expressions of visual communication such as architecture, statuary, and décor.
[47] A time not too distant from the usual dating of Revelation in the 90s, although this date has been vigorously challenged by Thomas Witulski, *Die Johannesoffenbarung und Kaiser Hadrian: Studien zur Datierung der neutestamentlichen Apokalpyse* (Göttingen: Vandenhoeck & Ruprecht, 2007).
[48] Barbara Burrell, 'Reading, Hearing, and Looking at Ephesos', in Johnson and Parker, eds., *Ancient Literacies*, 78–82.
[49] See Matthew Nicholls, 'Roman Libraries as Public Building in the Cities of the Empire', in *Ancient Libraries*, ed. J. König, K. Oikonomopoulou, and G. Woolf (Cambridge: Cambridge University Press, 2013), 267–70, 274–6. The presence of libraries in gymnasia is especially indicative of Greek education. Cf. Carr, *Writing*, 192.
[50] Victor M. Martínez and Megan Finn Sensensey, 'The Professional and his Books: Special Libraries in the Ancient World', in König, Oikonomopoulou, and Woolf, eds., *Ancient Libraries*, 403.
[51] Johnson, 'Elite Reading', 324. E.g. Pliny, *Nat. praef.* 18, 24; Cicero, *Cael.* 45; Seneca, *Ep.* 8.1.
[52] Ibid., 324.
[53] Ibid., 329.
[54] Cf. Athenaeus, *Deipnosophistae* 1.3a. On the origin and end of the Alexandrian library, see Yun Lee Too, *The Idea of the Library in the Ancient World* (Oxford: Oxford University Press, 2010), 31–40.

the *kritikoi* who worked there in its heyday surely used its textual holdings.[55] The collection of books and elite learning were closely related.[56]

Despite the importance of these institutions for elite circles, they have only minimal direct bearing on the question of scriptural access for the author of Revelation. There is almost no evidence that these libraries or others like them held Jewish or Christian literary material.[57] A possible exception exists in *Aristeas*' depiction of the patron relationship between the high priest Eleazar and Demetrius, the librarian of Alexandria, acting on behalf of the Ptolemy, and the production of the Septuagint (*Aristeas* 30–51; 301–311).[58] Although *Aristeas* is of dubious historical value, its ideology represents the cultural aspirations of at least a portion of the Jewish community in Alexandria in the first century BCE, displaying the desire to connect Jerusalem and important Jewish literature to the realm of Greek elite culture. At least some ancient Jewish communities living in the shadow of and closely enmeshed with Greek cultural icons were interested to acquire some of the social capital that these institutions offered. If the Ptolemies were to collect all the books of the world (*Aristeas* 9), surely Jewish scriptural texts must be a celebrated part of this collection. Even though this Greek library interacted with Jewish literature, at least in the *mythos* of the creations of the Septuagint, its burning in 48 BCE and eventual destruction (or slow decline to obsolescence)[59] and location apart from the working area of our author make the evidence for textual access less than helpful. However, the desire of Alexandrian Jews to participate in the textual world of the library at least raises the possibility that similar moves were made in other locations. In this way, the cultural boundaries between Hellenism and Judaism (if they existed at all) were transcended at the level of education and book culture in the Hellenistic and Roman periods. The myth surrounding the construction of the Septuagint represents an attempt to negotiate the cultural tensions of Jewish life in the diaspora.

Overall, Greco-Roman libraries demonstrate, among other things, that elite reading cultures were cultivated in these periods. Although John was not privy to this culture, and his anti-Roman polemic strongly suggests he would not have been interested, he was a part of a literary sub-culture enveloped in the shadow of the reading culture of

---

[55] Cf. Gregory Nagy, 'The Library of Pergamon as a Classical Model', in *Pergamon Citadel of the Gods: Archaeological Record, Literary Description, and Religious Development*, ed. H. Koester (Harrisburg: Trinity, 1998), 185–232; Wolfram Hoepfner, 'Die Bibliothek Eumenes' II. in Pergamon', in *Antike Bibliotheken*, ed. W. Hoepfner (Mainz am Rhein: von Zabern, 2002), 44–52.

[56] Samuel N. C. Lieu, 'Scholars and Students in the Roman East', in *The Library of Alexandria: Centre of Learning in the Ancient World*, ed. R. MacLeod (London: Tauris, 2000), 137–9.

[57] The book-list papyri also bear out this reality (e.g. Otranto, no. 16 [*PSILaur. Inv.* 19662v]). Cf. George W. Houston, 'Papyrological Evidence for Book Collections and Libraries in the Roman Empire', in Johnson and Parker, eds., *Ancient Literacies*, 233–67.

[58] For a brief overview of the library, see Monica Berti, 'Greek and Roman Libraries in the Hellenistic Age', in *The Dead Sea Scrolls and the Concept of a Library*, ed. S. White Crawford and C. Wassen (Leiden: Brill, 2016), 33–47. Stephen Pfann, 'Reassessing the Judean Desert Caves: Libraries, Archives, *Genizas* and Hiding Places', *Bulletin of the Anglo-Israel Archaeological Society* 25 (2007): 148, also indicates that material from the Jerusalem Temple was also likely stored in Vespasian's Library of Peace in Rome following its erection in 76 CE.

[59] Roger S. Bagnall, 'Alexandria: Library of Dreams', *Proceedings of the American Philosophical Society* 146 (2002): 359.

the imperial elites. His sub-culture was controlled not by the acquisition of intellectual cachet or the literature of classical Greece or the Augustan court, but by the Hebrew Bible, its versions, and the God about whom these texts speak.[60]

The elite status of text users in Greco-Roman reading cultures also suggests that text users in John's sub-culture (generically, 'Jewish reading culture') were also likely the elites of their community – those who held the keys to the community's 'classic' traditions. Reading in this community was tightly bound to the construction of identity, and John's reuse of scripture implements 'classic' texts to this end.[61] Revelation constructs a world that placed the ideology of Rome at odds with the received literary traditions of nascent Christianity. It is true that the transmission of early Christian literature provides evidence for the enfranchising readers of diverse social strata in contrast to the elite reading culture of the Empire, and indeed Revelation is not elite literature in the sense that it was composed only for a group of textual experts. Nor does the author play up the lugubriousness of composition, instead presenting the text as a series of passively received transcribed revelations, masking the complex literary and intellectual work that stands behind the work's composition.

But the way that scriptural traditions are handled indicates that the author was familiar with the literary works and modes of interpretation that defined early Jewish textual culture writ large.[62] The literary products of Christianity are more accessible to broader swathes of the community, but production of texts is still confined to the upper echelons of the communal elite. Although distinct in some ways, it is not possible to completely divorce the culture of textuality embodied in the libraries of the *polis* from the culture that defines early Christian text production.[63]

Although John did not access copies of Second Temple Jewish literature or scriptural manuscripts in monumental Greco-Roman libraries, and although he had no social impetus to take part in the elite reading cultures, it is plausible that he had access to textual artefacts in other contexts. The evidence indicates that John was party to an alternative and ambient culture of reading that also implicitly valued lucubration,

---

[60] As Teeter, *Scribal Laws*, 269, notes: 'This complex and multifaceted textual culture [of early Judaism] was simultaneously the product and producer of the scriptural text at its centre. Scribal copyists were thus firmly and necessarily imbedded within a cultural matrix wholly invested in engagement with that text and its meaning.'

[61] See William A. Johnson, 'Towards a Sociology of Reading in Classical Antiquity', *The American Journal of Philology* 121 (2000): 615–24, for a similar phenomenon in Roman reading in the first and second centuries CE.

[62] Allen, *Book of Revelation*.

[63] The lack of distinction indeed comes more into focus as Christianity develops into the religion of the empire. We know that later Christian authors, like Eusebius of Caesarea (born c. 260 CE), used library holdings attached to particular churches to compose their literary works (*Hist. eccl.* 6.20.1-2), and that Origen spawned an early Christian library in Caesarea Maritima. The two reading cultures merge as early Christianity develops, but the seeds of this union existed even at the end of the first century CE. Cf. Marco Frenschkowski, 'Studien zur Geschichte der Bibliothek von Cäsarea', in *New Testament Manuscripts: Their Texts and Their World*, ed. T. J. Kraus and T. Nicklas (Leiden: Brill, 2006), 52–104. For more on the presence of 'congregational libraries' and larger early Christian libraries, see Harry Y. Gamble, *Books and Readers in Early Christianity* (New Haven: Yale University Press, 1995), 144–202. Other evidence for Christian libraries, most which dates to the fourth century CE at the earliest, is located in the form of P. Ash. Inv. 3, an annotated list of Christian texts, and in the fact that Diocletian's edict in 303 presupposes that Christian communities collected books.

and which dominated early Judaism and Christianity. This culture valued a way of interacting with texts that included the controlling of detailed and precise knowledge of Jewish scriptural works. Many critics are content to say this much, but important socio-historical questions linger behind this portrait: if not the cultural monuments of the Greco-Roman library, where would an itinerant prophet from Judea active in western Asia Minor access scriptural material?

Synagogues

Despite the limits of our knowledge of these institutions in the first century, one answer is synagogues.[64] Some archaeological and rabbinic sources suggest that synagogues of the diaspora (or their 'study houses')[65] retained manuscripts, at least copies of the Torah stored in the 'Ark of the Law' used for liturgical purposes.[66] While local traditions differed, there is evidence that Jewish communities, to varying degrees, emphasized the study of scriptural texts as a vital part of religious experience (cf. Philo, *Mos.* 2.215-216; Josephus, *A.J.* 16.43).[67] Take Sardis, another city of western Asia Minor, as an example. Jews were known to have been in the city since the time of Babylonian exile (cf. Obad 20) and, as Josephus reports (*A.J.* 12.147-153; 14.235, 259-261; 16.171), a permanent Jewish community existed there from the third century BCE, blossoming into a group of some civic standing by the first century of the same era.[68] The Christian community in this city is addressed in Rev. 3:1-6.

A large building usually identified as a synagogue was discovered in 1962 excavations. It is part of the broader civic structure of the Sardis gymnasium complex. Its current architectural form dates to the third century CE, but it is likely older and shows evidence of multiple remodels.[69] In addition to liturgical and communal functions, the physical layout of the building indicates that it was a location of education. Kraabel argues that the *bema* installed in the centre of the Sardis hall served as the focal point of learning, and this in connection with the *aediculae* at the east of the hall – the likely location of manuscript storage.[70] Indeed a primary function of the synagogue,

---

[64] On the relationship of synagogues and libraries, see Gamble, *Books and Readers*, 189–92.
[65] Cf. Hezser, *Jewish Literacy*, 457–8.
[66] E. L. Sukenik, *Ancient Synagogues in Palestine and Greece* (London: British Academy, 1930), 52–3 (repr. Munich: Kraus, 1980).
[67] Paul R. Trebilco, *Jewish Communities in Asia Minor* (Cambridge: Cambridge University Press, 1991), 187. For an overview of ancient Judaism in Asia Minor, see Schürer, *History*, 3:17–36. Josephus also reports numerous events that centre on the destruction or movement of Jewish books in Judea: e.g. the Jews of Caesarea 'snatching up' (ἁρπάσαντες) their copy of the law when they flee the city (*B.J.* 2.291) and the exuberant response to the destruction of a copy of the Law (τὸν ἱερὸν νόμου) by a Roman soldier (*B.J.* 2.228-231).
[68] Cf. Alf Thomas Kraabel, 'The Diaspora Synagogue: Archaeological and Epigraphic Evidence since Sukenik', in *Ancient Synagogues: Historical Analysis and Archeological Discovery. Volume 1*, ed. D. Urman and P. V. M. Flesher (Leiden: Brill, 1995), 102; Tessa Rajak, *The Jewish Dialogue with Greece and Rome: Studies in Cultural and Social Interaction* (Leiden: Brill, 2001), 447–62.
[69] Kraabel, 'Diaspora Synagogue', 102–4. A potential dedicatory inscription to Lucius Verus (161–169 CE) possibly shows that the building was in use at least as early as the mid-second century CE. Josephus, *A.J.* 14.235, 259-261, also suggests that a Jewish gathering place had gained imperial imprimatur by the end of the first century CE.
[70] Ibid., 105; Yaacov Shavit, 'The "Qumran Library" in the Light of the Attitude towards Books and Libraries in the Second Temple Period', in *Methods of Investigation of the Dead Sea Scrolls and*

especially as we move later into the amoraic period, was a place of Torah study, a practice that likely goes back to the first century CE.[71] Although controversial in terms of historicity, the depiction of Jesus reading and expounding upon an Isaiah scroll in the Nazareth synagogue in Lk. 4:16-30 lends viability to the idea that a primary *raison d'être* of the synagogue was the reading and interpretation the Torah and Prophets,[72] a practice eventually idealised and codified in the reading cycles of the Mishnah and Toseftot.[73]

The communal dimension of synagogues also contributed to these buildings as a place of study. In addition to community administration, they functioned as places of extra-liturgical learning and modest libraries (cf. Josephus, *C. Ap.* 2.175; Philo, *Mos.* 2.216).[74] These libraries 'differed from congregation to congregation, depending upon local economic resources and local intellectual or cultural proclivities'.[75] Nonetheless, Jerome alludes to books borrowed from a synagogue (*Epist.* 36), suggesting that even into the fourth century CE Christians had access to Jewish libraries. Modest libraries were likely found in the synagogues of Asia Minor, particularly in wealthy communities in Ephesus and Sardis.

Returning to the Sardis synagogue, its location along the main street of a major city demonstrates that the Jewish community was engaged in civic life.[76] As we know from evidence in other regional centres, like Ephesus and Pergamum, access to large collections of textual objects was the privilege of the elite. (Of course this does not account for smaller private collections, which also certainly existed.) The prominence of the Jewish community of Sardis, persisting well into the common era, indicates that some of its wealthy members may have institutionally gathered small collections of important texts for personal or communal use. There seems little reason to believe that such 'libraries' did not exist.[77] In a cultural and religious setting where reading and writing engendered a certain social status,[78] the possession of textual artefacts increased social capital and were central to the life of the community.

Khirbet Qumran Site: Present and Future Prospects, ed. J. J. Collins, M. O. Wise, and N. Golb (New York: New York Academy of Sciences, 1994), 306.

[71] Zev Safrai, 'The Communal Functions of the Synagogue in the Land of Israel in the Rabbinic Period', in Urman and Flesher, eds., *Ancient Synagogues*, 182–7.

[72] Philo's description of the reading practices of Essenes also firmly places scriptural reading and learning in the context of a voluntary association, even if within Judea (*Prob.* 80–82). Cf. also Philo's extended discourse on the Therapeutae (*Contempl.* esp. 24–33), a Jewish group devoted, perhaps to an extreme, to the reading of Jewish scripture. For an overview of reading practices in synagogues, see Thatcher, 'Literacy', 128–30. The Theodotos inscription dating from the first century CE also indicates that reading the Torah was a primary facet of synagogue activities.

[73] So Anders Runesson, *The Origins of the Synagogue: A Socio-historical Study* (Stockholm: Almqvist & Wiksell, 2001), 193–207.

[74] See Lee I. Levine, *The Ancient Synagogue: The First Thousand Years* (London: Yale University Press, 2000), 366–81.

[75] Ibid., 380.

[76] Although, cf. Martin Goodman, *Judaism in the Roman World: Collected Essays* (Leiden: Brill, 2007), 237.

[77] Cf. Hezser, *Jewish Literacy*, 165–6.

[78] Ibid., 149, notes that Rabbinic literature suggests 'that just as in Graeco-Roman culture intellectuals and teachers of higher learning would be the one who were most interested in owning books. They would have recommended the purchase of these books to their wealthy fellow-Jews, although the latter may not have followed their advice.'

Furthermore, this type of evidence can realistically be extrapolated to other cities of western Asia Minor that had Jewish communities (cf. Josephus, *A.J.* 14.244-246). Evidence for a synagogue in Ephesus comes from numerous literary sources (Philo, *Legat.* 315; Josephus, *A.J.* 14.225-227; Acts 18:19-21, 24-26; 19:8-9). John also antagonistically identifies a 'synagogue of satan' in Smyrna (2:9) and Philadelphia (3:9). An inscription from the early second century CE in Thyatira (IJO II 146), also signifies the presence of a synagogue. More generally for the region, in *Legat.* 311, Philo describes an imperial decree allowing the Jews of Asia to gather in συναγώγια.

Evidence for the function of synagogues in Asia Minor in the first century remains circumstantial.[79] However, the archaeological, literary, and epigraphic data suggests the following. First, Jewish communities in Asia Minor, including many of the cities address in Revelation 2-3, boasted a location of voluntary religious association. The layout, adornment, and function of these buildings varied. Second, literary evidence and some archaeological features (e.g. Torah shrine) indicate that synagogues were locations of scriptural reading and learning. The precise mechanisms of access to textual artefacts are hazy at best before the amoraic period, but scriptural texts were routinely read aloud in communal gatherings and presumably accessible for private study. Third, the Jewish communities of Asia Minor, especially in Ephesus and Sardis, were well-off and enmeshed in the social world of the Greco-Roman *polis*.

This portrait of Jewish social and religious life centred on the synagogue suggests that John may have had access to textual artefacts through encounters with these associations, particularly at Ephesus if it served as his home base.[80] The scrolls used for liturgical or educational purposes may have been available for private usage on an informal basis. Additionally, wealthy and connected members of the community may have retained private copies, offering another potential point of access. And John's interactions with Christian communities may have offered access to scriptural texts either via manuscripts or oral recitation. Due to the relative paucity of direct evidence for the textual practices of Jewish communities in this region, exploring the most consequential extant Jewish library of the period, the scrolls found in the area of Qumran, provides some illuminating parallels. And here we begin to explicitly explore the idea of a special library in antiquity.

The Dead Sea Scrolls and Special Libraries

There continues to be a robust discussion on whether the manuscripts found in the eleven caves near Khirbet Qumran constitute a 'library', a conversation best exemplified by a recent collection of essays entitled *The Dead Sea Scrolls and the Concept of a Library*.[81] On the one hand, the lack of evidence for an overarching organizational structure or place of storage at the site (beyond the caves) suggests that

---

[79] However, see the Levine, *Ancient Synagogue*, 128, 159, who presents the known functions of synagogues in early Judaism.
[80] David E. Aune, *Apocalypticism, Prophecy and Magic in Early Christianity: Collected Essays* (Tübingen: Mohr Siebeck, 2006), 187.
[81] See Sidnie White Crawford and Cecilia Wassen, eds., *The Dead Sea Scrolls and the Concept of a Library*, STDJ 116 (Leiden: Brill, 2016).

the Dead Sea Scrolls do not represent the holdings of a library.[82] The physical trappings of ancient Hellenistic and Roman libraries, including inscriptions, statues, and other architectural features, indicate that if the scrolls discovered near Qumran are considered a library, it is not in the same sense as the cultural monument that is the Celsus library in Ephesus, for example.[83] The site is not a public space complete with a monumental building, but the location of a community that saw itself in conflict with its broader cultural environment (although, of course, deeply interconnected with it). However, the collection of over 900 manuscripts of literary works spread amongst the caves, some of which are sequestered based on language,[84] and the purported bookishness and priestly orientation of the community (Joseph, *B.J.* 2.136, 159), suggests that the scrolls were part of a 'special library' of sorts.[85]

A special library is a deliberate collection of thematically linked documents that transcends the inadequate labels of 'public' or 'private', models first disseminated during the Public Libraries Movement of the 1850s.[86] In terms of modern library sciences, a special library consists of a number of interlocking features designed to address the specific professional needs of a given guild, usually connected to an overarching institution. Small size, minimalistic setting, a thematically coherent collection, and limited clientele are the hallmarks of the special library.[87] A modern example is a small church library that provides religious sustenance to a congregation, retaining only volunteer staff, and holdings related to preaching or popular theology (or whatever congregants choose to offload there). Another example might be the legal library of a large law firm. The prominent characteristic of special libraries is their small scope (which Qumran is in comparison to the presentation of monumental

---

[82] So Corrado Martone, 'The Qumran "Library" and Other Ancient Libraries: Elements for Comparison', in White Crawford and Wassen, eds., *The Dead Sea Scrolls and the Concept of a Library*, esp. 68–9. His argument also compares Qumran to other grandiose ancient libraries like Ebla and Alexandria, and he seems to indicate that Qumran's modesty in comparison means that it is not a library. This argumentation may overplay the idea of the library as a physical space, rather than a collection of textual artefacts, and is not convincing in light of the evidence for small private or communal libraries in this period (cf. Gamble, *Books and Readers*, 144–202). See also Shavit, 'Qumran Library', 309.

[83] So Ian Werrett, 'Is Qumran a Library?', in White Crawford and Wassen, eds., *The Dead Sea Scrolls and the Concept of a Library*, 96–8, 101, who highlights the Greek cultural features of the Qumran site and manuscript collection, arguing that it too is a library similar to the Villa of the Papyri at Herculaneum. He notes also (p. 91) that the habits of the scholars and priest associated with the library of Alexandria are not entirely foreign to those of Qumran (common property, communal meals, overseen by a leading priest).

[84] Cf. the exclusively Greek nature of the scrolls in Cave 7.

[85] I also assume here a material connection between the community that inhabited Khirbet Qumran and the scrolls located in the cave. Cf. Mladen Popović, 'Qumran as Scroll Storehouse in Times of Crisis? A Comparative Perspective on Judaean Desert Manuscript Collections', *JSJ* 43 (2012): 551–94; contra Pfann, 'Reassessing', among others. Also, it should be pointed out that, if the materials of the eleven caves are heterogeneous in provenance, the literary makeup, evidence of shelving, and *in situ* decay of the material in Cave 4 (so Gamble, *Books and Readers*, 193–5) point to this cache particularly as a library of a particular community. Of course, the extant scrolls were produced over a period of about two centuries, so it is difficult to imagine that they ever made up a coherent library collection as such.

[86] Martínez and Senseney, 'Professional', 401.

[87] Esther Green Bierbaum, *Special Libraries in Action: Cases and Crises* (Engelwood: Libraries Unlimited, 1993), 7.

library collections in the ancient world),[88] usually organized around a particular field of study. In the case of Qumran, the 'field of study' was the literature of the Hebrew Bible, literature engaging with the Hebrew Bible, and the literature of a sect. The majority of the collection consisted either of scriptural manuscripts or literary works that engaged with the Hebrew Bible in some way.

The idea of a special library is admittedly a modern phenomenon, and the manuscripts from Qumran cannot be considered such a collection in a strict sense. Nonetheless, the trademarks of special libraries (i.e. an emphasis on efficiency, accessibility, limited collections, and thematic coherence) do correspond suggestively to the makeup of the collection, which lacks significant documentary material. In a general sense, the only users of ancient special libraries would have been 'professions with an intellectual tradition or a need for specific, and sometimes technical information'.[89] Physicians like Galen or priests who required information pertaining to specific rites would have been the primary users of such collections, but this observation extends also to exegetical attention to important communal documents, a reality witnessed not only at Qumran, but also in the ancient Greek commentaries on Homer and other works.

Victor Martínez and Megan Finn Senseney summarise the role of the special library thusly:

> Special libraries do not share the monumental characteristics of their public counterparts. They do not serve as a symbolic gesture to the power of knowledge and literary culture, nor do they provide the general community with gathering spaces or organized events. To the contrary, the contemporary special library is rarely more than a few crowded rooms housed within the context of a larger building. As such, the library is neither a prominent feature of the organization nor is it a primary element of the building's architecture. Despite this humble position, the library serves an essential role in assuring that the information needs of an organization are met efficiently and accurately.[90]

This description of a modern special library assuages some of the angst associated with identifying the Dead Sea Scrolls as a library. When considered a special library, the lack of monumental facades, inscriptions, and identifiable rooms dedicated to the use of texts is not so troubling. Like special libraries the scrolls were not part of a broader concerted effort to garner cultural prowess (at least not to those outside the community). Instead, the collection met the needs of a textual community that valued their religious documents and their interpretations of those documents. Production

---

[88] Numerous different, and likely mythical, numbers are given for the size of the Alexandrian library, for instance, including estimates from 40,000 to 700,000. Cf. Bagnall, 'Alexandria', 351–2, for discussion of ancient sources. The size of the collection also pales in comparison to royal libraries of the ancient Near East, including Ashurbanipal's library at Nineveh (c. 25,000 tablets) or the library at Ebla (17,000 tablets). See Martone, 'Qumran Library', 58–9.

[89] Martínez and Senseney, 'Professional', 405.

[90] Ibid., 404–5.

of new copies was likely undertaken in spurts and at a relatively slow pace over the life of the community,[91] indicating that universal assembly of material associated with ancient Judaism was not the goal of the collection. Even if Qumran is anomalous in light of comparative evidence, the isolated nature of the community ceases to be problematic if considered a special library, especially since its literary tastes were interconnected with similar collections in other Palestinian textual communities. Sidnie White Crawford concludes that the Scrolls are a 'scribal library', stating that 'the Qumran scrolls are demonstrably not only a particular Jewish sectarian collection, but a Jewish sectarian collection shaped by the particular interests of an elite group of scholar scribes attached to that community'.[92]

A parallel example to the special library at Qumran is the Villa of the Papyri at Herculaneum, destroyed and preserved by the eruption of Mt. Vesuvius in 79 CE, re-discovered in 1709.[93] This collection of about 1,700 scrolls is top-heavy with the works of Philodemus and other Epicurean philosophers.[94] The importance of this collection for this discussion rests in the fact that it demonstrates that 'a coherent collection could continue to exist for an extended period, well beyond a single person's lifetime, and that its essential contents and integrity as a specialized collection might remain intact throughout that period'.[95] There is also evidence that a professional group interested in Epicureanism used the library at Herculaneum.[96] Although the papyri differ in that they were the collection of a single wealthy family,[97] both Qumran and the Villa were multi-generational collections connected to a particular corpus of texts. Both the Villa and Qumran provide evidence that across the Greco-Roman world in the first century CE, textual collections designed around particular themes coalesced and were used by particular communities.

While the Scrolls and the Villa are the two largest and best examples of such collections, there seems to be no reason to doubt the existence of similar special libraries across the Roman world, suggesting that John may have had access to a similar, albeit modest collection of textual artefacts somewhere in Asia Minor. Although probably referring to a small personal collection of manuscripts, Paul's request of Timothy in

---

[91] Alexander, 'Literacy', 6–7.
[92] Sidnie White Crawford, 'The Qumran Collection as a Scribal Library', in White Crawford and Wassen, eds., *The Dead Sea Scrolls and the Concept of a Library*, 130, who additionally points out the archival function of the collection. She musters the following evidence for this argument: the collection is multi-lingual (e.g. Tobit in Aramaic 4Q196–199 and Hebrew 4Q200), shows evidence of a pattern of manuscript preparation and correction, occasionally employs paleo-Hebrew and cryptic scripts, contains translations, contains exegetical texts with interpretive goals, is interested in calendars and astronomical lore (4Q208–211), contains compositions that borrow or rely on scriptural idioms (e.g. *Songs of Sabbath Sacrifice* and *Hodayot*), contains lists (e.g. 4QMiscellaneous Rules), shows interest in magic and divination (4Q186, 4Q318, 4Q560, 4Q561), site has inkwells, multi-lingual ostraca inscriptions, and leather tabs in Cave 8.
[93] For an overview, see Sandra Sider, 'Herculaneum's Library in 79 A.D.: The Villa of the Papyri', *Libraries & Culture* 25 (1990): 534–42; David Sider, *The Library of the Villa dei Papiri at Herculaneum* (Los Angeles: J. Paul Getty, 2005), 16–23.
[94] Houston, 'Papyrological Evidence', 256.
[95] Ibid., 257.
[96] Martínez and Senseney, 'Professional', 415; Sider, *Villa dei Papiri*, 6.
[97] Likely founded by Lucius Calpurnius Piso Caesoninus or one of his offspring. Cf. Sider, *Villa dei Papiri*, 5–8.

2 Tim. 4:13 to bring him 'the books, above all the parchments' (τὰ βιβλία μάλιστα τὰς μεμβράνας) indicates that early Christian authors made use of manuscripts, sought out books, and were aware of collections of artefacts that might be beneficial to their own literary activity or intellectual sustenance.[98] Additionally, Paul's admonishment to Timothy to 'attend to the public reading of scripture, to preaching and to teaching' (1 Tim. 4:13) implies the presence of Christian book collections in Asia Minor by at least the early second century (cf. Justin, *Apol.* 1.67).

The idea of the special library corresponds also to private ownership of manuscripts in this period.[99] For example, the finds from the minor sites near Qumran that served as places of refuge during the Jewish wars (66–73 or 132–135 CE, Wadi Murabba'at, Nahal Hever, Masada, and Wadi Daliyeh)[100] evidence personal possession of scriptural manuscripts, even though the finds from these locations are primarily documentary and exceptional in their context of escaping imminent conflict.[101] Both Hebrew and Greek manuscripts (e.g. 8HevXIIgr) containing parts of Jewish scripture have been discovered. Perhaps literary texts were not confined to the urban 'elite' of the late Second Temple period, but textuality expanded to the upper strata of rural society as well, as wealthy individuals brought their documentary and literary possessions to the caves.[102]

This reality within Judea raises the possibility that well-connected Jewish families in the diaspora or patrons of early churches acted as text-brokers and retained copies of Jewish works, including portions of the Hebrew Bible and its early Greek versions. This is especially believable for locations like Pergamum and Ephesus, cities associated with textuality and books generally, and which boasted economically successful Jewish communities.[103]

The ways in which John reused scriptural texts stands in continuity with the type of interpretive engagement found at Qumran and in other early Jewish works like Ben Sira. He is intimately connected to the substance of Jewish scripture, aware of the internal tensions and connections between works (including existing exegetical and Jesus traditions), is familiar with cultic affairs, magical traditions, myths, gematria, and displays a developed cosmology.[104] Each of these points describes an author who was part of a textual community not unlike that attached to the Qumran scrolls. I am not at all arguing that John was associated with the sectarians, but that he likely was familiar with similar forms of an ambient Palestinian textual culture before his time in Asia Minor. In Ephesus and during the composition of the Apocalypse it is

---

[98] Bastiaan van Elderen, 'Early Christian Libraries', in *The Bible as Book: The Manuscript Tradition*, ed. J. Sharpe and K. van Kampen (London: British Library, 1998), 45, suggests that Paul is likely asking for copies of Jewish scriptural works.
[99] Cf. Gamble, *Books and Readers*, 174–6.
[100] Or in the case of Wadi Daliyeh, Samaritan refugees fleeing Alexander the Great's forces in the fourth century BCE.
[101] White Crawford, 'Qumran Collection', 117–20.
[102] Wise, *Language and Literacy*, 38–40.
[103] Trebilco, *Jewish Communities*, 186–90; John M. G. Barclay, *Jews in the Mediterranean Diaspora from Alexander to Trajan (323 BCE–117 CE)* (Edinburgh: T. & T. Clark, 1996), 268–9, 271–2, 276–7. Cf. also the evidence for textuality in Smyrna attributed to Polycarp and his dissemination of Ignatius' literary output (Gamble, *Books and Readers*, 153).
[104] Ryan, *Hearing*; Prigent, *L'Apocalypse*, 36–49.

probable that he sought a similar textual community, or at least a group or individual that had access to the artefacts that supported such engagement. Just as the Roman Empire enabled a situation where Greek intellectual culture was mobile between Rome and the eastern provinces,[105] so also the empire and a dispersed Jewish literary culture enabled the movement of Jewish and early Christian intellectual capital from Judea to the diaspora. Examples of special libraries preserved in rural Judea and urban Italy demonstrate the breadth of such collections across the empire in this period.

Concluding Thoughts

Where does this synthesis leave us when we consider a social context for John's engagement with scriptural traditions? The evidence from both Greco-Roman and Jewish sources indicates a serious interest in textuality. By this I mean that textual artefacts were important interlocutors in education and literary composition and readily available to the upper classes of society in Judea and the diaspora in both Hellenistic and Jewish circles. Even though Revelation claims to be a report of a vision received on an isolated island, text-centred events factored into its composition. A person who was able to write complex literary texts in a non-native language likely received a high level of education. Additionally, John's proficiency in cosmology, coded symbols, numerology, and his critiques of Roman economic systems further supports the idea that he was a well-educated individual. A writer of this calibre surely read manuscripts as part of his training and continued to do so when available during in the process of composition. When reading Revelation, it is important to distinguish between the governing voice's self-presentation as a lowly transcriber of visions and the high level literary care that stands unannounced behind the work's production.

The fact that John used manuscripts does not, however, indicate that he relied solely on physical forms of Jewish scriptural texts. Memory and orality were integral facets of his literary culture, complementing and encouraging textuality. As David Carr has argued, learning in Jewish antiquity was an oral/textual hybrid.[106] The cultivation of memory and appreciation for scriptural traditions were reinforced by aural experience of recitation and private encounters with manuscripts. High-level learners become 'walking libraries'; they 'embody the library through their memories'.[107] However, John's knowledge of scripture is more than the texts he was able to recall; his use of scriptural texts indicates continual reflection upon nearly every work that eventually became part of the Hebrew Bible. The use of manuscripts and appeal to memory function as partners in John's crafting of reused scriptural locutions.

The preceding discussion also illuminates the interrelationship between Jewish and Greco-Roman book collections. Differences remain – particularly the high level of cachet attached to elite Greco-Roman libraries – but similarities persist. Collections in both contexts were usually modest and organized around the needs of those at the

---

[105] Nicholls, 'Galen', 141.
[106] Carr, *Writing*.
[107] Too, *Idea*, 178, also 84–7. Cf. also Hezser, *Jewish Literacy*, 422–3.

Alexander, Philip S. 'Orality in Pharisaic-Rabbinic Judaism at the Turn of the Eras'. Page 159–84 in *Jesus and the Oral Gospel Tradition*. Edited by H. Wansbrough. Sheffield: Sheffield Academic, 1991.
Allison, Dale C. 'Was There a "Lukan Community?"' *IBS* 10 (1988): 62–70.
Allen, David. 'The Use of Criteria – The State of the Question'. Pages 129–41 in *Methodology in the Use of the Old Testament in the New: Context and Criteria*. Edited by D. Allen and S. Smith. LNTS 597. London: T&T Clark, 2019.
Allen, Garrick V. *The Book of Revelation and Early Jewish Textual Culture*. Cambridge: Cambridge University Press, 2017.
Allen, Garrick V. *Manuscripts of the Book of Revelation: New Philology, Paratexts, Reception*. Oxford: Oxford University Press, 2020.
Allen, Garrick V. 'Textual Pluriformity and Allusion in the Book of Revelation: The Text of Zechariah 4 in the Apocalypse'. *ZNW* 106 (2015): 136–45.
Alon, Gedaliah. *The Jews in Their Land in the Talmudic Age (70–640 C.E.)*. 3rd ed. London: Harvard University Press, 1989.
Anderson, Graham. *The Second Sophistic*. London: Routledge, 1993.
Anderson, P. N. 'Bakhtin's Dialogism and the Corrective Rhetoric of the Johannine Misunderstanding Dialogue: Exposing Seven Crises in the Johannine Situation'. Pages 133–59 in *Bakhtin and Genre Theory in Biblical Studies*. Edited by R. Boer. Atlanta: SBL, 2007.
Angel, J. L. 'Maskil, Community, and Religious Experience in the *Songs of the Sage* (4Q510–511)'. *DSD* 19 (2012): 1–27.
Aschough, Richard S. 'Forms of Commensality in Greco-Roman Associations'. *CW* 102 (2008): 33–45.
Aschough, Richard S. *Paul's Macedonian Associations: The Social Context of Philippians and 1 Thessalonians*. Eugene: Wipf & Stock, 2020.
Ascough, Richard. S., Philip A. Harland, and John S. Kloppenborg. *Associations in the Greco-Roman World: A Sourcebook*. Waco: Baylor University Press, 2012.
Atherton, C. *The Stoics on Ambiguity*. Cambridge: Cambridge University Press, 1993.
Aune, David E. *Apocalypticism, Prophecy and Magic in Early Christianity: Collected Essays*. WUNT 199. Tübingen: Mohr Siebeck, 2006.
Aune, David E. 'Jesus and the Cynics in First Century Palestine: Some Critical Considerations. Pages 176–92 in *Hillel and Jesus: Comparative Studies of Two Major Religious Leaders*. Edited by J. H. Charlesworth and L. L. Johns. Minneapolis: Fortress, 1997.
Aune, David E. 'Oral Tradition and the Aphorisms of Jesus'. Pages 211–65 in *Jesus and the Oral Gospel Tradition*. Edited by H. Wansbrough. Sheffield: Sheffield Academic, 1991.
Aune, David E. 'Prolegomena to the Study of Oral Tradition in the Hellenistic World'. Pages 59–106 in *Jesus and the Oral Gospel Tradition*. Edited by H. Wansbrough. Sheffield: Sheffield Academic, 1991.
Aune, David E. *Prophecy in Early Christianity and the Ancient Mediterranean World*. Grand Rapids: Eerdmans, 1983.
Aune, David E. *Revelation*. 3 vols. WBC 52a–c. Nashville: Thomas Nelson, 1997–1998.
Aune, David E. 'Septem Sapientium Convivium'. Pages 51–105 in *Plutarch's Theological Writings and Early Christians Literature*. Edited by H. D. Betz. Leiden: Brill, 1972.
Avi-Yonah, Michael. *Ancient Scrolls: Introduction to Archaeology*. Jerusalem: Jerusalem Publishing, 1994.
Avrin, Leila. *Scribes, Script and Books: The Book Arts from Antiquity to the Renaissance*. London: The British Library, 1991.
Bagnall, Roger S. 'Alexandria: Library of Dreams'. *Proceedings of the American Philosophical Society* 146 (2002): 348–62.

Bagnall, Roger S., and Rafaella Cribiore. *Women's Letters from Ancient Egypt: 300 BC–AD 800*. Ann Arbor: University of Michigan Press, 2006.

Baird, J. A. *Audience Criticism and the Historical Jesus*. Philadelphia: Westminster, 1969.

Baker, C. A. 'Peter and Paul in Acts and the Construction of Early Christian Identity: A Review of Historical and Literary Approaches'. *CBR* 11 (2013): 349–65.

Bakhos, Carol. 'Method(ological) Matters in the Study of Midrash'. Pages 161–87 in *Current Trends in the Study of Midrash*. Edited by C. Bakhos. Leiden: Brill, 2006.

Bakhos, Carol. 'Orality and Memory'. Pages 282–502 in *The Oxford Handbook of Jewish Daily Life in Roman Palestine*. Edited by C. Hezser. Oxford: Oxford University Press, 2010.

Bakke, Odd M. *'Concord and Peace': A Rhetorical Analysis of the Language of the first Letter of Clement with an Emphasis on the Language of Unity and Sedition*. WUNT 2/143. Tübingen: Mohr Siebeck, 2001.

Barclay, John M. G. *Jews in the Mediterranean Diaspora: From Alexander to Trajan (323 BCE–117 CE)*. Edinburgh: T. & T. Clark, 1996.

Bar-Ilan, Meir. 'Illiteracy in the Land of Israel in the First Centuries CE'. Pages 46–61 in *Essays in the Social Scientific Study of Judaism and Jewish Society*. Edited by S. Fishbane, S. Schoenfeld, and A. Goldschläger. New York: Ktav, 1992.

Barnett, Paul W. *The Corinthians Question: Why did the Church Oppose Paul?* Nottingham: Apollos, 2011.

Barrett, C. K. *A Critical and Exegetical Commentary on the Acts of the Apostles*. 2 vols. ICC. Edinburgh: T. & T. Clark, 1994–1998.

Barrett, C. K. *The Dialectical Theology of St John*. London: SPCK, 1972.

Bateman IV, Herbert W. *Early Jewish Hermeneutics and Hebrews 1:5–13*. New York: Peter Lang, 1997.

Bauckham, Richard. J. *Jesus and the Eyewitnesses: The Gospels as Eyewitness Testimony*. 2nd ed. Grand Rapids: Eerdmans, 2017.

Bauckham, Richard J., ed. *The Gospels for All Christians: Rethinking the Gospel Audiences*. Grand Rapids: Eerdmans, 1998.

Bauman, R. "'I'll Give You Three Guesses": The Dynamics of Genre in the Riddle Tale'. Pages 62–77 in *Untying the Knot: On Riddles and Other Enigmatic Modes*. Edited by G. Hasan-Rokem and D. D. Shulman. Oxford: Oxford University Press, 1996.

Beale, G. K. *John's Use of the Old Testament in Revelation*. JSNTSup 166. Sheffield: Sheffield Academic, 1998.

Beale, G. K. 'The Old Testament Background of Reconciliation in 2 Cor 5–7 and its Bearing on the Literary Problem of 2 Corinthians 6,14–7,1'. *NTS* 35 (1989): 550–81.

Beard, Mary, John North, Simon Price. *Religions of Rome*. 2 vols. Cambridge: Cambridge University Press, 1998.

Becker, Hans-Jürgen. *Die grossen rabbinischen Sammelwerke Palästinas. Zur literarischen Genese von Talmud Yerushalmi und Midrash Bereshit Rabba*. Tübingen: Mohr Siebeck, 1999.

Berti, Monica. 'Greek and Roman Libraries in the Hellenistic Age'. Pages 33–54 in *The Dead Sea Scrolls and the Concept of a Library*. STDJ 116. Edited by S. White Crawford and C. Wassen. Leiden: Brill, 2016.

Bierbaum, Esther Green. *Special Libraries in Action: Cases and Crises*. Englewood: Libraries Unlimited, 1993.

Bitner, Bradley J. *Paul's Political Strategy in 1 Corinthians 1–4: Constitution and Covenant*. SNTSMS 163. Cambridge: Cambridge University Press, 2015.

Bock, Darrell L. *Acts*. BECNT. Grand Rapids: Baker, 2007.

pinnacle of their given reading cultures. Special libraries like the Villa of the Papyri at Herculaneum and Qumran are thematically suited to the literary needs of a specific reading community. These collections are also multi-lingual: Latin and Greek in the case of the Villa, and Hebrew, Aramaic, and Greek at Qumran. The collection of literary works in multiple languages suggests that the users of these collections were educated to a very high standard within their particular sub-cultures, even if they lacked cultural prestige associated with wealth and Roman aristocratic status. Overall, the diffusion of book collections across the Empire, in both urban (Pergamum, Ephesus, Rome, Herculaneum) and rural (Judean Desert) settings, witnesses to the importance of reading for literary composition and the construction of cultural norms and boundaries. Within this context John recorded a visionary experience using Jewish scripture as an interpretive foundation to convey to the churches of Asia Minor the import of encounters with the machinations of empire. Books, book collections, and special libraries played an important role in this process, both in terms of John's past education and on-going encounters with literature in the process of composition. It is no longer appropriate to critique John's level of education based on this supposed ignorance of Greek grammatical norms or his handful of solecisms; instead, a broader range of factors must indeed be taken seriously in reconstructing his educational background.

Bibliography

Abasciano, B. J. 'Diamonds in the Rough: A Reply to Christopher Stanley Concerning the Reader Competency of Paul's Original Audiences'. *NovT* 49 (2007): 153–83.
Adams, Samuel L. 'Reassessing the Exclusivism of Ben Sira's Jewish *Paideia*'. Pages 47–58 in *Second Temple Jewish 'Paideia' in Context*. BZNW 228. Edited by J. M. Zurawski and G. Boccaccini. Berlin: de Gruyter, 2017.
Adams, Sean A. *The Genre of Acts and Collected Biography*. SNTSMS 156. Cambridge: Cambridge University Press, 2013.
Adams, Sean A. 'Luke's Preface (1.1–4) and its Relationship to Greek Historical Prefaces: A Response to Loveday Alexander'. *JGRChJ* 3 (2006): 177–91.
Adams, Sean A. 'What are Bioi/Vitae? Generic Self-Consciousness in Ancient Biography'. Pages 19–31 in *The Oxford Handbook of Ancient Biography*. Edited by K. De Temmerman. Oxford: Oxford University Press, 2020.
Ahearne-Kroll, S. P. 'Audience Inclusion and Exclusion as Rhetorical Technique in the Gospel of Mark'. *JBL* 129 (2010): 717–35.
Aitken, James K. 'Ben Sira's Table Manners and the Social Setting of His Book'. Pages 418–38 in *Perspectives on Israelite Wisdom: Proceedings from the Oxford Old Testament Seminar*. Edited by J. Jarick. LHBOTS 618. London: T&T Clark, 2015.
Aitken, James K., and Ekaterina Matusova. 'The Wisdom of Solomon'. Pages 599–615 in *The Oxford Handbook of Wisdom and the Bible*. Edited by W. Kynes. Oxford: Oxford University Press, 2021.
Alexander, Elizabeth Shanks. 'The Orality of Rabbinic Writing'. Pages 38–57 in *The Cambridge Companion to the Talmud and Rabbinic Literature*. Edited by C. E. Fonrobert and M. S. Jaffee. Cambridge: Cambridge University Press, 2007.
Alexander, Loveday. 'Luke–Acts in its Contemporary Setting with Special Reference to the Prefaces (Luke 1:1–4 and Acts 1:1)'. DPhil diss., University of Oxford, 1978.
Alexander, Loveday. 'Luke's Preface in the Context of Greek Preface-Writing'. *NovT* 28 (1986): 48–74.
Alexander, Loveday. *The Preface to Luke's Gospel: Literary Convention and Social Context in Luke 1.1–4 and Acts 1.1*. Cambridge: Cambridge University Press, 1993.
Alexander, Philip S. 'Jesus and the Golden Rule'. Pages 363–88 in *Hillel and Jesus: Comparative Studies of Two Major Religious Leaders*. Edited by J. H. Charlesworth and L. L. Johns. Minneapolis: Fortress, 1997.
Alexander, Philip S. 'Literacy among Jews in Second Temple Palestine: Reflections on the Evidence from Qumran'. Pages 3–24 in *Hamlet on a Hill: Semitic and Greek Studies Presented to Professor T. Muraoka on the Occasion of his Sixty-Fifth Birthday*. OLA 118. Edited by M. F. J. Baasten and W. Th. van Peursen. Leuven: Peeters, 2003.

Bohak, Gideon. 'Greek-Hebrew Gematrias in *3 Baruch* and in Revelation'. *JSP* 7 (1990): 119–21.

Bookidis, N. 'Ritual Dining in the Sanctuary of Demeter and Kore at Corinth: Some Questions'. Pages 86–94 in *Sympotica: A Symposium on the Symposion*. Edited by O. Murray. Oxford: Oxford University Press, 1990.

Borgen, Peder. 'Philo of Alexandria'. Pages 233–82 in *Jewish Writings of the Second Temple Period*. Edited by M. E. Stone. Assen: van Gorcum, 1984

Bouwman, Alan K. ed. *Literacy and Power in the Ancient World*. Cambridge: Cambridge University Press, 1997.

Bowe, Barbara E. *A Church in Crisis: Ecclesiology and Paraenesis in Clement of Rome*. Minneapolis: Fortress, 1988.

Beauchamp, Paul. 'Le salut corporel des justes et la conclusion du livre de la Sagesse'. *Biblica* 45 (1964): 491–526.

Becker, A. H. 'Bringing the Heavenly Academy Down to Earth: Approaches to the Imagery of Divine Pedagogy in the East-Syrian Tradition'. Pages 174–94 in *Heavenly Realms and Earthly Realities in Late Antique Religions*. Edited by R. Boustan and A. Yoshiko Reed. Cambridge: Cambridge University Press, 2004.

Benin, S. D. *The Footprints of God: Divine Accommodation in Jewish and Christian Thought*. Albany: SUNY Press, 1993.

Betz, Hans Dieter. 'Jesus and the Cynics: Survey and Analysis of a Hypothesis'. *Journal of Religion* 74 (1994): 453–75.

Bickerman, Elias J. 'The Seleucid Charter of Jerusalem'. Pages 315–356 in *Studies in Jewish and Christian History: A New Edition in English Including* The God of the Maccabees. Edited by A. D. Tropper. Leiden: Brill, 2007.

Bird, Michael F. 'The Markan Community, Myth or Maze? Bauckham's the Gospel for All Christians Revisited'. *JTS* 57 (2006): 474–86.

Boehm, O. *The Binding of Isaac: A Religious Model of Disobedience*. London: T&T Clark, 2007.

Boghossian, P. 'Socratic Pedagogy: Perplexity, Humiliation, Shame and a Broken Egg'. *Educational Philosophy and Theory* 44 (2012): 710–20.

Bowie, E. L. 'The Readership of Greek Novels in the Ancient World'. Pages 435–59 in *The Search for the Ancient Novel*. Edited by J. Tatum. Baltimore: Johns Hopkins University Press, 1994.

Boyarin, Daniel. 'Patron Saint of the Incongruous: Rabbi Me'ir, the Talmud, and Menippean Satire'. *Critical Inquiry* 35 (2009): 523–51.

Boyarin, Daniel. *Socrates and the Fat Rabbis*. Chicago: University of Chicago Press, 2009.

Brancacci, A. 'Dio, Socrates, and Cynicism'. Pages 240–60 in *Dio Chrysostom: Politics, Letters, and Philosophy*. Edited by S. Swain. Oxford: Oxford University Press, 2000.

Branham, R. Bracht. 'Authorizing Humour: Lucian's Demonax and Cynic Rhetoric'. *Semeia* 64 (1993): 33–47.

Branham, R. Bracht. 'The Cynics'. In *Routledge Encyclopedia to Philosophy*. London: Routledge, 1998.

Braun, W. *Feasting and Social Rhetoric in Luke 14*. Cambridge: Cambridge University Press, 1995.

Brawley, Robert L. *Text to Text Pours Forth Speech: Voices of Scripture in Luke-Acts*. ISBL. Bloomington: Indiana University Press, 1995.

Brunt, P. A. 'From Epictetus to Arrian'. *Athenaeum* 55 (1977): 19–48.

Bremmer, Jan N. 'Peregrinus' Christian Career'. Pages 729-47 in *Flores Florentino: Dead Sea Scrolls and Other Early Jewish Studies in Honour of Florentino García Martínez*. Edited by A. Hilhorst et al. Leiden: Brill, 2007.

Brenk, F. E. 'The Dreams of Plutarch's Lives'. *Latomus: Revue d'Etudes Latines* 34 (1975): 336-49.

Brenk, F. E. '"In learned conversation": Plutarch's Symposiac Literature and the Elusive Authorial Voice'. Pages 51-61 in *Symposion and philanthropia in Plutarch*. Edited by J. R. Ferreira. Coimbra: Classica Digitalia, 2009.

Brickhouse, T. C., and N. D. Smith. 'The Origin of Socrates' Mission'. *JHI* (1983): 657-66.

Brown, E. 'Socrates in the Stoa'. Pages 275-84 in *A Companion to Socrates*. Edited by S. Ahbel-Rappe and R. Kamtekar. Oxford: Blackwell.

Brown, R. E. *The Community of the Beloved Disciple*. New York: Paulist, 1979.

Burnyeat, M. F. 'Socratic Midwifery, Platonic Inspiration'. *Bulletin of the Institute of Classical Studies* 24 (1977): 7-16.

Burrell, Barbara. 'Reading, Hearing, and Looking at Ephesos'. Pages 69-95 in *Ancient Literacies: The Culture of Reading in Greece and Rome*. Edited by W. A. Johnson and H. N. Parker. Oxford: Oxford University Press, 2009.

Capelle, W. 'Diatribe'. *RAC* 3 (1957): 990-7.

Carr, David M. *The Formation of the Hebrew Bible: A New Reconstruction*. Oxford: Oxford University Press, 2011.

Carr, David M. *Writing on the Tablet of the Heart: Origins in Scripture and Literature*. Oxford: Oxford University Press, 2005.

Carter, W. 'Recalling the Lord's Prayer: The Authorial Audience and Matthew's Prayer as Familiar Liturgical Experience'. *CBQ* 57 (1995): 514-30.

Carston, Robyn. 'Lexical Pragmatics, Ad Hoc Concepts and Metaphor: A Relevance Theory Perspective'. *Italian Journal of Linguistics* 22 (2010): 153-80.

Carston, Robyn. *Thoughts and Utterances: The Pragmatics of Explicit Communication*. Oxford: Blackwell, 2002.

Cave, Terence. 'Towards a Passing Theory of Understanding'. Pages 167-83 in *Reading Beyond the Code: Literature and Relevance Theory*. Edited by T. Cave and D. Wilson. Oxford: Oxford University Press, 2018.

Cave, Terence, and Deirdre Wilson, eds. *Reading Beyond the Code: Literature and Relevance Theory*. Oxford: Oxford University Press, 2018.

Charles, R. H. *The Revelation of St. John*. 2 vols. ICC. Edinburgh: T. & T. Clark, 1920.

Charlesworth, James H. et al., eds. *The Dead Sea Scrolls: Hebrew, Aramaic, and Greek Texts with English Translations, Volume 6B Pesharim, Other Commentaries, and Related Documents*. Tübingen: Mohr Siebeck, 2002.

Christian, M. 'The Literary Development of the 'Treatise of the Two Spirits' as Dependent on Instruction and the Hodayot'. Pages 153-84 in *Law, Literature and Society in Legal Texts from Qumran*. Edited by J. Jokiranta and M. Zahn. STDJ 128. Leiden: Brill, 2019.

Ciampa, Roy E., and Brian S. Rosner. '1 Corinthians'. Pages 695-752 in *Commentary on the New Testament Use of the Old Testament*. Edited by G. K. Beale and D. A. Carson. Grand Rapids: Baker, 2007.

Ciampa, Roy E., and Brian S. Rosner. *The First Letter to the Corinthians*. Grand Rapids: Eerdmans, 2010.

Cirafesi, W. V. 'The Johannine Community Hypothesis (1968-Present): Past and Present Approaches and a New Way Forward'. *CBR* 12 (2014): 173-93.

Clark, Billy. *Relevance Theory*. New York: Cambridge University Press, 2013.

Clarke, Andrew D. *Serve the Community of the Church: Christians as Leaders and Ministers*. Grand Rapids: Eerdmans, 2000.
Clarke, M. L. *Higher Education in the Ancient World*. London: Routledge, 1971.
Clay, D. 'Lucian of Samosata, Four Philosophical Lives: Nigrinus, Demonax, Peregrinus, Alexander Pseudomantis'. *ANRW* 2.36.5 (1992): 3406–50.
Cohen, M. H. 'The Aporias in Plato's Early Dialogues'. *JHI* 23 (1962): 163–74.
Collins, Adela Yarbro. 'Mark and His Readers: The Son of God among Greeks and Romans'. *HTR* 93 (2000): 85–100.
Collins, Adela Yarbro. *The Combat Myth in the Book of Revelation*. Missoula: Scholars Press, 1976.
Collins, John J. 'The Reinterpretation of the Apocalyptic Traditions in the Wisdom of Solomon'. Pages 143–58 in *The Book of Wisdom in Modern Research*. Edited by A. Passaro and G. Bella. Berlin: de Gruyter, 2005.
Collins, John J. 'The Root of Immortality: Death in the Context of Jewish Wisdom'. *HTR* 71 (1979): 177–92.
Conzelmann, Hans. *Acts of the Apostles: A Commentary on the Acts of the Apostles*. Philadelphia: Fortress, 1987.
Conzelmann, Hans. *Die Apostelgeschichte*. 2nd ed. Tübingen: Mohr, 1972.
Cook, C. 'The Sense of Audience in Luke: A Literary Examination'. *New Blackfriars* 72 (1991): 19–30.
Coqueugniot, Gaëlle. 'Scholastic Research in the Archive? Hellenistic Historians and Ancient Archival Records'. Pages 7–30 in *Scholastic Culture in the Hellenistic and Roman Eras: Greek, Latin, and Jewish*. Edited by S. A. Adams. Berlin: de Gruyter, 2019.
Coqueugniot, Gaëlle. 'Where was the Royal Library of Pergamum?' Pages 109–23 in *Ancient Libraries*. Edited by J. König, K. Oikonomopoulou, and G. Woolf. Cambridge: Cambridge University Press, 2013.
Corbeill, Anthony. 'Education in the Roman Republic: Creating Traditions'. Pages 261–87 in *Education in Greek and Roman Antiquity*. Edited by Y. L. Too. Leiden: Brill, 2001.
Corley, Jeremy. 'Searching for Structure and Redaction in Ben Sira. An Investigation of Beginnings and Endings'. Pages 21–47 in *The Wisdom of Ben Sira: Studies on Tradition, Redaction, and Theology*. Edited by A. Passarro and G. Bellia. Berlin: de Gruyter, 2008.
Corrigan, K., and E. Glazov-Corrigan. *Plato's Dialectic at Play: Argument, Structure, and Myth in the Symposium*. University Park: Pennsylvania State University Press, 2004.
Cribiore, Raffaella. *Gymnastics of the Mind: Greek Education in Hellenistic and Roman Egypt*. Princeton: Princeton University Press, 2001.
Cribiore, Raffaella. *Writing, Teachers, and Students in Graeco-Roman Egypt*. Atlanta: Scholars Press, 1996.
Crossan, John Dominic. *The Historical Jesus: The Life of a Mediterranean Jewish Peasant*. Edinburgh: T. & T. Clark, 1991.
Cullmann, Oscar. *The Johannine Circle: Its place in Judaism, among the Disciples of Jesus and in Early Christianity: A Study in the Origin of the Gospel of John*. London: SCM, 1976.
Culpepper, R. A. *The Johannine School: An Evaluation of the Johannine-School Hypothesis based on an Investigation of the Nature of Ancient Schools*. Missoula: Scholars Press, 1975.
Damm, A. L. '"Speech Unhindered": A Study of Irony in the Acts of the Apostles'. PhD diss., Wilfrid Laurier University, 1998.
Danzig, G. 'Intra-Socratic Polemics: The *Symposia* of Plato and Xenophon'. *GRBS* 43 (2005): 331–57.

Danzig, G. 'Xenophon's *Symposium*'. Pages 132–51 in *The Cambridge Companion to Xenophon*. Edited by M. A. Flower. Cambridge: Cambridge University Press, 2017.

Darr, J. A. *Herod the Fox: Audience Criticism and Lukan Characterization*. Sheffield: Sheffield Academic, 1998.

Darr, J. A. 'Narrative Therapy: Treating Audience Anxiety through Psychagogy in Luke'. *PRSt* 39 (2012): 335–48.

Das, A. A. '"Praise the Lord, All you Gentiles": The Encoded Audience of Romans 15.7–13'. *JSNT* 34 (2011): 90–110.

Daube, David. *The New Testament and Rabbinic Judaism*. London: Athlone, 1956.

Davies, Philip R. *Scribes and Schools: The Canonization of the Hebrew Scriptures*. Westminster: John Knox, 1998.

Delcor, M. 'L'immortalité de l'âme dans le livre de la Sagesse et dans les documents de Qumran'. *NRTh* 77 (1955): 614–630.

de Pury, A. 'Yahwist Source'. Pages 6:1013–20 in *ABD*.

Deslauriers, M. 'Women, Education, and Philosophy'. Pages 343–53 in *A Companion to Women in the Ancient World*. Edited by S. L. James and S. Dillon. Oxford: Blackwell, 2012.

Desmond, W. D. *Cynics*. Stocksfield: Acumen, 2008.

Deutsch, C. 'Visions, Mysteries, and the Interpretive Task: Text Work and Religious Experience in Philo and Clement'. Pages 83–103 in *Experientia*. Volume 1. Inquiry into Religious Experience in Early Judaism and Early Christianity. Edited by F. Flannery et al. Atlanta: SBL, 2008.

Dewey, J. 'The Gospel of Mark as an Oral-Aural Event: Implications for Interpretation'. Pages 145–63 in *The New Literary Criticism and the New Testament*. Edited by E. S. Malbon and E. V. McKnight/ Sheffield: Sheffield Academic, 1994.

Dibelius, Martin. *Studies in the Acts of the Apostles*. London: SCM, 1956.

Dickey, Eleanor. *Ancient Greek Scholarship: A Guide to Finding, Reading, and Understanding Scholia, Commentaries, Lexica, and Grammatical treatises, from Their Beginnings to the Byzantine Period*. Oxford: Oxford University Press, 2007.

Dickey, Eleanor. 'What Does a Linguistic Expert Know? The Conflict Between Analogy and Atticism?' Pages 103–18 in *Scholastic Culture in the Hellenistic and Roman Eras: Greek, Latin, and Jewish*. Edited by S. A. Adams. Berlin: de Gruyter, 2019.

Dillon, J. *The Middle Platonists*. London: Duckworth, 1977.

Dobbin, R. *Epictetus. Discourses, Book 1*. Oxford: Oxford University Press, 1998.

Dochhorn, Jan. 'Ist die Apokalypse des Johannes ein Text des Christentums der Asia?' Pages 299–322 in *The Rise and Expansion of Christianity in the First Three Centuries of the Common Era*. WUNT 301. Edited by C. K. Rothschild and J. Schröter. Tübingen: Mohr Siebeck, 2013.

Dodd, C. H. *According to the Scriptures: The Sub-Structure of New Testament Theology*. London: Fontana, 1952.

Dodson, D. S. *Reading Dreams: An Audience-Critical Approach to the Dreams in the Gospel of Matthew*. London: T&T Clark, 2009.

Dorion, L. A. 'Xenophon's Socrates'. Pages 93–109 in *A Companion to Socrates*. Edited by S. Ahbel-Rappe and R. Kamtekar. Oxford: Blackwell, 2006.

Douglas, A. E. 'Form and Content in the *Tusculan Disputations*'. Pages 197–218 in *Cicero the Philosopher*. Edited by J. G. F. Powell. Oxford: Oxford University Press, 1995.

Dowd, S., and E. S. Malbon. 'The Significance of Jesus' Death in Mark: Narrative Context and Authorial Audience'. *JBL* 125 (2006): 271–97.

Downing, F. G. *Christ and the Cynics: Jesus and Other Radical Preachers in First-Century Tradition*. Sheffield: JSOT, 1988.
Downing, F. G. *Cynics and Christian Origins*. Edinburgh: T. & T. Clark, 1992.
Downing, F. G. *Cynics, Paul, and the Pauline Churches: Cynics and Christian Origins II*. London: Routledge, 1998.
Downing, F. G. 'Deeper Reflections on the Jewish Cynic Jesus'. *JBL* 117 (1998): 97–104.
Du Plessis, I. J. 'The Lukan Audience-Rediscovered? Some Reactions to Bauckham's Theory'. *Neotestamentica* 34 (2000): 243–61.
Dyck, A. R. *A Commentary on Cicero, De Officiis*. Ann Arbor: University of Michigan Press, 1996.
Eckhardt, Benedikt. *Private Associations and Jewish Communities in the Hellenistic and Roman Cities*. JSJSup 191. Leiden: Brill, 2019.
Eddy, P. R. 'Jesus as Diogenes? Reflections on the Cynic Jesus Thesis'. *JBL* 115 (1996): 449–69.
Edlow, R. B., ed. *Galen on Language and Ambiguity: An English Translation of Galen's 'De Captionibus (on Fallacies)' with Introduction, Text, and Commentary*. Leiden: Brill, 1977.
Edmundson, George. *The Church at Rome in the First Century: An Examination of Various Controverted Questions Relating to Its History, Chronology, Literature and Traditions*. London: Longman, Green and Co., 1913.
Edsall, Ben A. 'Paul's Rhetoric of Knowledge'. *NovT* 55 (2013): 252–71.
Edwards, M. 'Lucian and the Rhetoric of Philosophy: The *Hermotimus*'. *AC* 62 (1993): 195–202.
Eggenberger, Christian. *Die Quellen der politischen Ethik des 1. Klemensbriefes: Die Quellen der politischen Ethik des 1. Klemensbriefes*. Zürich: Zwingli, 1951.
Elliott, S. M. 'Paul and His Gentile Audiences: Mystery-Cults, Anatolian Popular Religiosity, and Paul's Claim of Divine Authority in Galatians'. *Listening* 31 (1996): 117–36.
Engberg-Pedersen, Troels. *Paul and the Stoics*. Edinburgh: T. & T. Clark, 2000.
Erler, M. 'Parrhesy and Irony: Plato's Socrates and the Epicurean Tradition'. Pages 155–69 in *How Should One Live?: Comparing Ethics in Ancient China and Greco-Roman Antiquity*. Edited by R. A. H. King and D. Schilling. Amsterdam: de Gruyter, 2011.
Eshel, H. 'The Historical Background of the Pesher Interpreting Joshua's Curse on the Rebuilder of Jericho'. *RevQ* 15 (1992): 409–20.
Esler, Philip F. 'Community and Gospel in Early Christianity: A Response to Richard Bauckham's Gospels for All Christians'. *SJT* 51 (1998): 235–48.
Fantin, Joseph D. *The Lord of the Entire World: Lord Jesus, a Challenge to Lord Caesar?* Sheffield: Sheffield Phoenix, 2011.
Fine, Steven. *Art, History and Historiography of Judaism in Roman Antiquity*. Leiden: Brill, 2014.
Fischel, H. A. *Rabbinic Literature and Greco-Roman Philosophy. A Study of Epicurea and Rhetorica in Early Midrashic Writings*. Leiden: Brill, 1973.
Fischel, H. A. 'Studies in Cynicism and the Ancient Near East: The Transformation of a Chria'. Pages 372–411 in *Religions in Antiquity: Essays in Memory of Erwin Ramsdell Goodenough*. Edited by J. Neusner. Leiden: Brill, 1968.
Fishman, Talya. *Becoming the People of the Talmud: Oral Torah as Written Tradition in Medieval Jewish Cultures*. Philadelphia: University of Pennsylvania Press, 2011.
Fitzmyer, Joseph A. *The Acts of the Apostles: A New Translation with Introduction and Commentary*. AB 31. New York: Doubleday, 1998.

Flusser, David. 'Hillel and Jesus: Two Ways of Self-Awareness'. Pages 71–107 in *Hillel and Jesus: Comparative Studies of Two Major Religious Leaders*. Edited by J. H. Charlesworth and L. L. Johns. Minneapolis: Fortress, 1997.

Foster, Paul. 'Echoes without Resonance: Critiquing Certain Aspects of Recent Scholarly Trends in the Study of the Jewish Scriptures in the New Testament'. *JSNT* 38 (2015): 96–111.

Fraade, Steven D. 'Interpretive Authority in the Studying Community at Qumran'. *JJS* 44 (1993): 46–69.

Fredrickson, D. E. 'Parrēsia in the Pauline Epistles'. Pages 163–83 in *Friendship, Flattery, and Frankness of Speech: Studies on Friendship in the New Testament World*. Edited by J. T. Fitzgerald. Leiden: Brill, 1996.

Frenschkowski, Marco. 'Studien zur Geschichte der Bibliothek von Cäsarea'. Pages 52–104 in *New Testament Manuscripts: Their Texts and Their World*. Edited by T. J. Kraus and T. Nicklas. TENT 2. Leiden: Brill, 2006.

Frey, Jean-Baptiste, ed. *Corpus Inscriptionum Judaicarum*. 2 vols. Rome: Pontifical Biblical Institute, 1936.

Frey, Jörg.. 'Das Corpus Johanneum und die Apokalypse des Johannes. Die Johanneslegende, die Probleme der johanneischen Verfasserschaft und die Frage der Pseudonymität der Apokalypse'. Pages 71–133 in *Poetik und Intertextualität der Johannesapokalypse*. Edited by S. Alkier, T. Hieke, and T. Nicklas. WUNT 346. Tübingen: Mohr Siebeck, 2015.

Friesen, C. J. P. *Reading Dionysus: Euripides' Bacchae and the Cultural Contestations of Greeks, Jews, Romans, and Christians*. Tübingen: Mohr Siebeck, 2015.

Fuellenbach, John. *Ecclesiastical Office and the Primacy of Rome*. Washington, D.C.: Catholic Press of America, 1980.

Furlong, Anne. 'Relevance Theory and Literary Interpretation'. PhD diss., University College London, 1996.

Gamble, Harry Y. *Books and Readers in the Early Church: A History of Early Christian Texts*. New Haven: Yale University Press, 1995.

García Ehrenfeld, C. 'Lucian's *Hermotimus*, Essays about Philosophy and Satire in Greek Literature of the Roman Empire'. PhD diss., King's College London, 2017.

Gärtner, Bertil. *The Areopagus Speech and Natural Revelation*. ASNU. Uppsala: Gleerup, 1955.

Gelb, Norman. *Herod the Great: Statesman, Visionary, Tyrant*. Lanham: Rowman & Littlefield, 2013.

Gibbs, Raymond W. *Intentions in the Experience of Meaning*. Cambridge: Cambridge University Press, 1999.

Gigerenzer, Gerd, and Peter M. Todd. 'Fast and Frugal Heuristics: The Adaptive Toolbox'. Pages 3–36 in *Simple Heuristics that Make us Smart*. Edited by G. Gigerenzer, P. M. Todd, and ABC Research Group. New York: Oxford University Press, 1999.

Gil, Moshe. *A History of Palestine, 634–1099*. Cambridge: Cambridge University Press, 1992.

Gill, C. 'Ancient Psychotherapy'. *JHI* 46 (1985): 307–25.

Glad, C. E. *Paul and Philodemus: Adaptability in Epicurean and Early Christian Psychagogy*. Leiden: Brill, 1995.

Glucker, J. *Antiochus and the Late Academy*. Göttingen: Vandenhoeck & Ruprecht, 1978.

Goff, Matthew. 'Students of God in the House of Torah: Education in the Dead Sea Scrolls'. Pages 71–89 in *Second Temple Jewish 'Paideia' in Context*. BZNW 228. Edited by J. M. Zurawski and G. Boccaccini. Berlin: de Gruyter, 2017.

Goff, Matthew. *The Worldly and Heavenly Wisdom of 4QInstruction*. Leiden: Brill, 2003.

Goldhill, Simon. 'The Anecdote: Exploring the Boundaries between Oral and Literate Performance in the Second Sophistic'. Pages 96-113 in *Ancient Literacies: The Culture of Reading in Greece and Rome*. Edited by W. A. Johnson and H. N. Parker. Oxford: Oxford University Press, 2009.
Gonzàlez Julià, L. Plutarch's *techne rhetorike* for the Symposium in *Quaestiones Convivales*: The Importance of Speaking Well to Cultivate Friendship'. Pages 63-74 in *Symposion and philanthropia in Plutarch. Edited by* J. R. Ferreira et al. Coimbra: Classica Digitalia, 2009.
Good, E. M. *Irony in the Old Testament*. London: SPCK, 1981.
Goodblatt, David M. *The Monarchic Principle: Studies in Jewish Self-Government in Antiquity*. Tübingen: Mohr Siebeck, 1994.
Goodman, Martin. 'Jews and Judaism in the Mediterranean Diaspora in the Late-Roman Period: The Limitations of Evidence. Pages 177-203 in *Ancient Judaism and its Hellenistic Context*. Edited by C. Bakhos. JSJSup 95. Leiden: Brill, 2005.
Goodman, Martin. *Judaism in the Roman World: Collected Essays*. AJEC 66. Leiden: Brill, 2007.
Goodman, Martin. 'Sacred Scripture and 'Defiling the Hands'. *JTS* 41 (1990): 99-107.
Goodman, Martin. 'Texts, Scribes, and Power in Roman Judaea'. Pages 99-108 in *Literacy and Power in the Ancient World*. Edited by A. K. Bowman and G. Woolf. Cambridge: Cambridge University Press, 1994.
Gorman, R. *The Socratic Method in the Dialogues of Cicero*. Stuttgart: Franz Steiner, 2005.
Goulder, Michael D. *A Tale of Two Missions*. London: SCM, 1994.
Gowler, D. B. 'The Chreia'. Pages 132-48 in *The Historical Jesus in Context*. Edited by A.-J. Levine et al. Oxford: Princeton University Press, 2006.
Grabbe, L. L. *Etymology in Early Jewish Interpretation: The Hebrew Names in Philo*. BJS 115. Atlanta: Scholars Press, 1988.
Graver, M. 'Philo of Alexandria and the Origins of the Stoic Προπάθειαι'. *Phronesis* 44 (1999): 300-325.
Gray, P. 'Implied Audiences in the Areopagus Narrative'. *TynBul* 55 (2004): 205-18.
Gregory, Andrew C. '*1 Clement*: An Introduction'. Pages 21-31 in *The Writings of the Apostolic Fathers*. Edited by P. Foster. London: T&T Clark, 2007.
Green, Gene L. 'Relevance Theory and Biblical Interpretation'. Pages 217-40 in *The Linguist as Pedagogue: Trends in the Teaching and Linguistic Analysis of the Greek New Testament*. Edited by S. E. Porter and M. B. O'Donnell. Sheffield: Sheffield Phoenix, 2009.
Green, Joel B. 'The Problem of a Beginning: Israel's Scriptures in Luke 1-2'. *BBR* 4 (1994): 61-86.
Green, Keith. 'Relevance Theory and the Literary Text: Some Problems and Perspectives'. *JLS* 22 (1993): 207-17.
Green, William Scott. 'Writing with Scripture. The Rabbinic Uses of the Hebrew Bible'. Pages 7-23 in *Writing with Scripture: The Authority and Uses of the Hebrew Bible in the Torah of Formative Judaism*. Edited by J. Neusner and W. S. Green. Minneapolis: Fortress, 1989.
Grelot, Pierre. 'L'eschatologie de la Sagesse et les apocalypses juives'. Pages 165-78 in *À la rencontre de Dieu. Memorial Albert Gelin*. Edited by M. Jourgion et al. Mappus: Le Puy, 1961.
Griffin, M. 'Cynicism and the Romans: Attraction and Repulsion'. Pages 109-204 in *The Cynics: The Cynic Movement in Antiquity and Its Legacy*. Edited by R. B. Branham and M.-O. Goulet-Cazé. Berkeley: University of California Press, 1996.

Griffith, Mark. 'Public and Private in Early Greek Institutions of Education'. Pages 23–84 in *Education in Greek and Roman Antiquity*. Edited by Y. L. Too. Leiden: Brill, 2001.

Grottanelli, C. 'On the Mantic Meaning of Incestuous Dreams'. Pages 143–68 in *Dream Cultures: Explorations in the Comparative History of Dreaming*. Edited by D. D. Shulman and G. A. G. Stroumsa. New York: Oxford University Press, 1999.

Guidorizzi, G. 'On Dreaming of One's Mother: Oedipal Dreams between Sophocles and Artemidorus'. Pages 219–32 in *Artemidor von Daldis und die antike Traumdeutung: Texte – Kontexte – Lektüren*. Edited by G. Weber. Berlin: de Gruyter, 2015.

Gupta, Nijay K. 'Mirror-Reading Moral Issues in Paul's Letters'. *JSNT* 34 (2012): 361–81.

Guthrie, W. K. C. *A History of Greek Philosophy*. Volume 3. Cambridge: Cambridge University Press, 1962.

Hachlili, Rachel. 'The State of Ancient Synagogue Studies'. Pages 7–46 in *Ancient Synagogues in Israel: Third–Seventh Century C.E.* Edited by R. Hachlili et al. Oxford: British Archaeological Review, 1989.

Haenchen, E. *The Acts of the Apostles: A Commentary*. Oxford: Blackwell, 1971.

Hafemann, Scott J. 'Paul's Argument from the Old Testament and Christology in 2 Cor 1–9: The Salvation-History/Restoration Structure of Paul's Apologetic'. Pages 277–303 in *The Corinthian Correspondence*. BETL 112. Edited by R. Bieringer. Leuven: Leuven University Press, 1996.

Hafemann, Scott J. *Paul, Moses, and the History of Israel: The Letter/Spirit Contrast and the Argument from Scripture in 2 Corinthians 3*. WUNT 81. Tübingen: Mohr Siebeck, 1995.

Hafemann, Scott J. '"Self-commendation" and Apostolic Legitimacy in 2 Corinthians: A Pauline Dialectic?' *NTS* 36 (1990): 66–88.

Hagner, Donald. A. *The Use of the Old and New Testaments in Clement of Rome*. NovTSup 34. Leiden: Brill, 1973.

Halbauer, O. *De diatribis Epicteti*. Leipzig: R. Noske, 1911.

Hammer, Reuven. *The Classic Midrash: Tannaitic Commentaries on the Bible*. Mahwah: Paulist, 1995.

Handis, Michael W. 'Myth and History: Galen and the Alexandrian Library'. Pages 364–376 in *Ancient Libraries*. Edited by J. König, K. Oikonomopoulou, and G. Woolf. Cambridge: Cambridge University Press, 2013.

Handy, D. A. 'The Gentile Pentecost: A Literary Study of the Story of Peter and Cornelius (Acts 10:1–11:18)'. PhD diss., Union Theological Seminary, 1998.

Haran, Menahem. 'Bible Scrolls in the Early Second Temple Period – The Transition from Papyrus to Skins'. *Eretz Israel* 16 (1982): 86–92 [Hebrew].

Haran, Menahem. 'Book-Scrolls in Israel in Pre-Exilic Times'. *JJS* (1982): 111–22.

Harnack, Adolf von. *Einführung in die alte Kirchengeschichte: Das Schreiben der Römischen Kirche an die Korinthische aus der Zeit Domitians (I. Clemensbrief)*. Leipzig: Hinrichs'sche, 1929.

Harrill, J. A. 'Cannibalistic Language in the Fourth Gospel and Greco-Roman Polemics of Factionalism (John 6:52–66)'. *JBL* 127 (2008): 133–58.

Harris, Murray J. *The Second Epistle to the Corinthians*. NIGTC. Grand Rapids: Eerdmans, 2013.

Harris, William V. *Ancient Literacy*. Cambridge, MA: Harvard University Press, 1989.

Harrison, S. J. *Apuleius: A Latin Sophist*. Oxford: Oxford University Press, 2004.

Hartog, Pieter B., and Jutta Jokiranta. 'The Dead Sea Scrolls in Their Hellenistic Context'. *DSD* 24 (2017): 339–55.

Hays, Richard B. *Echoes of Scripture in the Gospels*. Waco: Baylor University Press, 2016.

Hays, Richard B. *Echoes of Scripture in the Letters of Paul*. London: Yale University Press, 1989.
Hatch, E., and A. Redpath. *A Concordance to the Septuagint, And the Other Greek Versions of the Old Testament*. 2nd ed. Grand Rapids: Baker, 1998.
Heller, Marvin J. *Studies in the Making of the Early Hebrew Book*. Leiden: Brill, 2008.
Hempel, Charlotte. 'Bildung und Wissenswirtschaft im Judentum zur Zeit des Zweiten Tempels'. Pages 229-44 in *Was ist Bildung in der Vormoderne?* Edited by P. Gemeinhardt. Tübingen: Mohr Siebeck, 2020.
Hempel, Charlotte. 'Kriterien zur Bestimmung 'essenischer Verfasserschaft' von Qumrantexten'. Pages 85– 7 in *Qumran kontrovers: Beiträge zu den Textfunden vom Toten Meer*. Edited by J. Frey and H. Stegemann. Paderborn: Bonifatius, 2003.
Hempel, Charlotte. 'Maskil(im) and Rabbim: From Daniel to Qumran'. Pages 133-56 in *Biblical Traditions in Transmission: Essays in Honour of Michael A. Knibb*. Edited by C. Hempel and J. Lieu. JSJSup 111. Leiden: Brill, 2006.
Herron, Thomas J. 'The Most Probable Date of the First Epistle of Clement to the Corinthians'. *StPatr* 21 (1989): 106-21.
Hezser, Catherine. *Form, Function, and Historical Significance of the Rabbinic Story in Yerushalmi Neziqin*. Tübingen: Mohr Siebeck, 1993.
Hezser, Catherine. *Jewish Literacy in Roman Palestine*. TSAJ 81. Tübingen: Mohr Siebeck, 2001.
Hezser, Catherine. 'The Mishnah and Ancient Book Production'. Pages 167-92 in *The Mishnah in Contemporary Perspective, Part One*. Edited by A. J. Avery-Peck and J. Neusner. Leiden: Brill, 2002.
Hezser, Catherine. 'Private and Public Education'. Pages 465-81 in *The Oxford Handbook of Jewish Daily Life in Roman Palestine*. Edited by C. Hezser. Oxford: Oxford University Press, 2010.
Hezser, Catherine. *The Social Structure of the Rabbinic Movement in Roman Palestine*. Tübingen: Mohr Siebeck, 1997.
Himes, P. A. 'Rethinking the Translation of Διδακτικός in 1 Timothy 3.2 and 2 Timothy 2.24'. *BT* 68 (2017): 189-208.
Hock, R. F. 'Cynics'. Pages 1:1221-6 in *ABD*.
Hoepfner, Wolfram. 'Bibliotheken in Wohnhäusern und Palästen'. Pages 86-96 in *Antike Bibliotheken*. Edited by W. Hoepfner. Mainz am Rhein: von Zabern, 2002.
Hoepfner, Wolfram. 'Die Bibliothek Eumenes' II. in Pergamon'. Pages 41-51 in *Antike Bibliotheken*. Edited by W. Hoepfner. Mainz am Rhein: von Zabern, 2002.
Holford-Strevens, L. *Aulis Gellius*. London: Duckworth, 1988.
Holland, G. S. *Divine Irony*, Selinsgrove: Susquehanna University Press, 2000.
Holm, T. L. 'Literature'. Pages 253-65 in *A Companion to the Ancient Near East*. Edited by D. C. Snell. Oxford: Blackwell, 2005.
Holmes, Michael W. *The Apostolic Fathers: Greek Texts and English Translations*. Grand Rapids: Baker, 2007.
Holowchak, M. A. 'Education as Training for Life: Stoic Teachers as Physicians of the Soul'. *Educational Philosophy and Theory* 41 (2009): 166-84.
Horbury, William. 'Extirpation and Excommunication'. *VT* 35 (1985): 13-38.
Horrell, David G. *The Social Ethos of the Corinthian Correspondence*. Edinburgh: T. & T. Clark, 1996.
Houston, George W. *Inside Roman Libraries: Book Collections and Their Management in Antiquity*. Chapel Hill: The University of North Carolina Press, 2014.

Houston, George W. 'Papyrological Evidence for Book Collections and Libraries in the Roman Empire'. Pages 233–67 in *Ancient Literacies: The Culture of Reading in Greece and Rome*. Edited by W. A. Johnson and H. N. Parker. Oxford: Oxford University Press, 2009.

Howell, J. R. *The Pharisees and Figured Speech in Luke-Acts*. Tübingen: Mohr Siebeck, 2017.

Howland, J. *Plato and the Talmud*. Cambridge: Cambridge University Press, 2011.

Huffman, C. 'Pythagoras'. *SEP*.

Hultin, J. F. *The Ethics of Obscene Speech in Early Christianity and its Environment*. Leiden: Brill, 2008.

Hurd, John C. *The Origin of 1 Corinthians*. New ed. Macon: Mercer, 1983.

Hurtado, Larry W. *The Earliest Christian Artifacts: Manuscripts and Christian Origins*. Grand Rapids: Eerdmans, 2006.

Ilan, Zvi. 'The Synagogue and Study House at Meroth'. Pages 256–88 in *Ancient Synagogues: Historical Analysis and Archaeological Discovery*. Edited by D. Urman and P. V. M. Flesher. 2nd ed. Leiden: Brill, 1998.

Inkelaar, Harm-Jan. *Conflict over Wisdom: The Theme of 1 Corinthians 1–4 Rooted in Scripture*. CBET 63. Leuven: Peeters, 2011.

Jaffee, Martin S. *Torah in the Mouth. Writing and Oral Tradition in Palestinian Judaism, 200 BCE–400 CE*. Oxford: Oxford University Press, 2001.

Jastrow, Marcus. *A Dictionary of the Targumim, the Talmud Babli and Yerushalmi, and the Midrashic Literature*. Jerusalem: Horev, 1985.

Jaubert, Annie. *Clément de Rome*. Paris: Cerf, 1971.

Jauss, H. R. 'The Book of Jonah: A Paradigm of the Hermeneutics of Strangeness'. Pages 1–26 in *Contexts of Pre-novel Narrative: The European Tradition*. Edited by R. Eriksen. Berlin: de Gruyter, 1994.

Jipp, Joshua W. 'Paul's Areopagus Speech of Acts 17:16–34 as Both Critique and Propaganda'. *JBL* 131 (2012): 567–88.

Jocelyn, H. D. 'Diatribes and Sermons'. *Liverpool Classical Monthly* 7 (1982): 3–7.

Johnson, Luke Timothy. *The Acts of the Apostles*. SP 5. Collegeville: Liturgical, 1992.

Johnson, Luke Timothy. *The Gospel of Luke*. SP 3. Collegeville: Liturgical, 1991.

Johnson, Luke Timothy. 'On Finding the Lukan Community: A Cautious Cautionary Essay'. Pages 87–100 in *SBLSP 1979*. Volume 1. Edited by P. J. Achtemeier. Missoula: Scholars Press, 1979.

Johnson, William A. 'Constructing Elite Reading Communities in the High Empire'. Pages 320–30 in *Ancient Literacies: The Culture of Reading in Greece and Rome*. Edited by W. A. Johnson and H. N. Parker. Oxford: Oxford University Press, 2009.

Johnson, William A. 'Introduction'. Pages 3–10 in *Ancient Literacies: The Culture of Reading in Greece and Rome*. Edited by W. A. Johnson and H. N. Parker. Oxford: Oxford University Press, 2009.

Johnson, William A. *Readers and Reading Culture in the High Roman Empire: A Study of Elite Communities*. New York: Oxford University Press, 2010.

Johnson, William A. 'Towards a Sociology of Reading in Classical Antiquity'. *The American Journal of Philology* 121, no. 4 (2000): 593–627.

Johnson, William A., and Holt N. Parker, eds. *Ancient Literacies: The Culture of Reading in Greece and Rome*. Oxford: Oxford University Press, 2011.

Kahn, C. H. *The Art and Thought of Heraclitus: An Edition of the Fragments with Translation and Commentary*. Cambridge: Cambridge University Press, 1979.

Kahn, C. H. *Plato and the Socratic Dialogue: The Philosophical Use of a Literary Form*. Cambridge: Cambridge University Press, 1996.

Kahn, C. H. *Pythagoras and the Pythagoreans: A Brief History*. Indianapolis: Hackett, 2001.
Kalmin, Richard. *Migrating Tales: The Talmud's Narratives and Their Historical Contexts*. Berkeley: University of California Press, 2014.
Kanarfogel, Ephraim. *Jewish Education and Society in the High Middle Ages*. Detroit: Wayne State University Press, 1992.
Keith, Chris. *Jesus' Literacy: Scribal Culture and the Teacher from Galilee*. LNTS 413. London: T&T Clark, 2011.
Kelley, S. J. '"And Your Young Will See Visions": A Functionalist Literary Reading of the Visions to Saul and Peter in Acts'. PhD diss., Vanderbilt University, 1991.
Kennedy, G. A. *Progymnasmata: Greek Textbooks of Prose Composition and Rhetoric*. Leiden: Brill, 2003.
Kennedy, K. 'Cynic Rhetoric: The Ethics and Tactics of Resistance'. *RhetR* 18 (1999): 26–45.
Kent, John H. *The Inscriptions, 1926–1950*. Volume 8, Corinth. Princeton: American School of Classical Studies at Athens, 1966.
Kessler, E. *Bound by the Bible: Jews, Christians and the Sacrifice of Isaac*. Cambridge: Cambridge University Press, 2004.
Kirchheiner, H. I. 'Revitalization in Judea: An Anthropological Study of the Damascus Document'. PhD diss., University of Birmingham, 2018.
Klink, E. W. *The Audience of the Gospels: The Origin and Function of the Gospels in Early Christianity*. London: T&T Clark, 2010.
Kloppenborg, John S., and Richard S. Ascough. *Greco-Roman Associations: Texts, Translations, and Commentary*. Berlin: de Gruyter, 2011.
Klotz, F., and K. Oikonomopoulou. 'Introduction'. Pages 1–31 in *The Philosopher's Banquet: Plutarch's Table Talk in the Intellectual Culture of the Roman Empire*. Edited by F. Klotz and K. Oikonomopoulou. Oxford: Oxford University Press, 2011.
Klotz, F., and K. Oikonomopoulou, eds. *The Philosopher's Banquet. Plutarch's Table Talk in the Intellectual Culture of the Roman Empire*. Oxford: Oxford University Press, 2011.
Knoch, Otto. *Eigenart und Bedeutung der Eschatologie im theologischen Aufriß der ersten Clemensbriefes*. Bonn: Hanstein, 1964.
Knopf, Rudolf. *Das nachapostolische Zeitalter. Geschichte der christliechen Gemeinden vom Beginn der Flavierdynastie bis zum Ende Hadrians*. Tübingen: Mohr Siebeck, 1905.
Koch, Dietrich-Alex. *Die Schrift als Zeuge des Evangeliums: Untersuchungen zur Verwendung und zum Verständnis der Schrift bei Paulus*. Tübingen: Mohr Siebeck, 1986.
Koester, Craig R. *Revelation*. AYB 38A. London: Yale University Press, 2014.
König, Jason. *Saints and Symposiasts: The Literature of Food and the Symposium in Greco-Roman and Early Christian Culture*. Cambridge: Cambridge University Press, 2012.
König, Jason, Katerina Oikonomopoulou and Greg Woolf, eds. *Ancient libraries*. Cambridge: Cambridge University Press, 2013.
König, Jason, and Gregg Woolf. 'Encyclopedism in the Roman Empire'. Pages 23–63 in *Encyclopedism from Antiquity to the Renaissance*. Edited by J. König and G. Woolf. Cambridge: Cambridge University Press, 2013.
Konstan, D. *Philodemus: On Frank Criticism* Atlanta: Scholars Press, 1998.
Kowalski, Beate. *Die Rezeption des Propheten Ezechiel in der Offenbarung des Johannes*. SBB 52. Stuttgart: Katholisches Bibelwerk, 2004.
Krabbel, Alf Thomas. 'The Diaspora Synagogue: Archaeological and Epigraphic Evidence since Sukenik'. Pages 95–126 in *Ancient Synagogues: Historical Analysis and Archeological Discovery*. SPB 47/1. Edited by D. Urman and P. V. M. Flesher. Leiden: Brill, 1995.
Kraemer, David. 'The Intended Reader as a Key to Interpreting the Bavli'. *Prooftexts* 13 (1993): 125–40.

Kratz, Reinhard. 'Der 'Penal Code' und das Verhältnis von Serekh ha-Yachad (S) und Damaskusschrift (D)'. *RevQ* 25 (2011): 199–227.

Krueger, D. 'The Bawdy and Society: The Shamelessness of Diogenes in Roman Imperial Culture'. Pages 222–39 in *The Cynics: The Cynic Movement in Antiquity and its Legacy*. Edited by R. B. Branham and M.-O. Goulet-Cazé. Berkeley: University of California Press, 1996.

Krueger, D. 'Diogenes the Cynic among the Fourth Century Fathers'. *VC* 47 (1993): 29–49.

Labahn, Michael. 'Die Macht des Gedächtnisses: Überlegungen zu Möglichkeit unde Grenzen des Einflusses hebräischer Texttradition auf die Johannesapokalypse'. Pages 385–416 in *Von der Septuaginta zum Neuen Testament: Textgechichtliche Erörterungen*. ANTF 43. Edited by M. Karrer et al. Berlin: de Gruyter, 2010.

Labendz, J. R. *Socratic Torah: Non-Jews in Rabbinic Intellectual Culture*. New York: Oxford University Press, 2013.

Lageman, A. G. 'Socrates and Psychotherapy'. *Journal of Religion and Health* 28 (1989): 219–23.

Lamb, W. R. M., trans. *Plato in Twelve Volumes*. Cambridge, MA: Harvard University Press, 1925.

Lane, M. 'The Evolution of Eirôneia in Classical Greek Texts: Why Socratic Eirôneia is not Socratic Irony'. *OSAPh* 31 (2006): 49–83.

Lang, B. 'Jesus among the Philosophers: The Cynic Connection Explored and Affirmed, with a Note on Philo's Jewish-Cynic Philosophy'. Pages 187–218 in *Religio-Philosophical Discourses in the Mediterranean World: From Plato, through Jesus, to Late Antiquity*. Edited by A. K. Petersen and G. van Kooten. Leiden: Brill, 2017.

Langer, Gerhard. 'Rabbinic References to Asia Minor'. *JAJ* 5 (2014): 259–69.

Lappenga, Benjamin J. *Paul's Language of Ζῆλος: Monosemy and the Rhetoric of Identity and Practice*. Leiden: Brill, 2015.

Larcher, Chrysostomos. *Études sur le livre de la sagesse*. Paris: Gabalda, 1969.

Larcher, Chrysostomos. *Le livre de la sagesse, ou, La sagesse de Salomon*. 3 vols. Paris: Gabalda, 1984.

Larsen, K. B. *Recognizing the Stranger: Recognition Scenes in the Gospel of John*. Leiden: Brill, 2008.

LaVerdiere, E. A., and W. G. Thompson. 'New Testament Communities in Transition: A Study of Matthew and Luke'. *Theological Studies* 37 (1976): 567–97.

Leitzmann, Hans. *An die Korinther*. Tübingen: Mohr Siebeck, 1949.

Levine, Lee I. *The Ancient Synagogue: The First Thousand Years*. London: Yale University Press, 2000.

Lichtenberger, Hermann. 'Die Schrift in der Offenbarung des Johannes'. Pages 382–90 in *Die Septuaginta und das frühe Christentum*. WUNT 277. Edited by T. S. Caulley and H. Lichtenberger. Tübingen: Mohr Siebeck, 2011.

Liebermann, Saul. *Hellenism in Jewish Palestine*. 2nd ed. New York: The Jewish Theological Seminary of America, 1962.

Liebermann, Saul. *The Talmud of Caesarea*. Jerusalem: Supplement to *Tarbiz*, 1931 [Hebrew].

Lieu, Samuel N. C. 'Scholars and Students in the Roman East'. Pages 127–42 in *The Library of Alexandria: Centre of Learning in the Ancient World*. Edited by R. MacLeod. London: Tauris, 2000.

Lightfoot, Joseph B. *The Apostolic Fathers. Part I. S. Clement of Rome. A Revised Text with Introductions, Notes, Dissertations and Translations*. Volume 1. London: Macmillan, 1890.

Lindemann, Andreas. *Die Clemensbriefe*.Tübingen: Mohr Siebeck, 1992.
Liu, Yulin. *Temple Purity in 1–2 Corinthians*. WUNT 2/343. Tübingen: Mohr Siebeck, 2013.
Lona, Horacio E. *Der erste Clemensbrief*. Göttingen: Vandenhoeck & Ruprecht, 1998.
Long, A. A. *Epictetus, A Stoic and Socratic Guide to Life*. Oxford: Oxford University Press, 2002.
Lentz, J. C. *Luke's Portrait of Paul*. Cambridge: Cambridge University Press, 1993.
Lesher, J. H. 'Socrates' Disavowal of Knowledge'. *JHPh* 25 (1987): 275–88.
Lincicum, David. 'Mirror-Reading a Pseudepigraphical Letter'. *NovT* 59 (2017): 171–93.
Lukinovich, A. 'The Play of Reflection between Literary Form and the Sympotic Theme in the *Deipnosophistae*'. Pages 263–71 in *Sympotica: A Symposium on the Symposion*. Edited by O. Murray. Oxford: Oxford University Press, 1990.
MacFarlane, J. 'Aristotle's Definition of Anagnorisis'. *AJP* 121 (2000): 367–83.
MacMullen, Ramsay. 'The Epigraphic Habit in the Roman Empire'. *AJP* 103 (1982): 233–46.
Magness, Jodi. *The Archaeology of Qumran and the Dead Sea Scrolls*. Grand Rapids: Eerdmans, 2003.
Magness, Jodi. *Stone and Dung, Oil and Spit: Jewish Daily Life in the Time of Jesus*. Grand Rapids: Eerdmans, 2011.
Maier, J. *Die Qumran-Essener: Die Texte vom Toten Meer*. Munich: Reinhardt, 1995.
Malbon, E. S. and E. V. McKnight, eds. *The New Literary Criticism and the New Testament*. Sheffield: Sheffield Academic, 1994.
Malherbe, A. J. *The Cynic Epistles: A Study Edition*, Missoula: Scholars Press, 1977.
Malherbe, A. J. '"Gentle as a Nurse": The Cynic Background to I Thess II'. *NovT* 12 (1970): 203–17.
Malherbe, A. J. '"In Season and out of Season": 2 Timothy 4:2'. *JBL* 103 (1984): 235–43.
Malherbe, A. J. 'Medical Imagery in the Pastoral Epistles'. Pages 117–34 in *Light from the Gentiles: Hellenistic Philosophy and Early Christianity: Collected Essays, 1959–2012*. Volume 2. Edited by C. R. Holladay et al. Leiden: Brill, 2013.
Manson, T. W. *The Teaching of Jesus: Studies of its Form and Content*. Cambridge: Cambridge University Press, 1967.
Marchant, E. C., and O. J. Dodd. *Xenophon: Memorabilia, Oeconomicus, Symposium, Apology*. Loeb. Revised by J. Henderson. Cambridge, MA: Harvard University Press, 2013.
Marguerat, D. *The First Christian Historian: Writing the 'Acts of the Apostles'*. Cambridge: Cambridge University Press, 2002.
Marincola, J. *Authority and Tradition in Ancient Historiography*. Cambridge: Cambridge University Press, 1997.
Marrou, Henri-Irénée. *A History of Education in Antiquity*. Translated by G. R. Lamb. Madison: University of Wisconsin Press, 1981.
Marrow, S. B. '"Parrhēsia" and the New Testament'. *CBQ* 44 (1982): 431–46.
Marshall, I. Howard. 'Acts'. Pages 513–606 in *Commentary on the New Testament Use of the Old Testament*. Edited by G. K. Beale and D. A. Carson. Grand Rapids: Baker, 2007.
Marshall, I. Howard. 'Church and Temple in the New Testament'. *TynBul* 40 (1989): 203–22.
Marshall, L. A. 'Gadfly or Spur? The Meaning of ΜΥΩΨ in Plato's Apology of Socrates'. *JHelStud* 137 (2017): 163–74.
Martin, T. W. *By Philosophy and Empty Deceit: Colossians as Response to a Cynic Critique*. Sheffield: Sheffield Academic, 1996.
Martínez, Victor M., and Megan Finn Senseney. 'The Professional and his Books: Special Libraries in the Ancient World'. Pages 401–17 in *Ancient Libraries*. Edited by J. König, K. Oikonomopoulou, and G. Woolf. Cambridge: Cambridge University Press, 2013.

Martone, Corrado. 'The Qumran "Library" and Other Ancient Libraries: Elements for Comparison'. Pages 55–77 in *The Dead Sea Scrolls and the Concept of a Library*. STDJ 116. Edited by S. White Crawford and C. Wassen. Leiden: Brill, 2016.

Mason, Steven, and T. Robinson. 'A Letter from the Romans to the Corinthians'. Pages 44–51 in *Early Christian Reader: Christian Texts from the First and Second Centuries in Contemporary English Translations including the New Revised Standard Version of the New Testament*. Edited by S. Mason and T. Robinson. Atlanta: Scholars Press, 2013.

Matthews, G. B. *Socratic Perplexity and the Nature of Philosophy*. Oxford: Oxford University Press, 1999.

Matusova, Ekaterina. 'Genesis 1–2 in *De opificio mundi* and its Exegetical Context'. *SPhilo* 31 (2019): 57–94.

Matusova, Ekaterina. '"Seeing" God in Alexandrian Exegesis of the Bible: From Aristobulus to Philo'. Pages 63–86 in *Gottesschau-Gotteserkenntnis*. Edited by E. Dafni. WUNT 387. Tübingen: Mohr Siebeck, 2017.

McClure, L. *Courtesans at Table: Gender and Greek Literary Culture in Athenaeus*. London: Routledge, 2003.

McCracken, D. *The Scandal of the Gospels: Jesus, Story, and Offense*. Oxford: Oxford University Press, 1994.

McNamara, Martin. *Targum Neophiti 1: Deuteronomy*. Collegeville: Liturgical, 1997.

McPherran, M. L. 'Elenctic Interpretation and the Delphic Oracle'. Pages 114–44 in *Does Socrates have a Method? Rethinking the Elenchus in Plato's Dialogues and Beyond*. Edited by G. A. Scott. University Park: Pennsylvania State University Press, 2002.

Mehl, D. 'The Stoic Paradoxes According to Cicero'. Pages 39–46 in *Vertis in usum: Studies in Honor of Edward Courtney*. Edited by C. Damon et al. Munich: K. G. Saur, 2002.

Metso, Sarianna. *The Community Rule: A Critical Edition with Translation*. Atlanta: SBL, 2019.

Metso, Sarianna. *The Development of the Qumran Community Rule*. STDJ 27. Leiden: Brill, 1997.

Meyer, Marvin W. *The Ancient Mysteries. A Sourcebook of Sacred Texts*. Philadelphia: University Press, 1999.

Mikat, Paul. *Die Bedeutung der Begriffe Stasis und Aponoia für das Verständnis des 1. Clemensbriefes*. Cologne: Westdeutscher, 1969.

Millar, F. G. B. 'Epictetus and the Imperial Court'. *JRS* 55 (1965): 141–8.

Millard, Alan. *Reading and Writing in the Time of Jesus*. Sheffield: Sheffield Academic, 2001.

Miller, J. B. F. *Convinced That God Had Called Us: Dreams, Visions, and the Perception of God's Will in Luke-Acts*. Leiden: Brill, 2007.

Mintz, Sharon Liberman, and Gabriel M. Goldstein, eds. *Printing the Talmud: From Bomberg to Schottenstein*. New York: Yeshiva University Museum, 2005.

Mitchell, M. M. 'Patristic Counter-Evidence to the Claim that "The Gospels Were Written for All Christians"'. *NTS* 51 (2005): 36–79.

Mizrahi, Noam. 'The Songs of the Sabbath Sacrifice and Biblical Priestly Literature: A Linguistic Reconsideration'. *HTR* 58–33 :(2011) 104.

Moles, John L. 'Cynic Cosmopolitanism'. Pages 105–20 in *The Cynics: The Cynic Movement in Antiquity and Its Legacy*. Edited by R. B. Branham and M.-O. Goulet-Cazé. Berkeley: University of California Press, 1996.

Moles, John L. 'Cynic Influence upon First-Century Judaism and Early Christianity?' Pages 89–116 in *The Limits of Ancient Biography*. Edited by B. C. McGing and J. Mossman. Swansea: Classical Press of Wales, 2006.

Moles, John L. 'Jesus and Dionysus in 'The Acts of The Apostles' and Early Christianity'. *Hermathena* (2006): 65–104.
Möllendorff, P. von. *Lukian, Hermotimos oder, Lohnt es sich, Philosophie zu studieren.* Darmstadt: Wissenschaftliche Buchgesellschaft, 2000.
Morales, Nelson R. *Poor and Rich in James: A Relevance Theory Approach to James's Use of the Old Testament*. University Park: Eisenbrauns, 2018.
Morgan, Teresa. *Literate Education in the Hellenistic and Roman Worlds*. Cambridge: Cambridge University, 1998.
Morgan, Teresa. *Popular Morality in the Early Roman Empire*. Cambridge: Cambridge University Press, 2007.
Morris, Leon. *The Revelation of St. John*. TNTC. Grand Rapids: Eerdmans, 1984.
Morton, Stephen. 'The Subaltern: Genealogy of a Concept'. Pages 96–7 in *Gayatri Spivak: Ethics, Subalternity and the Critique of Postcolonial Reason*. Malden: Polity, 2007.
Mossman, Judith M. *Plutarch and His Intellectual World*. London: Duckworth, 1997.
Moxnes, H. 'The Social Context of Luke's Community'. *Union Seminary Review* 48 (1994): 379–89.
Moxon, J. R. L. *Peter's Halakhic Nightmare: The 'Animal' Vision of Acts 10:9 in Jewish and Graeco-Roman Perspective*. Tübingen: Mohr Siebeck, 2017.
Moyise, Steve. *The Old Testament in the Book of Revelation*. JSNTSup 115. Sheffield: Sheffield Academic, 1995.
Mroczek, Eva. *The Literary Imagination in Jewish Antiquity*. Oxford: Oxford University Press, 2016.
Muraoka, Takamitsu. 'Hebrew/Aramaic Index to the Septuagint'. In *A Concordance to the Septuagint and the other Greek versions of the Old Testament*. Grand Rapids: Baker, 1998.
Mussies, G. *The Morphology of Koine Greek as used in the Apocalypse of John: A Study in Bilingualism*. NovTSup 27. Leiden: Brill, 1971.
Nagy, Gregory. 'The Library of Pergamon as a Classical Model'. Pages 185–232 in *Pergamon Citadel of the Gods: Archaeological Record, Literary Description, and Religious Development*. Edited by H. Koester. Harrisburg: Trinity, 1998.
Nelson, S. A. *Aristophanes and his Tragic Muse: Comedy, Tragedy and the Polis in 5th Century Athens*. Leiden: Brill, 2016.
Nesselrath, H.-G. 'Kaiserzeitliche Skeptizismus in platonischen Gewand: Lukian's 'Hermotimos''. *ANRW* 2.36.5 (1992): 3451–82.
Newsom, Carol A. '"Sectually Explicit" Literature from Qumran'. Pages 167–87 in *The Hebrew Bible and its Interpreters*. Edited by W. H. Propp, B. Halpern, and D. N. Freedman. Winona Lake: Eisenbrauns, 1990.
Nicholls, Matthew. 'Galen and Libraries in the Peri Alupias'. *JRS* 101 (2011): 123–42.
Nicholls, Matthew. 'Roman Libraries as Public Building in the Cities of the Empire'. Pages 261–76 in *Ancient Libraries*. Edited by J. König, K. Oikonomopoulou, and G. Woolf. Cambridge: Cambridge University Press, 2013.
Nickelsburg, George W. E. *Resurrection, Immortality and Eternal Life in Intertestamental Judaism and Early Christianity*. Cambridge, MA: Harvard University Press, 2006.
Niditch, Susan. *Oral World and Written Word: Ancient Israelite Literature*. Louisville: WJK, 1996.
Nock, A. D. *Conversion: The Old and the New in Religion from Alexander the Great to Augustine of Hippo*. Lanham: University Press of America 1988.

Norton, Jonathan D. H. 'The Qumran Library and the Shadow it Casts on the Wall of the Cave'. Pages 40-74 in *Ancient Readers and Their Scriptures. Engaging the Hebrew Bible in Early Judaism and Christianity*. Edited by G. V. Allen and J. A. Dunne. Leiden: Brill, 2019.

Noy, David. *Jewish Inscriptions of Western Europe*. 2 vols. Cambridge: Cambridge University Press, 1993.

Nye, A. 'Irigaray and Diotima at Plato's Symposium'. Pages 197-215 in *Feminist Interpretations of Plato*. Edited by N. Tuana. University Park: Pennsylvania State University Press, 1994.

O'Brien, P. T. *Colossians, Philemon*. Waco: Word, 1982.

Oldfather, W.A., ed. and trans. *Epictetus: The Discourses as reported by Arrian, the Manual, and Fragments*. London: Heinemann, 1925.

Olson, S. D. *Athenaeus: The Learned Banqueters*. Volume 8. Loeb. Cambridge, MA: Harvard University Press, 2012.

Oltramare, A. *Les origines de la diatribe romaine*. Lausanne: Payot, 1926.

Pao, David W. *Acts and the Isaianic New Exodus*. Grand Rapids: Baker, 2000.

Pao, David W., and Eckhard J. Schnabel. 'Luke'. Pages 251-414 in *Commentary on the New Testament Use of the Old Testament*. Edited by G. K. Beale and D. A. Carson. Grand Rapids: Baker, 2007.

Park, Yoon-Man. *Mark's Memory Resources and the Controversy Stories (Mark 2:1-3:6): An Application of the Frame Theory of Cognitive Science to the Markan Oral-Aural Narrative*. Leiden: Brill, 2010.

Parry, Donald W., and Emanuel Tov. *The Dead Sea Scrolls Reader Part 1: Texts Concerned with Religious Law*. Leiden: Brill, 2004.

Parvis, Paul. '2 Clement and the Meaning of the Christian Homily'. Pages 32-41 in *The Writings of the Apostolic Fathers*. Edited by P. Foster. London: T&T Clark, 2007.

Patrick, D., and A. Scult. *Rhetoric and Biblical Interpretation*. Sheffield: Sheffield Academic, 1990.

Patte, D. 'A Structural Exegesis of 2 Corinthians 2.14-7.4'. Pages 40-49 in *SBLSP 1987*. Edited by K. H. Richards. Atlanta: Scholars Press, 1987.

Patte, D., ed. *Kingdom and Children: Aphorism, Chreia, Structure*. Chico: SBL, 1983.

Pattemore, Stephen W. *The People of God in the Apocalypse: Discourse, Structure and Exegesis*. SNTSMS 128. Cambridge: Cambridge University Press, 2004.

Pelling, B. R. *Plutarch: Life of Antony*. Cambridge: Cambridge University Press, 1988.

Pervo, R. I. *Acts: A Commentary*. Minneapolis: Fortress, 2009.

Peterson, David G. *The Acts of the Apostles*. Grand Rapids Eerdmans, 2009.

Pettem, M. 'Luke's Great Omission and his View of the Law'. *NTS* 42 (1996): 35-54.

Pfann, Stephen. 'Reassessing the Judean Desert Caves: Libraries, Archives, *Genizas* and Hiding Places'. *Bulletin of the Anglo-Israel Archaeological Society* 25 (2007): 147-70.

Pilkington, Adrian. 'Poetic Effects'. *Lingua* 87 (1992): 29-51.

Pilkington, Adrian. *Poetic Effects: A Relevance Theory Perspective*. Amsterdam: John Benjamins, 2000.

Polhill, J. B. *Acts*. Nashville: Broadman, 1992.

Popović, Mladen. 'Qumran as Scroll Storehouse in Times of Crisis? A Comparative Perspective on Judaean Desert Manuscript Collections'. *JSJ* 43 (2012): 551-94.

Popović, Mladen. 'Reading, Writing, and Memorizing Together: Reading Culture in Ancient Judaism and the Dead Sea Scrolls in a Mediterranean Context'. *DSD* 24 (2017): 447-70.

Popović, Mladen, Maruf A. Dhali, and Lambert Schomaker. 'Artificial Intelligence Based Writer Identification Generates New Evidence for the Unknown Scribes of the Dead Sea Scrolls Exemplified by the Great Isaiah Scroll (1QIsa a)'. *ArXiv* (2020).

Porton, Gary. 'Midrash and the Rabbinic Sermon'. Pages 461–82 in *When Judaism & Christianity Began: Essays in Memory of Anthony B. Saldarini*. Edited by A. J. Avery-Peck et al. Leiden: Brill, 2004.

Praeder, S. M. 'Jesus-Paul, Peter-Paul, and Jesus-Peter Parallelisms in Luke-Acts: A History of Reader Response'. Pages 23–39 in *SBLSP 1984*. Edited by K. H. Richards. Atlanta: Scholars Press, 1984.

Prigent, Pierre. *L'Apocalypse de Saint Jean*. 2nd ed. Paris: Labor et Fides, 2000.

Prince, S. 'Socrates, Antisthenes, and the Cynics'. Pages 75–92 in *A Companion to Socrates*. Edited by S. Ahbel-Rappe and R. Kamtekar. Oxford: Blackwell, 2006.

Puech, Émile. 'Exercices de deux scribes à Khirbet Qumrân: KhQ 161 et KhQ 2207', *RevQ* 32 (2020): 56–43.

Puech, Émile. 'Les fragments eschatologiques de 4QInsruction (4Q416 I et 4Q418 69 ii, 81–81a, 127)'. *RevQ* 22 (2005): 89–119.

Puech, Émile. 'Il Libro della Sapienza e i manoscritti del Mar Morto'. Pages 131–55 in *Il libro della sapienza (tradizione, redazione, teologia)*. Edited by G. Bellia and A. Passaro. Rome: Città Nuova, 2004.

Qimran, E. et al., eds. *Qumran Cave 4.V: Miqṣat Maʿaśeh Ha-Torah*. DJD 10. Oxford: Clarendon, 1994.

Rabin, Ira. 'Material Analysis of the Fragments'. Pages 61–77 in *Gleanings from the Caves: Dead Sea Scrolls and Artefacts from the Schøyen Collection*, Edited by T. Elgvin et al. London: T&T Clark, 2016.

Rajak, Tessa. *The Jewish Dialogue with Greece and Rome: Studies in Cultural and Social Interaction*. AGAJU 48. Leiden: Brill, 2001.

Rapp, U. 'You Are How You Eat: How Eating and Drinking Behaviour Identifies the Wise according to Jesus Ben Sirach'. Pages 42–61 in *Decisive Meals: Table Politics in Biblical Literature*. Edited by K. Ehrensperger, N. MacDonald, and L. Sutter Rehman. LNTS 449. London: Bloomsbury, 2012.

Rayo, Agustín. 'A Plea for Semantic Localism'. *Noûs* 47 (2013): 647–79.

Reese, J. M. *Hellenistic Influence on the Book of Wisdom and its Consequences*. Rome: Pontificio Instituto Biblico, 1970.

Reich, R. 'Confusion about the Socratic Method: Socratic Paradoxes and Contemporary Invocations of Socrates'. *Philosophy of Education Archive* (1998): 68–78.

Rendall, Gerald H. *The Epistle of James and Judaic Christianity*. Cambridge: Cambridge University Press, 1927.

Richardson, B. 'The Other Reader's Response: On Multiple, Divided, and Oppositional Audiences'. *Criticism* 39 (1997): 31–53.

Richardson, Peter. *Herod: King of the Jews and Friend of the Romans*. Columbia: University of South Carolina Press, 1996.

Riley, M. T. 'The Epicurean Criticism of Socrates'. *Phoenix* (1980): 55–68.

Robbins, Vernon K. *Jesus the Teacher: A Socio-Rhetorical Interpretation of Mark* Philadelphia: Fortress Press, 1984.

Robinson, John A. T. *Redating the New Testament*. London: SCM, 1976.

Rocca, Samuel. *Herod's Judaea: A Mediterranean State in the Classical World*. TSAJ 122. Tübingen: Mohr Siebeck, 2008.

Rodriguez, Rafael. *Structuring Early Christian Memory: Jesus in Tradition, Memory and Text*. London: T&T Clark, 2015.

Roemer, Cornelia. 'The Papyrus Role in Egypt, Greece, and Rome'. Pages 84–94 in *A Companion to the History of the Book*. Edited by S. Eliot and J. Rose. Oxford: Wiley Blackwell, 2009.

Rohrbaugh, R. L. 'The Social Location of the Markan Audience'. *Union Seminary Review* 47 (1993): 380–95.

Romero, Esther, and Belén Soria. 'Relevance Theory and Metaphor'. *Linguagem em (Dis)curso* 14 (2014): 489–509.

Rose, V. *Aristotelis qui ferebantur librorum fragmenta*. Leipzig: Teubner, 1886.

Roskam, G. 'Educating the young…over wine? Plutarch, Calvenus Taurus, and Favorinus as convivial teachers'. Pages 369–83 in *Symposion and Philanthropia in Plutarch*. Edited by J. R. Ferreira et al. Coimbra: Classica Digitalia, 2009.

Rosner, Brian S. *Paul, Scripture, and Ethics: A Study of 1 Corinthians 5–7*. AGAJU 22. Leiden: Brill, 1994.

Rostovtzeff, Michael Ivanovitch. *The Social & Economic History of the Hellenistic World*. 3 vols. Oxford: Clarendon Press, 1941

Rowe, Christopher. 'Socrates in Plato's Dialogues'. Pages 159–70 in *A Companion to Socrates*. Edited by S. Ahbel-Rappe and R. Kamtekar. Oxford: Blackwell, 2006.

Rowe, C. Kavin. 'The Grammar of Life: The Areopagus Speech and Pagan Tradition'. *NTS* 57 (2010): 31–50.

Rowe, C. Kavin. *World Upside Down: Reading Acts in the Graeco-Roman Age*. Oxford: Oxford University Press, 2009.

Rubenstein, Jeffrey L. *The Culture of the Babylonian Talmud*. London: The Johns Hopkins University Press, 2003.

Rubenstein, Jeffrey L. 'The Rise of the Babylonian Rabbinic Academy: A Reexamination of the Talmudic Evidence'. *Jewish Studies, an Internet Journal* 1 (2002): 55–68.

Runesson, Anders. *The Origins of the Synagogue: A Socio-historical Study*. CB 37. Stockholm: Almqvist & Wiksell, 2001.

Runesson, Anders, Ronald D. Binder, and Birger Olsson. *The Ancient Synagogue from its Origins to 200 C.E.: A Source Book*. AJEC 72. Leiden: Brill, 2008.

Runia, David T. *Philo of Alexandria and the 'Timaeus' of Plato*. Leiden: Brill, 1986.

Russel, D. A. *Plutarch: Selected Essays and Dialogues*. Oxford: Oxford University Press, 1993.

Ryan, Sean Michael. *Hearing at the Boundaries of Vision: Education Informing Cosmology in Revelation 9*. LNTS 448. London: T&T Clark, 2012.

Safrai, Zeev. 'The Communal Functions of the Synagogue in the Land of Israel in the Rabbinic Period'. Pages 181–204 in in *Ancient Synagogues: Historical Analysis and Archeological Discovery Volume 1*. SPB 47/1. Edited by D. Urman and P. V. M. Flesher. Leiden: Brill, 1995.

Salo, K. *Luke's Treatment of the Law: A Redaction-Critical Investigation*. Helsinki: Suomalainen Tiedeakatemia, 1991.

Sandbach, F. H. 'Plato and the Socratic work of Xenophon'. Pages 478–97 in *Greek Literature*. Edited by P. E. Easterling and B. M. W. Knox. Cambridge: Cambridge University Press, 1985.

Sauer, Georg. *Jesus Sirach/Ben Sira*. ATD Apokryphen B.1. Göttingen: Vandenhoeck & Ruprecht, 2000.

Sayce, A. H. 'Jewish Tax-Gatherers at Thebes in the Age of the Ptolemies'. *JQR* 2 (1890): 400–405.

Scarpat, G. *Libro della Sapienza*. Volume 1. Brescia: Morcellana, 1989.

Schäfer, Peter. 'Research into Rabbinic Literature: An Attempt to Define the Status Quaestionis'. *JJS* 37 (1986): 139–52.
Schams, C. *Jewish Scribes in the Second Temple Period*. Sheffield: Sheffield Academic Press, 1998.
Schlapbach, K. 'The Logoi of Philosophers in Lucian of Samosata'. *Classical Antiquity* 29 (2010): 250–77.
Schmidt, E. 'Diatribai'. *Kleine Pauly* 2 (1967): 1577–8.
Schnelle, Udo. 'Das frühe Christentum und die Bildung'. *NTS* 61 (2015): 113–43.
Schniedewind, William M. *How the Bible Became a Book*. Cambridge: Cambridge University Press, 2004.
Schürer, Emil. *The History of the Jewish People in the Age of Jesus Christ*. Rev. ed. 3 vols. London: Bloomsbury, 2014.
Schwartz, Seth. 'Hebrew and Imperialism in Palestine'. Pages 53–84 in *Ancient Judaism and its Hellenistic Context*. Edited by C. Bakhos. JSJSup 95. Leiden: Brill, 2005.
Schwartz, Seth. *Were the Jews a Mediterranean Society? Reciprocity and Solidarity in Ancient Judaism*. Princeton: Princeton University Press, 2010.
Scott, G. A., ed. *Does Socrates have a Method? Rethinking the Elenchus in Plato's Dialogues and Beyond*. University Park: Pennsylvania State University Press, 2002.
Sedley, D. N. 'The School, from Zeno to Arius Didymus'. Pages 7–32 in *The Cambridge Companion to the Stoics*. Edited by B. Inwood. Cambridge: Cambridge University Press, 2003.
Seeley, D. N. 'Jesus and the Cynics Revisited'. *JBL* 116 (1997): 704–12.
Segal, Eliezer. *From Sermon to Commentary: Expounding the Bible in Talmudic Babylonia*. Waterloo: Wilfrid Laurier University Press, 2005.
Segal, Michael. 'Biblical Exegesis in 4Q158: Techniques and Genre'. *Textus* 19 (1998): 45–62.
Shannon, Claude Elwood, and Warren Weaver. *The Mathematical Theory of Communication*. Urbana: University of Illinois Press, 1949.
Sharp, C. J. *Irony and Meaning in the Hebrew Bible*. Bloomington: Indiana University Press, 2009.
Shavit, Yaacov. 'The 'Qumran Library' in the Light of the Attitude towards Books and Libraries in the Second Temple Period'. Pages 299–317 in *Methods of Investigation of the Dead Sea Scrolls and Khirbet Qumran Site: Present and Future Prospects*. Edited by J. J. Collins, M. O. Wise, and N. Golb. New York: New York Academy of Sciences, 1994.
Sheridan, M. *Language for God in Patristic Tradition: Wrestling with Biblical Anthropomorphism*. Leicester: IVP, 2015.
Shiell, W. *Reading Acts: The Lector and the Early Christian Audience*. Leiden: Brill, 2004.
Sider, David. *The Library of the Villa dei Papiri at Herculaneum*. Los Angeles: J. Paul Getty, 2005.
Sider, Sandra. 'Herculaneum's Library in 79 A.D.: The Villa of the Papyri'. *Libraries & Culture* 25 (1990): 534–42.
Sim, Margaret G. *A Relevant Way to Read: A New Approach to Exegesis and Communication*. Cambridge: James Clark, 2016.
Skeat, T. C. 'Early Christian Book Production: Papyri and Manuscripts'. Pages 54–79 in *The Cambridge History of the Bible*. Volume 2. Edited by G. W. H. Lampe. Cambridge: Cambridge University Press, 1969.
Skehan, Patrick W., and Alexander A. Di Lella. *The Wisdom of Ben Sira: A New Translation with Notes*. AB 39. New York: Doubleday, 1987.
Small, Jocelyn Penny. *Wax Tablets of the Mind: Cognitive Studies of Memory and Literacy in Classical Antiquity*. London: Routledge, 1997.

Smend, Rudolf. *Die Weisheit des Jesus Sirach*. Berlin: Reimer, 1906.
Smith, Steve. *The Fate of the Jerusalem Temple in Luke-Acts: An Intertextual Approach to Jesus' Laments over Jerusalem and Stephen's Speech*. LNTS 553. London: Bloomsbury, 2017.
Smith, Steve. 'The Use of Criteria – A Proposal from Relevance Theory'. Pages 142–54 in *Methodology in the Use of the Old Testament in the New: Context and Criteria*. Edited by D. Allen and S. Smith. LNTS 597. London: T&T Clark, 2019.
Snyder, H. Gregory. *Teachers and Texts in the Ancient World: Philosophers, Jews and Christians*. London: Routledge, 2000.
Song, Nam Sun. 'Metaphor and Metonymy'. Pages 87–104 in *Relevance Theory: Applications and Implications*. Edited by R. Carston and S. Uchida. Amsterdam: J. Benjamins, 1998.
Sperber, Dan, and Deirdre Wilson. 'A Deflationary Account of Metaphors'. Pages 97–122 in *Meaning and Relevance*. Edited by D. Wilson and D. Sperber. Cambridge: Cambridge University Press, 2012.
Sperber, Dan, and Deirdre Wilson. 'Pragmatics, Modularity and Mind-Reading'. *Mind & Language* 17 (2002): 3–23.
Sperber, Dan, and Deirdre Wilson. *Relevance: Communication and Cognition*. 2nd ed. Oxford: Blackwell, 1995.
Squires, J. T. *The Plan of God in Luke-Acts*. Cambridge: Cambridge University Press, 1993.
Stacey, D. *Prophetic Drama in the Old Testament*. London: Epworth, 1990.
Stanley, Christopher D. *Arguing with Scripture: The Rhetoric of Quotations in the Letters of Paul*. London: T&T Clark, 2004.
Stanley, Christopher D. *Paul and the Language of Scripture: Citation Technique in the Pauline Epistles and Contemporary Literature*. SNTSMS 69. Cambridge: Cambridge University Press, 1992.
Stanley, Christopher D. '"Pearls before Swine": Did Paul's Audiences Understand His Biblical Quotations?' *NovT* 41 (1999): 124–44.
Stanley, Christopher D. ed. *Paul and Scripture: Extending the Conversation*. Atlanta: SBL Press, 2012.
Stadter, P. A. *Arrian of Nicomedia*. Chapel Hill: University of North Carolina Press, 1980.
Stadter, P. A. 'Flavius Arrianus: The New Xenophon'. *GRBS* 8 (1967): 155–61.
Stein, R. H. *The Method and Message of Jesus' Teachings*. Philadelphia: Westminster Press, 1978.
Stellwag, H. W. F. *Epictetus: Het Eerste Boek der Diatriben*. Amsterdam: H. J. Paris, 1933.
Stemberger, Günter. 'The Derashah in Rabbinic Times'. Pages 7–21 in *Preaching in Judaism and Christianity: Encounters and Developments from Biblical Times to Modernity*. Edited by A. Deeg et al. Berlin: de Gruyter, 2008.
Stephens, S. A. 'Who Read Ancient Novels?' Pages 405–18 in *The Search for the Ancient Novel*. Edited by J. Tatum. Baltimore: Johns Hopkins University Press, 1994.
Sterling, Gregory E. 'The Love of Wisdom: Middle Platonism and Stoicism in the Wisdom of Solomon'. Pages 198–213 in *From Stoicism to Platonism: The Development of Philosophy, 100 BCE–100 CE*. Edited by T. Engberg-Pedersen. Cambridge: Cambridge University Press, 2017.
Stern, David. 'The First Jewish Books and the Early History of Jewish Reading'. *JQR* 98 (2008): 163–202.
Stern, David. 'Imitatio Hominis: Anthropomorphism and the Character(s) of God in Rabbinic Literature'. *Prooftexts* 12 (1992): 151–74.
Stern, David. *Parables in Midrash: Narrative and Exegesis in Rabbinic Literature*. 2nd ed. London: Harvard University Press, 1994.

Steudel, Annette. 'Biblical Warfare Legislation in the War Scroll (1QM VII:1–7 and X:1–8)'. Pages 183–91 in *The Reception of Biblical War Legislation in Narrative Contexts: Studies in Law and Narrative*. Edited by C. Berner and H. Samuel. BZAW 460. Berlin: de Gruyter, 2015.

Steudel, Annette. 'The Damascus Document (D) as a Rewriting of the Community Rule (S)'. *RevQ* 100 (2012): 605–20.

Steudel, Annette. 'Dating Exegetical Texts from Qumran'. Pages 39–53 in *The Dynamics of Language and Exegesis at Qumran*. Edited by D. Dimant and R. Kratz. Tübingen: Mohr Siebeck, 2009.

Steudel, Annette. 'The Development of Essenic Eschatology'. Pages 183–191 in *Apocalyptic Time*. Edited by A. I. Baumgarten. Leiden: Brill, 2000.

Steudel, Annette. 'Testimonia'. Pages 936–8 in *The Dead Sea Scrolls Encyclopedia*. Edited by L. Schiffman and J. C. VanderKam. Oxford: Oxford University Press, 2000.

Stock, Brian. *The Implications of Literacy: Written Language and Models of Interpretation in the Eleventh and Twelfth Centuries*. Princeton: Princeton University Press, 1983.

Stökl Ben Ezra, Daniel. *Qumran: Die Texte vom Toten Meer und das antike Judentum*. Tübingen: Mohr Siebeck, 2016.

Stott, G. S. J. 'Jerome before the Judge: The Dialogic Nature of Reports of Dreams'. *Dreaming* 19 (2009): 7–16.

Stowers, Stanley K. *Letter Writing in Graeco-Roman Antiquity*. Philadelphia: Westminster, 1986.

Stowers, Stanley K. *A Rereading of Romans: Justice, Jews, and Gentiles*. London: Yale University Press, 1994.

Sukenik, E. L. *Ancient Synagogues in Palestine and Greece*. London: British Academy, 1930 [repr. Munich: Kraus, 1980].

Suleiman, S. R., and I. C. Wimmers. *The Reader in the Text: Essays on Audience and Interpretation*. Princeton: Princeton University Press, 1980.

Sweetland, D. M. 'The Lord's Supper and the Lukan Community'. *BTB* 13 (1983): 23–7.

Tan, Kim Huat. *The Zion Traditions and the Aims of Jesus*. SNTSMS 91. New York: Cambridge University Press, 1997.

Tannehill, R. C. *The Narrative Unity of Luke-Acts: A Literary Interpretation*. 2 vols. Philadelphia: Fortress Press, 1986.

Tannehill, R. C. *The Sword of His Mouth*. Philadelphia: Fortress Press, 1975.

Tassin, C. 'Conversion de Corneille et conversion de Pierre'. *Spiritus* 141 (1995): 465–75.

Taylor, A. 'The Riddle'. *CFQ* 2 (1943): 129–47.

Taylor, Joan E. 'The Archaeology of Qumran and the Dead Sea Scrolls'. Pages 32–108 in *The Archaeology of the Holy Land: From the Destruction of Solomon's Temple to the Muslim Conquest*. Edited by J. Magness. Cambridge: Cambridge University Press, 2012.

Taylor, Joan E. 'Spiritual Mothers: Philo on the Women Therapeutae'. *JSP* 23 (2002): 37–63.

Taylor, Joan E., and David M. Hay. *On the Contemplative Life*. Leiden: Brill, 2020.

Taylor, N. H. 'The Composition and Chronology of Second Corinthians'. *JSNT* 44 (1991): 67–87.

Teeter, David Andrew. *Scribal Laws: Exegetical Variation in the Textual Transmission of Biblical Law in the Late Second Temple Period*. FAT 92. Tübingen: Mohr Siebeck, 2014.

Tejera, V. 'The Hellenistic Obliteration of Plato's Dialogism'. Pages 129–36 in *Plato's Dialogues: New Studies and Interpretations*. Edited by G. A. Press. Lanham: Rowman & Littlefield, 1993.

Teugels, Lieve M. *Bible and Midrash: The Story of 'The Wooing of Rebeccah' (Gen. 24)*. Leuven: Peeters, 2004.

Thatcher, Tom. 'Literacy, Textual Communities, and Josephus' *Jewish War*'. *JSJ* 29 (1998): 123-42.
Thatcher, Tom. *The Riddles of Jesus in John: A Study in Tradition and Folklore*. Atlanta: SBL Press, 2000.
Thesleff, H. 'The Interrelation and Date of the *Symposia* of Plato and Xenophon'. *BICS* 25 (1978): 157-70.
Thomas, Rosalind. *Literacy and Orality in Ancient Greece*. Cambridge: Cambridge University Press, 1992.
Tigchelaar, Eibert. 'The Scribes of the Scrolls'. Pages 524-33 in *T&T Clark Companion to the Dead Sea Scrolls*. Edited by G. J. Brooke and C. Hempel. London: T&T Clark, 2018.
Todorov, Tzvetan. *Genres in Discourse*. Translated by C. Porter. Cambridge: Cambridge University Press, 1990.
Tomin, J. 'Socratic Midwifery'. *CQ* 37 (1987): 97-102.
Tomson, Peter J. *Paul and the Jewish Law: Halakah in the Letters of the Apostle to the Gentiles*. CRINT 3.1. Assen: Van Gorcum, 1991.
Toney, Carl N. 'The Composition of 2 Corinthians (1985-2007)'. Pages 50-69 in *2 Corinthians*, Ralph P. Martin. 2nd ed. WBC 40. Grand Rapids: Zondervan, 2014.
Too, Yun Lee. *The Idea of the Library in the Ancient World*. Oxford: Oxford University Press, 2010.
Tov, Emanuel. *Scribal Practices and Approaches Reflected in the Texts Found in the Judean Desert*. STDJ 54. Leiden: Brill, 2004.
Trapp, M. B. 'Lucianus's *Nigrinus* and the Anxieties of Philosophical Communication'. Pages 113-24 in *International Symposium on Lucianus of Samosata, 17-19 October 2008*. Edited by M. Cevik. Adiyaman: Adiyaman Universitesi, 2009.
Trapp, M. B. *Philosophy in the Roman Empire*. Aldershot: Ashgate, 2007.
Trebilco, Paul R. *Jewish Communities in Asia Minor*. SNTSMS 69. Cambridge: Cambridge University Press, 1991.
Trotter, David. 'Analysing Literary Prose: The Relevance of Relevance Theory'. *Lingua* 87 (1992): 11-27.
Turner, Eric G. *The Typology of the Early Codex*. Eugene: Wipf & Stock, 1977.
Tuval, Michael. *From Jerusalem Priest to Roman Jew: On Josephus and the Paradigms of Ancient Judaism*. WUNT 2/357. Tübingen: Mohr Siebeck, 2013.
Vaage, L. E. 'Cynic Epistles (Selections)'. Pages 117-28 in *Ascetic Behavior in Greco-Roman Antiquity: A Sourcebook*. Edited by V. L. Wimbush. Minneapolis: Fortress Press, 1990.
Vaage, L. E. 'Like Dogs Barking: Cynic Parresia and Shameless Asceticism'. *Semeia* 57 (1992): 25-39.
van der Henst, Jean-Baptiste, and Dan Sperber. 'Testing the Cognitive and Communicative Principles of Relevance'. Pages 279-306 in *Meaning and Relevance*. Edited by D. Wilson and D. Sperber. Cambridge: Cambridge University Press, 2012.
van der Horst, P. W. 'Philo and the Problem of God's Emotions'. *Études platoniciennes* (2010): 171-8.
van der Toorn, Karel. *Scribal Culture and the Making of the Hebrew Bible*. Cambridge, MA: Harvard University Press, 2007.
van Elderen, Bastiaan. 'Early Christian Libraries'. Pages 45-59 in *The Bible as Book: The Manuscript Tradition*. Edited by J. Sharpe and K. van Kampen. London: British Library, 1998.
van Engen, C. E. 'Peter's Conversion: A Culinary Disaster Launches the Gentile Mission'. Pages 133-43 in *Mission in Acts: Ancient Narratives in Contemporary Context*. Edited by R. L. Gallagher and P. Hertig. New York: Orbis, 2004.

van Henten, Jan Willem. 'The Intertextual Nexus of Revelation and Graeco-Roman Literature'. Pages 395–422 in *Poetik und Intertextualität der Johannesapokalypse*. Edited by S. Alkier, T. Hieke, and T. Nicklas. WUNT 346. Tübingen: Mohr Siebeck, 2015.

van Kooten, G. H. 'The Last Days of Socrates and Christ: Euthyphro, Apology, Crito, and Phaedo Read in Counterpoint with John's Gospel'. Pages 219–43 in *Religio-Philosophical Discourses in the Mediterranean World: From Plato, through Jesus, to Late Antiquity*. Edited by A. K. Petersen and G. H. van Kooten. Leiden: Brill, 2017.

van Unnik, Willem C. 'Studies on the So-called First Epistle of Clement'. Pages 115–81 in *Encounters with Hellenism: Studies on the First Letter of Clement*. Edited by L. L. Welborn, C. Breytenbach, and L. L. Welborn. AGAJU 53. Leiden: Brill, 2004.

Vermes, Geza. *The Dead Sea Scrolls in English*. London: Penguin, 2004.

Victor, Royce M. *Colonial Education and Class Formation in Early Judaism: A Postcolonial Reading*. LSTS 72. London: T&T Clark, 2010.

Vine, C. E. W. *The Audience of Matthew: An Appraisal of the Local Audience Thesis*. LNTS 496. London: Bloomsbury, 2014.

Vlastos, G. *Socrates, Ironist and Moral Philosopher*. Cambridge: Cambridge University Press, 1991.

von Wahlde, U. C. 'Community in Conflict: The History and Social Context of the Johannine Community'. *Interpretation* 49 (1995): 379–89.

Vulpe, N. 'Irony and the Unity of the Gilgamesh Epic'. *JNES* 53 (1994): 275–83.

Wacholder, Ben Zion. 'Greek Authors in Herod's Library'. *Studies in Bibliography and Booklore* (1961): 102–9.

Wacholder, Ben Zion. *The New Damascus Document. The Midrash on the Eschatological Torah of the Dead Sea Scrolls: Reconstruction, Translation and Commentary*. STDJ 56. Leiden: Brill, 2007.

Wallenfels, Ronald. 'Seleucid Babylonian 'Official' and 'Private' Seals Reconsidered: A Seleucid Archival Tablet in the Collection of the Mackenzie Art Gallery, Regina'. *JANEH* 2 (2015): 55–89.

Wassen, Cecilia. 'On the Education of Children in the Dead Sea Scrolls'. *Studies in Religion* (2012): 350–63.

Watson, D. F. 'Chreia/Aphorism'. Pages 104–6 in *DJG*.

Waltzing, Jean-Pierre. Étude *historique sur les corporations professionnelles chez les Romains depuis les origins jusqu' à la chute de l'Empire de l'Occident*. 5 vols. Hildesheim: Georg Olms, 1970.

Webb, William J. *Returning Home: New Covenant and Second Exodus as the Context for 2 Corinthians 6.14–7.1*. JSNTSup 85. London: Continuum, 1993.

Weeks, Kent R. 'Medicine, Surgery, and Public Health in Ancient Egypt'. Pages 1787–98 in *Civilizations of the Ancient Near East*. Edited by J. M. Sasson, G. M. Beckman, and K. S. Rubinson. Peabody: Hendrickson, 2000.

Wendt, Heidi. *At the Temple Gates: The Religion of Freelance Experts in the Roman Empire*. Oxford: Oxford University Press, 2016.

Werline, R. A. 'Ritual, Order and the Construction of an Audience in 1 Enoch 1–36'. *DSD* 22 (2015): 325–41.

Werner, Shirley. 'Literacy Studies in Classics'. Pages 333–83 in *Ancient Literacies: The Culture of Reading in Greece and Rome*. Edited by W. A. Johnson and H. N. Parker. Oxford: Oxford University Press, 2009.

Werrett, Ian. 'Is Qumran a Library?' Pages 78–105 in *The Dead Sea Scrolls and the Concept of a Library*. STDJ 116. Edited by S. White Crawford and C. Wassen. Leiden: Brill, 2016.

Wesseling, B. 'The Audience of the Ancient Novel'. Pages 67–79 in *Groningen Colloquia on the Novel*. Volume 1. Edited by H. Hofmann. Groningen: Egbert Forsten, 1988.

White, Adam G. *Where is the Wise Man: Graeco-Roman Education as a Background to the Divisions in 1 Corinthians 1–4*. LNTS 536. London: T&T Clark, 2015.

Whitenton, M. R. 'Feeling the Silence: A Moment-by-Moment Account of Emotions at the End of Mark (16:1–8)'. *CBQ* 78 (2016): 272–89.

White Crawford, Sidnie. 'The Qumran Collection as a Scribal Library'. Pages 109–31 in *The Dead Sea Scrolls and the Concept of a Library*. STDJ 116. Edited by S. White Crawford and C. Wassen. Leiden: Brill, 2016.

White Crawford, Sidnie. *Rewriting Scripture in the Second Temple Times* (Grand Rapids: Eerdmans, 2008

White Crawford, Sidnie, and Cecilia Wassen, eds. *The Dead Sea Scrolls and the Concept of a Library*. STDJ 116. Leiden: Brill, 2016.

Whitmarsh, Tim. *Greek Literature and the Roman Empire: The Politics of Imitation*. Oxford: Oxford University Press, 2001.

Wilkins, J. 'Dialogue and Comedy: The Structure of the *Deipnosophistiae*'. Pages 23–37 in *Athenaeus and his World: Reading Greek Culture in the Roman Empire*. Edited by D. Braund and J. Wilkins. Exeter: Exeter University Press, 2000.

Williams, H. H. Drake. 'From the Perspective of the Writer or the Perspective of the Reader: Coming to Grips with a Starting Point for Analyzing the Use of Scripture in 1 Corinthians'. Pages 153–72 in *Paul and Scripture*. Edited by S. E. Porter. Leiden: Brill, 2019.

Williams, H. H. Drake. 'Light Giving Sources: Examining the Extent of Scriptural Citation and Allusion Influence in 1 Corinthians'. Pages 7–38 in *Paul: Jew, Greek, or Roman*. Edited by S. E. Porter. Leiden: Brill, 2008.

Williams, H. H. Drake. *The Wisdom of the Wise: The Presence and Function of Scripture in 1 Cor. 1:18–3:23*. AGAJU 49. Leiden: Brill, 2001.

Wilson, Deirdre. 'Metarepresentation in Linguistic Communication'. Pages 230–58 in *Meaning and Relevance*. Edited by D. Wilson and D. Sperber. Cambridge: Cambridge University Press, 2012.

Wilson, Deirdre. 'Relevance and Understanding'. Pages 37–58 in *Language and Understanding*. Edited by G. Brown. Oxford: Oxford University Press, 1994.

Wilson, Deirdre, and Dan Sperber, eds. *Meaning and Relevance*. Cambridge: Cambridge University Press, 2012.

Wilson, Deirdre, and Dan Sperber. 'Truthfulness and Relevance'. Pages 47–83 in *Meaning and Relevance*. Edited by D. Wilson and D. Sperber. Cambridge: Cambridge University Press, 2012.

Winston, David. *The Wisdom of Solomon: A New Translation with Introduction and Commentary*. AB 43. Garden City: Doubleday, 1982.

Winter, Bruce W. 'On Introducing Gods to Athens: An Alternative Reading of Acts 17:18–20'. *TynBul* 47 (1996): 71–90.

Wirth, T. 'Arrians Errinerungen an Epiktet'. *Museum Helveticum* 24 (1967): 148–89, 197–216.

Wise, Michael Owen. *Language and Literacy in Roman Judaea: A Study of the Bar Kokhba Documents*. London: Yale University Press, 2015.

Witherington III, Ben. *The Acts of the Apostles: A Socio-Rhetorical Commentary*. Grand Rapids: Eerdmans, 1998.

Witherington III, Ben. *Letters and Homilies for Hellenized Christians: A Socio-Rhetorical Commentary on Titus, 1–2 Timothy and 1–3 John*. Downers Grove: IVP Academic, 2006.

Witulski, Thomas. *Die Johannesoffenbarung und Kaiser Hadrian: Studien zur Datierung der neutestamentlichen Apokalypse.* FRLANT 221. Göttingen: Vandenhoeck & Ruprecht, 2007.
Woolf, Greg. 'Ancient Illiteracy?' *BICS* 58 (2015): 31–42.
Wright, Brian J. 'Ancient Literacy in New Testament Research: Incorporating a Few More Lines of Enquiry'. *TJ* 36 (2015): 161–89.
Wright, Brian J. *Communal Reading in the Time of Jesus: A Window into Early Christian Reading Practices.* Minneapolis: Fortress Press, 2017.
Xenophontos, S. *Ethical Education in Plutarch: Moralising Agents and Contexts.* BZA 349. Berlin: de Gruyter, 2016.
Yassif, Eli. 'Oral Traditions in a Literate Society: The Hebrew Literature of the Middle Ages'. Pages 497–518 in *Medieval Oral Literature.* Edited by K. Reichl. Berlin: de Gruyter, 2012.
Yonder, Gillihan M. *Civic Ideology, Organisation and Law in the Rule Scrolls.* Leiden: Brill, 2012.
Yoos, G. E. 'The Rhetoric of Cynicism'. *RhetR* 4 (1985): 54–62.
Zagorin, P. 'The Historical Significance of Lying and Dissimulation'. *Social Research* (1996): 863–912.
Zahn, Molly M. *Rethinking Rewritten Scripture: Composition and Exegesis in the 4QReworked Pentateuch Manuscripts.* STDJ 95. Leiden: Brill, 2011.
Zanker, Paul. *The Mask of Socrates: The Image of the Intellectual in Antiquity.* Berkeley: University of California Press, 1995.
Zetterholm, Karin Hadner. *Jewish Interpretation of the Bible: Ancient and Contemporary.* Minneapolis: Fortress Press, 2012.
Zevit, Ziony. 'Echoes of Texts Past'. Pages 1–21 in *Subtle Citation, Allusion, and Translation in the Hebrew Bible.* Edited by Z. Zevit. Sheffield: Equinox, 2017.
Ziegler, D. *Dionysos in der Apostelgeschichte - eine intertextuelle Lektüre.* Münster: LIT, 2008.
Zurawksi, Jason M., and Gabriele Boccaccini. 'Introduction: Perspectives on Second Temple Jewish *Paideia* from the Fifth Nangeroni Meeting'. Pages 1–7 in *Second Temple Jewish 'Paideia' in Context.* BZNW 228. Edited by J. M. Zurawski and G. Boccaccini. Berlin: de Gruyter, 2017.

Index of References

Hebrew Bible/Old Testament

Genesis
1–3	51
1–2	32, 37, 52, 146
1	47
1:1	64, 65
1:3	176
1:5	45
1:8	45
1:10	45
1:26-27	32
1:26	31, 32, 44, 50
1:27	31, 32
2:7	32, 37, 44, 173
2:17	31, 37
2:24	173
3:9-14	159
3:10	159
3:19	31, 37
3:22-23	159
3:22	159
4:6	159
4:9	159
6:6	159
11:5	159
12:1-3	179
12:3	120, 131
13:14-16	179
15:5-6	179
18:16-33	160
18:21	159
18:27	37
19:17 LXX	140
19:19 LXX	140
22:1-19	179
22:18	120, 131
49:1-36	164

Exodus
9:19	45
16:18	176
20:21	24
25:8	174
29:45	174
32–34	176
32	173
34:34	176

Leviticus
18:30	46
19:17	40
20:23	46
20:25	46
21:14	46
22	66
22:6-7	66
22:7	67
26:11-12	174, 176
26:11	46

Numbers
5:18	40
5:19	40
5:23	40
5:24	40
5:27	40
12:6-8	160
24:15-17	24

Deuteronomy
1:31	159
7:22-24	43
7:26	46
8:10	68
9:3	43
12:29	43
13:5	174
17:7	173, 174
19:1	43
19:15	176
19:19	174
21:21	174
22:21	174
23:7	46
24:7	174
25:4	173
30:15	28
31:3	43
32:8	146
32:17	173
33:8-11	24

Joshua
23:4	43
23:9	43

Judges
1:34 LXX	140
2:10	40
6:2 LXX	140

1 Samuel
23:19 LXX	140
26:1 LXX	140

6:66	158	17:24-25	146	10:16	130
12:15	149	17:24	146, 148	11:2	173
12:38	130	17:25	146	11:13	152
13:1-17	159	17:26	146	11:26-27	131
16	157	17:28	145, 147	11:34-35	131
		17:29	146	12:7	125
Acts		18:1-8	172	15:4	125
1:20	141, 143	18:19-21	197	15:22-24	128
2:14-39	121	18:24-28	123–25	16:3-15	128
2:17-21	130	18:24-26	197	16:17	125, 130
2:34-35	119	19:8-9	197		
2:39	130	19:14	188	1 Corinthians	
3:12-26	121	20:2-3	181	1:2	175
3:25	120	22:3	172	1:7	127
4:8-12	121	26:12-18	162	1:11	172
5:29-32	121	26:14	163	1:12	181
5:39	165	26:22-23	124	1:19	173
6:2-4	123, 125			1:26-31	173
6:2	122	Romans		1:26-29	171
6:4	122, 125	1–4	132	1:26	127, 153
6:7	125	1:1-4	121	1:31	177
7	148	1:5	152	2:9	173
7:48	146, 148	1:8	130	2:10–3:1	127
7:55	119	1:10-13	128	2:16	173
8:32-33	142	1:12	152	3:16-17	173, 174
9:1-19	153, 162	1:17	130	3:19	173, 179
9:1-9	8	2:7	34	3:20	173
9:4	153, 162	2:17	152	3:21-23	181
9:5	162	2:24	110	4:6	128, 175
9:8	166	3	131	4:17	125
9:16	166	3:2	122	5	127, 174
10:9-16	8, 163	3:4	113	5:4-5	175
10:13	153	5–7	132	5:9-13	172
10:15	163	5:19	120	5:13	173
10:28	163	5:21	34	6	174
10:34-43	121	6	127	6:2-3	174
11:17	165	6:3	173	6:2	34
13:16-41	121	6:16	173	6:11	127
16:6-10	165	6:17	125, 130	6:12-21	127
17	135, 144, 145	6:22	34	6:16	173
		7:1	173	6:19-20	173, 174
17:2-3	124	8:34	119	8:1-11	128
17:6	166	9–11	131	8:7-13	161
17:10-12	123–25	9	120	9:1	127
17:16-34	145	9:33	120, 132	9:10	173
17:18	146, 147	10:9	127	9:13	173
17:21	147	10:13	130	9:24	173

1 Corinthians (cont.)		6:11	176	4:13	201
10:1-11	169	6:14–7:1	175	5:17-18	123, 125
10:1-10	173	6:16-18	176	5:17	123
10:20	173	8:15	176		
10:25-26	173	9:7	176	*2 Timothy*	
10:32	161	9:9-10	122	2:1-2	123, 125
12	127	9:9	176	2:2	123
12:7–11	127	10	180	2:14-15	123, 125
12:8	127	10:12-18	171	2:15	123
12:9-10	127	10:17	176	2:24-25	161
12:10	126	11:16-33	171	3:14–4:3	123, 125
12:28-30	126	11:22	172, 177	3:16-17	123
12:28-29	125, 127	12	127	4:2	161
12:28	127	12:14	181	4:13	201
14:6	125	13:1	176, 181		
14:21-22	165			*Philemon*	
14:21	131, 132, 173	*Galatians*		8–9	161
14:26	125, 175	3:8	120		
15	29, 119, 120	3:11	130	*Hebrews*	
		6:6	123, 125	1:3	119, 120
		6:8	34	1:13	119
15:1-58	128			2:6-8	120
15:2	127	*Ephesians*		8:1	119
15:3-8	121	1:20	119	10:12	119
15:10	127			10:37-38	130
15:17	127	*Philippians*		12:2	119
15:25	173	2	120, 131	13:7	123, 125
15:27	173	2:10	190		
15:32	173	4:3	178	*1 Peter*	
15:45	173			1:24–2:3	122, 123, 125
15:54-55	131	*Colossians*			
15:54	132, 173	3:1	119	1:24–2:2	125
15:55	173	3:21	161	2:6-8	120
15:56-58	127	4:16	181	3:22	119
16:11	175			5:1-2	123, 125
		1 Thessalonians		40:6-8	126
2 Corinthians		1:1	161		
1–7	176	1:10	121	*2 Peter*	
2:1-4	177	1:16	34	3:16	105
3	176	2:7	161		
3:6	176	2:8	121	*Jude*	
3:7-11	176	5:27	181	14–15	174
3:14-16	161				
3:16	176	*1 Timothy*		*Revelation*	
4:6	176	3:2	123, 125, 161	1:3	181
4:13	176			1:4	184
6:2	176	4:13-16	123, 125	1:8	189

1:9	184	14:17	189	2:23-24	28, 30, 31, 50
1:11	189	14:18	189		
1:13	189	15:5	189	2:23	29, 35–37, 43, 44
2–3	197	15:8	189		
2:1-7	192	16:1	189	2:24	31
2:1	189	16:19	189	3:1-9	32
2:8	189	17:5	189	3:2-4	28, 29
2:9	197	17:8-12	190	3:4	29, 32, 35
2:12-17	192	17:9	190	3:7-8	174
2:12	189	17:10-14	190	3:7	34
2:14	189	18:21	189	3:8	34
2:18	189	19:9	189	3:9	34
2:20	189	20:4	34, 174	3:13	34
2:26-27	174	21:1	190	4:15	34
3:1-6	195	21:6	189	5:6	34
3:1	189	21:17	190	5:15-23	32
3:7	189	22:13	189	5:15-16	28
3:9	197			5:15	32, 34, 36
3:14	189	Apocrypha/Deutero-Canonical Books		5:18	34
4–5	190			6:7	49
4:2	190	1 Esdras		6:18	29
5:3	190	9:45	181	6:19	29
5:13	190			7:26	49
7:15	189	Tobit		8:13	29
8:3-5	184	1:4	174	8:20	29
8:3	189	14:6-7	174	11–12	47, 51
8:5	189			11	43, 47
9:11	190	Judith		11:15-23	43
9:13	189	9:8	174	11:17–12:22	43, 46
10:4	189			11:17	49
10:5	190	Wisdom of Solomon		11:23–12:1	43, 44
10:6	190	1–2	47	11:24	36, 44, 46
11:1-3	184	1:5	42	11:25	43–45, 50
11:1-2	189	1:7	44, 49	11:26	44
11:1	189	1:12-16	28, 43	11:27–12:22	45
11:8	189	1:12	28	12:1	29, 43, 49
11:18	189	1:13-16	36, 43	12:3-22	43
11:19	184, 189	1:13-15	39	12:4	47
12	190	1:13-14	36, 49	12:8	43
12:12	190	1:13	38–40, 43, 48, 50	12:10-11	47
13:1	190			12:19	43
13:3	190	1:14	39, 42, 43	12:20	43
13:18	190	1:15	29	12:22	49
14:6	190	1:16	28, 50	14:3	49
14:8	189	1:23	44	15:3	29
14:15	189	2:11	42	15:11	44
14:16:7	189	2:22	35	17:2	49

Ecclesiasticus		14:31	174	*Testament of Benjamin*	
4:11	174	14:46	35	9:1-5	174
4:15	174				
14:12	42	Pseudepigrapha		*Testament of Levi*	
14:17-19	39, 42, 43, 49	*1 Enoch*		3:28	174
		1:9	174	5:1	174
14:17	37, 38	1:38	174	8:1-19	174
14:19	38	12:4-5	174	9:9-10	174
17	38	14:22-25	174	14:1-8	174
17:30–18:1	43	15:3-4	174	15:1-2	174
17:30-32	38, 39, 49	17–19	190	16:1-5	174
17:30	37, 38	38:5	174	18:6	174
17:31	38	95:3	174		
17:32	37	96:1	174	*Testament of Moses*	
18	38	98:12	174	3:1-3	174
18:1	38, 39	108:12	174	5:3	174
19:13-15	42				
20:29	40	*3 Baruch*		*Testament of Solomon*	
21:6	40	4:7	190	16:3	190
28:21	42	4:10	190		
31:12–32:13	81			Dead Sea Scrolls	
32:7-9	81	*4 Ezra*		1QS	
32:17	40	10:21-22	174	III 13–IV 26	23
35:22 LXX	41	14:44-46	169	III 13	81
35:24	41			III 25–IV 1	46
41:1-4	39	*4 Maccabees*		4:7	34
41:1-2	39	5:4	188	IV 22–23	81
41:3-4	39	18:10-19	168	IV 7–8	36
41:4	40, 41, 48			IX	25
41:13	45	*Aristeas*		IX 10–11	24, 25
49:12	174	9	193	IX 12–25	81
		30–51	193	V 9	25
Prayer of Azariah		187–300	81	V–VII	23
1:16	174	250	79	VI	23, 27
		301–311	193	VI 2–5	82
1 Maccabees		310	188	VI 6–8	82
2:28	140			VI 6	23
2:49	40	*Jubilees*		VIII 12	24
4:49	174	1:27-29	174	VIII–IX	23
		3:10-13	174		
2 Maccabees		4:26	174	*1QSa*	
5:15	174	8:19-20	174	I 6–8	188
5:27	140	24:29	174		
6:18	188			*1QpHab*	
7:21-23	29	*Psalms of Solomon*		7:3-6	81
7:23	35	10:1	40	II	26
13:10	174			V 4	3

4Q258		II 1 1	45	*Legatio ad Gaium*	
frag. 6 6–8	24	II 6–13	46	80	187
		II 7	46	210	168, 187
4Q266		II 8	46	311	197
frag. 11 20	25	II 11–12	45	315	197
		II 13	46		
4Q270		II 20	45	*De migratione Abrahami*	
frag. 7 ii 15	25	III 1	45	80	160
		III 6	45		
4Q417		III 9–12	45	*Quod omnis probus*	
1 i 7	34	III 17	45, 48	*liber sit*	
2 i 10–11	35	3:20	34	31	187
		IV 3–4	45	80–82	196
4Q418				*De opificio mundi*	
69 ii 6	32	Philo		69	31
69 ii 7	34	*De Abrahamo*			
69 ii 8	35	10	187	*De plantatione*	
69 ii 9	34			111	160
69 ii 10	34	*De aeternitate mundi*			
69 ii 14	34	13	49	*Quaestiones et solutiones*	
69 ii	29, 33–35			*in Genesin*	
69 ii, ll: 6–7	33	*De agricultura*		1.34	160
69 ii, ll: 7–15	33	16	160	1.45	159
frag: 102		136	160	1.54-55	159
a+b 3	34			1.68-69	159
		De cherubim			
4Q504		49	185	*Quis rerum divinarum*	
col: 1 frag: 8, l: 4	32			*heres sit*	
		De confusione linguarum		262	160
4Q509		4	187		
VII 3	46			*De specialibus legibus*	
		Quod Deus sit		2.64	187
4Q521		*immutabilis*			
2 ii 12–14	29	70	47	*De vita contemplativa*	
5 ii + 7	29			17	187
frag. 2 ii +		*De ebrietate*		31	81
4 5	45	51	78	32	82
		139	160	33	80
CD				40	80
A VII 14–15	119	*Hypothetica*		57–58	84
I–III	47, 51	7.13	188	59	85
I 1	45			60–61	85
I 2–4	45	*Legum allegoriae*		64–90	80
I 6–7	45	3.103	160	75	81
1:8–11	81	3.226	160	82	188
I 17–18	45			88–89	80
II	46				

De vita Mosis
2.215-216   195
2.216   196

JOSEPHUS
Antiquitates judaicae
Praef 24   160
12.147-153   195
12.210-214   81
14.225-227   197
14.235   195
14.244-246   197
14.259-261   195
16.43   195
16.171   195
20.262-263   187
20.263-265   186

Contra Apionem
1.38-42   169
1.38-41   187
1.46   82
1.53-55   82
2.37   82
2.62   82
2.175   168, 196
2.178   168, 187
2.204   168, 189

Vita
1-2   187
7-12   188
357-360   82

Bellum judaicum
2.136   198
2.159   198
2.228-231   195
2.291   195
3.252   188
3.325   160

MISHNAH
Berakot
1.1   66

Nedarim
5.5   64

BABYLONIAN TALMUD
Baba Batra
21a   188

Baba Meṣiʿa
59b   160
86a   160

Giṭṭin
6b   160

JERUSALEM TALMUD
Baba Meṣiʿa
2:11, 8d   66

Berakot
1:1, 2a   66

Ḥagigah
1:8, 76d   58

Ketubbot
2:4, 26c   59

Megillah
4:1, 74d   56

Nedarim
5:5, 39b   64

Peʾah
2:6, 17a   58

Šabbat
16:1, 15c   56, 60

TOSEFTA
Berakot
1:1   67

OTHER RABBINIC WORKS
Genesis Rabbah
1:1   64, 65

APOSTOLIC FATHERS
1 Clement
1:1   177
1:2   181
3:4–6:4   177
4   179
5-7   178
7:6-7   179
7:6   179
7:7   179
10:3   179
13:1   171
13:3   180
13:4-5   179
13:6   179
16–19   177
16:2   180
17–19   179
17   179
19:1   180
21:5   171
31–32   179
31:1   180
31:2-4   180
32:4   171
38:2   171
40–43   179
44:2   178
45   179
45:8   179
46:1   179
46:4   179
46:7-9   177
47:1   180, 181
47:2-3   181
47:6   178
53:1   180
56:1-2   180
56:3-4   180
56:3   180
57:3   180
62   180
62:3   180
63:1   177
63:2   177
63:3   178

Index of References

2 Samuel		114:2	174	27:9	131
7:8	176	116:1	176	28:11-12	173
7:14	176	117:26 LXX	149	28:11	131, 132, 165
11:24–12:6	159	118	47		
24:1-9	15	118:90	45	28:16	120, 131
		118:91	45	28:16 LXX	120
1 Kings		119:32	176	29:14	173
17:17-24	140	119:90 ET	45	33:20	34
22:17 LXX	140	149:7	40	37:3	40
				37:15	40
2 Kings		*Proverbs*		40–66	131
6:25	15	1:10-19	28	40	47
19:3 LXX	40	1:17-19	28	40:3-5	148
24:33	15	2:12-19	28	40:3	24
		3:12	180	40:13	131, 173
2 Chronicles		3:18	28	40:18-20	146
1:16	15	3:22	28	40:26	45
2:1	15	4:14-16	28	41:4	45
24:20-21	142	4:22-23	28	42:5	146
		5:5	28	43:1	45
Job		7:26-27	28	45	119
5:13	173	8:30	64, 65	45:3-4	45
26:6	190	8:35	28	45:23	119, 131
28:22	190	8:36	28	45:23 LXX	120
31:12	190	10:2-3	28	46:5-7	146
41:3	131	10:10-17	28	48	47
		11:7 LXX	29	49:1	45
Psalms		11:19	28	49:8	176
8:4-6	120, 131	11:30	28	52–53	142
8:6	173	12:28	28	52:4	176
17:7	42	14:27	28	52:5	110
18:10	45	15:11	190	52:11	176
24:1	173	18:6	28	53	120, 142
38:12	40	22:8	176	53:1	130
81:6-7 LXX	31	23:1-8	81	53:12	142
82:6-7	31	24:1-2	28	55:10	176
88	41	24:8	28	59:20	131
88:12	190			64:4	173
94:11	173	*Isaiah*		65:17	173
101:27	45	5:1-7	149	66	47
108:8 LXX	141	6:9-10	160, 165	66:22	45
110	119	8:14	120, 131, 132		
110:1	120, 130, 131, 142, 173	15:5 LXX	140	*Jeremiah*	
		22:13	173	7:9	174
		25:8	120, 131, 132, 173	9:23-24	173, 180
110:1 LXX	122			9:23	176
112:9	176			9:24	176

Jeremiah (cont.)		Joel		Mark	
16:16 LXX	140	2:28-32	130	2:5-7	158
21:8-10 LXX	140			4:10-12	157
26:20-23	142	Amos		4:11	151
27:6 LXX	140	5:19-20 LXX	140	4:33-34	151
27:39 LXX	34	5:26-27	119	10:17-23	152
30:2 LXX	140			10:22	158
31:31-34	176	Jonah		10:24	158
34:21 ET	140	3:15	34	10:25-26	158
41:21 LXX	140	4:6	132	10:30	34
45:4-6	142	4:14	34	11:15-19	159
49:8 ET	140	4:36	34	12:12	158
50:6 ET	140	5:39	34	12:36	119
50:39	34	6:27	34	14:63	119
52:7 LXX	140	6:40	34		
		6:47	34	Luke	
Lamentations		10:28	34	1:1-4	145
4:19 LXX	140	17:2	34	1:5-20	165
				1:26-38	165
Ezekiel		Nahum		2:23	139
4:14	163	3:18 LXX	140	3:4-6	148
7:16 LXX	140			3:10-14	152
11:16	174	Habakkuk		4:16-30	196
20:34	176	2:4	130	7:11-17	140
33:10-20	51			10:25	34
36:26-27	176	Zechariah		11:49-51	142
37:26-28	174	9:9	149	12:13-15	152
		14:5 LXX	140	13:33-34	142
Daniel				17:26-30	143
2	165	Malachi		18:30	34
2:18	35	3:8	153, 165	19:38	149
2:19	35			19:41-44	148
2:28	35	NEW TESTAMENT		20:9-19	149
5	165	Matthew		20:42	142
5:1-31	160	5:43-48	51	21:20-24	148
5:25	165	13:57	161	21:21	140
7:22	34, 174	15:12	158, 161	22:30	174
12:2	34	18:6	161	22:37	142
		18:10-14	161	24:25-27	161
Hosea		19:16	34		
3:2-3	174	19:28	34, 174	John	
3:3	174	19:29	34	3:4	158
8:12	58	21:5	149	3:9	158
13:14	173	25:46	34	3:16-17	51
13:14 LXX	120, 131	26:61	158	5:18	158
13:15	42			6:60	158
				6:61	161

Classical and Ancient Christian Writings

Apollodorus
173b	73
196d	73
197c	73
198a	73
198c	73

Aristotle
Ethica nicomachea
8	71
9	71

Problemata
956b	95

Rhetorica
2.12-17	152
3.7, 1408a-b	81

Artemidorus
Oneirocritica
4.22.36-45	164
4.71.11-13	164

Athenaeus
Deipnosophistae
1.1a-b	75
1.1b	74
1.1f	84
1.3a	192
1.4c	75
1.13c	75
2.64a	83
2.64e-f	83
2.67e	83
3.127a	75
3.127b	78
3.79e-80a	83
3.97a	79
3.97a-b	72
3.97c	76
3.97d	75
4.129a	79
4.129d	79
5.179d	84
5.182a	84
5.186e	76, 81, 84
5.187b-188d	84
5.187b	84
9.366b	75
9.398c	75
9.407d	75
10.449d-e	78
10.450e-451b	78
10.458a-d	75
11.505b	73
11.506c	73
11.782d-11.509e	75
13.555b-612f	85
13.563-565f	85
13.577e-f	78
13.578a-579d	78
13.579e-581a	78
13.583f	78
13.584b-585b	78
13.584a-b	79
13.585b	78
13.588a-b	78
13.588b	78
13.596e	78
13.601e-605b	85
15.671c	82
15.673d-e	82
15.675f	82
15.676f	76
15.678f	82

Augustine
Contra mendacium
24	161

Confessionum libri
6.3.3	116

De doctrina christiana
2.9.14	116
2.14.21	116

Chrysippus
SVF
3.161.3-6	159

Cicero
Pro Caelio
45	192

De divinatione
2.49	164
2.101-102	164
2.64.132-65.135	164

De inventione rhetorica
1.28	81

De officiis
1.128	158
1.148	161

Tusculanae disputationes
1.43.104	158

Demetrius
De elocutione
197-198	81

Dio Chrysostom
8.9-10	171
32.11	158
51.1	159
52.16	159

Diogenes Laertius
1.91	79
3.2	74
3.34	73
4.5	74
4.36	78
6	156
7.174	74
8.8	80

Index of References

Diogenes Laertius (cont.)
8.21	80
36.6-10	156, 163
54.2	156

Dionysius of Halicarnassus
Antiquitates romanae
1.7.3	82
7.68.3–7.69.2	164

Epictetus
Diatribai (Dissertationes)
1.4	101
1.4.9	98
1.4.14	98
1.7	99
1.7.32	99
1.17.4-12	99
1.17	99
1.25.6	101
1.26	100
1.26.13	100
1.29.56	101
2.6.23	99
2.13	99
2.13.21	99
2.14	96
2.16.34	101
2.17.27	99
2.17.34-35	101
2.19.10	101
2.23.41	100
3.2.13-15	101
3.9.14	96
3.21	98
3.22	99
3.23	98
3.23.20-21	101
3.23.30-32	103

Eunapius
Lives of the Philosophers and Sophists
454	74

Euripides
Bacchae
778–795	162

Iphigenia aulidensis
89–91	160

Eusebius
Historia ecclesiastica
3.4.8-9	178
3.15.1	178
3.20.9	184
3.23.1-19	184
3.24.1	184
3.24.17	184
3.25.4-6	184
3.34.1	178
3.39.4	57
4.18.8	184
4.22.1	177
4.23.11	177
6.20.1-2	194
6.25.9-10	184
7.25.1-27	184

Galen
De compositione medicamentorum secundum locos
6	192

Gellius
Noctes atticae
1.2.1-13	84
1.26	93
2.2	93
5.18.1-6	82
7.13	94
7.13.1-12	84
7.14	93
12.5	95
17.8	94
17.20	91
17.8.1-17	84
19.6	92
20.4	95

Herodotus
Historiae
2.154	78

Hippocrates
Epidemics
5.81	79

Homer
Iliad
2.408	85
23.810	75

Horace
Ars Poetica
333–346	71

Iamblichus
De anima
1.378.25	95

Irenaeus
Adversus haereses
3.3	177

Isocrates
Panegyricus
11	76

Jerome
Epistulae
36	196
75.7	132
75.22	132

Julian
Orationes
5.171b	155

Justin
1 Apologia
1.67	201

2 Apologia
3	154

Justin			Macrobius			176e	76, 79
Haer.			*Saturnalia*			177a–201c	85
2.14.5	154		1.1.3	76		177a	77
2.32.2	154		7.3.23	83		178a	77
						178b	77
Libanius			Origen			179b	77
Epistulae			*Commentarii in*			180a	77
1097	18		*evangelium Joannis*			181d	85
			6.36	178		183e	77
Lucian						184d	85
Fugitivi			Petronius			185d-e	74
27.16	158		*Satyricon*			188e	74
			26–78	84		190b	77
Hermotimus						192a-b	85
1	88		Philoponus			195b	77
2	88		*De aeternitate mundi*			195d	77
11	88		520.20-23	95		196c	77
86	89					196e	77
			Plato			201d-215a	76
Historiae			*Apologia*			201d	80
29	82		30e–31a	164		206b	75
47	82		33c	164		207c	75
						214b	77
De mercede conductis			*Charmides*			218c	85
23	78		157a.ff	164		220c	77
						221b	77
Nigrinus			*Protogoras*				
2–3	89		347c-d	72		*Timaeus*	
37–38	89		347c	76		29d	48
						29d–30a	48
Symposium			*Republic*			29e	50
3	77		2.377a	78		30a	49
6–7	85		379b1	48		30b	49
8–9	85		379c2-7	48		41a	50
10	85		379c2	48		41a7-b6	49
12	77, 85		381b	36			
17	77		382a	36		Pliny the Elder	
25	77		409b	78		*Naturalis historia, praef*	
34	83		617e4-5	48, 50		18	192
35	79, 85					24	192
37	77, 85		*Sophista*				
41	77		251b	78		Plutarch	
44	77					*Quaestionum*	
48	77		*Symposium*			*convivialum libri IX*	
			174b	77		1.1, 612e-	
			176a	84		615c	95

Caesar
32.7-9   166

Cato Major
25.1-3   71

Demosthenes
2.3   78

[De liberis educandis]
1.1.1   183
1.1.4f   183
1.1.8b   183
1.1.9e-f   183

Moralia
3e-f   78
147f   79
148c-e   80
148d   84
148f   84
150a   84
150b   80
152a-b   75
154b   80
154b-c   80
154e-f   75
154f–155e   75
155e   80
334c   78
612d   71, 83
612d-e   83
612e   74
612e–615c   83
613d   77
613e   76
614a   77
614b   71
614c   77
614d   76
614f   76
615b   75
615d   77
615e   77
616a   77
617b   77
617c   77

617d   77
618b   77
618f   77
619a   77, 85
619e   77
621b   76
621c   71
622a   77
622c   77
627a   77
628b   75
629d   75
630a   76
631d   77
631e   77
634c   78
635e   77
636e   77
644a   71
644c   81
644f   75
645b   71, 77
645c   75, 81
646f   77
647e   77
653b   86
653c   86
653f   86
654d   77
658b   77
659b   77
660a   71
660b   75
660d   81
662d   77
666f   77
669–672c   77
670c   77
671e   77
673a-b   76
676e   75, 83
677a   75, 77
677b   77
684f   77
686d   84
691c   85
700e   77

705d   77
707e   77
710b   76
710b-d   79
712a   76
712c   85
713e-f   76
713f   75
726e   77
732f   77
736c   81
736e   75
737d-e   76

Pericles
11.1   72
13.12   82

Polybius
Historiae
4.1.1-4   82
4.2.2-3   82
12.4c.3-5   82
12.25b.1-5 82
12.25e.1-7 82

Philostratus
Vita Apollonii
1.15.54-56   156
1.16.18-20   156
1.16.24-26   156
1.19–3.58   156
1.20.5-7   156
3.16-25   156
3.34-37   156
3.41-49   156
6.11.132-135   156

Quintilian
Institutio oratoria
1.1.4-24   78
1.1.6   79
4.2.31   81
8.4.23   86
10.1.123   84
11.1.1   81

Seneca			Xenophanes			INSCRIPTIONS	
Epistulae			B 26 DK	36		*CIJ*	
6.3-5	57					I.256	18
8.1	192		Xenophon			I.533	18
			Symposium			II.741	18, 20
Stobaeus			1.2-3	73			
Florilegium			2.1	84		*CIL*	
III.6.58	79		2.4	77		1.1214	79
			2.9	79			
Strabo			2.11-12	79		*CPJ*	
Geographica			2.16	75		I 43	15
13.1.54	192		3.1–4.64	73		I 104-111	17
13.4.2	192		3.5	75		I 104	17
			4.6	77		I 105	17
Suetonius			4.10-17	73		I 106	17
Nero			4.34-35	73		I 107-111	17
20.1	78		4.45	77		I 107	16, 17
41.1	78		8.1-43	73		I 108	16
			8.1-41	85		I 109	17
Theocritus			8.30	77		I 110	17
Idylls						I 111	16
14	79		Papyri				
			P.Rylands			*IJO*	
Thucydides			578	15		II 33	188
Historiae						II 44	188
1.22.2-3	82					II 146	197

Index of Authors

Abasciano, B. J. 113–15, 122, 123, 125, 131, 152
Abegg, M. 24
Adams, S. A. 80–4
Ahearne-Kroll, S. P. 152
Aitken, J. 52
Aitken, J. K. 81
Alexander, E. S. 60
Alexander, L. 57, 152
Alexander, P. S. 188, 200
Allen, D. 139
Allen, G. V. 184, 190, 194
Allison, D. C. 151
Alon, G. 54
Angel, J. L. 81
Ascough, R. S. 10, 72, 171
Asher, J. R. 128
Ashton, J. 119
Aune, D. E. 74, 121, 163, 189, 190, 197
Avi-Yonah, M. 65
Avrin, L. 65

Bagnall, R. S. 79, 193, 199
Baird, J. A. 151
Bakhos, C. 12, 13, 65
Barclay, J. M. G. 107, 201
Barnett, P. W. 172
Barrett, C. K. 142
Bateman, H. W. 43
Bauckham, R. 144, 145, 151
Bauman, R. 162
Beale, G. K. 123, 175, 176, 185
Beard, M. 10
Beauchamp, P. 29
Becker, H.-J. 56
Benin, S. D. 160
Berti, M. 193
Bickerman, E. J. 19

Bierbaum, E. G. 198
Bitner, B. J. 171
Bloom, H. 107, 108
Bock, D. L. 145, 146
Boghossian, P. 155
Bohak, G. 190
Bookidis, N. 79
Bowman, A. K. 2
Boyarin, D. 157
Branham, R. B. 158
Brawley, R. L. 149
Brenk, F. E. 72, 166
Brooke, G. J. 118
Brown, E. 156
Brown, R. E. 151
Brunt, P. A. 90, 96
Burrell, B. 192

Cain, A. 132
Capelle, W. 98
Carr, D. M. 13, 168, 186–8, 192, 202
Carston, R. 135–7, 141, 143
Carter, W. 150
Cave, T. 139, 143
Charles, R. H. 184, 185
Charlesworth, J. H. 23
Christian, M. 23
Ciampa, R. E. 173–5
Clark, B. 136, 143
Clarke, A. D. 170
Clarke, M. L. 90
Clay, D. 89
Collins, A. Y. 190
Collins, J. 29, 119
Cook, E. 24
Coqueugniot, G. 77
Corbeil, A. 191
Corley, J. 38

Corrigan, K. 73
Crawford, S. W. 3, 10, 43, 63, 197, 200, 201
Cribiore, R. 1, 13, 14, 79, 170, 186–8
Cullmann, O. 151
Culpepper, R. A. 151

Damm, A. L. 155
Danzig, G. 73
Darr, J. A. 150
Das, A. A. 151
Daube, D. 157
Delcor, M. 29
Deslauriers, M. 79
Dewey, J. 152
Dhali, M. 25
Di Lella, A. A. 41
Dibelius, M. 145
Dickey, E. 76
Dillon, J. 90, 91
Dobbin, R. 90, 91, 100
Docchorn, J. 184
Dodd, C. H. 118
Dodd, O. J. 73, 119–21, 124, 125, 130, 175
Dodson, D. S. 150
Donfried, K. P. 107
Dorion, L. A. 154
Douglas, A. E. 98
Dowd, S. 150
Downing, F. G. 157

Eckhardt, B. 10
Edmundson, G. 178
Edsall, B. A. 173
Edwards, M. 88
Eggenberger, C. 178
Ehrenfeld, C. G. 88
Elderen, B. van 201
Elliott, N. 132, 133
Ellis, E. E. 131, 132
Engberg-Pedersen, T. 157
Engen, C. E. van 153
Erler, M. 158
Eshel, H. 25

Fantin, J. D. 139, 148
Fee, G. G. 128
Feldman, L. H. 112
Fine, S. 66

Fischel, H. A. 157
Fishman, T. 61
Fitzmyer, J. A. 145
Floyd, M. 56
Flusser, D. 157
Foster, P. 108, 110, 139
Fox, R. L. 58
Fraade, S. D. 63
Fredrikson, D. E. 159
Frenschkowski, M. 194
Frey, J.-B. 18, 184
Friesen, C. J. P. 152
Furlong, A. 144

Gamble, H. Y. 111, 168, 181, 194, 195, 198, 201
Gärtner, B. 145
Gelb, N. 19
Gibbs, R. W. 134
Gigerenzer, G. 141
Gil, M. 53
Gillihan, Y. M. 10
Glad, C. E. 159
Glazov-Corrigan, E. 73
Glucker, J. 91
Goff, M. J. 35, 37
Goldhill, S. 191
Goodblatt, D. M. 53
Goodman, M. 66, 196
Gorman, R. 156
Goulder, M. D. 166
Grabbe, L. L. 77
Green, G. L. 135
Green, J. B. 148
Green, K. 138
Green, W. S. 55
Gregory, A. C. 177, 178
Grelot, P. 29
Griffin, M. 156, 158, 161
Gupta, N. K. 150

Haak, R. D. 56
Hachlili, R. 64
Hafemann, S. J. 176, 177
Hagner, D. A. 178–80
Halbauer, O. 98, 99, 101
Hammer, R. 65
Hanson, A. T. 105

Haran, M. 63
Hard, R. 90
Harland, P. A. 171
Harnack, A. von 178
Harris, M. J. 169
Harris, W. A. 111
Harris, W. V. 13, 170, 181
Harrison, S. J. 84
Hartog, P. B. 10
Hatch, E. 34
Hay, D. 80
Hays, R. B. 105, 107-9, 113-16, 128-32, 139, 140
Heller, M. J. 69
Hempel, C. 22, 81
Henst, J.-B. van der 135
Hewitt, J. T. 119
Hezser, C. 14, 53-5, 59, 60, 62-4, 66, 186-8, 195, 196, 202
Hidary, R. 64
Hock, R. F. 156
Hoepfner, W. 193
Holford-Strevens, L. 90, 102
Holland, G. S. 153, 159
Hollander, J. 107
Holm, T. L. 155
Holmes, M. W. 180
Hooker, M. D. 128
Horbury, W. A. 119
Horrell, D. G. 178
Houlden, L. 106
Houston, G. W. 60, 85, 193, 200
Hübner, H. 131
Hultin, J. F. 156
Hurtado, L. 62, 119, 131, 170
Hurtado, L. W. 118

Ilan, Z. 63
Inkelaar, H.-J. 169

Jaffee, M. S. 55, 60
Jastrow, M. 58
Jipp, J. W. 145
Jocelyn, H. D. 98
Johnson, L. T. 142, 145, 149
Johnson, W. A. 2, 3, 13, 19, 116, 117, 120, 121, 144, 168, 185, 192, 194
Jokiranta, J. 10
Julià, L. G. 86

Kahn, C. H. 154, 155
Kalmin, R. 69
Kanarfogel, E. 53
Keener, C. S. 145
Kennedy, G. A. 156
Kennedy, K. 156
Kent, J. H. 171
Kirchheiner, H. I. 25
Kloppenborg, J. S. 10, 171
Klotz, F. 74, 83, 95
Knopf, R. 181
Koch, D.-A. 115, 131, 132, 169, 173
Koester, C. R. 184, 185
König, J. 2, 10, 58, 82, 86
Kraabel, A. T. 195
Kraemer, D. 56
Kratz, R. 23

Labahn, M. 184, 185
Labendz, J. R. 155
Lane, M. 155
Lappenga, B. J. 139
Larcher, C. 29, 30
Leitzmann, H. 174, 175
Lesher, J. H. 155
Levine, L. I. 196, 197
Lichtenberger, H. 184
Lieberman, S. 59, 66
Lieu, S. N. C. 193
Lightfoot, J. B. 178
Lincicum, D. 151
Lindemann, A. 178
Liu, Y. 174
Lona, H. E. 180, 181
Long, A. A. 90, 96, 97
Lukinovich, A. 72

MacMullen, R. 2
Magness, J. 63, 66
Maier, J. 23
Malbon, E. S. 150
Malherbe, A. 132, 158, 161
Manson, T. W. 151
Marchant, E. C. 73
Marguerat, D. 162
Marincola, J. 82
Marrou, H. I. 78
Marshall, I. H. 146
Martínez, V. M. 192, 198-200
Martone, C. 198, 199

Matusova, E. 31, 46, 52
McClure, L. 78
McKnight, E. V. 150
McNamara, M. 43
McPherran, M. L. 155
Meeks, W. A. 107, 132
Metso, S. 23
Meyer, M. W. 10
Michel, O. 130
Millar, F. G. B. 96
Miller, J. B. F. 165
Mintz, S. L. 69
Mitchell, M. M. 151
Mizrahi, N. 23
Moles, J. 153
Möllendorff, P. von 88
Morales, N. R. 139, 140, 144
Morgan, T. 1, 79, 85
Morris, L. 185
Morton, S. 2
Mossman, J. M. 74
Moxnes, H. 152
Mroczek, E. 13
Muraoka, T. 42
Mussies, G. 184

Nagy, G. 193
Nelson, S. A. 151
Nesselrath, H.-G. 88
Nicholls, M. 191, 192, 202
Nickelsburg, G. W. E. 29
Niditch, S. 56, 168
Norton, J. 10, 11, 118, 119, 121, 131
Norton, J. D. H. 114
Noy, D. 18
Nye, A. 80

Oakes, P. 129, 132
Oikonomopoulou, K. 2, 10, 74, 83, 95
Oldfather, W. A. 102
Olson, S. D. 77
Oltramare, A. 98

Pao, D. W. 142, 145, 148
Park, Y.-M. 57
Parker, H. N. 2, 13, 19
Parsons, M. C. 145
Patrick, D. 150
Pattemore, S. W. 138–40
Pelling, B. R. 72

Peterson, D. G. 145, 146
Pfann, S. 193, 198
Pilkington, A. 137, 138, 142–4
Popović, M. 25, 120, 198
Porton, G. 64
Price, S. 10
Prigent, P. 185, 201
Puech, E. 27, 29, 31, 32, 36

Qimron, E. 22

Rabin, I. 63
Räisänen, H. 106, 115
Rajak, T. 195
Rapp, U. 81, 82
Rayo, A. 136
Redpath, A. 34
Reese, J. M. 51
Reich, R. 155
Rendall, G. H. 178
Richardson, P. 19, 151
Riley, M. T. 156
Rocca, S. 19
Roemer, C. 62
Rohrbaugh, R. L. 151
Romero, E. 143
Rose, V. 83
Roskam, G. 75
Rosner, B. S. 168, 169, 173–5
Rostovtzeff, M. I. 13, 16
Rowe, C. K. 145, 146, 167
Rubenstein, J. L. 53, 59
Runesson, A. 196
Runia, D. T. 52
Russell, D. A. 74
Ryan, M. 186
Ryan, S. 1, 188, 190, 201

Safrai, Z. 196
Sanders, E. P. 115, 130
Sauer, G. 41
Sayce, H. A. 16
Scarpat, G. 31
Schäfer, P. 56
Schlapbach, K. 89
Schmidt, B. B. 56
Schmidt, E. 98
Schnabel, E. J. 142
Schnelle, U. 170
Schniedewind, W. M. 13

Schomaker, L. 25
Schürer, E. 186, 188, 195
Schwartz, S. 18
Schwarz, S. 189
Scott, G. A. 155
Scott, M. 108
Scult, A. 150
Segal, E. 61
Segal, M. 43
Sensensey, M. F. 192, 198–200
Shannon, C. E. 135
Sharp, C. J. 153
Shavit, Y. 195, 196, 198
Shiell, W. 152
Sider, D. 200
Sider, S. 200
Sim, M. A. 136, 138, 139
Skeat, T. C. 63
Skehan, P. W. 41
Small, J. P. 66
Smend, R. 41
Smith, S. 139, 140, 142, 143, 148, 149
Snyder, G. H. 191
Song, N. S. 143
Soria, B. 143
Sperber, D. 135–8, 140, 141
Stadter, P. A. 90, 96, 102
Stanley, C. D. 107, 111, 112, 114–16, 122, 129, 131, 132, 149, 151, 152, 169, 173, 176
Stellwag, H. W. F. 91
Stemberger, G. 64, 65
Stephens, S. A. 151
Sterling, G. E. 30
Stern, D. 53, 61, 68, 159, 160
Stern, M. 112
Steudel, A. 23, 25, 26
Stock, B. 170
Stökl Ben Ezra, D. 27
Stowers, S. K. 57
Sukenik, E. L. 195
Suleiman, S. R. 150
Sweetland, D. M. 151

Talbert, C. H. 145
Tan, K. H. 149
Taylor, J. 27
Taylor, J. E. 80
Taylor, N. H. 175
Teeter, D. A. 188, 194

Tejera, V. 156
Thatcher, T. 170, 188, 196
Theissen, G. 107, 132
Thesleff, H. 73
Thielman, F. 120
Thomas, R. 13
Tigchelaar, E. 25
Todd, P. M. 141
Todorov, T. 138
Too, Y. L. 192, 202
Toorn, K. van der 13
Tov, E. 188
Trapp, M. B. 89, 103
Trebilco, P. R. 195, 201
Trotter, D. 139
Tucci, P. L. 121
Tuckett, C. M. 111
Tuegels, L. M. 61
Turner, E. G. 62, 63
Tutrone, F. 121
Tuval, M. 187, 188

Vaage, L. E. 156
Vermes, G. 23
Victor, R. M. 186
Vine, C. E. W. 151
Vollmer, H. 130
Von Wahlde, U. C. 151

Wacholder, B. Z. 27, 187
Wagner, J. R. 112, 113, 115, 116, 128–30
Wallenfels, R. 19, 20
Waltzing, J.-P. 170
Wassen, C. 10, 187, 188, 197
Weaver, W. 135
Webb, W. J. 175
Weeks, K. R. 20
Wendt, H. 10, 122, 128
Werline, R. A. 152
Werner, S. 2
Werrett, I. 198
Whitenton, M. R. 152
Whitmarsh, T. 9, 77
Whote, A. G. 171
Wilk, F. 131
Wilkins, J. 74
Williams, H. H. D. 173, 175
Wilson, D. 135–41
Wimmers, I. C. 150
Winston, D. 29, 30, 34

Winter, B. 148
Wirth, T. 90, 91
Wise, M. O. 24, 189, 201
Witulski, T. 192
Woolf, G. 2, 10, 19, 58
Wright, B. J. 171, 175
Wright, N. T. 110, 115, 129

Xenophontos, S. 76

Yassif, E. 69

Zahn, M. M. 43
Zanker, P. 54
Zetterholm, K. H. 62
Zevit, Z. 140